THE
LOST
CHRONICLES
OF THE
MAYA KINGS

David Drew

University of California Press

Berkeley · Los Angeles

University of California Press
Berkeley and Los Angeles, California

Published by arrangement with
Weidenfeld & Nicolson

© 1999 David Drew

ISBN 0–520–22612–7

Typeset by Selwood Systems, Midsomer Norton

Set in Monotype Garamond

Printed in Great Britain by
Butler & Tanner Ltd, Frome and London

9 8 7 6 5 4 3 2 1

Contents

For my family
Post Tenebras Lux

Illustrations

Structure 5c-2nd at Cerros, partly
excavated.
(By permission of David Friedel)

Stela 11 from Kaminaljuyú.
(Photograph © Stuart Rome; courtesy
Albuquerque Museum)

Yuri Knorosov.
(Courtesy Valery Gulayev, Akademiya
Nauk, Russia)

Between pages 242 and 243

Temple II at Tikal.
(Author's photograph)

The North Acropolis at Tikal.
(Author's photograph)

Teotihuacan, looking south from the
Pyramid of the Moon.
(Photograph © Ursula Jones)

Rio Azul, tomb I.
(Photograph by Ian Graham; courtesy
Peabody Museum of American
Archaeology and Ethnology, Harvard
University, USA)

Copán. Watercolour reconstruction
drawng by Tatiana Proskouriakoff.
(Courtesy Peabody Museum of
American Archaeology and
Ethnology, Harvard University, USA)

Detail of Altar Q at Copán.
(Author's photograph)

The remains of Yax K'uk Mo in his
tomb chamber beneath the Acropolis
at Copán.
(Photograph © Kenneth Garrett;
courtesy National Geographic
Society)

A reconstruction drawing of the buried
Rosalila temple and the structures
and tombs beneath it.

(Drawing by Christopher Klein;
courtesy National Geographic)
Calakmul Dynasty Vase.
(Photograph © Justin Kerr)

The north face of Structure II at
Calakmul.
(Photograph courtesy Simon Martin)

The Ballcourt at Copán.
(Courtesy Peabody Museum of
American Archaeology and
Ethnology, Harvard University, USA)

Stela H at Copán.
(Author's photograph)

The Popol Na, or Council House, at
Copán.
(Author's photograph)

Temple 33 at Yaxchilán.
(Author's photograph)

A reconstruction drawing of the
Hieroglyphic Stairway at Copán by
Tatiana Proskouriakoff.
(Courtesy Peabody Museum of
American Archaeology and
Ethnology, Harvard University, USA)

Between pages 338 and 339

The Temple of the Inscriptions at
Palenque.
(Author's photograph)

The Palace at Palenque.
(Author's photograph)

One of the piers from the Temple of
the Inscriptions.
(Author's photograph)

The Cross Group of buildings,
Palenque.
(Author's photograph)

Images of captives from the East Court
of the Palace at Palenque.
(Author's photograph)

ILLUSTRATIONS IN TEXT

CHAPTER ONE: The Discovery of the Maya

Acknowledgements

My debts to the large community of Mayanists are evident in the bibliography, but in the preparation of this book I have also greatly benefited from conversations with Mary Miller, the late Linda Schele, Robert Sharer, William Fash, Peter Mathews, David Freidel, David Webster, Nikolai Grube, Simon Martin, Richard Hansen and Ian Graham. Some have given me access to their unpublished material, for which I am extremely grateful. Needless to say, none bears any responsibility for the interpretations that appear here.

In Mexico and Guatemala, my thanks for hospitality and support go to Susanna Ekholm, Dona Betty of Na Bolom, Wiggie Andrews, Ana Smith and Vinicio Pena. I am grateful to Alan and Sarah Ereira, Martin Randall and Fiona Urquhart for presenting me with opportunities for productive visits to the Maya area and companionship in Maya travels. In this country, I am indebted in particular to the Millers of Cheltenham, the Mungos of Membury, Edward Few, the extremely helpful staff of the Royal Anthropological Institute library and to Elizabeth Carmichael, Warwick Bray and Ann Kendall for introducing me to the ancient Americas many years ago. I have much appreciated the encouragement and remarkable forebearance of Rebecca Wilson and Catherine Hill of Weidenfeld & Nicolson while this book has been long in the writing. I am very grateful to John Gilkes for his work on the maps and many of the drawings that appear here. Finally, I wish to express my love, as always, to my wife Anne, and my thanks to her, and to Emma and Thomas, for their patience and fortitude. Without their support, and the generosity of the rest of my family, this volume would not have seen the light of day.

Author's Note

A brief note on the spellings and pronunciations of Maya words is necessary here. For most archaeological sites and place names I have retained the traditional Spanish usages which still appear in guide-books and maps of the Maya region. The letter *x*, as in Uxmal or Yaxchilán, is to be pronounced *sh*, as in early Colonial Spanish. All *c*s, irrespective of the following vowel, are hard. When a *u* precedes another vowel, as in Uaxactún, the sound is *w*. Most other vowels or consonants are pronounced as they are in Spanish and stresses, as in Spanish, tend to fall on the last syllable, unless they end in a vowel or an *n*, or on occasion an *s*. Where this is not the case, accents are employed. For many Maya personal names and a number of nouns such as *ahaw* for 'lord', I have adopted, with what may be a degree of inconsistency, and on occasion inaccuracy, the orthographies used by the practicioners of Maya decipherment. I say orthographies because there is still a degree of inconsistency between epigraphers themselves. Modern Mayan languages distinguish, in particular, between glottalized and non-glottalized consonants. Thus, for example, what is written as *k* is pronounced as in English, but the glottalized form distinguished by a glottal stop *k'* should be pronounced with the glottis or voice box closed. Though alien to us, the difference is an important one to the Maya and serves to distinguish words of completely different meaning. I would also point out here that the adjective 'Mayan' is only conventionally used, as above, when referring to languages. Otherwise plain 'Maya' is employed both as a noun and adjectivally, singular and plural. Thus we talk here of Maya art and Maya people, not the 'Mayas' of long ago.

The Ancient Maya

We sat down on the very edge of the wall, and strove in vain to penetrate the mystery by which we were surrounded. Who were the people that built this city? In the ruined cities of Egypt, even in the long-lost Petra, the stranger knows the story of the people whose vestiges are around him. America, say historians, was peopled by savages; but savages never reared these structures, savages never carved these stones. We asked the Indians who made them, and their dull answer was 'Quien Sabe?' 'who knows?'.

– John Lloyd Stephens, 1841[1]

A 'lost' civilization, the 'mysterious' Maya. These are two of the adjectives still commonly used to describe the most brilliant and complex of all ancient societies of the Americas, whose cities first arose before the time of Christ across much of present-day Mexico, Guatemala, Belize and Honduras.

The greatest glories of the Maya – the palaces, temples and vast pyramids of stone from the golden age of their civilization – were indeed hidden in the Central American jungles and lost to the world for almost a thousand years. They have only been discovered by explorers and archaeologists over the last two centuries. The first intrepid explorers, leading their mule-trains through the undergrowth and towering trees from one forgotten ruin to another, were confronted by a host of mysteries. How could any civilized society have emerged in the tropical forest, which seemed such a hostile setting for the development of human culture? Who could these people have been? Had they grown up here, in this very environment, or come from somewhere else? How old were the ruins? What were the strange stone images depicted in elaborate costume that they came upon? Were they priests, kings, heroes or gods? Above all perhaps, why, at the time of the Spanish Conquest in the sixteenth century, had all knowledge of the inhabitants of these great cities been lost?

Despite the increasing encroachments of the twentieth century, much of the ancient Maya lands remains shrouded by great expanses of jungle, which continue to yield up their secrets. Every year fresh reports emerge of the finding of magnificent and often unexpected monuments from the past: pyramids adorned with vast polychromed masks of the gods from the dawn of Maya civilization, broad limestone causeways that linked one city with another, the tell-tale grid pattern of ancient fields seen from the air on the edge of swamp land and, most popularly appealing of all, the rich tombs of Maya rulers accompanied by spectacular caches of jade and finely painted pottery. The pursuit of the ancient Maya in their exotic location seems synonymous still with adventure and romance, and provides an alluring backdrop for that enduring journalistic compulsion to cast modern archaeologists as stereotypes from years gone by. In the Central American backyard of the USA, Indiana Jones appears to be alive and well, hacking his way through television documentaries and across the pages of glossy magazines.

Yet beyond the pure drama of discovery, there is ample justification for the media attention that Maya archaeology has generated, for palpable excitement amongst professional archaeologists themselves and for the rapidly increasing fascination with the Maya among the public at large. For quite astonishing advances have accompanied discoveries in the field. The product of the patient labour of a great number of scholars, recent years have witnessed a transformation in our understanding of one of the world's most original civilizations, a transformation more pronounced perhaps than in any other comparable area of modern archaeology. Most of the older 'mysteries' of the Maya have now been answered, though as we shall see, many new ones have emerged to take their place.

From the 1840s, when the best-selling books of the great American explorer John Lloyd Stephens first brought the existence of Maya civilization to the attention of the world, an enduring riddle was to be posed by the ancient Maya script, the only fully developed written language to appear anywhere in the pre-Columbian Americas. This alien yet singularly beautiful form of writing is made up of 'glyphs', graphic elements combined in individual blocks that have been found carved in stone and other materials, painted on pottery and the walls of buildings and tombs and with which Maya scribes filled so-called 'codices' or folding books made from the bark of the wild fig-tree.

Hundreds of inscriptions were to be found among Maya ruins, and it was obvious to men like Stephens that comprehending them would offer answers to many of the perplexing questions. Maya languages are spoken to this day, but the tradition of writing in hieroglyphs was stamped out soon after the Spanish conquest. This explains, in part, why decipherment was to prove painfully slow. A few significant advances had been made by the beginning of this century. Scholars could understand Maya numbers and had unravelled most of the complexities of their calendrical systems, added testimony to the sophistication of Maya culture. Furthermore, one of these, a cumulative count of time known as the 'Long Count' was successfully correlated with the Christian calendar. The plentiful dates on Maya monuments revealed that they had all been set up between about AD 300 and AD 900. Thus, while Europe had been struggling through the Dark Ages, Maya civilization, during what was to become known as the 'Classic' period, had reached its greatest heights. Yet any more substantial progress in decipherment remained frustratingly elusive. So much so that by the 1950s many scholars came to believe that, like those few other lost and forgotten ancient scripts such as Etruscan or the writings of the Harappan civilization of the Indus valley, the bulk of Maya texts might never be understood.

Over the last few decades, however, the pace of decipherment has quickened dramatically. Now, from reliefs on temple walls and magnificently carved 'hieroglyphic stairways', from inscribed limestone lintels and vertical slabs of stone known as 'stelae', planted in the plazas of their cities, we can read the chronicles of Maya kings and put names to the otherworldly faces of Maya sculpture. Out of prehistoric anonymity, the Maya have emerged as a historical people whose rulers left records of themselves and their families, their deeds and the great events in their lives, along with the dates down to the very day when such events occurred. Described by Michael Coe, the recent historian of Maya decipherment, as 'one of the most exciting intellectual adventures of our age'[2] alongside the exploration of space and the discovery of DNA, the cracking of the Maya code compares with the decipherment of Egyptian hieroglyphs or Linear B as one of the 'great decipherments' of the writing system of an ancient civilization.

The breakthroughs of recent years have brought a revolution in perceptions of the political history and organization of the Maya world.

Enabling great strides to be made in understanding of the contents and intricate symbolism of Maya art, they have led to a completely new view of the nature of Maya kingship and the aristocratic culture that surrounded it. An older, romanticized image of a quite unique society of benevolent and scholarly priest–kings, artists and farmers who lived in peace with each other and worshipped the passage of time, has been replaced by a vivid and very different picture of competitive city-states headed by aggressive dynasts regularly at war and for whom the centrepiece of religious observance was blood-letting and human sacrifice. Rarely has the perceived character of a whole civilization been so comprehensively turned upside down.

However profound the impact of the unravelling of their writing, our picture of the ancient Maya has not been changed by decipherment alone. Maya archaeology, interpreting mute material remains, has undergone its own revolution over the last half century, becoming more scientific and sophisticated in methodology and more ambitious in its aims. The attention of most scholars was once fixed exclusively on the great art, architecture and inscriptions of the jungle cities of the Classic period. Today, however, armed with more advanced techniques for the dating and analysis of archaeological materials, scholars are concerned as much with hand-axes, potsherds, pollen samples and the patterns of more humble ancient settlement spread out across the landscape. The result has been an infinitely greater understanding of both the chronological development of Maya civilization and the more day-to-day functioning of their society as a whole. The full scope and variability of the Maya past can now be reconstructed, during which, over many millennia, a succession of communities and kingdoms rose and fell across the variegated geography of their world.

The Maya lands cover a compact block of some 325,000 square kilometres (see map on page 5) and include the whole of the Yucatán peninsula and much of the Mexican states of Chiapas and Tabasco, all of Guatemala and Belize and the westernmost parts of Honduras and El Salvador. This vast area encompasses stark contrasts, from the humid Pacific slopes and volcanic highlands of Guatemala to the lush tropical forests of what is known as the Southern Lowlands at the base of the Yucatán peninsula and the flat, dry Northern Lowlands at its top, covered in stunted forest and dense undergrowth, without rivers or streams and where surface water is only to be found in *cenotes* or natural wells in the underlying limestone.

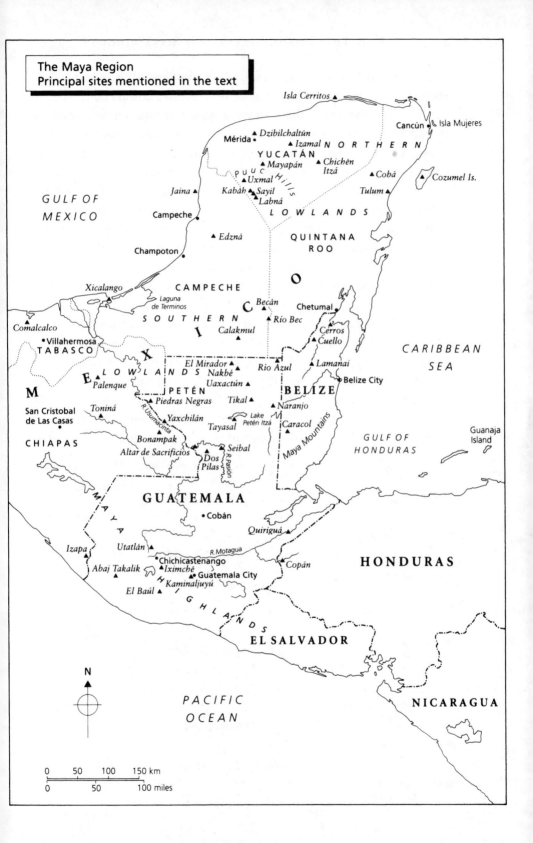

The Maya Region
Principal sites mentioned in the text

Isla Cerritos ▲

Cancún ● — Isla Mujeres

Mérida ● — *Dzibilchaltún* ●

Izamal ▲ NORTHERN

YUCATÁN

Mayapán ▲ — *Chichén Itzá* ▲

PUUC HILLS

Uxmal ▲ — *Cobá* ▲

Jaina ▲

Kabáh ▲ — *Sayil* ▲

Labná ▲

Tulum ▲

Campeche ●

LOWLANDS

GULF OF MEXICO

Edzná ▲

QUINTANA ROO

Champoton ●

CAMPECHE

Xicalango ▲

O

Laguna de Terminos

Becán ▲

Chetumal ●

C *Río Bec* ▲

Comalcalco ▲

SOUTHERN

I *Calakmul* ▲

Cerros ▲

Cuello ▲

● Villahermosa

TABASCO

X

CARIBBEAN SEA

E LOWLANDS

El Mirador ▲ — *Nakbé*

Río Azul ▲

Lamanai ▲

M *Palenque* ▲

Uaxactún ▲

● Belize City

PETÉN

BELIZE

San Cristobal de Las Casas

Piedras Negras ▲

Tikal ▲

Toniná ▲

Yaxchilán ▲

Naranjo ▲

CHIAPAS

R. Usumacinta

Tayasal

Lake Petén Itzá

Caracol ▲

Bonampak ▲

Seibal ▲

Maya Mountains

GULF OF HONDURAS

Guanaja Island

Altar de Sacrificios ▲

Dos Pilas ▲

R. Pasión

GUATEMALA

● Cobán

Quiriguá ▲

MAYA

HONDURAS

Izapa ▲

Utatlán ▲

R. Motagua

Abaj Takalik ▲

Chichicastenango ●

Iximché ▲

Copán ▲

Guatemala City ▲

El Baúl ▲

Kaminaljuyú ▲

H I G H L A N D S

EL SALVADOR

N

PACIFIC OCEAN

NICARAGUA

0   50   100   150 km

0   50   100 miles

The very first people to enter the Maya area were hunters and gatherers, who were roaming here by at least 10,000 BC, at the end of the last Ice Age, descendants of those original Americans who had crossed the Bering Straits from Asia. At first shifting with the seasons, they began, during the so-called 'Archaic' period from about 6000–1800 BC (see table) to congregate more permanently in the most favourable locations such as the mangrove swamps and lagoons along the Pacific coast and the shores of Belize, where sources of food were available all year round. Very slowly, through tending and ultimately domesticating wild plants, foragers became farmers. Around 1800 BC, the beginning of the 'Preclassic' period, village communities had already become established above the Pacific coast, cultivating what would become the staple Maya crops of maize, beans, squash and peppers, weaving and producing pottery, the universal accompaniment of a sedentary existence.

By 1000 BC farming villages were to be found across the Maya Highlands and groups of pioneers, descending from the mountains and following the great river systems such as the Usumacinta and its tributaries and the broad, winding rivers of Belize, had spread out within the Southern Lowlands, carving their maize fields from the forests and swamps. Populations increased rapidly and soon they were building

DATE	PERIOD	MAYA HIGHLANDS AND PACIFIC COAST	SOUTHERN LOWLANDS	NORTHERN LOWLANDS
				Spanish conquest
1520	Colonial	Spanish conquest	Cortés crosses the lowlands	
		Quiché and Cakchiquel Kingdoms		Chichén Itzá abandoned
900	Postclassic			
800	Terminal Classic		The 'Collapse' of the vast majority of cities	Rise of Chichén Itzá, Uxmal and the Puuc sites
			Maya Civilization at its height	
600	Late Classic			
				Growth of Coba and other centres
AD 250	Early Classic	Spread of Teotihuacan influence	Dynasties established at the major cities	
0			Rise of Tikal	
400 BC	Late Preclassic	Writing systems and dynastic rule develop	Growth of Cities with impressive monumental architecture	Coastal trade flourishing
1000 BC	Middle Preclassic	Olmec influence		
		Farming communities established in highlands and lowlands		
1800 BC	Early Preclassic	Settled village life along Pacific coast		

much more than simple houses of pole and thatch. By 500 BC, in the northern Petén region of Guatemala the first great stone pyramids were being constructed from the abundant outcrops and beds of limestone that, when first quarried, were easy to cut with axes of flint or chert.

The Late Preclassic, from about 400 BC to AD 250, was the most crucial, formative time of change, when the template for Maya civilization was created. Cities grew up in both the highlands and the lowlands, and in some of them forms of monumental architecture were created that were more colossal than anything built by the Maya in later centuries. Indeed, by the time of Christ most of the diagnostic ingredients of the Classic period were already in place, including hieroglyphic writing, first emerging in the highlands but slowly developed in the lowlands as well.

But it was the Classic period which saw the full florescence of Maya civilization, best defined by the establishment of ruling dynasties who ordered the erection of inscribed monuments to commemorate their achievements. This was the time when most of the fabric of the great cities that can be seen today such as Tikal, Palenque and Copán was constructed and when the Maya were to reach unequalled heights of artistic and intellectual expression.

Perhaps the most striking overall impression today is of the sheer scale of Maya civilization at its height in the eighth century AD. Forty or so major cities have been documented, some of them with populations of up to 100,000 people. The total population of the Maya area at this time has been put by some scholars at more than ten million, a staggering figure, second only to that of T'ang dynasty China at the same period and which makes the contemporary England of the Anglo-Saxon kings and the continental Europe of Charlemagne models of underdevelopment by comparison.

That anything like these figures could have been supported is testimony to an often overlooked achievement, yet one of quite fundamental importance – the productivity of Maya agriculture. Their natural surroundings offered a range of sources of food: fish, shellfish and marine fauna along the coasts and in lakes and rivers, and from the forests an enormous variety of wild plant foods and sources of protein such as peccary, deer, monkeys, tapir and a host of smaller rodents, birds and other creatures. But, as populations grew, much of the wild resources of the forest would have been hunted out or significantly reduced and their inventory of domesticated animals is a paltry one, limited to the turkey and a small variety of edible dog. Meat-eating would have been an irregular luxury among the bulk of the population. The diet was essentially vegetarian and based principally on maize.

Farming in the fertile volcanic soils that covered much of the highlands was a relatively straightforward matter and could support substantial settlements. In the Northern Lowlands, apart from the small, anomalous area of the Puuc hills to the west, the situation was quite the opposite. The meagre earth, only a few inches deep in many places, was rapidly exhausted. The forests to the south offer a much more complex picture. Drainage and soils are extremely variable from place to place and scientists still debate the carrying capacity of much of the landscape over long periods of time, complicated by evidence for cycles of climate change, markedly wetter periods followed by dry, throughout Preclassic and Classic times. But the forest was not as hostile a prospect for farmers as was once believed. It demanded adaptability and acute sensitivity to local conditions. The Maya learnt well through centuries of experience. Shifting cultivation, slash and burn farming, was common practice everywhere, but this was supplemented by more intensive methods. Alluvial lands along the major rivers to the south could have been cultivated almost continuously and surpluses even exported to other areas. Agricultural terraces were constructed on hill slopes, and in swampy areas close to some of the slow-running rivers, especially in Belize, raised field cultivation was practised. This involved digging networks of small canals or drainage channels, the excavated earth piled up in between to produce elevated planting platforms. A similar technique was also widely applied to the large areas of *bajos* or seasonal swamps that existed away from the rivers, for example in the area around Tikal in the forests of the Petén in northern Guatemala. So, in this versatile way, exploiting every niche in the landscape, the Maya managed to thrive in the forest, producing the surpluses that fuelled the growth of cities and supporting ever-increasing numbers of people who did not have to work on the land and could turn their minds to other things.

Contrasting environments also meant diverse natural resources or finished products that were exchanged for those from other regions. Trade networks, local and long-distance, in utilitarian and luxury items, ranged across the Maya world from Preclassic times. From highlands to lowlands, for example, went grinding stones of granite or volcanic lava and obsidian, much sought after for spear-points, knives and blades for a multiplicity of craft and ritual uses. In return travelled lowland products such as feathers, beeswax, cotton and animal skins. Salt, a dietary necessity, was a particular speciality of the northern Yucatán, where it was produced in pans along the coast. Cacao, or chocolate, made into the frothy ancestor of the modern mug of cocoa and the high-status drink of the aristocracy, was an extremely sought-after trade item which only grew in regions of high rainfall such as the lower slopes above the Pacific and around the Gulf of Honduras.

Maya kings themselves controlled the acquisition and use of particularly precious commodities such as jade, only to be found in the Motagua valley of eastern Guatemala, and the tail-feathers of the resplendent quetzal bird, whose habitat was the remote cloud forests of the transitional zone between mountains and jungle. The status and authority of Maya rulers was expressed by the personal use of such rare materials. Each had a particular symbolic value, decorating and accompanying the lord in life and going with him to his grave. The gift-giving of rare jades and finished objects such as finely painted pottery to retainers and subordinates was another token of the ruler's power, and the wider circulation of these objects helped to cement political relationships between kingdoms.

For each Maya city had its own political realm or surrounding dependent territory. Often no more than a day's walk apart, they formed a patchwork of independent local traditions, jostling in uneasy equilibrium. Through trade, endlessly shifting alliances and the waging of war – for tribute and sacrificial victims, it would seem, rather than the all-out conquest war of territorial expansion with which we might be more familiar – they were constantly aware of each other. New ideas and ways of doing things travelled through the tracks in the forest and by canoe along the coasts and rivers: agricultural techniques and other technologies, modes of warfare, religious concepts and symbols used by rulers to buttress their authority. Such constant exchange and communication made for a hot-house of competitive emulation and creative energy.

Earlier this century the Maya tended to be viewed largely in isolation in their remote jungles and the importance to them of contact with other contemporary peoples minimized. But in reality they were an integral part of a much wider world. This is known as Mesoamerica, which, along with the Andes, was one of the two great cradles of civilization in the Americas (see map on page 10). Geographically, Mesoamerica is defined as the whole land mass stretching from northern Mexico, close to the modern border with the USA, down into Central America as far as the fringes of Nicaragua and Costa Rica. But the use of the term is

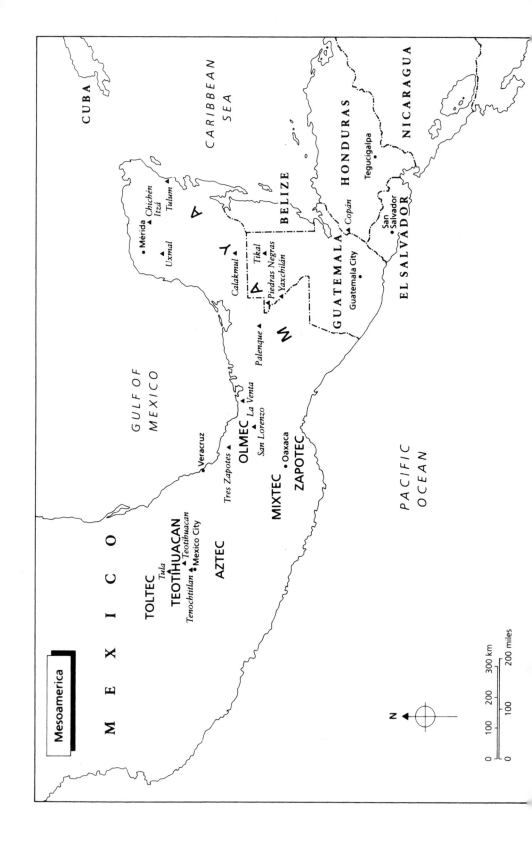

essentially a cultural one, referring to peoples who, though they spoke different languages and had quite separate ethnic identities, shared a number of practices and beliefs and had more in common with one another than they did with other, less complex cultures further to the west and east. They all, for example, used a 260-day ritual calendar, combined with a solar calendar of 365 days. They held certain gods and underlying views of the cosmos in common, practised human sacrifice and also auto-sacrifice, the letting of blood from one's own body as an act of piety. Mesoamerican peoples played a game with a rubber ball in a special court that was of great ritual significance, they wrote in codices of bark paper or deer skin, and all depended on the cultivation of maize and the accompanying triad of beans, squash and peppers. Many of these shared traits date back to very early times but, as archaeological research is making increasingly apparent, across the whole of Mesoamerica there was a continuous and vigorous flow of people and ideas.

The Maya straddled Mesoamerica from coast to coast and became intermediaries, and major players as producers, in long-distance trade routes that stretched many hundreds of kilometres along the Pacific and through the southern Maya lowlands. And, at certain periods, they came to be strongly influenced by others in ways which contributed both to the growth and the particular character of Maya civilization. The Olmec, the first complex society to emerge in Mesoamerica, along the Gulf Coast of Mexico at the turn of the first millennium BC, had a powerful, though still much debated impact upon the initial development of Maya civilization. In the Early Classic period, parts of the Maya world established a close relationship with the great metropolis of Teotihuacan in central Mexico. Connections with this region remained strong through succeeding centuries, with the Toltecs and, ultimately, with the Aztecs. Indeed, parts of the southern periphery of the Maya world, the Pacific coast in particular, became so thoroughly 'Mexicanized' that they are today regarded as anomalous and outside the Maya mainstream.

Yet the vast bulk of Maya peoples kept their individuality and essential Mayaness across the centuries. They were never conquered. The fearsome empire of the Aztecs bordered Maya lands, they traded with the Maya but never reduced them to the level of cowed tribute-payers as they did other ancient societies of Mexico. The Maya retained their idiosyncratic political system, religious beliefs, distinctive styles of art and architecture and, uniquely, they wrote down their own histories of the affairs of their world using a script markedly more sophisticated than those of their neighbours.

Language was, of course, the most important element of their shared cultural identity. Today there are as many as thirty-one different languages that make up the Mayan language family, the best known being Yucatec, spoken over most of the Yucatán peninsula, Tzeltal, Tzotzil and Chol in Chiapas and Cakchiquel, Quiché and Kekchí found in the Guatemalan highlands. Studies by linguists of the patterns of divergence amongst these languages, whose mutual intelligibility decreases uniformly with geographical distance, suggest that they all descend from a single 'Proto-Mayan' ancestor which existed around 2000 BC. By the Classic period it is probable that two main languages were spoken over most of the lowlands – what is known as Cholan across much of the Southern Lowlands and Yucatecan further to the north. The language of Maya inscriptions is, however, a more complex question. It has recently been proposed, on the basis of compelling linguistic evidence, that the vast majority were written in Choltí, a now-extinct sub-division of Cholan which, like Latin or diplomatic French, seems to have become accepted as the highly esteemed medium of royal or official communication right across the Maya area.[3]

If the destiny of the Maya in Precolumbian times remained in their own hands, so their downfall at the end of the Classic period was of their own making. Although Maya civilization, in a different guise, was maintained in northern Yucatán and the highlands of Guatemala until the Spanish conquest, in the ninth century AD, in what is commonly known as the 'Maya Collapse', it came to a terrible halt in their jungle heartland. There was no more construction in the great cities, the records of Maya rulers ceased to be carved. The cities themselves were largely abandoned, to be taken over by the jungle. Before their fall there may indeed have been little jungle left. The consensus now is that environmental depredation was a prime cause of the catastrophe, brought on by the pressure of population on limited and fragile natural resources. The story of the end of the tropical-forest Maya thus seems to offer a tragic lesson for our own times – a people who grew up in an intimate, symbiotic relationship with the forest that they had tamed and developed so successfully, but who in the end managed to destroy both their environment and themselves. Yet, as an explanation for the Maya Collapse this is by no means the complete answer, however appealing, to what we shall see was a complex phenomenon. The same is true of many other elements of the Maya story. For if, little by little, scholars are getting closer to a grasp of the reality of ancient Maya society, the very increase of knowledge in recent years only serves to introduce new uncertainties and underline how much work remains to be done.

Despite many colourful theories that have suggested otherwise, the Maya developed over the centuries in isolation from the civilizations of Europe, Asia or Africa. No one would seriously doubt today that they too were a complex, 'civilized' society. They share many of that check-list of characteristics traditionally observed among the ancient civilizations of the Old World. They had large populations concentrated in and around urban centres and fed by systems of intensive agriculture. They possessed an hierarchical social structure with full-time specialists such as priests, administrators and scribes and were governed by an élite class that had control of surplus goods and the labour of the population at large. The ruling élite organized great public works of temple and pyramid building in the service of an institutionalized religion harnessed to what, by the Classic period, one can legitimately call the power of the state. They produced great art in a variety of media, and of course they had writing.

Indeed, earlier this century the Maya were welcomed into the fold of conventionally defined civilization almost as long-lost cousins. A number of scholars, impressed in particular by the technical quality and appealing naturalism of much Maya art, so different and so advanced it seemed compared to that of other pre-Hispanic societies, referred to them as the 'Greeks' of the New World or the 'Classical' civilization of the Americas. Certain elements of this comparison still hold. Like the cities of Classical Greece or Renaissance Italy, the Maya were never truly unified in any political sense. The essence of their civilization was inde-pendence, in an abundance of city-states which expressed their shared culture in brilliant but varying religious and artistic traditions. Many of the greatest accomplishments of the Maya were also achievements of the mind. Their script was as complex and versatile as any writing system ever devised. As mathematicians they developed place-system numerals and the concept of zero, which neither the Greeks nor the Romans ever arrived at. Without the use of telescopes or other optical instruments, simply with the naked eye, they plotted the movements of planets and stars, predicted astronomical events such as eclipses way into the future and devised calendars that were almost as accurate as our own.

For those scholars keen to formulate universal laws of human behaviour, it is clearly essential to compare ancient societies who have grown up independently around the globe. Yet any attempt to categorize or characterize the Maya through analogy with other civilizations with which we are familiar, highlighting the similarities, is of course potentially misleading. The Maya are intriguing, not just because they are like us or our forebears in many ways, but because they are also profoundly different. Perhaps the most significant result of the breakthroughs in Maya studies of recent years is that scholars are now in a position to approach the ancient people on their terms. Through the advances of decipherment, combined with analysis of texts written down by Maya soon after the conquest and the work of anthropologists among traditional communities today, we can begin to understand their beliefs and thought processes and that Maya society was built on a set of premises far removed from our own.

They accumulated a vast amount of systematic knowledge of the world around them. But they used this information to develop their own individual vision of how it functioned and their place in the scheme of things. Tracking the revolutions of planets and stars, observing the changing of the seasons, the extraordinary speed of growth and decay in the tropical environment, they concluded that everything went through continuously recurring, cyclical processes of life, death and rebirth. If the workings of the world were revealed in cycles, then through the formulation of calendars, pattern and order could be established and acted upon. For, to the Maya, time future was contained in time past. If history did not literally repeat itself in every detail, they were convinced that drought, flood, disease, war, the texture of events in the lives of humans were liable to recur, mirroring the observed reality of the natural order itself.

They possessed an array of gods, with many different aspects, most of whom appear to have been associated in one way or another with the forces of nature. The gods had created the world and established the particular era, one of many cycles of creation, in which men lived. Broadly, the heavens were conceived as the home of the gods, the earthly realm that of humans and an underworld as the abode of the dead. But in effect there was no real division between these domains and between what we would conceive as the natural and supernatural. Everything operated concurrently. The dead, for example, merely moved from one plane of existence to another and could still manifest themselves in the day-to-day lives of their descendants.

Gods constantly involved themselves in the affairs of men, and certain humans, through the religious rituals which pervaded every aspect of Maya life, could communicate with the gods. Such men were special individuals, men of knowledge and power. At the lesser, local level this would be the village shaman. But the key figure came to be the Maya ruler himself. Through the right performance of elaborate ceremonial he was seen to actively participate in keeping the world on its course, guaranteeing the regular cycle of the seasons and the productivity of the Maya farmer's fields of maize. In all important rituals there was one key component. In order to ensure that human life was maintained, the gods who had made the world had to be nourished in return with the most sacred commodity that humans had received at their creation, the gift of blood. In Maya art of the Classic period, the ruler was portrayed as the central intermediary with the gods, under whose auspices the debt of blood was constantly repaid. He was himself semi-divine and he dressed in the attire of the gods.

In many respects Maya beliefs appear quite alien to us. Yet they demonstrate that there are many coherent, considered ways of seeing the world besides our own. For the Maya they provided answers to their special concerns, above all the relationship between humans and those natural forces which so dominated their lives. Their system of beliefs, elevated to the level of state religion, enabled the few to dominate the many, but it worked for a very long time. The social and religious order of the Maya, headed by what was in effect the cult of the ruler, endured in its essentials for some eight hundred years.

They produced a society as creative and original as any in the Old World, but developing along their own independent trajectory as they did, they simply found no need or did not happen upon certain items of technological hardware that were commonplace in other ancient civilizations across the oceans. They remained an essentially stone-age society. Even when some metals were introduced into the Maya area from the ninth century onwards, principally gold and copper, these were only adopted as luxury, ornamental items. Metals never replaced obsidian, the 'disposable razor' of Mesoamerica, and other stones for both practical and ritual purposes. As a precious material gold remained secondary to blue-green jade, the colour of fertility and the essence of life itself. The Maya did not use the wheel, though it seems they knew the principle of it, since they had no draught animals to make it of any practical use. Lacking anything approximating to a horse, they used the phrase 'tapir of Castile' to identify the fearsome beasts that brought their conquerors among them.

Like all native peoples of the Americas, the Maya proved terribly vulnerable. They did not have the political coherence, the advanced military technology nor, above all, the resistance to European-imported diseases to withstand the onslaught of the Spanish conquest. The Spanish moved them into new towns and villages, their books and 'idols' were burnt and concerted efforts were made to eradicate the ancient ways. Over the post-conquest period their lands have been taken from them and they have been forced to work on the plantations of Mexican and Guatemalan landowners. In more recent times, military regimes have persecuted and massacred the Maya as if the original conquest had never ended.

Yet it would be wrong to view the Maya since the Spanish conquest simply as tragic victims or anachronistic remnants of a once-glorious past. With a population that has increased rapidly in recent years and may now reach some seven million speakers of Maya languages across Mexico, Guatemala, Belize and Honduras, the Maya today are the largest group of native Americans north of the Andes. They are a distinctive living culture, revealing an intriguing mixture of both ancient beliefs and practices and those adopted since the Spanish conquest. Recent studies have helped us to understand the processes of their survival as they adapted to changing circumstances. They did not passively accept the subordinate roles assigned to them. In remote parts, independent Maya groups, and one whole forgotten kingdom, survived in isolation. Armed resistance was to be violent and effective until the turn of this present century and when the Maya did adapt to Spanish ways they managed to outwardly transform themselves yet, subtly, to remain in many essential ways the same. More recent sufferings have only served to reinforce their ethnic identity and solidarity and today a cultural revival is underway that has begun to unite different groups across international boundaries. An increasingly important element in this is a fuller consciousness of the achievements of the Maya past.

The words of John Lloyd Stephens that head these introductory pages refer to Copán in Honduras, one of the jewels among Maya cities. It is renowned for the elegant layout of its architecture, the imposing and intricately beautiful sculpture that sorely tested the skills of Stephens' draughtsman companion, Frederick Catherwood, and panel upon panel of magnificent hieroglyphs. Excavations and intensive study of Copán began more than a hundred years ago. But it is only in the last two decades that a series of international projects and the collaboration of a number of leading scholars have begun to reveal to us in detail the city's more human story, from the lives of the very earliest Maya farmers in outlying settlements in the Copán valley to the illustrious careers of the great lords of the Classic period. It is projects such as this that are leading the way in a uniquely productive era for Maya research, the like of which, the participants agree, may never come again. The atmosphere of anticipation and expectation must compare with those exhilarating years after Champollion's breakthroughs, when the past of ancient Egypt began to open up like a flower.

Those presently working among Maya ruins also agree on something else, which gives an added relevance to the study in which they are engaged. To Stephens, no 'remembrance' of the ancient race hung around the ruins of Copán; the sullen Maya he questioned appeared to know nothing. It made the seemingly vanished ancient people an even greater mystery. Here, of course, he was wrong. Like Stephens, we are familiar enough with the story of ancient Egypt or that of the Nabatean traders of the deserts of the Near East. But since the spread of Islam centuries ago, the fellahin who cultivate the silts of the Nile valley close to the ruins of Thebes or the few Bedouin tribesmen who still sell souvenirs to tourists amongst the rock-cut temples and tombs of Petra, have had little connection back, in their language or religious beliefs, to the original inhabitants of these cities. Their ancient civilizations have truly vanished. Among the Maya the situation is very different. The Maya past that is being reconstructed today is not a dead history, as the Mexican archaeologist Ignacio Bernal once put it, but a living one: 'it is the past tense of a story which exists nowadays'.[4]

The following pages will largely be concerned with what we know today about the ancient Maya. But in this next chapter we will look at the history of Maya discovery, at the various attempts of outsiders to come to terms with the Maya past. For the revelations of recent years and the approaches of modern archaeologists can best be understood as the latest stage in a long, colourful and often contentious process of observation and study. When this began, the Maya world was much changed from its heyday of the Classic period. The great cities of the tropical lowlands had already been engulfed by the forests for centuries.

The Discovery
of the Maya

CONQUISTADORES AND FRIARS

In August 1502, on his last voyage of discovery, Christopher Columbus anchored his ships off the island of Guanaja in the Gulf of Honduras. His son, Ferdinand, later described what they saw one morning not long after sun-up:

> there came at that time a canoe as great as a galley, 8 feet wide, all of a single trunk loaded with merchandise from western parts. Amidships it had a canopy of palm leaves, like that of gondolas in Venice. Under this canopy were the children, women and all the baggage and merchandise. The crew of the canoe, although they were twenty-five, did not have the spirit to defend themselves against the batels sent in pursuit. The canoe thus taken fast by us without a fight was brought to the ships where the Admiral gave many thanks to God, seeing that in one moment, without effort or danger to his own men, he had been provided with a sample of all the things of that land.[1]

Amongst the cargo was cotton cloth and ready-made clothing, including sleeveless shirts and 'pantaloons' that were dyed with different designs. There were wooden 'swords' or clubs with stone blades set into them, copper axes and bells, pottery, wood and stone carvings and small knives made from a translucent yellow stone. The terrified occupants of the canoe allowed the Spaniards to rummage through everything, only becoming animated when cacao beans, a universal means of exchange used literally as chocolate money, spilt into the bottom of the boat and they scrabbled after them 'as if their eyes had dropped out of their sockets'. Keeping a few items as souvenirs, particularly some of the cotton clothing, the Spaniards let the canoe on its way, retaining one old man as a guide whom they were later to release on the Honduras coast.

This momentous, and peacable, meeting was the first encounter, not just of Spaniards with Maya but between Europeans and any more advanced civilization of the Americas. Compared with the miserable 'savage' Indians from the simpler tribal societies of Cuba and Hispaniola, with whom the Spaniards had become familiar since 1492 and who were to be reduced to slavery and die out with terrible speed, the occupants and contents of the canoe provided evidence of a more sophisticated kind of society. The well-dressed merchant 'from a province called Maiam' who was the master of the vessel and drove on twenty-five chained and naked paddlers, may have been from a city along the Yucatán coast or perhaps from Xicalango, a great commercial entrepôt on the Gulf Coast of Mexico. Much of the cargo would have come from central Mexico, notably the copper bells and axes and the 'translucent yellow stone' or obsidian. The cotton cloth would almost certainly have been collected on their way round the Yucatán peninsula.

Columbus, however, seems not to have attached any great importance to the incident. It was only mentioned later among many other curiosities of the voyage. The reason was very simple and came from the famous delusion with which he was burdened – that they were somewhere off the mainland of Asia and must soon find immense wealth. The canoe with 'all the things' of the Maya lands contained interesting handicrafts, but little evidence of the rightful riches of the Orient. And so he sailed away.

It was not until nine years later, by which time they were more established in the Caribbean, with their principal base in Havana, that the Spaniards met the Maya again, under very different circumstances. In 1511 a Spanish ship was taking Juan de Valdivia, a crown official, from Darien in Panama to Hispaniola when it sank off Jamaica. Valdivia and eighteen others got away in a small boat and drifted helplessly westwards for two weeks until they hit the east coast of Yucatán. By this time seven men had already died and the rest were quickly captured by Maya. Valdivia and four others were almost immediately sacrificed and eaten, so the Spanish story goes, in a cannibalistic ritual.[2] The remainder were kept in a cage to be fattened up for another festival. Only two Spaniards, Gerónimo de Aguilar and Gonzalo de Guerrero, managed to survive. Aguilar became the slave of the lord of a neighbouring territory. Guerrero, however, went completely native, marrying the daughter of the Maya ruler of Chetumal to the south and becoming so committed to his new people that he led Maya resistance to the Spanish. Much later, in

1535, the body of a white man was discovered after a Maya raid on the Spanish in Honduras. It was Guerrero, his hair long and matted, lips, nose and ears pierced for jade ornaments and his body tattooed. The true story, and above all perhaps the motivation of this extraordinary figure, who became Maya for a quarter of a century, will probably never be told. In post-revolutionary Mexico he became a hero and today he is hailed as one of the founders of the Mexican nation and as father of the first *mestizos.*

These two isolated initial encounters with the Maya were followed in 1517 by a more purposeful expedition led by Francisco Hernández de Córdoba, who set out west with three ships in search of new lands and slaves to replenish the stocks that had become so depleted in Cuba.[3] They landed first on a small island off the northern tip of Yucatán. After some skirmishes with the inhabitants they were amazed to find houses and temples built of stone and finished with lime plaster. Inside one of them they saw many images of women, almost certainly the Maya goddess Ix Chel, which gave the island its Spanish name, Isla Mujeres. From there they continued further west and then south, hugging the Yucatán coastline, until they arrived at the bay of Campeche and landed at the town of Champoton. Despite the novel experience of Spanish firepower, the Maya resisted bravely. Taking heavy casualties, the Spanish retreated to their boats and in due course returned to Cuba. Hernández later died of his wounds, but not before making exaggerated claims for the riches of the lands, the fine cities he had seen and above all the quantities of gold that the natives possessed, based on the few items they had come away with from the Isla Mujeres. But here at least was the scent of greater possibilities.

Another expedition was immediately made ready for the following year. Juan de Grijalva returned with a larger force, establishing himself first on the island of Cozumel off the north-east coast where the Maya fled without offering any resistance. Believing the Yucatán peninsula to be an island and that he could sail round it, he continued south along the coast, sighting a number of native towns on the way: 'We followed the shore day and night, and the next day toward sunset we perceived a city or town so large, that Seville would not have seemed more considerable nor better'.[4] This optimistic impression, typical of Spanish hyperbole of the time, almost certainly refers to the town of Tulum, whose modest but well-preserved ruins are still impressively perched on a rocky promontory overlooking the sea (see p.22, plate section). Discovering that Yucatán was perhaps not an island after all, they turned about and retraced Hernández' route north around the peninsula and down towards Tabasco and the Gulf Coast. Here they formed better relations with the local Indians, exchanging glass beads for items of gold and fresh supplies. And then, further north along the coast of Veracruz, a group of Indian chiefs came down to the shore and paddled out to the boats. They wore fine cotton clothing and were adorned with magnificient featherwork and gold jewels. They entertained Grijalva and his captains with a banquet of turkey, tortillas and exotic fruit. Grijalva had no interpreter on this occasion, but even so, from this meeting and other contacts along the coast, it became apparent that where the sun set to the west lay the heart of a great empire. It turned out later that the chiefs with whom they had dined were Aztecs, envoys of their emperor Montezuma. Grijalva's force turned for home, and on reaching Cuba the excitement was intense.

Now, of course, the story becomes one of the genuinely momentous 'turning points' in world history. For in 1519 Hernán Cortés set off with eleven ships, five hundred soldiers, a hundred sailors, horses and artillery. His first stop was Cozumel, where the Maya fled once more into the interior. Maya idols in their temples were destroyed and a cross set up in one of them. But Cortés made efforts to make peace with the inhabitants and good relations were finally established with Naum Pat, the local ruler. Over the next few years Cozumel became the base for Spanish ships to resupply on their way to Mexico. It was on Cozumel, too, that Cortés heard of the existence of Spaniards on the mainland, the two survivors from 1511. He sent messages urging them to rejoin their countrymen. Guerrero refused, but Aguilar managed to reach the island, where he 'wept for joy, and kneeling down he thanked God, and asked the Spaniards if the day was Wednesday'.⁵ Guerrero was no doubt observing the Maya calendar by now, but Aguilar, a lay brother, had been devoutly counting off the Christian days, one by one, for eight years. It was gently explained to him that it was in fact a Sunday.

Cortés' expedition rounded the peninsula and reached Tabasco, where they defeated a local force sent against them. The chiefs submitted and offered the Spaniards gold, food and women. Among them was a girl whom the Spanish named Doña Marina, who was to become Cortés' mistress and bear him a son. She spoke both Maya and the Aztec language Nahuatl. Aguilar by now spoke fluent Maya. Together they became Cortés' indispensable interpreters on the road to the city of

Tenochtitlan and the conquest of the Aztec empire. To Cortés' good fortune, that great tribute empire was inherently unstable. Those other Mexican peoples conquered by them hated their overlords and were only too willing to side with the Spaniards. This was the key to Cortés' success. He marched inland with only a few hundred Spaniards but on the way acquired a large army of native auxiliaries.

Tenochtitlan dwarfed every other native city that the Spanish found in the Americas. An island metropolis of 200,000 people that could only be reached by great causeways across Lake Texcoco, it was truly one of the wonders of the world at that time. Only Constantinople or Venice in the Old World could remotely compare with it. London had a population of some 50,000 in the early sixteenth century, Seville a mere 30,000. The Maya towns and cities that the Spanish had seen were villages by comparison. And above all, the precious metals the Maya possessed were negligible compared with the magnificient loot that the Aztec empire offered. So, exploration of Yucatán by the Spanish was at first only a preliminary to the conquest of the Aztecs. For a few years the Maya lands were by-passed, their coastline no more than an occasional watering-place as Spanish ships hurried on to join the Aztec enterprise. But, of course, the Spaniards had not gone away for good. After the fall of Tenochtitlan in 1521, news of the fantastic exploits of Cortés and the gold, lands and glory he had acquired, were to bring thousands of men from Europe to 'New Spain', as the newly discovered lands were called. These adventurers were very soon to be swarming all over Mesoamerica looking for their own empires to conquer. Spanish attentions turned once more to the Maya.

Between 1524 and 1527 the Quiché, Cakchiquel and other smaller Maya kindoms in the highlands of Guatemala were subdued by Cortés' brutal lieutenant Pedro de Alvarado in a series of vicious and bloody campaigns. Supported by thousands of native allies from Mexico and using the familiar principle of divide and rule employed by Cortés in his defeat of the Aztecs, he first overcame the Quiché with Cakchiquel aid and then turned on the Cakchiquel themselves. With the highlands quiet, it was the turn of the Maya in Yucatán.

The conquest here was to be led by Francisco de Montejo, a member of the Grijalva expedition of 1518 who had returned with Cortés the following year. He did not, however, join the assault on the Aztec capital. Instead he was sent back to Charles V in Spain to deliver the 'Royal Fifth', the crown's official share of the booty that the expedition had already accumulated. It included loot from along the Gulf Coast and some magnificient treasures of gold, silver, mosaics and featherwork that had been sent as a present to Cortés from Montezuma before the Spaniards had begun their march inland. There were also items that had been plundered from the Maya in Yucatán, including some bark-paper books that may well have been taken from Cozumel island. Among them, quite possibly, was the Dresden Codex, the most informative of the four Maya books that survive, named after the city where it now resides.

Having delivered the royal share, Montejo then waited seven years in Spain in order to secure exclusive title to his own conquests. He was made *Adelantado* of Yucatán, literally 'the man who goes ahead', which gave him hereditary licence to lead its conquest and exploitation. Yet, in the end, all that this precious dispensation produced was twenty years of hardship and disenchantment. Experience might have already taught Montejo how fiercely resistant and politically unpredictable the Maya were. Unlike Cortés and Alvarado, he was quite unable to work out any pattern in the shifting alliances and local allegiances and manipulate them to his own advantage. His first attempt at conquest in 1527 began at Cozumel island and along the north-east coast. Some Maya resisted fiercely, others simply withdrew into the dense bush of the interior. Even when Maya chiefs surrendered, they would rise up again and massacre Spanish garrisons when Montejo himself had gone away. The following year he gave up his attempt on the east and tried from the west, founding Salamanca, the first Spanish town in Yucatán, at Xicalango, the Maya trading-post on the northern coast of Tabasco. From there he moved further north in the early 1530s and established a base at Campeche. Over the next few years they made inroads across the endless monotony of the Yucatán landscape and gained the allegiance of some of the myriad local lords. Montejo's son, Francisco the Younger, even occupied the great Maya city of Chichén Itzá for a short period, though it had largely been deserted by this time, before being forced to retreat and rejoin his father to the west. Conquest of the Maya here was hard and inglorious and there seemed little prospect of material reward to make it worthwhile. Those toiling in northern Yucatán only became more embittered when they began to hear the news of Pizarro's breathtaking exploits in Peru. These had begun with a curious parallel to the first contact with the Maya – a trading raft that Pizarro's men encountered off the coast of Ecuador.

But this one was loaded with precious metals. The Inca empire was to prove a mother-lode richer by far than the treasures of the Aztecs and most of Montejo's men were to head off in that direction. By 1535 there was not one Spaniard left in Yucatán. Montejo, now sixty-seven, was exhausted.

> In these provinces there is not a single river, although there are lakes, and the hills are of live rock, dry and waterless. The entire land is covered by thick bush and is so stony that there is not a single square foot of soil. No gold has been discovered, nor is there anything from which advantage can be gained. The inhabitants are the most abandoned and treacherous in all the lands discovered to this time, being a people who never yet killed a Christian except by foul means and who have never made war except by artifice.[6]

When the conquest was resumed once more in 1540 by the younger Montejo, the men who followed him had no more illusions about what they might discover. The best they could hope for was to finally subdue the native population, settle down and live off their labour. Since 1515, if not earlier, they had had one formidable ally. Biological warfare had been waged silently on their behalf, diseases that apparently had not crossed the Bering Straits thousands of years before and to which the Maya had no immunity. Smallpox in particular took a terrible toll on the Maya of Yucatán. By 1547 the population was reduced to little more than a quarter of what it had been thirty years before. Demoralised by disease, worn down by Spanish persistence, Maya lords submitted little by little during the 1540s. In 1542 Mérida, the future capital of Yucatán, was founded amongst the ruins of the Maya city of Tihoo. In 1546 the lord of the Tutul Xiu of Maní, the most powerful kingdom at that time in the north-west, swore allegiance to the Spanish and was publicly converted to Christianity. Many others then followed and, despite one last burst of resistance in the east late that year, conquest of most of the northern part of the peninsula was completed by the end of 1547.

Once they were established, conquistadores, Spanish administrators and settlers, few of whom were natural scholars, had little practical reason to be curious about the people they had subjugated, or about their history, aside from the administrative necessity to assess the human and material resources at their disposal. Any more active speculation and curiosity about these new lands and their people came from elsewhere.

Thousands of miles away across the Atlantic, the humanists and antiquarians of sixteenth-century Europe were intrigued by the arrival of the art objects and curios such as Montejo had accompanied. The textiles, featherwork, turquoise inlaid masks and gold ornaments were most famously praised by Albrecht Dürer when he saw them exhibited in Brussels in 1520: 'All the days of my life I have not seen anything that gladdened my heart as these things did. For I saw among them wonderful works of art and marvelled at the subtle ingenuity of people in strange lands.'[7]

The Renaissance revival of learning and interest in the remains of Classical antiquity now extended tentatively outward towards contemplation of the products of another, very different culture, and many European princes and noblemen showed themselves keen to acquire examples of New World art and artifice. Yet these were destined not for the sculpture gallery, to be set alongside their collections of Classical antiquities, which represented the exclusive yardstick of all artistic achievement, but for the 'Cabinet of Curiosities', that indiscriminate repository for shells, fossils, gems, stuffed animals, giant's teeth – objects to gawp and marvel at, so strange that they fitted within no easy frame of reference. And if it was difficult to categorize the objects, it was just as hard to come to terms with the people who had created them.

In the Caribbean, during the initial plundering phase between 1492 and 1520, the Spanish had felt themselves on firm ground about the brutes who were set to work panning for gold. The Indians 'went naked and had no shame; they were like idiotic asses, mad and insensate... they had no art or manners of men'.[8] They were by nature servile beasts and were to be treated as such, fitting a lingering medieval vision of half-human beings, wild men in the woods on the edges of the civilized world. But the very need for more slaves had prompted expeditions further afield and ultimately to the lands of the Maya and Aztec. Here, on the American mainland, they had now discovered populous and well-organized societies with towns and cities, rulers and ruled and systems of agriculture, trade and tribute upon which settled life was based.

Thoughtful laymen such as Cortés himself or Bernal Díaz del Castillo, the great eye-witness chronicler of the conquest of Mexico, sought to convey for posterity, somewhat self-consciously, their amazement at first witnessing the scale and nature of American civilization. It was almost inexpressible, the words would not come. 'And some of our soldiers even asked whether the things that we saw were not a dream? It is not to be wondered at that I here write it down in this manner, for there is so much to think over that I do not know how to describe it, seeing things as we did that had never been heard of or seen before, not even dreamed about.'⁹ Such was Díaz' famous description of first setting eyes on Tenochtitlan, that vast metropolis seen shimmering in the thin, clear light from a pass through the surrounding volcanoes. Much of the shock, however, was at recognition, the familiarity of much that they witnessed: the palaces and other buildings of plastered masonry, the gardens and canals, the markets where people exchanged goods from the orderly tilling of their fields to feed their families. Here was a civilization manifestly comparable to, and which in many repects surpassed in its brilliance and scale, contemporary society in Europe.

The conquistadores were hardly strangers to brutality and to killing on a spectacular scale. The wars of sixteenth-century Europe and the ferocious genocide that they had already begun to unleash upon innocent populations in the Americas, both through murder and disease, are testimony enough to their willing subscription and inurement to violence and horror. But there was one totally alien feature which appalled the Spaniards – the rituals of bloodshed and human sacrifice practised not just by the Aztecs, but on a less notable scale by the Maya as well. Bernal Díaz had been introduced to this early on among the Maya of Yucatán, as a member of Hernández de Córdoba's expedition: 'They led us to some large houses very well built of masonry which were the Temples of their Idols, and on the walls were figured the bodies of many great serpents and snakes and other pictures of evil-looking idols. These walls surrounded a sort of altar covered with clotted blood.'¹⁰ The 'priests' who officiated within these temples had hair thickly matted with human blood and the putrid odour of sacrifice was everywhere.

What could account for this? The fundamental teachings of the Christian church were that all men were descended from Adam and Eve and from the sons of Noah after the Flood. So, where had these societies come from originally? Had there been two separate creations? Were these innocents from the main body of humanity who had somehow colonized these regions in remote times and then strayed into grievous error? Or had these peoples been placed here by the Devil himself as a cunning mockery of Christian society? The nature of the peoples of the New World would continue to be a source of academic debate throughout the sixteenth century and the question of their origins, as we shall see, would exercise scholarly, and not so scholarly, minds for a good deal longer. But in 1537 the Papal Bull of Pope Paul III, *Sublimis Deus*, formally declared that the Indians of the Americas were indeed rational humans, 'true men'. They were not to be treated as dumb beasts. They were capable of civilized life and had the evident potential for entry into the Commonwealth of Christians. So, hard on the heels of conquest and the establishment of a system for economic exploitation came the great campaign of religious conversion, the 'Spiritual Conquest'.

For the missionary friars, the strategists and shock troops of that conquest, the propagation of the faith was a daunting but uplifting challenge for which they were well prepared. The task of reforming the pagan nations of the Americas would have as its reward the establishment of a pure New Jerusalem among the teeming millions of a whole continent. This would more than compensate for any Catholic losses to the Protestants in Europe. In New Spain the pioneers of evangelization were the Franciscans. Rejuvenated at home after the Reconquista of the Moorish territories, the favoured order of the Spanish crown and of Cortés himself, their first mission was established in Mexico City in 1524. They were men in a great hurry, fortified by the millenarian conviction that they, and they alone, had been appointed to achieve the complete Christianization of the world before the Second Coming, a cyclical, determinist view of history that was comparable to that of the Maya themselves. In order to succeed, to completely remould Indian culture, they first had to understand the people who were now their charges. The languages of native peoples must be learnt, their traditional customs and beliefs fully comprehended, and the scale of their error assessed.

The best known of all the Fransciscans who worked at this time in the New World, among the Aztecs, is Fray Bernardino de Sahagún. He arrived in Mexico in 1529 and spent more than a decade studying Aztec culture and documenting it through a series of interviews with members of the defeated native nobility, which were carried out and recorded by young mission-trained Indian scribes. The end-product of his labours was the *Historia General de las Cosas de Nueva España*, better known as the

Florentine Codex. A massively comprehensive work in twelve separate books, written both in Spanish and the Aztec language Nahuatl and including almost two thousand illustrations, it is the most detailed account that exists of any indigenous people of the Americas at the time of the conquest. For the Maya, the documentary sources are much more scanty. Apart from brief accounts of the process of conquest and the records of Spaniards who compiled administrative surveys from the later sixteenth century onwards, we have to rely in the main on the writings of one controversial Franciscan who led missionary work in the northern Yucatán, Fray Diego de Landa.

The compelling, paradoxical figure of Landa will reappear a number of times in these pages. He is notorious above all as the prime extirpator of Maya 'idolatries' who in 1562, incensed at the reversion of supposed Christian converts to their ancient religious practices, organized the torture of thousands of Maya, the burning and hanging of their leaders and in a tremendous bonfire destroyed countless 'pagan idols', ancient pots, bones and other 'abominations'. Yet, recalled to Spain to answer charges of excessive zeal and exceeding his authority, he wrote as part of his defence and, as some would like to see it, as a genuine act of atonement, a long and sympathetic account of the people he had persecuted, describing their history, religious practices, their customs, craft traditions, dress, their trade and agricultural practices, indeed most of the details of Maya daily life in remarkable detail.

Naturally enough, one has to approach Landa with great caution given his very particular perspective and the biases of his own sources. The manuscript was also copied a number of times and we do not possess anything like the complete original. Even so, the *Relación de las Cosas de Yucatán* or 'Account of the Things of Yucatán' still provides a unique insight into Maya society in this region in the decades immediately following the Conquest. Combined with the evidence of archaeology, many of his descriptions can be legitimately projected back to give flesh and blood to Maya society of earlier centuries.

Landa arrived in northern Yucatán in 1549. A man of extraordinary energy and natural curiosity, he quickly taught himself Maya and in the early years of his mission travelled alone from village to village, enjoying the intimate access to Maya people and the trust of his informants of a modern anthropologist. He moved principally among the Maya nobility, learned men and the keepers of traditional knowledge. By this period the Maya were no longer producing the kind of written history on monuments of stone that they had done in the Classic period, but his informants were still literate in the Maya script. It was such men who related to him their traditional histories of the centuries before the Conquest and provided Landa with information that has been of fundamental importance to Maya studies. Firstly, he was able to record the names of the Maya days and months from the ancient calendar, accompanied by drawings of their respective hieroglyphs. He also noted a certain date in the Maya calendar along with the equivalent in his own Julian calendar of the time. More than three hundred years later this was to prove one of the keys to the correlation of the Christian and Maya calendrical systems. But other details he recorded have proved even more momentous in recent times. For Landa sat down one day with a Maya noble called Gaspar Antonio Chi and asked him to explain the letters of the Maya alphabet and write them down. The Maya had no alphabet, since their writing system did not work like that, but the confused response of the baffled Chi, and the Maya glyphs that he did copy out for Landa, would turn out, four hundred years later, to be the key to much of modern Maya decipherment.

Landa described traditional Maya society at the very point when it was being irrevocably changed. But he also came to some conclusions of his own about the the Maya past. He recognized the considerable time-depth of Maya culture and suggested the likelihood that there had been a 'better' time in preceding centuries. He was greatly struck by the remains of Maya architecture:

> If Yucatán were to gain a name and reputation from the multitude, the grandeur and the beauty of its buildings, as other regions of the Indies have obtained these by gold, silver and riches, its glory would have spread like that of Peru and New Spain. For it is true that in its buildings and the multitude of them it is the most remarkable of all the things which up to this day have been discovered in the Indies; for they are so many in number and so many are the parts of the country where they are found, and so well built are they of cut stone in their fashion, that it fills one with astonishment.[11]

In a further passage he describes the urban nature of pre-Hispanic Maya society as he conceived it, the kind of 'garden city' planning that archaeologists recognize today, and makes some broad observations on Maya social structure:

Before the Spaniards had conquered that country, the natives lived together in towns in a very civilized fashion. They kept the land well cleared and free from weeds, and planted very good trees. Their dwelling place was as follows: in the middle of the town were their temples with beautiful plazas, and all around the temples stood the houses of the lords and the priests... and at the outskirts of the town were the houses of the lower class.[12]

Landa evidently took notes on his visits to Maya sites, and drew sketches of some of the more prominent architectural elements, such as the great pyramid of the Castillo at Chichén Itzá and the layout of the original Maya plaza at Tihoo, noting orientations and features such as the number of steps and levels to the Castillo. Chichén Itzá as a whole was 'a very fine site', 'with many and magnificent buildings'. He acutely observed that open plaza areas were all paved with a lime cement and that a 'wide and handsome causeway runs, as far as a well which is about two stone's throw off. Into this well they have had, and then had, the custom of throwing men alive, as a sacrifice to the gods, in times of drought... They also throw into it a great many other things, like precious stones and things which they prized.'[13]

This description of the famous 'Sacred Cenote' is pleasingly free of reference to sacrificial virgins cast into its depths, who make their full romantic appearance, prompted by a contemporary of Landa's, much closer to our own day. He also observes that both Chichén Itzá and the island of Cozumel were sacred sites at the time of the Conquest, even though Montejo had found Chichén largely uninhabited: 'they held Cozumel and the wells of Chichén Itzá in the same veneration as we have for the pilgrimages to Jerusalem and Rome'.[14]

Landa had an eye for telling detail. He was impressed by the clothing depicted in Maya sculpture, which accorded with the way that sixteenth-century Maya dressed, and on one occasion he was present when:

there was found in a building... a large urn within which there were the ashes of a burned body, and among them we found three good beads of stone and made like those which the Indians now today use for money; all of which shows that it was the Indians (who were the constructors of these buildings). It may well be that... they were people superior to those of the present time and of very much greater size and strength.[15]

He based this theory on the unusually large size of the bones that they discovered and a feeling that the steps of Maya pyramids were adjusted to a taller race of men. Although we cannot be sure about the date of the particular bones that he found, recent analyses of Maya skeletons support Landa's notion that the Maya of earlier centuries were generally more robust than their descendants of the Conquest period. However, to characterize Landa as an enlightened proto-archaeologist would be wide of the mark. His more 'archaeological' observations are very few and betray little more than an enthusiastic, generalized curiosity about what he saw on his travels. His judgements appear impressively matter-of-fact today compared with the more elaborate conjecture of later times, but to him it no doubt seemed natural enough that the buildings he saw were constructed by the ancestors of the Maya that he knew.

The town of Izamál, halfway between Mérida and Chichén Itzá, was a major pre-Hispanic centre which Landa himself says boasted eleven or twelve formidable pyramids, with temples 'of such height and beauty that it astonishes one'. Izamál was Landa's base for most of his missionary career and it was here 'the Indians obliged us with importunity to establish in the year 1549 a house on one of these edifices, which we call St Antonio, which has been of great assistance in bringing them to Christianity'.[16] The Franciscans built their church and monastery on one of the biggest of the Maya platforms, flattening the buildings that had stood there and quarrying further stone from other nearby pyramids. The church that survives today is unremarkable, but the arcaded precinct approached by a ramp that extends to the west is vast, seemingly out of all proportion. It was largely Landa's own design. He was well aware of the symbolic power of architecture and across this great parade ground of the faith would have processed the massed ranks of the converts he thought he had gained. Yet if the Spaniards believed they had successfully levelled the old culture and constructed another out of its rubble, they were mistaken. The foundations of Maya beliefs had not been eradicated.

In 1562 it became only too clear to Landa and his colleagues that their initial high hopes for the success of their mission had been misplaced. Caves were discovered where 'idols' were still being worshipped and further investigation revealed the full scale of persisting superstitions and idolatries, even of human sacrifice. The result was an orgy of floggings, fiendish tortures and purges. The full horror of the Spanish Inquisition was unleashed in the small town of Maní, a reign of terror that lasted three months. It was crowned by an elaborate 'Auto da Fe' or 'Act of Faith' during which every sacrilegious object that the friars could lay their hands on was destroyed by fire.

In the early days, in displays of reckless confidence, Landa's Maya friends and informants had shown him their precious manuscripts – histories, sacred prophecies and books of divination. These were the native books of bark paper, which were coated in a thin layer of lime plaster and painted with hieroglyphs. The pages were joined up and folded within covers of wood or jaguar skin and when opened out like a small folding screen could be up to twenty feet in length. In these books, Landa observes, they recorded Maya 'antiquities and their sciences'. But, as he also says, casually and pitilessly, 'we found a large number of books of these characters, and as they contained nothing in which there were not to be seen superstition and lies of the devil, we burned them all, which they regretted to an amazing degree, and which caused them much affliction'.[17]

The loss to modern science in Landa's bonfires and the wider process of cultural destruction in the early Colonial period is incalculable. Hundreds of Maya books must have been destroyed, along with count-less monuments and images conceived to have a pagan, diabolical message. All trace of the ancient ways had to be expunged. The uncom-fortable paradox today is that archaeologists and historians have to make do with what remains – Landa's own priceless *Relación*, which, however tainted, still stands as the first account of the Maya in their context as a native people of the Americas with a considerable history and who were worthy of European interest and admiration.

In 1563 Landa was ordered to return to Spain, where three years later he wrote the *Relación*. For most scholars the reputation of this enigmatic figure is sullied by falsified documents that Landa appended to his own text which claimed that his purges had the approval of local people. In due course, however, he was acquitted by his peers of the charges against him and returned to Yucatán as its first bishop in 1572.

Landa does not stand completely alone in this early period as an observer of Maya antiquities. There were other clerics and travellers who have left brief accounts of Maya sites in northern Yucatán such as Uxmal and Chichén Itzá. The very first reference of all to the ruins of a pre-Conquest Maya city comes from the man who was initially Landa's Superior, Lorenzo de Bienvenida, describing a part of ancient Tihoo or Mérida :

in all the discoveries in the Indies none so fine has been found; buildings of big and well carved stones; there is no record of who built them. It seems to us that they were built before Christ, because the trees on top of the buildings were as high as the ones around them. Amongst these buildings, we, monks of the Order of Saint Francis, settled.[18]

He clearly expresses the idea of the great antiquity of the buildings and the admiration commonly shown for the quality and sophistication of Maya architecture, compared with the remains of other pre-Hispanic societies that the Spanish observed. More unusually, from the other side of the Maya world, comes a unique early description of the great Classic Maya city of Copán. In 1576 a colonial official called Diego Garcia de Palacio wrote in a letter to Philip II of Spain, 'in the first town within the province of Honduras, called Copán, are certain ruins and vestiges of a great population, and of superb edifices...' He identified Copán's main plaza and was the first to comment upon the famous standing sculptures or stelae:

In this square are six great statues: three representing men covered with mosaic work, and with garters around their legs, their weapons covered with ornaments; the others are of women with long robes and head dresses in the Roman style. They seem to have been idols, for in front of each of them is a large stone used as a basin and a channel cut into it where they executed the victim and the blood flowed off... Besides these things, there are many others which prove that here was formerly the seat of a great power, and a great population, civilized and considerably advanced in the arts, as is shown in the various figures and buildings.[19]

Besides description of Maya antiquities, a number of other friars engaged in documentary and linguistic studies that would prove invaluable for more recent efforts at Maya decipherment. Antonio de Ciudad Real was a Franciscan working in the Yucatán whose study of the Maya language resulted in a great dictionary of Yucatec Mayan known as the Motul Dictionary. Writing in the late seventeenth century, Fray Diego López de Cogolludo described many of the ruins of Yucatán, wrote a biographical sketch of his predecessor Diego de Landa and supplemented the latter's work by recording the Yucatec names for the months and some of the days in the Maya calendar. At the turn of the eighteenth century, in Chichicastenango in the highlands of Guatemala, Fray Francisco

Ximénez made the only copy that survives of the Popol Vuh or 'Book of Council' of the Quiché Maya, which now apears in good part to be a transcription or a descendant of a pre-Hispanic Maya codex and a unique key to much of ancient Maya religion and cosmology.

Yet despite documentation of living Maya culture and admiration for a small number of pre-Hispanic cities expressed by a few rare individuals, there was no more systematic attempt to mount expeditions, find more ruins and learn any more about the Maya past. The dawn of 'archaeology' as we know it today was far off and, as we have seen, the underlying motive behind most attempts to study and understand Maya culture was to hasten its ultimate destruction. The early observers were also quite unaware that what they saw was but a part of the Maya heritage, whose most glorious physical remnants lay buried for centuries in the forests of the Southern Lowlands. Few Spaniards cared to enter there because there seemed nothing worth pursuing. There was no gold to seize from the natives, nor could there be mines in the unbroken shelf of limestone that underlay the whole of the Yucatán peninsula.

A single epic crossing of the lowlands had been made soon after the downfall of Tenochtitlan by that Odysseus of the New World himself, Hernan Cortés. To quell a revolt in Honduras by one of his commanders, he set out in late 1524 from the Gulf Coast with some 230 Spaniards and 3000 Mexican warriors along with artillery, 150 horses and herds of pigs as a mobile larder. They plunged into the swamps of Tabasco, followed the Usumacinta River as far as its junction with the Rio San Pedro and then headed north and south-east straight into the forests of the Petén. Six months later the exhausted remnants of the original force emerged on the shore of Lake Izabal and descended to the Gulf of Honduras. Tormented by insects, sometimes unable to march more than five miles a day, totally lost for a time when their Indian guides fled, this remarkable feat of endurance is still a little-known episode in Cortés' career, but it ranks alongside the exploits of those searchers after El Dorado in the Amazon Basin, as one of the great achievements in Spanish exploration of the Americas.[20]

Halfway across the Petén Cortés had an appropriately mythic encounter, at Tayasal, modern Flores, on Lake Petén Itzá. Here they came upon a Maya kingdom still remaining within the forests, which the evidence now suggests had survived continuously since the Classic period. Cortés met Kan Ek, the ruler of the 'Itzá' people, on the shore of the lake and was then escorted by canoe to Tayasal. There, a group of

Spanish friars was allowed to celebrate a sung mass. Kan Ek was apparently delighted by the music and vowed to destroy his heathen idols and become a vassal of Spain. So accommodating was he that he also agreed to look after Cortés' sick horse, a fearsome creature of supernatural proportions which of course the Itzá had never set eyes on before, until such time as Cortés and Kan Ek should meet up again. Whether this encounter was quite so cosy in reality is debatable, since we do not have any Maya account of these events. But Cortés and Kan Ek never met again. Indeed, Tayasal was to remain as an independent, living Maya city, untouched by the Spanish for many more years.

Besides Tayasal there is no mention in the Spanish sources of any other major Maya town still existing in the forests at this time. Neither is there any reference to the sighting of ruins of an earlier period, though the Cortés expedition passed close to a number of Maya sites known today. Apart from the lonely missionary activities of the friars, who would slowly begin to probe the forests in the seventeenth century, these regions remained an area of wilderness and of refuge, where Maya from the areas of Spanish occupation could flee to maintain in isolation the traditional practices of their forefathers.

As the years passed and crumbling Maya cities became ever more firmly embedded in the jungle, so too all the earlier accounts of Maya culture and antiquities themselves turned into archaeological material, buried in libraries and forgotten. The great archival sleep of Landa's *Relación* was to last for almost three hundred years. This did not happen simply by chance, suggests the Mexican historian Enrique Florescano, but originated as official policy. If Landa and other zealots who came after him attempted to eliminate the remnants of paganism and destroy the Maya's own histories, the Spanish crown would seek to ban and bury even Spanish documentation of native 'superstitions' and the indigenous past. Thus Philip II, for example, knowing of the great collections of testimonies about the Aztecs formed by Bernardino de Sahagún, ordered the Viceroy in New Spain in 1577 to 'get hold of these books ... and send them forthwith and with great care to the Consejo de Indias so that they may be examined, and be well advised that no one in any language or under any circumstances be allowed to write things that touch upon superstitions and the way of life that these Indians had.' The effects of this 'annihilation of the past' were to last until the late eighteenth century.[21]

'IT MAY REASONABLY BE CONJECTURED'

Charles III, the Bourbon king who ruled Spain and its American possessions from 1759 to 1788, was an energetic man who attempted to
reform and liberalize the creaking structure of the Spanish empire and, a
hopeless task in the end, to bind the colonies more closely to the home
country. One element of this was an attempt at what one might call cultural integration and the encouragement within Spanish America of the
new approaches and ideas of the Enlightenment, that spirit of intellectual curiosity and more outward-looking scientific enquiry into the
workings of the world that had emerged during the course of the
eighteenth century in Europe. Cosmetic gestures they may have been,
but in this vein Charles supported a number of natural history expeditions to New Spain to collect specimens of native flora and fauna and
encouraged the application of new technologies to local industries.

Charles was himself an enthusiastic antiquarian who, as King of
Naples before acceding to the Spanish throne, had sponsored the first
excavations, of a rather crude nature, at Pompeii. From this and other
sources he had acquired a fine collection of Graeco-Roman antiquities.
But besides this classical antiquarianism in the narrower Renaissance
tradition he now began to encourage interest in the past of his more
remote dominions and appointed Juan Bautista Muñoz, originally Royal
Cosmographer, to be official 'Historiographer of the Indies'. To some
degree this was a response to local initiatives. For by the 1770s a few
scholars in New Spain itself were beginning to embark upon their own
histories and for the first time to consider the remains of the native
peoples of Mesoamerica, not as a potentially threatening phenomenon,
but as a worthy subject for study and a part of the heritage of what
would soon be independent New World nations.

This more positive outlook established, a whole new beginning was
about to be made with the emergence from the forests of the first of the
great 'lost' cities of the Maya Classic period, the incomparably beautiful
city of Palenque (see plate section, pp.17–18). Few ancient sites, anywhere
in the world, can match Palenque's setting. Still nestling in thick forest, the
ruins are perched among the lower slopes of a small range of hills on the
very edge of the Chiapas highlands. To the north, two hundred feet
below, the immense floodplain of the Usumacinta spreads far away to the
horizon towards the Laguna de Terminos and the Gulf Coast.

Palenque appears modest in size, though, like many Maya sites, much of it remains hidden in jungle and even today the full extent of its outlying structures is unclear. The core area of best preserved stone buildings, bisected by the canalized stream of the Rio Otolum, ranges along the hillside upon a series of natural and artificial terraces. The most impressive complex is the 'Palace', built on a rectangular platform some ninety metres long and seventy metres wide and consisting of a series of vaulted rooms and galleries around open courtyards, one of which surrounds a three-storeyed tower, unique in Maya architecture (see plate section, p.17).

The Palace almost certainly represents the ancient heart of Palenque. Immediately surrounding it are the famous temples, including the Temple of the Inscriptions (see overleaf), set into the hillside on a nine-levelled pyramid to the south-west, and the so-called 'Cross Group' to the east, made up of the Temple of the Cross, the Temple of the Sun and the Temple of the Foliated Cross, each perched at different elevations and facing onto a small, secluded plaza.

Palenque is renowned for the human scale, the delicacy and grace of its buildings and for the profusion here of architectural ornament, notably modelled stucco and limestone carved in low relief. The façades of buildings and many of the interior walls in the Palace and principal temples were originally brightly painted and adorned with panels of Maya hieroglyphs and portrait and narrative scenes depicting men, women and elaborate supernatural images executed in a remarkably elegant and realistic style. Such scenes were to defy accurate interpretation for a very long time, but they have always appeared tantalisingly accessible. No other Maya site could have been better calculated to provoke or fascinate those who stumbled upon it. It was here that the first generations of visitors began to ponder the mysteries of the Maya.[22]

The ancient city takes its name from the small town some seven kilometres away which was founded as Santo Domingo de Palenque in 1567. But the ruins kept their secrets for almost two hundred years more until, in 1746, the relations of Antonio de Solís, a local priest, are said to have come upon 'casas de piedra' or stone houses while cutting their way up the forested hillside to clear new maize fields. It was another thirty years before Ramón Ordoñez y Aguiar from Ciudad Real, today San Cristóbal de las Casas, who had been a schoolfellow of one of the Solís family, organized a preliminary expedition and then reported the discovery to José Estachería, President of what was then the Royal

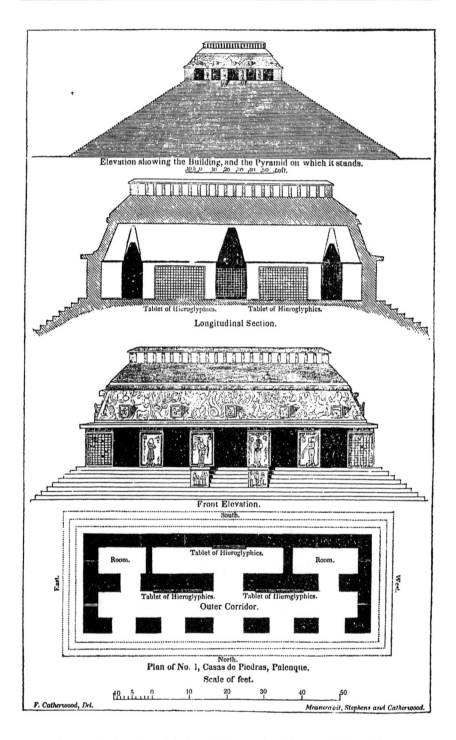

Catherwood's drawings and plan of the Temple of the Inscriptions, Palenque.

Audiencia of Guatemala. Estachería instructed José Antonio Calderón, a local government official in Palenque, to have a close look at the ruins and send him a report.

Calderón spent three days hacking his way through the forest, astonished and mystified at the appearance of 'la gran Ciudad Palencana' as he termed it, 'the great City of Palenque'. He was the first to give the name to the 'Palace' at the centre of the city, 'which from its construction and size could not be anything less'. Besides this large Palace, he also claimed to have counted twenty-eight lesser 'palaces' and 197 other houses. He reported the remarkable preservation of the buildings and described the different architectural elements including the spacious vaulted rooms, the patios and corridors, T-shaped windows and 'beds' of stone. He also remarked upon 'figures sculpted with much delicacy on the walls of the Palace'.[23] He made two ink drawings of these, another of the tower in the Palace and a fourth of a relief in the Temple of the Sun (see below). Although what they are trying to depict is recognizable, the best that can be said of Calderón's sketches is that they possess a certain naïve charm. As to any conclusions about the identity of the original inhabitants, he could only suggest that the style of the sandals that some of the figures wore looked to him rather Roman. Estachería, however, could hardly have expected anything more from the mayor of a small provincial town.

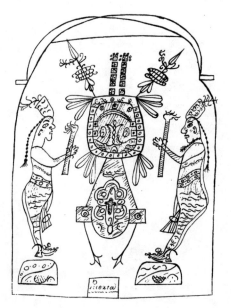

The main scene from the Tablet of the Temple of the Sun, drawing by José Calderón.

Sufficiently intrigued, Estachería sent another expedition the following year, headed by the noted Spanish architect Antonio Bernasconi, who was in Guatemala at the time working on the construction of a new capital city after a disastrous earthquake in 1773 had destroyed the previous capital, now known as Antigua. Calderón was to act as Bernasconi's guide and provide local labour to clear some of the jungle. As one might imagine, Bernasconi's report was more professionally presented and included a general map of the area and sketched plans, elevations and cross-sections of some of the principal structures (see below), including the Palace and the Temples of the Cross and the Sun. He also attempted to render some of the sculptural reliefs, a stone throne and a panel of hieroglyphs. However, there was very little text to go with the drawings. Perhaps Bernasconi felt he could add little more to the untutored Calderón's conclusions. The city appeared to have been naturally abandoned, rather than destroyed by fire or earthquake, there was something 'gotico' or Gothic about the vaulting in the Palace, but otherwise he was at a loss. He could see in the ruins no 'order' of architecture, either ancient or modern, with which he was familiar.[24]

Estachería now sent copies of both reports to the court of Charles III, where they were first seen by Juan Bautista Muñoz. Muñoz never set foot in New Spain, but he was nonetheless to play an important role. He was evidently an enterprising and conscientious scholar whose

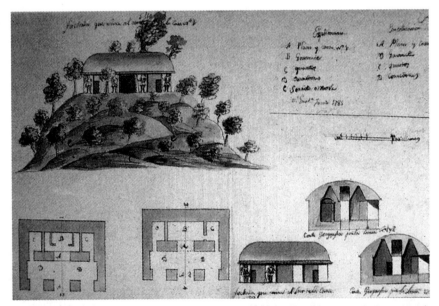

Sketches of the Temple of the Sun and the Temple of the Cross by Antonio Bernasconi.

researches in the Spanish archives convinced him of Palenque's importance. After reading the reports, he sent them on to the king, accompanied by observations of his own.

He says that the work of both Calderón and Bernasconi has 'borne not inconsiderable fruit'. Their investigations had provided an 'eye-witness demonstration of the veracity of our conquistadores and earliest historians with respect to the buildings discovered in New Spain and surrounding areas'. Palenque, he suggests, may well have been the capital 'of a great power some centuries before the conquest'. Revealing his familiarity with some of the early sources, he goes on to note famous buildings previously found to the north-east in Yucatán, 'covered with earth and supporting trees of great size' just like those of Palenque, and he mentions that to the east, just within the province of Honduras, were discovered 'vestiges of another great city with superb edifices adorned with statues and reliefs very like those which have now been found'. Here he is referring to the 1576 report of Diego Garcia de Palacio on the ruins of Copán. Muñoz says that he is including a copy of this report so that the king can compare it with those of Calderón and Bernasconi. He expresses generous praise for Estachería's 'laudable zeal in ordering the detailed investigation of the ruins, which may illustrate the origins and history of the Ancient Americans'.[25]

Muñoz and the king agreed that further explorations were warranted and gave precise instructions as to how future investigations should be undertaken. These are informative in themselves in revealing the more 'scientific' method now being advocated. They were to distinguish 'between doors, niches and windows... to study any stones that are found like those described or walls of stoned mortar or of similar mixed materials; to make detailed descriptions and drawings of shapes, sizes and the cut of the stones and bricks, particularly in arches and vaults.' They were also to send what one might call 'archaeological' evidence back to Spain, 'samples of plaster mixture, stucco, bricks (baked or otherwise), pots or any other utensils or tools that may be found, digging where necessary'.

As a result, in May 1786, Estachería sent two men to the ruins – Antonio del Río, a bright and diligent Captain of Artillery in the Spanish army, and Ricardo Almendáriz, a professional artist. Dismayed to find the buildings completely overgrown once more, they were initially delayed while scores of local labourers were hired to clear the ruins with axes and machetes. Then, with gusto they began to follow their orders.

In the Palace, where they started work, 'there remained neither a window nor a doorway blocked up; a partition that was not thrown down, nor a room, corridor, court, tower, nor subterranean passage in which excavations were not effected'.[26] Fortunately their excavations were not as radical or destructive as Del Río suggests. In the end thirty-two objects were to be sent to Spain, including pottery and stone tools as well as fragments of stone sculpture, some stucco glyphs and the leg of a throne from the Palace.

Almendáriz produced a series of thirty drawings, the best-known of which are the major relief panels from the Cross Group (see below). Although his rendering of the hieroglyphs is quite inaccurate, and indeed purely notional, he was the first man to represent competently the rich and complex iconography of Palenque. Del Río drew up a substantial, largely descriptive report. Echoing Muñoz and having also consulted a local historian of the Yucatán, he reckoned that the remains of Palenque belonged to the same people who had built the monuments of Chichén Itzá and Uxmal. As to who these people might have been, his conclusions were judiciously phrased but significant none the less:

> The conclusion... must be that the ancient inhabitants of these structures lived in extreme darkness, for, in their fabulous superstitions, we seem to view the ideology of the Phoenicians, the Greeks, the Romans and other

The Tablet from the Temple of the Cross by Ricardo Almendáriz.

primitive nations most strongly portrayed. On this account it may reasonably be conjectured, that some one of these nations pursued their
conquests even to this country, where it is possible they only remained long
enough to enable the Indian tribes to imitate their ideas and adapt, in a rude
and awkward manner, such arts as their invaders thought fit to inculcate.[27]

Here we have a statement of the basic assumption that was to underlie
all interpretations of Palenque over the next few decades. When Del Río
uses the word 'primitive' here, 'primitivo' in Spanish, he does not mean
it in the oft-used, more modern sense of 'simple' or 'undeveloped'. To
him it meant 'early' or 'ancient'. He is talking about the early nations or
civilizations of Greece and Rome and so on. The only simple or undeveloped people were the Indians, who were indeed so simple, rude and
awkward that they could not possibly have created Palenque on their
own. The questing intellectual spirit of the Enlightenment, the encouragement of Charles III and Muñoz had initiated the investigation of this
great Maya city but it could not alter the fundamental preconception of
scholars of the time, absorbed with the first Latin verbs learnt at school,
that all true civilization had its origins in the Old World.

One can begin to understand these attitudes by looking at the question
another way. At least men such as Diego de Landa were closer to the pre-
Conquest Maya, and could associate more easily the Maya they knew with
the achievements of the past. But for those explorers of the eighteenth and
nineteenth centuries who saw the wretched remnants of great pre-Hispanic
civilizations slaving in the fields for the new lords of the land, reduced over
two hundred years of subjugation to a dependent and seemingly inarticu-
late peasantry, it was difficult to believe that their ancestors had been
capable of anything better. The solution to the conundrum of the ruins was
that it had to be someone else: Egyptians, attractive because of pyramids
and hieroglyphs; Hebrews; Carthaginians; wandering Welshmen; peoples
from the lost continent of Atlantis – the list would be endless.
Unfortunately, these appealingly simple answers, approaching racism
at times in their dismissal of indigenous abilities, have continued on in
unbroken succession down to the extra-terrestrial fantasies of our own day.

Charles IV maintained the official encouragement of exploration and
in 1804 commissioned a retired army officer, Guillermo Dupaix, to
survey not just the Maya area but all the major ruins of New Spain. In
1807, on his third journey, Dupaix reached Palenque with his accompanying artist, José Castañeda. Dupaix seems to have been a scholarly

and sensitive man, familiar at first-hand with the ancient heritage of Greece and Rome. Twenty years spent in the New World, the previous two among the ruins of Central Mexico, had also equipped him with considerable experience of pre-Hispanic art and architecture. He could see that Maya art was quite different to that of the Aztecs or the Zapotec of Oaxaca. He, too, produced a thorough description of Palenque and a better technical appreciation than Del Río of the methods and materials employed in the construction of buildings and in their ornament. The stucco and limestone reliefs impressed him technically, but above all aesthetically and for the story they might tell:

> Most of the figures are erect and well-proportioned: all of them are in profile, portly and almost colossal, their height exceeding six feet; while their attitudes display great freedom of limb, with a certain expression of dignity... Many of the figures hold a kind of rod or staff in one hand; at the feet of others smaller figures are placed in reverential postures, and some are surrounded with rows of hieroglyphics.[28]

Dupaix imagined that many of these figures might have been lords of the city and the hieroglyphs perhaps told something of their history. If this was writing, however, it bore little resemblance to what he knew of Egyptian hieroglyphs or to the forms of picture writing used by other later peoples of Mexico. The elongated, flattened heads of many of the figures also suggested to him a quite original, distinctive race of people. They could not, he felt, be related to the present Indians of the region. Among the limestone and stucco reliefs that he looked at long and hard, he found the central panel in the Temple of the Cross quite mystifying. The heavily ornamented cruciform image between the two human figures seemed if anything like a 'Greek' cross, 'not the holy Latin Cross which we adore'. He concluded in the end that it was probably related 'to the religion of the country,' whatever that might have been.

Like Bernasconi, Dupaix could see little stylistic connection with the art of any other civilization. He also entertained, in common with Del Río, the notion of an initial influence or impact from another part of the world at some point way in the past. But if this had been so, only many centuries of independent development could have produced the strange beauty and magnificient originality of what he saw. He felt unable to come to any firmer conclusions, but he was remarkably close to the suggestion of purely indigenous origins.

The reports of both Del Río and Dupaix were conscientiously delivered and filed and for a long while little was heard of them. Dupaix's was
lodged in Mexico City for many years, larger events having prevented its
reaching Europe. For in 1808 Napoleon invaded Spain, forced the abdi-
cation of Charles IV and put his brother Joseph Bonaparte on the
throne. Although the Bourbons were restored in 1814, a brief taste of
self-government had encouraged an irresistible desire for permanent
independence, which Mexico gained in 1821. During these uncertain
early years of the nineteenth century, little more Maya exploration was
undertaken.

Meanwhile, it is instructive to look at the wider world of early archaeology at this time as a gauge of the limited and tentative progress that
had been made in the Americas. Due also to the impact of Napoleon
Bonaparte, Europe's antiquarian gaze was firmly fixed on the Near East,
more precisely along the valley of the Nile. Napoleon's forces appeared
in Egypt in 1798. In their wake followed his 'Commission of Arts and
Sciences', a body of scholars, cartographers and artists who in three
years followed the army up and down the Nile recording the monuments of ancient Egypt. It was an extraordinary idea, and in the annals
of archaeology an expression of state support for learning that has never
been equalled. The published results began to appear in 1809 in the
magnificent *Description de l'Egypte*, twenty volumes of precise recording
and learned text, illustrated with engraved plates of extraordinary
quality. The *Description* still represents the greatest panorama of ancient
Egypt ever produced and one of the glories of the French
Enlightenment. Although Europeans had been studying and speculating
about the antiquities of Egypt for centuries, the work of Napoleon's
Commission effectively began Egyptology as we know it today, drawing
other scholars and such archaeological adventurers as Giovanni Belzoni
to the Nile valley, whose dramatic discoveries and adventures ignited
popular interest in Europe. No such systematic scholarly work was to
take place in the Maya area for many years. But, significantly, the archaeological awakening of ancient Egypt formed the education of two
men who would in turn begin the modern era of Maya studies.

In 1822, towards the end of this very first bout of European
'Egyptomania', came Champollion's initial breakthrough in the decipherment of Egyptian hieroglyphs. It was in that same year that a slim
volume entitled *Description of the Ruins of an Ancient City ...* was published
in London. The ancient city in question was not Memphis or Thebes,

but Palenque. It would appear that a copy of Del Río's report left in Guatemala had been seen by Paul Felix Cabrera, an Italian emigré with a taste for antiquarian speculation. He had been inspired to write his own treatise on the Transatlantic origins of American peoples, *Teatro Critico Americano*, which suggested that the first seeds of civilization in the New World had been sown by Votan, son of Hercules. A shadowy Dr M. Quy then brought the two texts to London, where they were translated and printed together by the publisher Henry Berthoud, along with seventeen of the Almendáriz drawings that had accompanied the Del Río report, engraved by the artist Jean Frédéric 'Count' Waldeck.

This was the first illustrated description of a Maya ruin ever to appear in print. But interest in the book was slow to pick up, Brunhouse notes, and when it did, due perhaps to the dubious company that Del Río's account was in, excited even more outlandish comment, like this review from one John Ranking: 'Guatemala and Yucatán have been proved by the remarks on the ruins at Palenque, to bear strong evidence of their having been peopled by Asiatics, Turks, Mongols and Calmucs. The arrival of the Tartars in America in considerable numbers from 544 to 1283... are sufficient to account for everything of importance that is yet known with regard to America'.[29]

Dupaix's report and Castañeda's drawings were also first published in London. Edward King, Lord Kingsborough, included them in Volume VI of his *Antiquities of Mexico*, nine enormous and luxurious volumes, vastly expensive to produce, that appeared between 1830 and 1848. They reproduced Mexican manuscripts in European collections, including the Maya Dresden Codex. Of considerable importance as source material for scholars, Kingsborough's own written contribution was not so valuable. It was a confused attempt to prove that the progenitors of native American peoples had been the Lost Tribes of Israel, a fashionable theory that had been going about in one form or another since the Conquest. Yet again the more sober and modest accounts of the explorers who had actually seen the ruins were hi-jacked by armchair theorists eager to put forward their more eccentric, ambitious views on the origins of American civilization.

In 1834 Dupaix and Castañeda's work appeared in two volumes published in Paris, entitled *Antiquités Mexicaines*, where it generated considerable interest. Even here, though, it was accompanied by the commentaries of a variety of scholars who theorized heavily on the links between ancient America and other civilizations. But at least one

Frenchman, Alexandre Lenoir, refrained from the more exclusive pursuit of origins and produced instead what he believed was a viable chronology which, working backwards, was the following:

1. Mexican antiquities, that is to say those belonging to the Aztecs... whose ancestry goes back to the twelfth century. 2. pre-Aztec antiquities, for example those of the Toltecs... 3. antiquities of Palenque and others of the same nature throughout Guatemala, Yucatán, the origins of which go so far back in time and are totally unknown.[30]

This was indeed a very reasonable, state-of-the-art summary of what people could generally agree on at this time. What was needed above all was more purposeful exploration and more effective critical analysis of Maya ruins on the spot.

By the later 1820s circumstances in Central America had changed dramatically. Mexico was now independent and Guatemala and Honduras were to form part of a new Central American Confederation, an unstable entity that would eventually break up into the modern nation states of Central America. With Spanish imperial restrictions removed, the region now opened its arms to the outside world. As in the Eastern Europe of the 1990s, traders and entrepreneurs descended on the area in search of commercial opportunity and to set up new industries. Along with them came diplomats and consular representatives to protect their national interests. Foreigners constantly bumped into each other, searching for mines, for logging rights, for preferment from competing political factions among the volatile new republics. Some were pure travellers in search of a wilder alternative to the more convential Grand Tour of Europe and the Middle East, attracted by the romantic mythology of the independence movements and by a few significant published descriptions of the area, the most influential being Alexander von Humboldt's magnificient atlas *Vues des cordillères et monuments des peuples indigènes de l'Amérique*, published in Paris in 1810. Humboldt's plates vividly conveyed the wonders of the scenery and ancient monuments of Latin America, and also included, though Humboldt never visited the Maya area, a remarkably accurate copy of five pages of the Dresden Codex and an engraving of one of the reliefs from Palenque, which must somehow have been a copy of one of the original Almendáriz drawings.

This exciting new era of opportunity for foreigners threw up two unusual characters who have each made a name for themselves in the story of Maya discovery. The first, and most extraordinary of all, was without doubt Jean Frédéric Waldeck (see p.2, plate section). He it was who produced the engravings of the Almendáriz drawings which accompanied the English publication of Del Río's report in 1822. This is one of the undoubted facts in his incredible life about which those who have attempted Waldeck's biography, such as Robert Brunhouse and Claude Baudez, can be certain.[31] For 'Count' Waldeck claimed many things. According to him, he was born in 1766, in either Paris, Prague or Vienna. He was of Austrian noble descent and boasted a number of titles, including Duke but most commonly Count, and a variety of nationalities, depending on where he happened to be at the time. He said that at the age of fourteen he had set off with a scientific expedition to explore much of southern Africa. He had then returned to Paris to develop his skills as an artist under the tuition of the great neo-Classical painter Jacques-Louis David, or perhaps David's own teacher, Joseph Vien. He would recount how in 1794 he had been at Napoleon's side at the siege of Toulon. He had accompanied him on the Italian campaign and in due course to Egypt. Many other international adventures followed and in 1819 he had supposedly joined Lord Cochrane in the liberation of Chile.

Such a brilliant career had made him the confidant of all the great and good, the high and mighty of Europe. In England, for example, he was friends with George III, Pitt and Fox, Beau Brummel and with Lord Byron who, when they met up at a Scottish castle, 'would swim and leave me to fish alone'. Across the Channel he had somehow managed to be on intimate terms with both Robespierre and Marie Antoinette, whom he visited frequently in prison while she awaited her execution. These, as Brunhouse says, were merely the adventures of Waldeck's 'youth', until his mid-fifties. But his fantastic life as a charming self-publicist and bare-faced liar lasted until 1875, when at the age of 109, settled in Paris on a modest pension from the Institut de France, the self-appointed 'First Americanist' is said to have died of a stroke in a Montmartre café after turning over-energetically to watch a pretty girl walk by. As Brunhouse nicely puts it, 'It is a typical Waldeck anecdote, and one suspects that he might have invented it, if that were possible.'[32]

Waldeck's fifteen or so years devoted to the Maya, however, can be followed with reasonable accuracy. After preparing the plates for Del Río's report, which he dismissed as 'a very incomplete work', he says that he was determined one day to investigate and draw the ruins himself. Four years later he took a job with an English company as a mining engineer in a remote part of western Mexico, many miles from Palenque. It was curious thing to do, but here we can detect the more prosaic reality of Waldeck's life intruding, for he was never a rich man and had a wife and child to support in Europe, to whom he despatched sums of money when he could. He left the mine after a year and moved to Mexico City, where he got by painting portraits and giving drawing lessons. He mixed with Mexican scholars, became more acquainted with other pre-Hispanic antiquities and attempted to raise money by subscription to support his own expedition to Palenque. He raised a third of it and felt confident enough of the rest to leave for the ruins in May 1832.

Waldeck spent a year at Palenque, living in the Palace until the bats became too bothersome and then in a hut that he had built for him beneath the Temple of the Cross. He did not, it seems, occupy what is popularly known today as the Temple of the Count, to the north of the Palace. Working conditions were terrible, especially since he had arrived at the beginning of the rainy season, and he complained continuously of the ticks, the mosquitoes and the draining humidity. Yet, for a man in his sixties he did a remarkable amount of work. In all he produced about a hundred drawings, some now in France and others in the Newberry Library in Chicago.

Many of his first drafts and pencil drawings on squared paper are by all accounts extremely impressive. They include plans and elevations of buildings, copies of hieroglyphic panels and details of reliefs and stone carvings, some of which are of great value to archaeologists today since the originals have been lost or destroyed. Unfortunately, Waldeck's paintings and published lithographs, executed after he left Mexico, are much less reliable. He produced a number of neo-Classical landscapes in the Paris salon style, immensely attractive as works of art since Waldeck was an extremely good painter, but none too helpful archaeologically. In these he modified the topography of the ruins for Romantic effect and placed picturesquely savage wild-life and semi-naked figures in the foreground, one of whom was reputedly his local Palenque mistress, Nicté. He rendered relief panels in a beautifully finished but misleading 'Graeco-Egyptian' style, and in his representations of Maya hieroglyphs (see p.51) introduced certain interpretations or modifications to fit his own theories about the ruins. These inevitably involved Old World origins and Waldeck's choice, as one might expect, was more exotic than most: 'To all appearances the Chaldeans were the original stock, and the main body consisted of Hindoos'. To help these ideas along a little he managed to detect sections of cuneiform script among the glyphs, which Henry Rawlinson and other scholars in Europe were puzzling over at the time Waldeck was working up his drawings. There are other bizarre, disconnected features such as a hieroglyphic rendering of the *marimba*, a musical instrument introduced into the Maya area in the colonial period by African slaves. But the most notorious introduction of all was elephants, which would have provided Waldeck's most direct piece of evidence for the 'Hindoo' connection. Elephants have a long history on the fringes of Maya studies. The Maya could on occasion treat the head of a macaw in such a stylized way that its beak came to resemble an elephant's trunk. This is particularly true on the stelae of Copán, so much so that certain enthusiastic diffusionists were still seeing Indian elephants here as late as the 1920s.

After Palenque, Waldeck proceeded to the ruins of Uxmal, financed by one of his patrons, the ever-generous Lord Kingsborough who was soon to die in a debtor's prison, bankrupted largely by his devotion to pre-Hispanic America. Of Uxmal's architecture, too, Waldeck was to produce some beautiful but extremely imaginative interpretations.

Waldeck was an engaging opportunist and much of his invention was calculated to appeal to the audience for publications that he planned after his return to Europe. For by the 1830s romantic travelogues combining antiquarian 'researches' with descriptions of adventures and hardships encountered in exotic, little-known parts of the world were greatly in demand. On his return to France after eleven years in Mexico he immediately began working up his drawings into lithographs and in 1838 his *Voyage pittoresque et archéologique dans la province d'Yucatán* was published, which was neither a commercial nor critical success. Much later, in 1866 when Waldeck reached his 100th birthday, more than fifty of his lithographs were used in *Monuments Anciens du Mexique, Palenque et autres ruines de l'ancienne civilisation du Mexique* to accompany a text by the French scholar Brasseur de Bourbourg. By then, however, Waldeck's work had long been eclipsed by other less fanciful approaches to Maya monuments. Waldeck's brief but marginal value was as a publicist, for himself and for the Maya as well, and as a catalyst to encourage others to find out the truth for themselves.

The second and more original figure in this period was Juan, originally John, Galindo (see plate section, p.2).[33] Born in Dublin in 1802, his

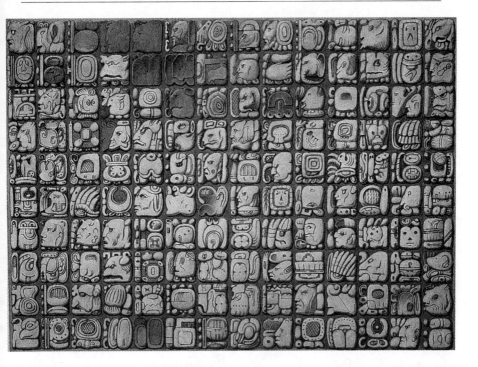

Jean Frédéric Waldeck's drawing of hieroglyphs from the
Temple of the Inscriptions, Palenque.

father, Philemon, was English but of Spanish ancestry and his mother
Irish. Both his parents were unsuccessful actors, Philemon the fencing-
master and occasional lover of the actress Sarah Siddons. Dissatisfied
with this bohemian but penniless background, Galindo set off for the
Americas before he was twenty, to his uncle's sugar plantation in
Jamaica or perhaps to join the liberation struggle in Chile like so many
other Irishmen of the time. Little is certain about his early career. But in
1827 he appeared in Guatemala and through his success in the army of
General Morazán, founder of the Central American Confederation, he
was made Governor of the Petén and given a large grant of land there,
one of his responsibilities being to pacify the 'wild' Lacandón Maya
Indians of the region.

In April 1831 he visited Palenque and wrote an account which
appeared in *The Literary Gazette* in London later in the same year.[34] Most
of it adds little to previous reports, and Galindo's own claims of
discovery reveal a pretended or quite genuine ignorance of earlier exploration there. But he does provide some original insights of his own.

From observation of the physiognomy and perhaps elements of the dress of the figures in the reliefs, he felt, in contrast to Dupaix, that there was an evident continuity between the ancient people and the Maya of his own day: 'Everything bears testimony that these surprising people were not physically dissimilar from the present Indians...' Furthermore, reflecting on the hieroglyphs: 'I have seen sufficient to ascertain the high civilization of their former inhabitants and that they possessed the art of representing sounds by signs, with which I hitherto believed no Americans previous to the Conquest were acquainted... I also presume that the Maya language is derived from them: it is still spoken by all the Indians, and even by most of the other inhabitants throughout Yucatán, the district of Petén and the eastern part of Tabasco.'

In 1834 Galindo was sent by the Government of Central America to make an official report on Copán and was the first to draw an on-the-spot comparison between these two great Maya cities: 'it can be seen immediately that their similarity suggests a common origin, in spite of the fact that they differ in essential points'.[35] He felt that the 'superior architecture' of Palenque had led to the markedly better preservation of the buildings there. He noted differences in construction techniques and architectural style and how the Copán tradition of carving elaborate stone stelae in the round contrasted with the Palenque preference for sculptural relief. But what most united them were 'their writings always placed in almost square blocks containing faces and hands and other identical characters', and he returned here to the point he had made at Palenque: 'This writing is hieroglyphic–phonetic, representing sounds, and is greatly superior to the paintings of the Mexicans and the symbolic hieroglyphs of the Egyptians, which only represented things'. We shall return to the subject of phoneticism in Maya writing in due course, but here Galindo, in the 1830s, is speculating in an astonishingly modern way not just whether this is writing at all, but about the very nature of Maya hieroglyphs as a written language.

Galindo spent ten weeks at Copán preparing his report and letters to the *Literary Gazette*, the American Antiquarian Society and the Société de Géographie in Paris. He also undertook a little archaeological excavation. On the eastern side of the ruins the changing course of the Copán River had sliced away a section of the city over the period of almost a thousand years between its abandonment and Galindo's arrival, producing the sheer cut or *corte*, thirty metres high, that you see today. Noting the remains of stonework all along it, he imagined that it had originally been one long retaining wall pierced by 'windows'. He dug a little way into one of these and discovered a vaulted burial chamber. He found more than fifty pieces of pottery, many of them containing human bones, and obsidian points, shells, jade beads and a small jade mask. All of this material had been laid on a stone floor covered with lime plaster. He measured the chamber and observed that it was aligned 'directly from north to south, in accordance with the compass, which in these countries has a variation of 9° to the east...' Apart from Del Río's diggings at Palenque, this was the first recorded excavation at any Maya site. It also anticipated some of the most dramatic of all recent discoveries in Maya archaeology, to be described in Chapter 4, which have been made by tunnelling through the *corte* into the heart of some of the very earliest Temple structures at Copán.

Galindo was an extremely effective and intelligent self-taught observer, who well deserves his place as one of the pioneers of Maya archaeology. He managed to combine his amateur work and extensive communication with learned societies – he wrote thirty-two letters in all to the Société de Géographie – with a very different career as an extremely ambitious political operator and entrepreneur in his adopted country. It can only have been his political ambitions and the desire to ingratiate himself with the government which led him to open his report on Copán with some quite extraordinary conclusions about both the past and the future of the Americas. In brief, he claimed that Central America was the birthplace of all civilization and that, in his analysis of the cycles of world history where civilization and political power had thence spread around the globe in a westerly direction, the young, emerging republics of the Americas were poised to lead the world once more and take over from the inevitably waning power of European empires.

One would not take this political clarion call too seriously, save for one unsavoury side to it. There was little place in all this for the Maya of his own day, the very people whom Galindo, uniquely among his contemporaries, had correctly identified as the heirs of the creators of Maya civilization. Prospects were grim for the sorry descendants of the builders of Palenque and Copán: 'The Indian race is in the last centuries of its age and soon will dissappear from the earth.' The days of their glory were long gone and they were 'incapable of regeneration'. The new Central America belonged to people like Galindo, the man who had unearthed and appropriated their past simply as an accoutrement worthy of the glittering future of another race of men.

Galindo wrote this unfortunate thesis at the high point of his fortunes, when destiny had seemed to beckon. He had a million acres in the Petén which he hoped to settle with colonists, and plans to exploit an island off Panama amongst a number of other ventures. He was also, it seemed, well in with the right factions in the government. But this was not to last. As the 1830s came to a close he found that he had backed the wrong side. The Central American Confederation broke up in turmoil and violence and in 1839 Galindo was killed in the aftermath of a military skirmish in Honduras. That very year saw the arrival in Central America of two men whose names are as synonymous with Maya discovery as those of Schliemann or Carter and Carnarvon amongst the monuments of the Old World.

INCIDENTS OF TRAVEL

John Lloyd Stephens and Frederick Catherwood transformed the study of the Maya, indeed they began it in the modern scientific sense. It is hard to overestimate the scale of their achievement. On two great expeditions they plunged into the forests and came back with vivid accounts and superbly detailed drawings of unknown cities that were published in four best-selling volumes between 1841 and 1843. Previously, explorers, scholars and a variety of dilettanti, in our more modern sense of the word, had simply been talking amongst themselves about the very limited number of ruins that had been investigated. Stephens' and Catherwood's sheer energy and devotion to their task led them to cover vastly more territory than anyone before them and to reveal the existence of Maya civilization to the world.

Although they were strictly amateurs, since there were of course no 'professional' archaeologists at this time, their methods and publications were models of professionalism. They described, planned and reproduced Maya art and architecture to a standard that was on a completely different plane to that of their predecessors. All too conscious of the wild, unwarranted speculation that had beset the subject, they employed nothing more than reasoned analysis and the evidence of their eyes.

Their different talents complemented each other perfectly and as a team they are unique in the annals of archaeology.

In 1839, when they set off on their first trip to Central America, Stephens was thirty-four (see plate section, p.2). Trained as a lawyer and from a wealthy and well-connected New York family, he had sailed for Europe five years previously to recover from a persistent illness. His recuperation seems to have been swift, since for the next two years he travelled with typical enterprise and sense of adventure through Eastern Europe, Turkey, Russia and on an antiquarian tour of the Middle East. He explored the monuments of the Nile valley and, travelling in Arab disguise, was the first American ever to reach Petra. This was still an extremely dangerous journey and he was one of the very few to have accomplished it since the ancient city's rediscovery in 1812 by Jean Louis Burckhardt. His travels left him fascinated by antiquity and by the explosion of archaeological activity being accomplished in those years. No doubt, too, it inspired in him the desire to research further into the antiquities of his own American continent.

Returning from the Middle East to Paris, he found that his long letters back to the USA describing his travels had been published by their recipient in the *American Monthly* magazine. In due course he wrote up his diaries as *Incidents of Travel in Arabia Petraea*, which was published in 1837 to great critical and popular acclaim. Overnight he became a successful, and wealthy, author.

In London in 1836 he had met Catherwood, who was exhibiting his famous panorama 'The Ruins of Jerusalem' in Leicester Square. This was an enormous circular mural illuminated by gaslight, that was eventually to be destroyed by fire, but which was one of the great London attractions of the time. Stephens had visited Jerusalem and had used a map made by Catherwood to get himself around. It was a good enough introduction and they established an immediate friendship that was to last all their short lives. They were very different people, Stephens by all accounts the gregarious and compulsively energetic personality that comes across in his books, Catherwood six years older, a gangling figure, shy and self-effacing in the extreme. Stephens was always to refer to him in print as 'Mr. Catherwood', typical enough of the period but somehow suiting his diffident nature, the Englishman abroad.[36]

Catherwood was born in north London, trained first as an architect and then attended classes at the Royal Academy, where he would have been taught by John Soane, Turner, Fuseli and other great artists of the day. Though clearly affected by the drama, the light and shade of his artistic training, Catherwood was never to be overwhelmed by his Romantic tutors as was Waldeck. In 1823 he went on his first, short journey to the Middle East to sketch and survey ancient monuments with the antiquarian traveller Henry Westcar. A few years later he returned with the famous Nile expedition led by Robert Hay and remained in Egypt until 1833, working alongside some of the best Egyptological scholars of the day and completing hundreds of extremely fluent and accurate drawings of the great monuments of Giza, Memphis and Thebes. They survive amongst the collections of manuscripts in the British Museum, and in these little-known drawings one can appreciate Catherwood's love of architecture, his excellence as a draughtsman and the patient care he devoted to detail. There are pages here devoted purely to the delineation of Egyptian hieroglyphs. In the years immediately following Champollion's decipherment the value to future research of faithful copying was all too apparent. If Hay, the indolent aristocrat, had got around to publishing his material, Catherwood would today be more widely appreciated as one of the pioneers of Egyptology.

Stephens was clearly impressed by Catherwood's work and in London they were already discussing the prospect of working together on some future expedition. When Stephens returned to New York, Catherwood was soon to follow him, setting up as an architect and creating another Jerusalem panorama on Broadway. Apparently prompted by the bookseller John Russell Bartlett, they began to read together the few published accounts of Maya ruins: Del Río, Dupaix, the Kingsborough volumes and finally, in 1838, Waldeck's *Voyage pittoresque*. In truth it was a motley and confusing collection of work, but it was that very confusion, the welter of speculation, that intrigued them. Stephens also immersed himself in as many other histories and Spanish chronicles as he could find.

With the success of *Arabia Petraea* behind him, and a second volume he had brought out on his eastern European travels, the commercial decision could not have been difficult. There must surely be money to be made on a book about the mysterious ruins in Central America. Commercial enterprise it was, and Stephens drew up a very modern style of book deal or contract for Catherwood to sign. He was to be paid all expenses and a fee of $1500. In return, he made over all rights in his material to Stephens: 'he will not in any way interfere with the right of the said Stephens to the absolute and exclusive use of all the information, drawings and material collected on the said journey'.[37]

These niceties dealt with, Stephens, an active and well-connected Democrat, was also entrusted at the last minute by President Van Buren with a 'Special Confidential Mission' to the government of Central America. Since the political situation there was so unstable and the US representative had recently died, Stephens was to close down the American legation, ship its archives back home and then locate the government, present his credentials and enter into preliminary discussions about a trade deal. It should not take up too much of his time, would provide him with official status on his travels and when his diplomatic duties were done, he could proceed with his archaeological explorations.

On 3 October 1839 the two explorers set sail for the town of Belize, the nearest deep-sea port to their first goal, Copán. There, in what was now the de facto British Honduras, the 'Special Agent' and his English companion were entertained with great formality by the Superintendent of the 'Colony', Colonel McDonald, a veteran of the Peninsula War and Waterloo, 'one of the most military-looking men I ever saw', as Stephens put it, whose conversation 'was like reading a page of history'.[38] McDonald quizzed them about their plans and they told him openly about their itinerary. McDonald no doubt felt that the British should not be outdone here. The combination of the American and the 'yankified' Englishman seemed a formidable outfit, but if they were heading for Copán and then going in search of the elusive government of Central America they could be gone for some time. There was a good chance that an overland expedition from British Honduras could reach Palenque first, complete their own survey and gain what he imagined would be the resultant prestige.

As Stephens and Catherwood went on their way to thirteen-gun salutes and much flag-waving, McDonald was composing a letter to Lord John Russell, Secretary of State for the Colonies:

It is not unknown to your Lordship that in the province of Tabasco, a portion of the Mexican Republic in Central America, there exist some far-famed remnants of ancient architecture called the 'Ruins of Polenki'. These ruins, I believe, form now a great object of interest among the enlightened in the U.S., and I am led to understand that similar sentiments pervade the curious in Europe... It has been my intention for some considerable time past to bring the subject before the Secretary of State.[39]

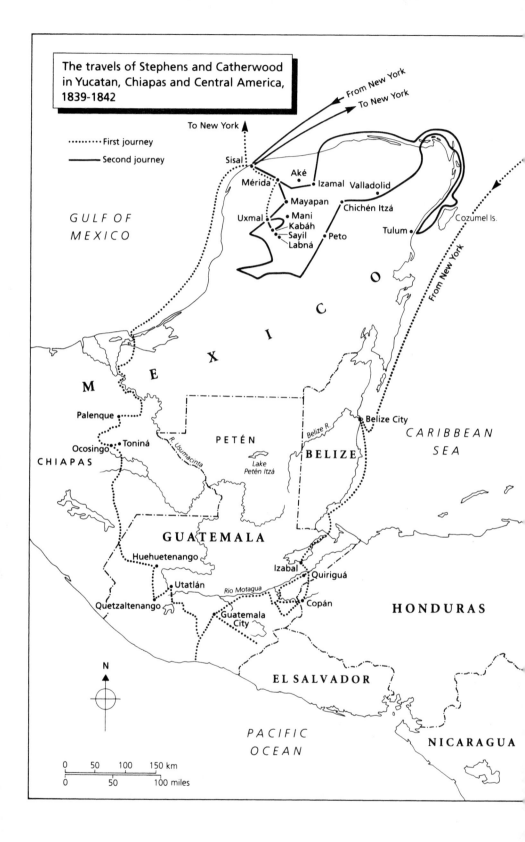

The travels of Stephens and Catherwood in Yucatan, Chiapas and Central America, 1839-1842

.... First journey
———— Second journey

From New York
To New York
To New York

GULF OF MEXICO

Sisal
Aké
Mérida
Izamal
Valladolid
Mayapan
Chichén Itzá
Uxmal
Mani
Kabáh
Sayil
Labná
Peto
Tulum
Cozumel Is.

From New York

M E X I C O

Palenque
Ocosingo
Toniná
CHIAPAS

R. Usumacinta

PETÉN

Belize R.
Belize City

CARIBBEAN SEA

BELIZE

Lake Petén Itzá

GUATEMALA

Huehuetenango

Izabal
Quiriguá

Utatlán
Rio Motagua

Quetzaltenango
Copán

HONDURAS

Guatemala City

N

EL SALVADOR

PACIFIC OCEAN

NICARAGUA

0   50   100   150 km
0   50   100 miles

The last sentence would seem to have been a downright untruth. Apart from vague rumours of ruins in the interior, McDonald had almost certainly only heard about Palenque from Stephens. Indeed his curious spelling, 'Polenki', suggests a direct rendering of the way the American would have pronounced it.

At least McDonald made it clear to Stephens that the Colony would be mounting its own expedition. Two men were swiftly selected: Patrick Walker, an 'exemplary' army officer, and John Caddy, a gifted draughtsman. At the height of the rainy season they headed off on a direct route up the Belize river and then straight across the Petén. The early stages of the journey were gruelling, but the southern Petén was now more extensively settled and their passage relatively untroubled. On Lake Petén Itzá, where they spent Christmas, they even met an Englishman called Bartlet who had married a local woman and lived on the lake in a 'neat cottage with a small garden attached'.[40] Walker was ordered to prepare an official report and Caddy wrote his own more lively diary. They decribed their adventures with local officialdom, the flourishing cattle ranches they came upon and the game they shot in profusion, but little of archaeological interest, though their route took them close to the ruins of Xunantunich and even Tikal, which slept on, awaiting the arrival of more questing, motivated explorers.

In two months they were at Palenque, well ahead of Stephens and Catherwood, where they were led around the ruins by Juan, the same guide that had accompanied Waldeck. Caddy produced a number of very passable drawings, but Walker's report did little but reiterate previous descriptions and opinions. He wrote of 'Egypto-Indian origins' and that 'each building marks the despotic character of Egyptian architecture, while many of the figures of warriors and idols are demonstrative of the East – both together forming a character sombre yet fantastic'.[41] This kind of thing had all been heard before.

Although Caddy gave a presentation at the Society of Antiquaries in London in 1842, no other record of the expedition was published until the detective work of archaeologist David Pendergast tracked down the material in the 1960s. The report was insufficient, the British Colonial office showed little interest, and Colonel MacDonald in Belize received an official reprimand from the British Treasury about the expense. Although it is extremely interesting as a description of the early, frontier days in the Petén, the Walker–Caddy expedition served as little more than a throwback to earlier times in its limited achievements while being something of a presentiment of the nationalistic rivalry in Maya exploration that would reappear on occasion later in the century.

Meanwhile, Stephens and Catherwood had had their first experience of Maya ruins. They took a steamboat down the coast from Belize and sailed up the delightful Rio Dulce to Izabal. Here they equipped themselves with a mule-train and headed off with their servant and translator Augustin into the 'distracted' country of Guatemala, which was now in a confused state of civil war. Briefly detained and threatened by an undisciplined party of soldiers, their reception at Copán was initially hostile, while the local hacienda owner Don Gregorio studiously ignored them. Eventually one of his sons provided a guide to take them to the ruins.

After all their preparations and the 'vague and unsatisfactory' stories they had heard, Stephens was nervous about what lay in store. 'Mr. C. and I were somewhat sceptical, and when we arrived at Copán, it was with the hope, rather than the expectation, of finding wonders.'[42] Stephens knew that he was 'entering abruptly upon new ground'. Until his arrival at Copán he had had to read the 'volumes without number' suggesting one or other origin for the civilizations of the Americas. Old prejudices still held sway in many minds, like those who still subscribed to the views of William Robertson, who in his well-known *History of America* had claimed that 'The inhabitants of the New World were in a state of society so extremely rude as to be unacquainted with those arts which are the first essays of human ingenuity in its advance toward improvement.'[43]

They picked their way through Don Gregorio's fields of maize and into the woods along the Copán River. From the River, rearing up a hundred feet high on the far bank, they saw a mass of stonework with vegetation growing out of the top. 'This was part of the wall of Copán, an ancient city on whose history books throw but little light.' They forded the river and cut their way upwards into the ruins, passing walls of finely cut stone and following stone steps which took them onto a wide, densely overgrown terrace. Struggling through further thick forest they then suddenly came upon 'a square stone column, about fourteen feet high and three feet on each side, sculptured in very bold relief... The front was the figure of a man curiously and richly dressed, and the face evidently a portrait, solemn, stern, and well fitted to excite admiration. The back was of a different design, unlike anything we had ever seen before, and the sides were covered with hieroglyphics.'[44]

Any misgivings Stephens might have had were now immediately

extinguished. The evident scale of the city and this first, magnificent monument revealed to him that they were in the presence of an unknown and original civilization. 'The sight of this unexplored monument put at rest at once and forever, in our minds, all uncertainty in regard to the character of American antiquities, and gave us the assurance that the objects we were in search of were interesting, not only as the remains of an unknown people, but as works of art, proving, like newly-discovered historical records, that the people who once occupied the Continent of America were not savages.'[45]

As they continued on that first day, they saw fourteen further monuments 'of the same character and appearance, some with more elegant designs, and some in workmanship equal to the finest monuments of the Egyptians'. They ascended a pyramidal structure to a square 'with steps on all sides like a Roman amphitheatre', where on one side lay a colossal head 'evidently a portrait', and then proceeded to a terrace high above the river. There they sat, he says, and 'strove in vain to penetrate the mystery by which we were surrounded'. It elicited some of the extraordinary prose for which Stephens is famous.

> There were no associations connected with the place... but architecture, sculpture and painting, all the arts which embellish life, had flourished in this overgrown forest; orators, warriors and statesmen, beauty, ambition and glory, had lived and passed away, and none knew that such things had been, or could tell of their past existence...

He then reached a crescendo of lament:

> The city was desolate... it lay before us like a shattered bark in the midst of the ocean, her masts gone, her name effaced, her crew perished, and none to tell whence she came, to whom she belonged, how long on her voyage, or what caused her destruction... All was mystery, dark impenetrable mystery, and every circumstance increased it.[46]

The first day was an astonishing, moving experience, but now they had major practical tasks ahead – to work out the full extent of the ruins and to plan and draw them. What is more, it was the middle of the rainy season. The priority was to set Catherwood up to record the major monuments, principally the stelae, which presented a formidable challenge: 'The designs were very complicated, and so different from

anything Mr. Catherwood had ever seen before as to be perfectly unintelligible. The cutting was in very high relief, and required a strong body
of light to bring up the figures.' With only a small number of local
people to help them, with machetes but few axes, full-scale clearance of
the forest was out of the question. In the end they managed to cut down
the trees immediately around the stelae, which produced sufficient light,
when it was not raining, for Catherwood to get to work. The conditions
that the great illustrator faced were indeed quite terrible. He stood all
day with his feet deep in mud and wearing gloves to protect his hands
from the mosquitoes. Yet throughout their journeys of exploration, in
the days when of course there were no insect-repellents, anti-malaria
tablets or the range of potions and accessories available to the modern
explorer, he seems to have complained very little. Both Catherwood and
Stephens suffered debilitating bouts of malaria for the rest of their lives.

Catherwood maintained his exacting standards of draughtsmanship.
As in Egypt, he used the 'camera lucida' as an aid, a piece of optical
equipment that projected the image of a subject through a prism onto
paper where it could effectively be traced. But at Copán, like many a
novice coming to Maya art for the first time, he found it impossible to
get to grips with the daunting complexity of the ornament and
inscriptions, with or without the camera lucida. Through trial and error
he acclimatized and was to produce illustrations that remain useful to
this day.

Survey of the site was done with a compass and Catherwood's old
tape that he had used to map the ruins of Jerusalem and Thebes. They
cut straight lines through the forest and measured off a simple grid
made of wooden poles stuck in the ground. Stephens explored the ruins
for most of the two weeks they spent at Copán together, finding courts,
terraces, pyramids and monuments that extended some two miles along
the river. Catherwood eventually produced a plan of the core of the site
including the central 'Temple' area, now known as the 'Acropolis', and
most of the Main Plaza, including the principal stelae. It would not be
bettered before Alfred Maudslay's arrival much later in the century.

Stephens also set himself a rather different challenge – that of buying
the ruins. This may sound ridiculous today, a parody of traditional
American commercial enterprise, like the tycoon so taken with the
battery razor that he buys the company. But Stephens was perfectly
serious. He was also to attempt, without success, to buy Palenque and
the ruins of Quiriguá. He and Catherwood, of course, had witnessed

first-hand the international open-season of archaeological plunder during their time in the Eastern Mediterranean. The early years of the nineteenth century had seen boat-loads of ancient objects shipped back to the museums and private collections of Europe by Napoleon's agents, Lord Elgin, Belzoni and many others. The major justification was that such monuments were little regarded in their own country. In the freebooting, colonialist spirit of the age, Stephens had no qualms about following their example. He travelled with a mixture of intent – literary, antiquarian, diplomatic and commercial – and was always on the look-out for an opening, be it a railroad here or a grandiose plan for a canal there. As for antiquities, it seemed natural enough that the United States, already the acknowledged power in the hemisphere, had a proprietary right over the neglected remains of the Americas.

Mulling the idea over in his mind, one night he suggested to Catherwood 'an operation ... To buy Copán! remove the monuments of a by-gone people from the desolate region in which they were buried, set them up in the "great commercial emporium" [New York City] and found an institution to be the nucleus of a great national museum of American antiquities'. They 'belonged of right to us', he wrote, otherwise 'the friends of science and the arts in Europe would get possession of them'.[47]

His first idea, floating the major monuments down the river to the sea, was ruled out when impassable rapids were discovered a little downstream. But Stephens formally purchased Copán for $50 and concluded the deal dressed in his official diplomatic frock-coat with sparkling eagle buttons. Although Stephens removed nothing from Copán, it was a hint of the inevitable future consequences of world-wide interest in Maya archaeology. In due course Maya antiquities would begin to flee the region like so many tons of minerals, rubber or bananas.

After two weeks, Stephens' initial wonderment gave way to more considered thoughts about the nature and significance of Copán. The challenge was intoxicating: 'The ground was entirely new; there were no guide-books; the whole was virgin soil.' It all 'created an interest higher, if possible, than I had ever felt among the ruins of the Old World'.[48] And his experience with the monuments of the Old World he constantly drew on.

The city had clearly been built by a process of accretion. 'Probably... additions were made and statues created by different kings, or perhaps, in commemoration of important events in the history of the city.' The central area of pyramids and temples he envisaged crowned with 'buildings or altars now ruined'. They had noticed the remains of red pigment on some of the stelae and he believed quite rightly that the structures themselves were once painted, 'and the reader may imagine the effect when the whole country was clear of forest, and priest and people were ascending from the outside to the terraces, and thence to the holy places within to pay their adoration in the temple'.

Due to the richness and realism of its many sculptures, Copán, even more so than Palenque, always appeals to visitors as a peopled, human place. Some of the images Stephens found grotesque and threatening and felt were 'intended to inspire terror… and sometimes suggested the idea of a blind, bigoted, and superstitious people, and sacrifices of human victims'. Others gave a very different impression. One monument in particular, at the foot of one of the pyramids of the Acropolis, 'presents as curious a subject of speculation as any monument in Copán'. This was a large block of stone, some two metres square and one and a half metres high, now known prosaically as Altar Q, which is carved in low relief with thirty-six blocks of hieroglyphs on its top and sixteen seated human figures around its sides (see below). These converged on two 'principal personages' on the west side who faced each other: 'Each of the two principal figures is seated cross-legged… on a hieroglyphic which probably designates his name and office, or character'.[49] Stephens noted their elaborate individual head-dresses, the sceptre of office, or so it seemed, grasped by one of the prominent figures and the mysterious objects which all of the other figures held in their hands.

Catherwood's drawing of the West Side of Altar Q.

The glyphs he felt 'beyond doubt record some event in the history of the mysterious people who once inhabited the city'.

Altar Q is a crucial monument in Maya studies and interpretations of its meaning have varied widely over the years. But Stephens' intuition that it recorded historical events and real people, namely Maya rulers, just like the monuments of ancient Egypt with which he was familiar, is borne out by more recent interpretations. Indeed, the most powerful overall impression that Copán created in his mind was that here 'the people who reared it had published a record of themselves, through which we might one day hold conference with a perished race... One thing I believe, that its history is graven on its monuments. No Champollion has yet brought to them the energies of his inquiring mind. Who shall read them?'[50]

Catherwood had much to do at Copán, so it was decided that he would remain while his companion went off to perform his diplomatic duties. Stephens successfully packed up the archives in Guatemala City and then headed off into lower Central America, to where the government semed to have moved. While he was away, and acting on the advice of a hacienda owner in Guatemala City, Catherwood briefly investigated the site of Quiriguá, which possesses elaborate stelae similar to those of Copán, but very much taller. These Catherwood found very difficult to draw without his camera lucida. Quiriguá was the first site that they could claim to have discovered themselves. After months of separation they met up again in Guatemala City and prepared to travel on to their second major goal, Palenque.

They left at Easter 1840 and headed north-west through the Guatemalan highlands, across the border and into Chiapas. By early May they had reached the small Mexican town of Ocosingo, where they took a brief side trip to the ruins of 'Tonila', or Toniná, a great rival to Palenque in the later Classic period and which shared a taste for elaborate architectural stucco decoration. They saw the remains of a number of reliefs still clinging to the walls, including figures of humans and even a monkey. These have since perished, but in recent years archaeologists have made great discoveries of stucco friezes at Toniná, including the large, arresting image of a skeletal figure clutching a decapitated head (see plate section, p.19). Toniná was a substantial site, and though Stephens and Catherwood stayed here only briefly, it helped to build up in their minds an idea of the density of ancient settlement and the prospects that lay ahead for future exploration.

The timing of their visit to Palenque could not have been worse, for the rains had begun in earnest once again. On arrival in the town, they found that Walker and Caddy had left only recently. Using once more the same guide, Juan, who must by now have been on the point of setting up his own tour agency, they hired such labourers as were available, since most of the men were occupied planting, bought all the provisions they could and made for the ruins. The trail was poor. It entered the forest soon after they left the town and was swamped by streams that had overflowed with the torrential rains, leaving their mules floundering in the mud. But within three hours they began a stony ascent up the hillside and their guides were soon shouting 'El Palacio'. 'Through openings in the trees we saw the front of a large building richly ornamented with stuccoed figures on the pilasters, curious and elegant; trees growing close against it, and their branches entering the doors; in style and effect unique, extraordinary and mournfully beautiful.'

They set up camp in the Palace, Stephens commenting that since no structures remained intact at Copán, 'For the first time we were in a building erected by the aboriginal inhabitants, standing before the Europeans knew of this continent, and we prepared to take up our abode under its roof.'[51]

They worked in the same methodical fashion as at Copán and here Catherwood found that he could draw more rapidly, the lower relief being much easier to copy. Stephens cleaned and prepared the monuments and saw to the construction of scaffolding where Catherwood could set up the camera lucida. He then proceeded to make an annotated plan of the Palace, indicating those walls still standing, those in ruin and the position of the principal sculptures. Apart from drawing most of the major reliefs in the Palace and the Cross Group and spending hour upon hour copying all the panels of hieroglyphs in the Temple of the Inscriptions, which no one had attempted before, Catherwood also made painstaking elevations, cross-sections and plans of the principal temples. As at Copán, the end result was archaeological documentation of the highest order. Given the conditions in which they worked, it was another remarkable achievement.

Some of Stephens' conclusions were similar to those of Galindo. Though there were obvious differences in architectural and artistic style, a cultural unity over a wide area was apparent, best expressed by the hieroglyphs: 'the hieroglyphics are the same as we found at Copán and

Quiriguá... There is room for the belief that the whole of this country was once occupied by the same race, speaking the same language, or at least having the same written characters.'[52] The latter was a typically acute distinction. The stucco and stone reliefs were 'incomprehensible', Stephens admitting that he had no idea what they conveyed, but that these were real individuals and that the hieroglyphs 'give the history of these incomparable personages' he had no doubt.

He was satisfied that they had investigated the heart of the city and the site of the temples and public buildings. Its full extent was difficult to judge given the dense forest on every side. He rightly supposed that the houses of ordinary inhabitants would have been 'like those of the Egyptians and the present race of Indians, of frail and perishable materials'. These would have disappeared altogether and the city may originally have covered a large area. But he could see little to justify previous extravagant claims that a massive stone metropolis continued for miles along the hilside. He was dismissive, too, of any claims for the great antiquity of Palenque:

> The reader is perhaps disappointed, but we were not. There was no necessity for assigning to the ruined city an immense extent, or an antiquity coeval with that of the Egyptians or of any other ancient or known people. What we had before our eyes was grand, curious and remarkable enough. Here were the remains of a cultivated, polished and peculiar people, who had passed through all the stages incident to the rise and fall of nations; reached their golden age, and perished, entirely unknown.[53]

Their privations and sufferings at Palenque were worse than those at Copán. Within a couple of weeks Stephens' feet became infected by insect bites and burrowing chiggers. They swelled up so much that he was forced to retire to the town to recover. When he returned, Catherwood was in a terrible state: 'He was wan and gaunt; he was lame, like me, from the bites of insects, his face was swollen with his left arm hung with rheumatism as if paralyzed.' But their dedication to the task they had set themselves remained undaunted and Stephens was keen to counter the fashionably romantic but quite misleading impression given by previous visitors that getting to Palenque was beset by terrible dangers: 'there is no difficulty in going from Europe or the United States to Palenque. The only danger might be from the revolutionary state of the country.'

By the end of May the rains had made it impossible for them to carry on. They broke up their sodden camp and left, Catherwood weakly slumped over the back of a mule which stumbled and rolled on top of him between the ruins and the town. They waited two days for him to recover a little and then began the last stage of their journey. This took them down the Usumacinta by boat with a cargo of logwood to the Gulf of Mexico and then northwards by sea along the coast of the Yucatán to Sisal and thence to Mérida. Here their aim was to visit the ruins of Uxmal, which were on the vast hacienda lands owned by Don Simeón Peón, whom Stephens had met the previous year in New York. Catherwood gamely struggled to the hacienda but then spent most of the time in bed. It was Stephens alone who first saw Uxmal. Emerging from a patch of scrubby forest he 'came at once upon a large open field strewed with mounds of ruins and vast buildings on terraces, and pyramidal structures, grand and in good preservation, richly ornamented, without a bush to obstruct the view, in picturesque effect almost equal to the ruins of Thebes.'[54]

Catherwood accompanied him the next day and was equally excited. That year the land around the ruins had all been cleared and planted and unlike Copán and Palenque here they could appreciate the layout of the core of the city. There were steep pyramids such as the 'Pyramid of the Magician' but also elegant ranges of buildings on wide platforms such as the 'House of the Governor' and 'House of the Nuns'. These curious names had been given to the structures by a variety of visitors over the Colonial period, since the site had never been 'lost' and had been described a number of times since the 1560s.

They found no stelae or figures in stucco. Instead the glory of the buildings were their façades, covered in 'rich and elaborate sculptured ornaments' of grotesque masks, frets and lattice-work that formed striking patterns in the bright sunlight. The lavish use of surface ornament was unlike anything they had seen before, but Stephens noted on one wooden lintel the same hieroglyphs that they had seen in greater profusion at other sites. In counterpoint to the complexity of surface, many of the groups of buildings, notably the House of the Governor on its expansive platform 350 feet wide, had an extraordinarily clean simplicity of line and form. 'There is no rudeness or barbarity in the design or proportions; on the contrary, the whole wears an air of architectural symmetry and grandeur... If it stood at this day on its great artificial terrace in Hyde Park or the Garden of the Tuileries it would form a new order... not unworthy to stand side by side with the remains of Egyptian, Grecian and Roman art.'⁵⁵

There was an immense amount of work to be done at Uxmal. But although Catherwood made a start, he was in no state to continue. On 24 June 1840 the explorers were to sail for home. They had been almost ten months away. Stephens immediately busied himself writing, and a year later *Incidents of Travel in Central America, Chiapas and Yucatán* was published. But already they had begun to plan another expedition to resume their work at Uxmal and explore other parts of Yucatán. This time Stephens had no diplomatic mission and it was a journey of pure archaeological discovery.

They spent six weeks at Uxmal where Catherwood was to produce some of his very finest work (see plate section, p.1). The strikingly beautiful architectural forms and intricate façades with their mosaics of stone fascinated him and though the scrubby jungle of the region had grown back to conceal some of the buildings, he was able to achieve a well-nigh complete survey of the ruins. Along with their regular range of equipment Catherwood had in his baggage a Daguerreotype camera, which he practised with briefly on their arrival in Mérida by taking portraits of local society ladies. Daguerre had publicized his discovery of the process only two years previously and the adoption of the technique by Catherwood, who can claim to be the first photographer of Maya ruins, illustrates his inquiring mind and the desire to experiment with any technique that might aid the process of recording. Unfortunately, it seems not to have worked well with the strong contrasts in lighting presented by the architecture, and the few photographs that he did take were lost in a disastrous fire in New York in 1842, which destroyed Catherwood's panorama along with many drawings and other material from their expeditions.

Close to Uxmal, in the upland region of the Puuc hills, they visited a dozen other Maya sites including such cities as Sayil, Labná, with its extraordinary arched gateway, and Kabáh, where Stephens found a series of wooden lintels covered with hieroglyphs and briefly explored a section of a *sacbe*, or ancient Maya road built of packed limestone, that connected this city with Uxmal. The style of architecture, with the elaborate use of mosaic ornament and the characteristic 'monster' masks on façades, the long-nosed visage of the rain-god Chak, was very similar in all these cities. Here was more evidence of the local diversity but overall cultural unity of Maya culture.

From the Puuc region they travelled north-east towards Chichén Itzá.

On the way they made some important discoveries of a different but extremely important kind through a warm friendship they struck up with a local scholar, Juan Pío Pérez. For a number of years Pío Pérez had carried on his own quiet but extremely productive research into the history of the Maya in the region. He had talked to older members of leading families and searched in the archives of towns and villages for early manuscripts and traditional Maya histories, written in Maya but in the Latin alphabet, which had survived the purges of the Colonial period or had been more recently written down. He generously gave Stephens copies of much of his work, including a dictionary of the Yucatec Mayan language with some 4000 words and his 'Ancient Chronology of Yucatán', an explanation of the mechanics of the Maya calendar, which included the names of the months and a list of the twenty day-names. Stephens was fascinated:

> I am able to state the interesting fact, that the calendar of Yucatán, though differing in some particulars, was substantially the same with that of the Mexicans. It shows common sources of knowledge and processes of reasoning, similarity of worship and religious institutions, and in short, it is a link in a chain of evidence tending to show a common origin in the aboriginal inhabitants of Yucatán and Mexico.[56]

He thus began to realize that besides the unity of Maya culture over a wide area, there were also many underlying elements originally held in common by the different peoples of Mesoamerica. He was also given a part of a manuscript from the town of Maní which Pío Pérez had laboriously copied. This was one of the Maya chronicles now known generically as the Books of Chilam Balam, written down and constantly added to in the centuries after the Conquest and which recounted prophecies, riddles, astrology and fragments of history associated with the passing of each *katun* or period of twenty years. As we shall see in Chapter 7, the Chilam Balams are notoriously difficult to understand since they represent a peculiarly Maya way of looking at the past which is quite different from our own. It is also very hard to correlate the *katuns* with our own calendar, since by this time the Maya had given up using the Long Count. But in the Maní book Stephens noted references to the founding of Chichén Itzá and other cities, to the wars between them in the centuries before the Conquest and to the arrival of the Spaniards. Here was a record that was potentially of great value, which 'if genuine and authentic, throws more light upon aboriginal history than any other known to be in existence.'

The Maní chronicle certainly is genuine and many other Chilam Balam books are now known. Pío Pérez, recognized today as an unsung Mexican pioneer of Maya documentary studies, was himself to discover two other such books, which were not published until 1949. But the section of the Maní chronicle and his essay on Maya chronology were both appended to Stephens' account of the Yucatán explorations and published under Pío Pérez's name, providing him with some contemporary recognition.

The great city of Chichén Itzá, today the most visited of all Maya cities, was well enough known in Stephens' and Catherwood's day, with its enormous pyramid of the Castillo that towered some thirty metres above the surrounding plain. Stephens noted the immense scale of the city and that politically it must have dominated much of northern Yucatán in pre-Hispanic times. He suggested that the forbiddingly plain architecture of the centre around the Castillo might signify that it was older than other sections of the site, notably the buildings in the 'Nunnery' or 'Las Monjas' area, where he noticed a more elaborate style of architecture similar to that of the Puuc sites. Differential dating of elements of Chichén Itzá has proved a bone of contention that has continued down to the present day.

At Uxmal they had identified a curious arrangement of constructions with parallel walls some twenty metres apart and with the remains of stone rings fitted into them. They reckoned that this formed a space for some kind of 'public games'. At Chichén Itzá there was a massive and more obvious version of the same thing, which Stephens called the 'Gymnasium'. In the writings of the Spanish chronicler Herrera, he found a description of a ball-game called *tlachtli* played at the time of the Conquest by the Aztecs, which suggested what might have gone on here:

The ball was made of the gum of a tree that grows in hot countries. They struck it with any part of their body... but sometimes he lost that touched it with any other part but his hip, which was look'd upon among them as the greatest dexterity... The place where they played was a ground room, long, narrow... and they kept it very well plastr'd and smooth... On the side walls they fix'd certain stones, like those of a mill, with a hole quite through the middle, just as big as the ball, and he that could strike it through this won the game.[57]

This is a good example of a combination of acute observation and research into the available documentary sources, methods of the modern archaeologist, helping to explain the function of the monuments they saw. Here, too, Stephens deduced 'an affinity between the people who created the ruined cities of Yucatán and those who inhabited Mexico at the time of the conquest'. Doubtless, if he had returned to the more ruined and overgrown sites of Copán, Palenque and Toniná with this knowledge, he would have noted the ball-courts there. The ball-game and its associated mythology were central features of Maya life throughout their pre-Conquest history.

Stephens and Catherwood spent three weeks at Chichén Itzá, documenting the site and making copies of hieroglyphic inscriptions, and of murals in the temples close to the ball-court that have now been almost completely destroyed. They then set out to Valladolid and on to the north-east coast, finally reaching Tulum, overlooking the sea, where Stephens imagined himself among 'the same buildings which the Spaniards saw entire and inhabited by Indians' at the time of Grijalva's expedition in 1518.

They returned to Mérida through Izamal and the site of Aké. At Izamal they were impressed by the great pyramids that still towered above the town. One of them possessed an imposing stucco mask of the sun-god, since destroyed, which they located in the back-yard of the house of a Senora Méndez and which Catherwood enthusiastically sketched. They also toured Diego de Landa's monastery. But of Landa himself they made only passing mention. It would be another twenty years before the *Relación* saw the light of day.

In May 1842 Stephens and Catherwood sailed for home and in the spring of the following year appeared *Incidents of Travel in Yucatán*. Both sets of *Incidents* volumes were a resounding popular success. Tens of thousands of copies were sold within the space of a few years, both in the USA and Europe, and they have been reprinted ever since. Reasonably priced and containing more than two hundred engravings in all, they gave an eager public the first extensive graphic record of a vanished and unknown civilization. Catherwood's illustrations in these volumes are often dramatic and atmospheric, inevitably touched with the Romanticism of the period, but compared with the work of his predecessors they are models of accuracy. Stephens' easy text, without a hint of the pomposity that so affects other travel writings of the period, is deceptively brilliant. A gripping narrative of adventures on the road,

gentle and humorous commentary on the passing scene, on the personalities and curiosities of Central American politics – all are adroitly
integrated with a rigorous scholarly purpose, which became more
disciplined and acute over time as his experience grew.

At Copán the vacuum of knowledge about the ruins had seemed
daunting. How to make anything of them? But the quantity and quality
of documentation and insight accumulated over the course of the journeys enabled Stephens to come to conclusions that, all archaeologists
today agree, were way ahead of his time. The first question was the age
of the ruins and he made a number of initial practical points to counter
previous assertions that they were extremely ancient, if not antediluvian.
Accumulation of earth and forest growth, the presence of enormous
trees growing out of walls, were no guarantee of great antiquity. In a
matter of a few years in the jungle environment sites became swiftly
overgrown. Indeed, the argument could be turned around. If these cities
were thousands of years old, then how could sites like Palenque or
Uxmal have survived in such remarkable condition 'it seems impossible
that, after a lapse of two or three thousand years, a single edifice could
now be left standing'.[58]

He then turned to the chronicles and the accounts of conquistadores
such as Bernal Díaz de Castillo, who had themselves seen fully functioning Maya cities. He quoted references to 'buildings of lime and stone
with steps', 'figures of serpents and idols upon the walls'. And of course
Stephens had visited Tulum on the Yucatán coast, one of the first Maya
cities seen by the Spaniards. There was no doubt, he thought, that all the
ruins they had examined were part of the same cultural tradition. Some
were still flourishing at the time of the Conquest; others, it appeared,
were already in ruins. Beyond these broad conclusions, he would not be
drawn any further. Why some cities might have declined earlier, he
could not say. The limits of the evidence would not allow him to hazard
a guess.

The second issue was the origin of the ruins and the identity of the
builders. Could the art and architecture they had documented be compared with that of the peoples of the Old World? Systematically, he went
about scotching any thought of such comparisons, with Greece or
Rome, or with what he knew about Oriental architecture, or Hindu
sculpture such as Waldeck and his ilk had postulated. Finally, he came
to the Egyptians; even today, some people are persuaded that this is a
relevant comparison:

The point of resemblance upon which the great stress has been laid is the pyramid. The pyramidal form is one which suggests itself to human intelligence in every country as the simplest and surest mode of erecting a high structure upon a solid foundation. It cannot be regarded as a ground for assigning a common origin to all people among whom structures of that character are found, unless the similarity is preserved in its most striking features.[59]

Stephens puts the argument with great clarity and Maya pyramids do in fact differ fundamentally from those of Egypt. In a purist sense they are not pyramidal. They do not have sloping sides that meet at the apex, which is the case with most Egyptian pyramids, if not some of the earlier stepped examples. But the essential difference is that they are temple platforms that invariably had structures built on top of them. Egyptian pyramids do not support other structures and are monuments in themselves, whose primary purpose was funerary, containing mortuary chambers deep within them. In Stephens' day no chambers or burials had been found within or beneath Maya pyramids and he believed that 'probably none exist'. He was wrong here, although it is only since the 1950s that spectacular discoveries of the tombs of Maya rulers have proved that Maya pyramids did indeed have a funerary function.

Turning from pyramids to Egyptian art and architecture in general, he explained that despite some quite superficial resemblances, in the use of profile figures in relief sculpture for example, they otherwise had nothing whatsoever in common. He included 'a plate of Egyptian sculpture taken from Mr. Catherwood's portfolio' to demonstrate this. Maya remains were quite unique.

They are different from the works of any other known people, of a new order, and entirely and absolutely anomalous: they stand alone... we have a conclusion far more interesting and wonderful than that of connecting the builders of these cities with the Egyptians or any other people. It is the spectacle of a people skilled in architecture, sculpture and drawing... not derived from the Old World, but originating and growing up here, without models or masters, having a distinct, separate, independent existence; like the plants and fruits of the soil, indigenous.[60]

Central to many of Stephens' thoughts were, of course, the hieroglyphs, and his conviction that through them 'we might one day hold conference with a perished race'. They were evidently used in different media. For in the course of his research he had come upon the copies of pages of the Dresden Codex, published by both Humboldt and Lord Kingsborough. He set a section of glyphs from the Codex next to the text from the top of Altar Q at Copán copied by Catherwood (see below). One was carved in stone and the other was originally painted on bark paper. There were slight differences, but the clear similarities outweighed them: the same layout in blocks, the same bars and dots, heads and hands among the signs. They represented the same system of writing, used both on the monuments and in Maya books.

This in turn led him on to the consideration of what future documentary studies might offer, the kind of work that Pío Pérez had only

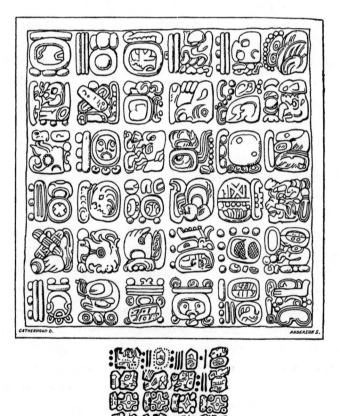

The inscription from Altar Q (top), compared to a detail from the Dresden Codex (below).

recently begun: 'Throughout the country the convents are rich in manuscripts and documents written by the early fathers, caciques and Indians, who very soon acquired the knowledge of Spanish and of writing.' These might help to cast more light on 'the history of some one of these ruined cities'. They might do even more than that: 'I cannot help believing that the tablets of hieroglyphs will yet be read... though not perhaps in our day, I feel persuaded that a key surer than that of the Rosetta Stone will be discovered.'[61] The key itself, Landa's *Relación*, would soon appear, but it would be more than a century before it unlocked the door of Maya decipherment.

Their expedition to the Yucatán marked the end of Stephens' and Catherwood's journeys among Maya ruins. Exactly why they did not return is unknown, but the toll on their health must have been a major factor. They planned to publish another book, a more expensive, lavishly illustrated volume to be called 'American Antiquities' and to include contributions by other scholars such as Humboldt and the great historian William Prescott, whose classic *Conquest of Mexico* was published in 1843 and who had introduced Stephens to many of the Spanish chronicles. But as it was planned to retail at $100, Stephens could not find the 900 subscribers to finance it. In 1844, however, in London, Catherwood published on his own, at considerable expense, a folio of twenty-five lithographs, *Views of Ancient Monuments in Central America, Chiapas and Yucatán*, with brief explanatory texts and a dedication to Stephens. They were reworkings of engravings from the original books, but here Catherwood allowed himself rather more Romantic indulgence, with dramatic lighting effects, savage vegetation, compositions of exotic native figures and a certain licence with archaeological exactitude to heighten the impression of mystery and fallen grandeur. In his lithograph of the great stucco mask at Izamal, for example, Senora Méndez' backyard had mysteriously disappeared, to be replaced by two shadowy figures of hunters in the jungle, a prowling jaguar and an eerie Gothic moon. Yet these are quite distinct from the fabrications of Waldeck, powerful, picturesque yet essentially faithful images that are the equivalent for the Maya area of David Roberts' lithographs of ancient Egypt.

In the following years Catherwood resumed his architectural practice and then tried his hand at engineering, returning to Latin America to work on railroad projects, one of them run by Stephens in Panama. Stephens himself was involved in politics for a while and in a number of the profitable business ventures of the day, including mining and investment in a steamboat company. But the malaria they had contracted in the jungles of Central America never left them and finally diminished even Stephens' seemingly inexhaustible energies. In 1852 he is said to have been found unconscious under a giant ceiba tree in Panama. He was brought back to New York, where he died soon afterwards. He was only forty-seven. Catherwood met his end tragically two years later. Returning from England to the USA on the SS *Arctic*, the ship struck another vessel in dense fog off Newfoundland and he was among the 300 passengers lost.

Today, archaeologists look back on these two remarkable men with veneration as the originators of Maya studies. With a certain envy, too, perhaps. For these were the heroic early days of archaeological adventure and of quite extraordinary revelation, when in remote parts of the globe whole lost worlds still lay in wait for those brave and inquisitive enough to search. And it was the romance and mystery of the Maya which was to be Stephens' and Catherwood's most durable legacy, a brilliant civilization whose spectacular remains had become unaccountably lost amidst the savagery of the jungle. This heady popular image began a process which, in the minds of both public and scholars alike, was to elevate the Maya to a plane all of their own among the ancient peoples of the Americas.

SCHOLARS AND EXPLORERS

In the second half of the nineteenth century, with the world-wide attention that Stephens' books received, other dedicated scholars would be drawn to the Maya area. Soon Maya researches began to bifurcate, breaking down into that of explorers, who would continue the task of discovery and the recording of ruins, and less physically active individuals whom one might call 'desk men', who hunted in libraries for manuscripts that touched on Maya history or Maya writing and tried to make what they could of the inscriptions. These were the twin approaches that Stephens himself had recommended for the future and this division of labour largely continues to this day.

Firstly we shall look at the work of the scholars in studies and libraries from the 1850s until the turn of the century. But before we do this, in order to give one extraordinary character due recognition, we must briefly go back a little in time. George Stuart, and latterly Michael Coe, have rescued from obscurity a remarkable pioneer of hieroglyphic decipherment, Constantine Samuel Rafinesque Schmaltz, to give him his full title, reflecting his French and German parentage. He was born in 1783 and was thus only three when Antonio Del Río was sent to Palenque. Rafinesque became a notable botanist and zoologist, but was evidently a scientific polymath of extraordinary precocity. After a decade spent studying, among many other things, the marine life of the Mediterranean, around 1820 he went to live permanently in the USA. Here he began to turn his considerable mind to early writing systems. A compulsive subscriber to journals and reader of scientific literature, he had obviously seen, by the mid-1820s, both the illustrations of hieroglyphs from Palenque engraved by Waldeck in Del Río's published report, as inaccurate and fanciful as they were, and the copies of the pages of the Dresden Codex in Humboldt's *Vues des cordillères*.

At that time no one had made any connection between the two. The Codex had simply been catalogued in Dresden as a 'painted Mexican manuscript' and was often referred to as 'Aztec'. But in collaboration with the American antiquarian James H. McCulloh, Rafinesque realized that the glyphs in the Codex and the inscriptions from Palenque were the same written language. He worked out the basic notation used by the Maya to represent numbers, and not only distinguished the Maya form of glyphic writing from the less developed Aztec picture writing, but also suggested a direct connection between the ancient Maya writing system and contemporary Chontal and Tzeltal Mayan languages.

Rafinesque published his own scientific periodical, the *Atlantic Journal and Friend of Knowledge*, for which he himself seems to have written nearly all of the articles. In 1832 he used its pages to pen his 'Second Letter to Mr. Champollion, on the Graphic systems of America and the Glyphs of Otolum or Palenque, in Central America...'. It is a summation of the advances that he had made.

> Besides this monumental alphabet, the same nation that built Otolum, had a Demotic alphabet... which was found in Guatimala and Yucatán at the Spanish conquest. A specimen of this has been given by Humboldt... from the Dresden Library, and has been ascertained to be Guatimalan instead of Mexican, being totally unlike the Mexican pictorial manuscripts. This page of the Dresden Codex has letters and numbers, those represented by strokes meaning 5 and dots meaning unities, as the dots never exceed 4. This is nearly similar to the monumental numbers. The words are much less handsome than the monumental glyphs; they are uncouth

glyphs in rows formed by irregular or flexous heavy strokes, inclosing within, in small strokes, nearly the same letters as in the monuments... It might not be impossible to decypher some of these manuscripts... since they are written in languages yet spoken and the writing was understood in Central America, as late as 200 years ago. If this is done, it will be the best clue to the monumental inscriptions.[62]

Stuart, Coe and the modern fraternity of Maya epigraphers all salute this remarkable individual who, some years before Stephens' and Catherwood's journeys and working with the slimmest amount of evidence, had taken the first positive steps along the road of decipherment. It seems none too clear whether Stephens and Rafinesque communicated, though it has been suggested that before Rafinesque died in poverty in 1840, Stephens had written to acknowledge his pioneering contribution. Certainly both men thought along similar lines, believing that one day, once enough documentary resources had been accumulated, the inscriptions would be read.

The principal provider of that documentary material and the greatest of the nineteenth century manuscript hunters was the French Abbé Etienne Charles Brasseur de Bourbourg. In 1854, the year that Catherwood died, Brasseur began his third and most productive visit to Central America. He was there until 1857, one year being spent as parish priest in the small town of Rabinal in the highlands of Guatemala. Brasseur was a man upon whom his ecclesiastical duties, as he put it, 'rested very lightly'. Earlier in life he had been a journalist and a writer of romantic novels, but in 1845 at the age of thirty-one he took Holy Orders largely, it seems, to pursue more serious, scholarly ambitions under the convenient, privileged cover of the cloth.

Soon appointed Vicar-General in Boston, he read the *Conquest of Mexico* by the famous Bostonian William Prescott and this appears to have been the spur to a passion for ancient Mesoamerica. By 1854 he had already acquired a good working knowledge of most of the available manuscripts and sources on both sides of the Atlantic. His aim now was to find more. Brasseur had two great attributes. Firstly, he possessed an easy facility with languages. He rapidly learnt the Aztec language, Nahuatl, and Quiché and Cakchiquel Maya, which equipped him to track down, identify and translate native documents. He was also, by all accounts, a tremendously engaging personality, with the ability to charm his way into any library or private archive that he came upon. He made key discoveries in Guatemala and Mexico, and in the libraries of Europe.

In Rabinal itself Brasseur heard of a unique pre-Conquest Quiché dance-drama, now known as the Rabinal-Achi, which only survived in oral tradition and which was dictated to him by a local Maya informant. He painstakingly transcribed and published this along with a grammar of the Quiché language. The 'Annals of the Cakchiquel', a history of the Cakchiquel Maya which is particularly valuable as a native account of the Spanish conquest of the highlands, was also tracked down by Brasseur in Guatemala City. There too, in a university library, he was introduced to the only manuscript copy of the magnificent 'Popol Vuh'.

The Popol Vuh or the 'Book of Council' of the Quiché Maya was written down in Maya, but in the Spanish alphabet, by members of the ruling lineages of the Quiché kingdom soon after the Spanish conquest. It includes much of the later pre-Conquest history of the Quiché. But it is the earlier section of the work which provides the unique and truly priceless account of the genesis of the Maya world, whose heroes and epic stories scholars today can trace in Maya art of the Classic period and even earlier centuries. The sixteenth-century version is now lost, but a copy of it had been made at the turn of the eighteenth century by the Dominican priest Francisco Ximénez, who came upon the original in Chichicastenango. Ximénez also produced a Spanish translation. It was the Ximénez manuscript which Brasseur saw in Guatemala City. To be accurate, it was in fact another scholar, the Austrian Karl Scherzer, who discovered the Ximénez translation and then published it in 1857. But Brasseur was the first to publish the original Quiché with a French translation four years later. Brasseur succeeded in 'borrowing' the manuscript in order to translate it and then duly took it to France, from where in 1911 it eventually found its way to the Newberry Library in Chicago.

Brasseur returned to Europe in 1857 with a large number of documents, not all of them related to the Maya. But amongst the Maya material there was also a 1200-page manuscript which he had bought at a bookstall in Mexico City for four pesos. This was the so-called Motul dictionary, an extremely important sixteenth-century dictionary of Yucatec Mayan which has proved of immense value to Maya 'epigraphers', or decipherers of hieroglyphs, in recent years, since many sixteenth-century Maya words and their meanings can now be used to help in the translation of the Classic period texts. Brasseur busied himself publishing this hoard of material and compiling his own four-volume *Histoire des Nations Civilisées du Mexique et de l'Amérique Central....* But he also now stepped up his search for other Central American documents in European archives. It was in 1863 that he made his greatest discovery of all. Lying unrecognized in the library of the Academy of History in Madrid he found an edited copy of Diego de Landa's *Relación de las Cosas de Yucatán.* This was a truly great moment in the study of the Maya. He published most of the *Relación* in 1864 and its value as an incomparable insight into Maya society of the Conquest period was immediately recognized.

As Brasseur first pored over the wealth of information that it contained, his pulse would have quickened at two key passages. Firstly, he found illustrations of the Maya signs for the names of the days in the 260-day *tzolkin* or sacred calendar and for the months in the 365-day approximate solar year (see Appendix 1 for a discussion of the Maya calendar). The names themselves were already known, since Pío Pérez had provided Stephens with them. But now here were both the names and reproductions of actual Maya hieroglyphs in use, or at least still memorized, soon after the Conquest. This was not all, however. Landa announced, in no uncertain terms, that he was going to provide the reader with a Maya ABC, a Maya alphabet (see below). And there it was:

Diego de Landa's Maya 'alphabet'. A page from his *Relación de las Cosas de Yucatan.*

A to Z with Maya signs set next to each of Landa's letters. These were
the signs that had been drawn for Landa by his informant Caspar
Antonio Chi. There were a few missing, though Landa explained that
the Maya language lacked equivalents to certain of our letters and, rather
curiously, there were a number of different Maya signs for the same
letter and one or two that stood for a consonant plus a vowel. But no
matter. This was it, Brasseur must have thought. The great mystery of
the hieroglyphs must soon be solved. Stephens' longed-for Rosetta
stone was staring him in the face.

Before following Brasseur's efforts at decipherment, we must briefly
move sideways to the subject of Maya codices.[63] Three of them survived
the Conquest and Landa's bonfires and somehow found their way to
Europe, taking the names of the cities where they have come to rest.
The first, the Dresden Codex, may well have been sent back from
Mexico in 1519 by Cortés, as we have seen. From then on its movements are a mystery, until in 1739 the Director of the Saxon Royal
Library in Dresden 'obtained it from a private person, for nothing, as
being an unknown thing' while travelling through Vienna. It was catalogued the following year as 'an invaluable Mexican book with
hieroglyphic figures' and remained in obscurity in the Dresden Library
until Alexander Von Humboldt heard about it and in 1810 published
five pages in his *Vues des cordillères*. It was these few pages that were seen
by Rafinesque. All seventy-four pages were copied by the Italian artist
Agostino Aglio and published by Viscount Kingsborough in the 1830s.

The Dresden Codex is the most informative of the ancient Maya
books that survive and, until it suffered water damage during the
bombing of Dresden in the Second World War, it was also the best preserved (see p.3, plate section). It consists in part of almanacs or
instructions for the timing of religious ritual within the 260-day sacred
calendar. Lengthy texts and groups of numbers were painted in black or
red and illustrated with pictures of those gods associated with particular
days. These were picked out with washes of colour or sometimes set
against a ground of red, yellow or blue. The Dresden Codex also contains a series of astronomical tables, related in particular to the synodical
periods of Venus and to eclipses.

In 1859 a second Codex suddenly came to light in Paris. It was discovered by a young scholar of ancient scripts, Léon de Rosny, who is
said to have noticed it lying in a basket of dusty and neglected
manuscripts in the corner of a chimney in the Bibliothèque Imperiale.

The Paris Codex is a twenty-two page fragment of a Maya book, comparable in subject matter to the Dresden. Much of it concerns the particular deities and ceremonies that are connected with specific *katuns*. Modern researchers also believe that it represents certain elements of the Maya 'Zodiac'. It appears that the Paris Codex had in fact been catalogued and seen by a few scholars a quarter of a century previously, but its origins and how it first arrived in Paris are totally unknown.

It was Brasseur de Bourbourg himself who in 1866, when on a visit to Spain, discovered part of a third Maya book, the Madrid Codex. Another fragment, of seventy pages, it was in the possession of Juan de Troy y Ortolano, Professor of Palaeography in Madrid, a collector of manuscripts who claimed to be a descendant of Cortés. Brasseur borrowed it for study and published it in 1869, calling it the Codex Troano after elements of the owner's name. Now it was that Brasseur, the great Maya linguist and collector of manuscripts, felt well-equipped, with Landa and the codices to hand, to settle down and make substantial inroads into the mysteries of Maya writing.

Today I lack nothing: I am master of all the inscriptions, despite the numerous variations of each character, and the same key that I use to read the Troano manuscript will allow me to read the Dresden manuscript, the Mexican Manuscript number 2 of the Imperial Library (The Paris Codex) as well as the Inscriptions of Palenque and the monoliths of Copán.[64]

So he applied his key, Landa's alphabet, to the Troano manuscript. But, as he very soon must have realized, it didn't work. Though he tried hard to disguise the fact, it was of no help whatsoever in making sense of the text. He found a similar sign here, and another over there, but words, sentences, Maya voices from across the centuries simply did not materialize. Another problem that Brasseur had, although one can hardly blame him for it and it would have made very little difference, was that he was attempting to read the Maya text backwards. He read down one column of glyphs and then up the next, from right to left, whereas what he should have done was read top to bottom left to right in pairs of glyph blocks. It was not until 1882 that the American scholar Cyrus Thomas established this reading order to be correct. Deeply frustrated, Brasseur was reluctant to admit failure. Instead, he took refuge in his imagination and simply declared that he had translated the text without explaining how. And what he had discovered, the mystery of the

hieroglyphs that he had 'unlocked' seemed pure fantasy to most other
scholars. The major theme of all the codices, according to Brasseur, was
nothing less than the story of Atlantis. In effect the codices were Maya
origin myths, telling of the time thousands of years ago when survivors
from the stricken, sunken continent had struggled ashore in the
Americas and planted civilization in the Maya lands. The story of
Atlantis, along with various delvings into comparative mythology,
became the overpowering enthusiasms of Brasseur's last years, before
his death in 1874.

None of this, of course, should detract from Brasseur's considerable
and lasting achievements. He provided the tools for other scholars,
tracking down and publishing many of the major documentary pillars of
present-day Maya research. But his failure with Landa's alphabet meant
that in the years to come, few returned to it. It was widely regarded as a
dead end and in 1880 one scholar even suggested that it was a meaningless fabrication. The only way to progress, it seemed, was to pick away at
the internal structure of the Maya codices, armed with what was now
known, namely Landa's day and month signs and Maya numerals. This
is what Brasseur himself evidently did, to his credit, alongside his more
outrageous claims and speculations. He managed to locate and confirm
many of these signs where they appeared in the codices, as well as
making some more specific decipherments. He worked out the *kin* sign
for a day, the *tun* or period of 360 days and was the first, according to
George Stuart, to correctly identify the sign 'u' which appeared in
Landa's alphabet, for the possessive pronoun.[65]

After Brasseur's death, De Rosny continued to devote much of his
energies to Maya writing. Indeed, the following year, in 1875 another
fragmentary Codex, the so-called 'Codex Cortesianus', after the story
that it had been brought back to Europe by Cortés himself, was sold to
the Archaeological Museum in Madrid. De Rosny travelled to see it and
was amazed to find that it was in fact the missing portion of the Troano.
The two sections now reside together in the Museo de America in
Madrid and the whole manuscript of the Madrid Codex is also known
today somewhat confusingly as the 'Tro Cortesianus'. From his own
study of the codices, De Rosny managed to come up with the successful
decipherment of the signs for the Maya world directions. But perhaps
his greatest significance today, though of little relevance at the time, was
that he remained open-minded about Landa's alphabet, in the belief that
it might represent more than just an 'ABC'. He was one of the few who

thought as much at the time and, in the longer term, he proved to be right.

The first systematic progress in decipherment between 1880 and the turn of the century was made by one remarkable man, the German scholar Ernest Forstemann. He was ideally placed for the task since he was the Royal Librarian at Dresden, custodian of the Codex, and could thus sit with the original on his desk in front of him, though he also organized the production of a magnificent facsimile edition of the manuscript, immensely valuable today given the more recent damage to the book itself. Forstemann was fifty-eight when he began his efforts, but over the next quarter of a century he produced fifty publications on Maya hieroglyphs. A linguist, the son of an eminent mathematician, and an immensely patient and disciplined scholar, he is regarded as a towering genius by modern epigraphers. He saw that Landa's alphabet had produced very little, so he worked on with the months, the days, the bar and dot numbers, the texts of the codices and using Pío Pérez's initial work on calendrics published by Stephens. By his death in 1906 he had elucidated the whole basis of the Maya calendar, Maya maths and much of their astronomy. He demonstrated that the calendar was founded on the two major cycles, the 260-day *Tzolkin* and the 365–day *Haab* or vague year, the combination known as the Calendar Round that repeats itself every fifty-two years. He unravelled the mechanics of the Long Count and discovered its origin or base date as 4 Ahau 8 Cumku in the Calendar Round. In achieving this, he recognized that the Maya used a vigesimal or base 20 system of arithmetic in place of our decimal system. Forstemann also worked out the way that the Maya in the Dresden Codex had calculated the cycles of Venus, the so-called Venus tables, and their predictions of lunar eclipses.

By the end of the century, Forstemann was increasingly able to turn from the codices to the evidence from Maya monuments. In 1894, for example, he successfully read the Long Count dates from copies of the inscriptions on seven of the stelae at Copán. For by now precise recording had begun of sculpture and inscriptions in the field. It is this parallel work, undertaken by explorers in the forests of the Southern Lowlands, that we shall now follow.

Stephens had been very conscious of the enormous amount of exploration that remained to be done. For in truth, in their own journeys, they had only penetrated the fringes of the Southern Lowlands. This must have been brought home to him in one of the most romantic highlights of the first *Incidents* volumes. Here he recounts how, during their journey overland across the mountains from Guatemala City to Palenque, they had come upon a Spanish padre in the town of Santa Cruz del Quiché. They spent a day with this cigar-smoking, eccentric cleric, an immensely knowledgeable antiquarian with much of the Brasseur de Bourbourg about him, who had lived in the Guatemalan highlands for thirty years. He had started off as a cura in the town of Cobán in the Alta Verapaz and it was there that he was told by local people the fantastic story that beyond the mountains, way to the north, 'was a living city, large and populous, occupied by Indians, precisely in the same state as before the discovery of America'. What is more, the padre himself, then a young man, had climbed a ridge in the sierra and saw 'at a great distance a large city spread over a great space, and with turrets white and glittering in the sun'.[66] He had never gone in search of this place – it was said that the inhabitants would kill any intruder – and neither did Stephens and Catherwood. In 1839, Stephens wrote, they did not have the time nor the resources for such an expedition. On their second journey, to northern Yucatán, he had toyed with the idea of trying to penetrate from there into the tropical forests to the south. But again, the sheer immensity of the task forestalled them. The vision of a lost, living Maya city obviously haunted Stephens. But it was something for younger men, a future generation of explorers, for without doubt, in the vast, uncharted region that stretched from Belize right across the Petén to the Usumacinta valley, great ruins, and maybe more than mere ruins, still lay waiting to be discovered.

Walker and Caddy had crossed the southern Petén, recording very little, on their way to Palenque. Galindo had been based in Flores on Lake Petén Itzá for a while and from here he had visited the ruins of Topoxte just to the east of the lake. But no outsider had penetrated any further north. Until, in 1848, Ambrosio Tut, the 'Governor' of the District of Petén and Colonel Modesto Méndez, Chief Magistrate and doubtless the real power in Flores at the time, explored the great city of Tikal. Tut was himself Maya, from the Itzá-speaking village of San José across Lake Petén Itzá from Flores. There is no doubt that his people already knew about the ruins, but the six days Tut spent at Tikal with Méndez amount to the first officially recognized visit in modern times, about a thousand years since Tikal's demise at the end of the Classic period. These were not foreign explorers, bent like Stephens on publishing their discoveries abroad, and Eusebio Lara, the so-called artist who accompanied them, produced drawings of monuments and statuary as naïve and unimpressive as those of José Calderón at Palenque (see below). This may account for the very limited attention that the discovery received at the time. Méndez' report appeared the same year in Guatemala and some of Lara's drawings were published in Germany in 1853. But world-wide recognition of Tikal's existence had to wait. A Captain John Carmichael visited briefly in 1869 and eight years later the Swiss Dr Gustave Bernoulli reached the ruins and removed some of the carved wooden lintels from Temples I and IV, which are now to be found in the Museum für Volkerkunde in Basel. But in 1881, outfitted by 'Mr Sarg', a German living in the town of Cobán who had already facilitated Bernoulli's lintel-lifting expedition, there appeared at Tikal the English explorer Alfred Maudslay.

Maudslay arrived on Easter Sunday with a sizeable mule train and a contingent of Maya *mozos* or porters and assistants to help clear the jungle. It was Maudslay's first journey among Maya ruins. He had met Sarg at the beginning of his trip who had excited him with 'an account of a newly discovered and undescribed ruined city near Flores which is said to be as fine as Palenque'. It had taken more than two weeks to get to Tikal from Cobán. Maudslay was weary and had had stomach trouble for days. His porters were disinclined to work over Easter and his first reaction to Tikal was candidly unenthusiastic. It is somewhat refreshing to find that not every explorer, stumbling upon a 'lost' city, wipes his brow, takes a large slug from his canteen and emits a long 'wow' of amazement:

A temple at Tikal by Eusebio Lara.

On the whole I must own to being much disappointed. The forest was over everything. The work of clearing would be much more than I could do and there appeared to be very little hope of taking satisfactory photographs. No doubt I was on the site of a very large city, larger than anything mentioned by Stephens.[67]

The following day, however, his mood had changed. His *mozos* returned to work and Maudslay began the very first mapping and photography at Tikal. He climbed one of the principal pyramids, probably Temple I, clinging to tree roots and vines until he made it to the top and could appreciate the roof-combs of other pyramids protruding through the sea of forest and even taller than the one he was on. His workmen made remarkably swift progress and his photographs of Tikal were to reveal the truly impressive scale of the 'Rome' of the Maya world (see plate section, p. 5).

Tikal was the last stop on a journey that had begun in December the previous year. He had come to Guatemala, so he wrote, through a 'desire to pass the winter in a warm climate'. Maudslay was a shy, modest and deceptively under-stated character and his presence in Guatemala was in fact more than a mere holiday in the sun. He had been in Central America once before, in 1870, when while studying anatomy and botany at Cambridge University he had been advised by the eminent naturalist Osbert Salvin that Guatemala was a good place to visit to experience a rain-forest and its bird life, Maudslay being a keen ornithologist. He had spent a month there but, on that occasion, did not visit any ruins.

According to the modern-day Maya explorer Ian Graham, Maudslay suffered early in life from a form of chronic bronchitis.[68] After graduating in 1872 he thus decided that he should follow a career that took him to warmer climates. He entered the Colonial Service and spent time in Trinidad, Australia and finally in Fiji, where it seems that he began to take an interest in ethnography. By 1880 he no longer wished to be a civil servant and returned from the Pacific to England to think about his future. Now his mind evidently turned to archaeology. Years before, Salvin had shown him photographs of Copán and Quiriguá and Maudslay says himself that his 'interest had been roused by reading Stephens' account of his travels'. Money was not a consideration, since his family was comfortably off. He headed back to Guatemala in December 1880 to visit Copán and Quiriguá and see whether he could perhaps make a contribution to the work that Stephens and Catherwood had begun.

Maudslay's port of arrival in January 1881 was Livingstone on Guatemala's Caribbean coast. From there he travelled first to Quiriguá, briefly visited by Catherwood. When he arrived here with some local villagers the site was covered in jungle. But as they cut away the branches of trees, the vines and creepers, magnificent stelae and stone monuments were revealed. These monuments were much more important, he later wrote 'than any account of them had led me to expect'. Catherwood had made his trip alone, without his camera lucida, and had published only two illustrations, which were extremely poor by his own high standards. The remains of buildings at Quiriguá are few but some of the stelae here are the largest ever carved by the Maya, standing up to 9 metres high. They possess awe-inspiring sculptural images of elaborately ornamented human figures and extremely beautiful panels of hieroglyphs. Already it had dawned on Maudslay that there was indeed work to be done. This was confirmed when he reached Copán, where he found that the numerous stelae were very comparable to those at Quiriguá, deeply carved in relief and depicting similarly costumed figures flanked by hieroglyphs. Catherwood's drawings, however admirable for his day, were rarely detailed or quite accurate enough to serve as a permanent record of monuments and texts. A more systematic, scientific approach was needed.

In his self-effacing way, Maudslay never advertised himself as a great expert or major scholar. He developed no particular theories about the Maya and offered very few answers to their myriad mysteries. Indeed, in reading his published works some might find him frustratingly devoid of opinions. But this was not the task he set himself. His job, the vocation that he discovered in 1881, was to provide others with information, to document Maya sites with plans, drawings, photographs and copies of the monuments and inscriptions in order, as he later put it, to 'enable scholars to carry on their work of examination and comparison, and to solve some of the many problems of Maya civilization, whilst comfortably seated in their studies at home'. It was typical of the new, classificatory scientific spirit of the later nineteenth century and an ideal of selfless service suited to a British colonial servant and a gentleman.

So, by early 1881, before the coming of the rains in late April, Maudslay had visited Quiriguá, Copán and Tikal. He returned to England for the summer and was back in Guatemala in December, spending another week at Tikal and five days at Quiriguá. Through his old friend Mr Sarg of Cobán he also now heard reports of unknown ruins on the banks of the Usumacinta. In March 1882 he set off down the river with *mozos*, a guide and two canoes. They entered a remote, little-explored region of pristine beauty, that can still be experienced to this day. They passed numerous rapids, took pot-shots at crocodiles, and here and there saw signs of the unacculturated Indians, the Lacandón or *Caribes* as Maudslay's men called them. At one point they saw a canoe that had been left by the water on a sand-bank and stopped to examine it. As they did so the owner, a woman and child emerged from the forest:

> The man was an uncouth-looking fellow with sturdy limbs, long black hair, very strongly marked features, prominent nose, thick lips and complexion about the tint of my half-caste canoemen. He was clothed in a single long brown garment of roughly-woven material, which looked like sacking, splashed over with blots of some red dye...[69]

Later they went to a Lacandón *caribal* or small settlement, two miles from the river, along a path through the jungle marked by jaguar skulls on poles and sticks here and there laid across the track. They came upon three houses near the bank of a small stream, in a clearing planted with cotton, maize, squash and tobacco. Maudslay observed their simple hunting equipment of bows and stone-tipped arrows. On another visit he was very struck by the 'sloping forehead and skull' of the Lacandón, so like many of the images on ancient Maya sculpture.

A day's journey further downstream they encountered a heap of stones by the riverside which marked the spot where the ruins were located. 'We scrambled up the bank and began to cut our way through the undergrowth in search of the ancient buildings which we found on a succession of terraces rising in all about 250 feet above the river... It was some time before we could find a house good enough for me to live in, but at last we came upon one at the top of many terraces and steps which was in fairly good preservation and rather wider than any I had seen at Tikal...'.

The Maya city they had encountered is known today as Yaxchilán. It lies on the southern, Mexican bank of the Usumacinta, surrounded by a horseshoe-shaped bend in the river which provides a natural, moated defence. The architecture here is impressive and distinctive. Instead of the taller temple-pyramids found at Tikal, the buildings are modest in scale, more comparable with those of Palenque. Most have very thick walls, multiple entrances and many, like Palenque, have 'mansard' roofs with very large perforated roof combs which have the look of enormous pigeon lofts (see plate section, p.15). The relief sculpture of Yaxchilán is prolific and world-famous, due indirectly to Maudslay. In place of the wooden lintels seen at Tikal, those at Yaxchilán were of limestone and quite magnificently carved with inscriptions and narrative scenes. Edwin Rockstroh, a German friend of Sarg's who had been employed by the Guatemalan government to explore this part of the Usumacinta and had come upon the ruins, had noticed a fallen lintel and attempted to remove it, without success. Maudslay decided to take it away himself and later received permission from the Guatemalan Government to remove a number of others. At the time the area was so remote and inadequately surveyed that the Guatemalans believed Yaxchilán to be in their territory. Today the finest of the lintels that Maudslay removed are to be seen in the Mexican Gallery of the British Museum.

Once his men had cut down the trees and undergrowth, the fine preservation of the ruins was such that Maudslay could well imagine how they had once looked: 'The view from the river in the old days of the white terraces and brightly coloured houses with their rows of sculpted figures must have been both picturesque and imposing'. There were signs, too, that the site was being used by the Lacandón, who were evidently burning incense and making offerings in front of a headless statue in one of the buildings. It brought to mind the account by Stephens' padre of lost cities flourishing in the midst of the jungles 'with turrets white and glittering in the sun'. Maybe this hidden town by the river, still frequented by the Lacandon with their fine Maya profiles and flowing robes, was indeed the source of all the stories.

Maudslay called Yaxchilán 'Menche', a name of Lacandón derivation given to the ruins by Rockstroh. However, if he had arrived a week later Yaxchilán might have become known as 'Lorillard City'. It would have been a little like naming the ruins 'Marlboro' or 'Benson and Hedges'. For, on their fourth day at the site, as Maudslay's men worked away clearing the buildings, another expedition was approaching overland from the west. It was headed by the French explorer Desiré Charnay, who was sponsored by the French government and the Franco-American tobacco manufacturer Pierre Lorillard, after whom Charnay had promised to name the rumoured lost city that he confidently expected to discover.

Charnay, already in his late fifties, is deservedly known today as an important pioneer of archaeological photography who much earlier, between 1858 and 1860, had already toured Palenque, Uxmal, Chichén Itzá and other sites with his enormously bulky photographic apparatus and fragile glass plates. On this second expedition he had returned to take more photographs and to make papier-mâché moulds of monuments. In a vivid contrast to Maudslay, which approaches that of national stereotypes, Charnay was also a considerable showman, not averse to cutting a dash as the fearless lone explorer in the books about his travels and with no qualms about letting the bulk of his own personality get in the way of his subject (see plate section, p.6). David Adamson, in his account of Maya discovery, has aptly called him 'the nineteenth century's equivalent of those intrepid impresarios of the remote or primitive who lead television teams into the jungles or mountains'.[70] He had hoped to crown this, his last expedition, with a major discovery of his own. Alas, it was not to be. As they neared Yaxchilán, they came upon some of Maudslay's men who, since supplies were low, were out foraging for food among the Lacandón. They talked of the European with them called Don Alvarado. Charnay's heart must have sunk. He was also suffering from a bout of malaria at the time, but with dignity and generosity he sent back with them half a pig, rice and some biscuits along with his visiting card 'M. Desiré Charnay. Mission Scientifique Franco-Americaine'. Two days later, at the ruins there ensued a famous meeting, in the style of Stanley and Livingstone, described by Charnay:

> We shook hands. He knew my name, he told me his: Alfred Maudslay Esq. from London; and as my looks betrayed the inward annoyance I felt: 'It's all right', he said, 'there is no reason why you should look so distressed. My having had the start of you was a mere chance, as it would have been mere chance had it been the other way. You need have no fear on my account for I am only an amateur, travelling for pleasure. With you the case of course is different. But I do not intend to publish anything. Come, I have a place got ready for you; and as for the ruins I make them over to you. You can name the town, claim to have discovered it, in fact do what you please …'. I was deeply touched with his kind manner and am only too charmed to share with him the glory of having explored this city. We lived and worked together like two brothers and we parted the best of friends in the world.[71]

In truth, however, despite the outward display of courtesy, Maudslay was 'not best pleased' at Charnay's presence. It interfered with his work and in his unpublished field notes he writes of Charnay that 'he does not strike me as a scientific traveller of much class – he is a pleasant, talkative gentleman, thirsting for glory and wishes to be Professor of the history of American civilization in Paris… he is just my idea of a French traveller, not of a careful scientific observer'.[72]

But at Yaxchilán Charnay did Maudslay one great service. He added to his own 'scientific' armoury by providing an answer to the problem of recording the Maya monuments in detail: 'he immediately set his secretary at work to take paper moulds of some of the carved lintels. It is a very easy process and I wish I had known of it before.'

Between 1881 and 1894 Maudslay mounted seven expeditions in all to the Maya area. Apart from Tikal and Yaxchilán, he devoted his attentions to Copán, Quiriguá, Palenque, Chichén Itzá and the lesser-known site of Ixkún in the Petén, attempting to achieve as complete a documentation of their monuments and inscriptions as possible through photography and two different kinds of mould-making. Firstly, there were the papier-mâché moulds or paper 'squeezes', the technique Charnay employed. He used old newspapers, but Maudslay chose a special tissue like orange wrappers that travelled out from England in large bales. Such a technique was adequate for some low relief sculpture and inscriptions but for stelae and sculpture in the round in particular, the only answer was plaster of Paris. The second half of the nineteenth century was of course the great age of cast-making for international exhibitions and museum exhibits. For the work at Copán and Quiriguá he hired a Mr Guintini from an established Italian firm of cast-makers in London, and bought tons of plaster from a supplier in Carlisle.

The logistical problems were formidable. Besides photographic and survey equipment, and supplies for many weeks in the field, he had to arrange for the shipment of the plaster, the bales of paper, wrapping materials for the moulds and specially designed boxes to transport them. The journey from England by steam boat was the easy part. For everything had then to travel by mule or on the backs of human porters to the sites themselves. The return trip to the coast was even more taxing. The plaster moulds had to be packed with extreme care, and there were hundreds of them. At Copán, Maudslay and Guintini used four tons of plaster and produced some 1400 separate piece moulds and at Quiriguá one enormous zoomorphic sculpture alone, the 'Great Turtle', required 600 separate moulds and 2 tons of plaster. Occasional accidents, the sudden, unseasonal arrival of rains while the moulds were still open to the elements meant that on occasion the work had to be done all over again. The costs, too, were considerable and apart from his last visit to Copán in 1894, which was supported by the Peabody Museum of Harvard University, Maudslay financed everything and worked on his own behalf. In contrast to the French, for whom state support of archaeological and cultural endeavour had become an enduring tradition since the time of Napoleon, the British way, as it so often still is, was to leave such things to private initiative, to the philanthropy or cultural noblesse oblige of the wealthy.

The immense trouble and patient care that Maudslay took in his photography and the making of moulds has rarely been paralleled in the history of archaeology. The original moulds and the casts taken from them now reside in the collections of the British Museum. Aside from their use for display purposes, the most obvious benefit is that they serve as permanent copies of monuments and inscriptions that have since suffered a century of weathering and erosion, and on occasion of vandalism and looting. Another great virtue of the casts, in Maudslay's own day, was that they enabled a skilled illustrator to produce accurate drawings from them under working conditions vastly better than the tropical forest could offer. Back in England, Maudslay's principal artist Annie Hunter produced a magnificient series of drawings (see p.235), consulting with Maudslay, who checked them against the casts, his photographs and in the earlier years when he returned to Central America, against the monuments themselves. Aside from accurate rendering of the inscriptions, Hunter and Maudslay also helped the understanding of Maya iconography by the simple technique of using different coloured washes to highlight elements of the designs. Thus the 'baroque' complexity of Maya art, so difficult to get to grips with, was made more intelligible.

Maudslay's plans, descriptions, drawings and photographs were published between 1889 and 1902 as part of the *Biologia Centrali-Americana*. This was a massive, many-volumed work principally concerned with the flora and fauna of Mexico and Central America. But its editors, one of whom was Maudslay's biologist friend Osbert Salvin and the other Frederick Du Cane Godman, a Trustee of the British Museum, enabled Maudslay to include his material as a special four-volume archaeological appendix, the *Archaeologia*. The quality of Maudslay's published work is outstanding and the photographs and drawings remained unmatched until the 1970s when Ian Graham began his own quiet and unsung work on the 'Corpus of Maya Hieroglyphic Inscriptions', an ongoing project to compile a complete record of Maya inscriptions in drawings and photographs. Graham and his colleagues have continued in the tradition begun by Maudslay, to produce a body of information for others to work on 'in their studies at home'.

Maudslay was the greatest of the late nineteenth century Maya recorders. But alongside Maudslay and Charnay must be included Teobert Maler, a naturalized Austrian of German parentage who in 1846 joined the French forces sent to establish Maximilian as Emperor of Mexico. He stayed on beyond the collapse of the regime, became entranced with the Maya on a visit to Palenque and, after returning home to fight for his inheritance, bought a house near Mérida in 1884 and devoted the rest of his years to Maya exploration. Maler was a prickly, misanthropic, difficult individual but he was undoubtedly the most effective pure explorer of his day. He made no moulds or drawings of hieroglyphic inscriptions, but produced plans, extensive notes and descriptions of many unknown sites and magnificent photographs that are the equal of Maudslay's. In the 1880s Maler began work in the northern Yucatán and then turned to the Usumacinta Valley. There he discovered the cities of Altar de Sacrificios and Piedras Negras and continued Maudslay's work at Yaxchilán. But it was in the unexplored forests of the Petén that he made his greatest pioneering contribution. In the 1890s the area began to open up, largely due to the American demand for chewing gum, whose raw ingredient, before the advent of synthetic alternatives, was *chicle* or the sap of the Chicozapote tree. *Chicleros*, chewing-gum tappers, criss-crossed the jungle and Maler went with them. Perhaps his greatest discovery in the Petén was the important but still little-known city of Naranjo. But travelling light, unlike the more cumbersome field expeditions of Maudslay or Charnay, and suffering terrible privations, he found countless other ruins. He also spent a long and productive period at Tikal, where Maudslay's time had been limited. In 1898 the Peabody Museum employed him to undertake explorations on their behalf and for ten years his reports and photographs appeared in the Peabody Memoirs. In the end Maler's erratic behaviour and non-delivery of promised materials led the Museum to break off relations. He died in Mérida in 1917, not a time to expect extensive and laudatory obituaries if you were a German, and his intense application and contribution to Maya exploration has only been fully appreciated in recent years. His large and detailed photographic archive of Maya monuments and inscriptions stands as another critical corpus of material with which Maya scholars have continued to work. His lengthy descriptions of work in the field, full of fine archaeological detail and at times forthright and not entirely flattering observations about those who toiled alongside him, are an exciting and colourful read and have proved of great value to more modern archaeologists and explorers.

The period from 1880 to 1910 was thus a great era for the discovery and documentation of Maya ruins. The jungles still held many secrets but the frontiers of that vast, uncharted blank on the map were being pushed back on every side. New technology and improved means of documentation and representation also meant that Maya discovery could now be presented to the public in a more vivid and tangible way. The World's Fair in Chicago in 1893 is a good example. Here, in a special section devoted to the civilizations of the New World, were exhibited Maudslay's evocative photographs of ruins emerging from the jungle, Charnay's casts of Maya monuments and casts too of the sculpture and architecture of Uxmal and Labná in the Puuc region made by another pioneer, Edward Thompson, later to achieve fame through his dredging of the Sacred Cenote at Chichén Itzá. Reproductions of some of Labná's striking buildings were exhibited in the open air and even enveloped in cacti and forest plants native to the Yucatán. To the visiting public, the remains of Maya civilization appeared just as wondrous as Stephens' books had suggested.

But where did all this rich accumulation of data lead? The significance of Maudslay's work to the study of Maya hieroglyphs was immediate. It was his recording of the inscriptions of Copán which led to Forstemann's decipherment of the Long Count dates on the stelae there, and Maudslay's material also now enabled the German scholar's work on the calendar to be taken a crucial stage further. He had defined its workings, but correlation with the Christian calendar had not yet been achieved. This vital breakthrough was made in 1905 by the American newspaper proprietor, one of the increasing band of expert amateur epigraphers, Joseph Goodman. Basing his work on Forstemann, on Maudslay's publications and upon Landa and other colonial sources, Goodman achieved a correlation which, with minor modifications, has survived until today. It meant that Maya civilization, quite suddenly, was given a chronology and anchored within our own system of time. From the range of dates on their monuments it appeared that the Maya in the tropical forests had flourished between about 300–900 AD, which soon became known as the Classic period.

It was all too evident that recording the passage of time was of vital importance to the Maya. On some stelae, for example, half of the texts consisted of calendrical information. But what did this seemingly obsessive concern actually mean? The trouble was that the rest of the inscriptions, the so-called 'non-calendrical glyphs', could not be understood. A step in this direction seemed to have been taken by another German scholar, Paul Schellhas, who successfully identified a large number of Maya gods and the glyphs for their names that appeared in the codices. In 1904 he published a list of fifteen distinct deities, an impressive 'pantheon', and to each one he gave an alphabetical label A–P. The codices date from the centuries just before the Spanish conquest. But what Schellhas' work suggested at the time was the likelihood that on the stone monuments of the Classic period many of the unidentified and anthropomorphic hieroglyphs – of figures and human heads set alongside the dates – also represented gods or mythical beings. The impression thus began to grow that Maya texts were solely concerned with time and the gods.

The pace of discovery by the early decades of the twentieth century, both in the field and at the desks of Maya scholars, had revealed much of the scale, the temporal and geographical spread and the sophistication of ancient Maya society. The ultimate yardstick of civilization remained the familiar classical cultures of the Old World. But the Maya, because of their perceived intellectual capacities – their possession of literacy, numeracy and their abilities as astronomers and empirical 'scientists' – seemed at least to have been approaching western achievements. This was true also of their art. Maya architecture possessed a splendour, and in the case of such cities as Palenque or Uxmal, a grace and aesthetic refinement unmatched by any other pre-Columbian culture of the Americas. Their sculpture and pottery painting, though somewhat cluttered with ornament, depicted the human figure in a realistic and accessible manner that was very pleasing to European and American sensibilities. In 1913 the Maya received their first art-historical treatment from Herbert Spinden, who declared:

> At first glance too exotic and unique to be compared to the Old World, nevertheless Maya art furnishes upon examination many analogies to the earlier products of the Classic Mediterranean lands. Indeed, upon technological grounds, such as knowledge displayed of foreshortening, composition and design, Maya art may be placed in advance of the art of

Assyria and Egypt and only below that of Greece in the list of great national achievements.[73]

The idea of the ancient Maya as a very special people, and a little like us, began to take hold. It was at this point that they began regularly to be termed the 'Classical' civilization of the Americas. Their golden age appeared to have come to an abrupt and unexplained end by AD 900, which only added to the mystique that surrounded them. But what they had created was a touchstone for all that followed in Mesoamerica, and no later people could match them.

JUNGLE UTOPIA

One might imagine that the study of the Maya in the twentieth century, which saw the gradual establishment of the more scientific techniques of a true archaeology, would have brought steady progress towards a deeper understanding of the character and functioning of Maya civilization. Today, it is easy enough for us to see that this did not happen. Instead, a view of the Maya developed that was as romanticized as any that had gone before.[74]

After the First World War the nature of research changed. The great era of the lone explorer was coming to a close. Now American institutions entered the field in force, introducing programmes of archaeological excavation and restoration, as well as funding exploration for new sites and the recording of hieroglyphic inscriptions. The Peabody Museum had been involved in Maya archaeology since the 1890s, but the major player for the next thirty years was to be the Carnegie Institution of Washington. Fired by the great American Mayanist and archaeological impresario Sylvanus Morley, Carnegie began two major projects in the 1920s, at Chichén Itzá and Uaxactún. Morley himself directed investigation and restoration at Chichén Itzá in its early stages and this was later combined with an impressive multi-disciplinary study of the natural and human environment of the northern Yucatán. Uaxactún was a much more remote and little-known site lying some forty kilometres north of Tikal in the forests of the Petén. A stela had been discovered here with a date of AD 328. This was for some time the earliest dated monument known, and so in 1926 it was decided to begin a systematic programme of excavation there which lasted more than a decade.

The work at Uaxactún proved extremely important. Inscriptions with dates, found in different contexts in archaeological excavation, helped to build up a chronology for the site. The architectural development of the city could be charted over time and, even more significant, a dated sequence of Maya pottery was also determined, which was to become an important reference collection for comparison with material from other sites. Four separate ceramic phases were identified, reaching back into what was now termed a Preclassic period, to as early as 500–600 BC it was thought, though little attention was paid to this early era, the general presumption being that before the beginning of the erection of dated monuments Maya society had consisted of little more than simple farming villages. Once a chronology had been defined at Uaxactún, the emphasis thereafter was to be on building up comparable ones at other sites. Carnegie initiated field-work at cities such as Tulum and Cobá and continued work at Copán, and other institutions began to play a role. For example, the University of Pennsylvania worked at Piedras Negras through the 1930s; Mexican archaeologists systematically investigated Palenque at the same time and, slightly earlier, the British Museum had started to excavate at the sites of Lubaantun and Pusilha in British Honduras.

The recording of Maya inscriptions proceeded rapidly, largely driven by Morley whose great enthusiasm this was. As early as 1920 he had completed *The Inscriptions at Copán*. The multi-volumed *Inscriptions of the Petén* appeared in the late 1930s, a massive contribution whose value at the time lay in helping to build up the series of relative chronologies for lowland sites, both large and small. Morley was certainly very industrious in his pursuit of inscriptions, offering the *chicleros* prize money to lead him to new ones. But today scholars express serious doubts about the quality and underlying presumptions of his work. Firstly, his photographs and drawings were well below the exacting standards set by Maudslay and Maler. Second, Maudslay, even though he might not understand the inscriptions he was reproducing, ensured that Annie Hunter faithfully copied every element of a Maya text. When Morley drew monumental inscriptions, however, he tended to ignore those sections of text which did not deal with the calendar, the tantalizing hieroglyphs between the dates which still could not be understood. It was as if he felt that these glyphs would never be deciphered, and thus there was little point in recording them.

So, until the 1950s, the practice of Maya archaeology principally involved the collection and logging of dates from monuments, which gave archaeologists a very broad idea of the careers of Maya cities, of their rise, florescence and fall within the Classic period, the comparison of pottery styles and styles of architecture and a certain amount of speculation about what the structures within the major centres might have been used for. Thus the tallest and most elaborate buildings were termed 'temples' and the ranges of single and sometimes double-storey buildings on lower platforms, often with multiple entrances, dispersed around the centre of a city were called 'palaces'.

Alongside this comparative, descriptive and speculative kind of archaeology there developed a different approach. This was ethnographic analogy, the observation of contemporary Maya communities and the use of presumed continuities over time to make various assumptions about pre-Hispanic Maya society. Firstly, it was evident that there were certain remarkable continuities in Maya beliefs. The Maya of the northern Yucatán, for example, still made offerings to the Rain God Chak to ensure the coming of the rains and a plentiful harvest, and in highland Guatemala the religious practitioners in a number of communities kept to the traditional 260-day Sacred Calendar observed by their ancient ancestors. More generally it was felt that the living Maya were intensely 'religious' people. They had enthusiastically adopted the Catholic observances of their Spanish conquerors and welded them onto a rich Precolumbian inheritance. This richness and complexity could be seen at such Maya towns as Zinacantan or Chamula in the Chiapas highlands. With no sizeable population for much of the year, at the time of certain fiestas they would fill up for many days of music, dance and religious ritual. At the end of a festival, Maya families would return to their hamlets and maize fields in the surrounding area. This image of a largely vacant religious centre that serviced the rural hinterland became an appealing model for what had perhaps prevailed in ancient times. This idea became even more persuasive when Maya agricultural practices were considered. Contemporary Maya uniformly practised slash-and-burn or 'swidden' farming, as they still do, and this also appeared to be the only method that Diego de Landa had observed at the time of the conquest. It involves clearing an area of land, known locally as a 'milpa', by cutting down and burning as much of the trees and undergrowth as possible, planting for a few years until soil fertility is depleted and then moving on to another patch of land. This kind of shifting cultivation normally demands large tracts of available land and can only support relatively small and dispersed populations.

So it was that after the Second World War a particular vision of Maya society began to emerge in the writings of Sylvanus Morley and in particular of the Englishman Eric Thompson, who came to dominate Maya research for a quarter of a century after Morley's death in 1948. If Alfred Maudslay is often defined as an archetypal English gentleman of the late Victorian period, then Thompson has been characterized as a slightly more dashing example for the succeeding era (see plate section, p.6). The son of a well-to-do doctor, he went to public school, served underage in the trenches and was wounded during the First World War, worked for a spell as a gaucho on the cattle ranch of a branch of his family in Argentina and then returned to read Anthropology at Cambridge. Encouraged by Maudslay's example, he too became fascinated by the Maya and taught himself all he could about hieroglyphs, which earned him a job with Morley at Chichén Itzá in 1926. He then conducted archaeological excavations in British Honduras for a number of years on behalf of the British Museum and the Field Museum of Natural History in Chicago, before returning to work for Carnegie from 1935 onwards. Thompson was a prodigious all-round scholar, one of the greatest Mayanists of all time. He was a field archaeologist, became the acknowledged authority on Maya writing of his day and was also a great ethnographer who spent long periods living and studying among contemporary Maya and tracing connections in technology, domestic life and religious beliefs between the ancient and modern people. It was the very breadth of his knowledge, coupled with his own deep personal attachment to the Maya with whom he worked, that enabled him in his more popular books of synthesis to draw an extraordinarily persuasive picture of what Maya society had been like during the Classic Period.

Thompson felt that the Maya had been a peaceable people living alongside one another in orderly city states. However, these were not true cities in the way we would think of them. They were empty 'ceremonial centres' presided over by priest–kings who devoted most of their days to astronomy and divination on behalf of their people. The Maya social structure was very simple. It was a paternalistic society of wise and benevolent rulers, who interceded with the gods, and a sturdy peasant class of slash-and-burn farmers spread throughout the surrounding landscape, who would only leave their cornfields for the ceremonial centres on feast days to worship the gods and celebrate the significant dates in the Sacred Calendar. Both rulers and ruled were perceived to be a deeply religious, modest kind of people. What they wrote about on their monuments was exclusively to do with religion and their obsessive charting of the passage of time. Politics or more conventional 'secular' concerns were of little interest to them. The possibility that the dates recorded on Maya monuments might be connected with historical events or the deeds of individuals was, as Thompson put it,

> well nigh inconceivable, the dates surely narrate the stages of the journey of time with a reverence befitting such a solemn theme... To add details of war or peace, of marriage or giving in marriage, to the solemn role call of the periods of time is as though a tourist were to carve his initials on Donatello's David.[75]

Thus the images on Maya stelae were defined by Thompson and others as 'calendar priests' or perhaps even as 'gods'. It is worth recalling here the monument known as Altar Q from Copán. Stephens, with his experience of other civilizations of the Old World, had thought that the sixteen seated figures carved around it were probably Maya rulers, a very reasonable suggestion as it turned out. But by the 1950s it was felt that something so simple and mundane was highly unlikely. A view that gained wide currency for many years was that the Altar represented nothing less than a convocation of priestly astronomers meeting to discuss certain necessary adjustments to the Maya system of time reckoning. Indeed, so appealing and so authoritatively promoted was this idea that Jacob Bronowski was to pass it on enthusiastically to the public at large in his *Ascent of Man* of 1973:

> The Maya temple complexes, with their step pyramids, housed some astronomers, and we have portraits of a group of them on a large altar stone that has survived. The altar commemorates an ancient astronomical congress that met in the year AD 776. Sixteen mathematicians came here to the famous centre of Maya science, the sacred city of Copán in Central America...[76]

The most striking element of Thompson's overall thesis, however, was the belief in the essentially peaceful nature of Maya society, the idea that, unlike most other early civilizations around the globe, the Maya were largely unaffected by warfare or competition between one Maya city state and another. Scholars find this particularly remarkable today, given that warlike imagery should have been all too apparent both in Maya sculpture and, most vividly of all, in an astonishing and unique set of Maya wall paintings, known as the Bonampak murals. In 1946 a British journalist, Giles Healey, was commissioned by the United Fruit Company in the USA to make a film about the Lacandón Indians. It was during his time with the Lacandón that they took him to the ruins of Bonampak, situated in Chiapas thirty kilometres south of Yaxchilán, and at that time unknown to the outside world. There he made one of the great Maya discoveries. Wall paintings are known to have covered the interiors of many Maya buildings, from the fragmentary remains and traces of pigment that archaeologists have found over the years. In the forest environment one would not expect to find them intact. But at Bonampak, by a freak of nature that had deposited a protective layer of calcite over them, the murals in the three rooms of one building were miraculously preserved. They include magnificent scenes of pageantry, music, dance and the court of a Maya ruler in all their elaborate finery (see plate section, pp. 5, 23). These are startling and rare images that today one has to transplant to the stillness of Maya ruins to recreate in the mind's eye the true colour and vibrancy of Maya life. Much of the impact of the murals, however, lies in the level of violence that is represented. This includes a frenzied battle scene, the capture of prisoners and explicit depictions of torture and ritual slaughter. One clear message of the paintings at the time they were discovered was, or at least should have been, that the Maya were deeply concerned with militarism, power and blood. This, of course, did not fit too well with the Thompson thesis, yet the peaceful vision managed to survive.

In one of Thompson's classic books, *The Rise and Fall of Maya Civilization*, published in 1954, he gave his views on Maya warfare. One has to remember that this was a popular synthesis and Thompson undoubtedly felt that in a book of this nature, unlike his more cautious academic works, he had a duty to chance his arm a little.

> Perhaps we can assume that relations between city states of the Classic Period were, on the whole, quite friendly. Presumably their rulers were related; certainly they shared the same upbringing, education, taste in art and religious beliefs. That does not necessarily lead one to conclude that relations were always cordial. I think one can assume fairly constant friction over boundaries, sometimes leading to a little fighting, and occasional raids on outlying parts of a neighbouring city state to assure a supply of sacrificial victims, but I think the evidence is against the assumption of

regular warfare on a considerable scale... the Maya motto was ' live and let live', and somehow I don't see too much bullying of a small city state by a big one, although affection for the Maya may have influenced that opinion.[77]

He is not, of course, denying the existence of warfare, or of the practice of human sacrifice, but he gently dismisses the thought of it. What the Bonampak murals represented, then, was little more than an occasional raid, something of an aberration among people who were generally a friendly sort. Poor Thompson! His admission that he was 'assuming' all sorts of things, his rather cosy, period style has guaranteed him harsh treatment from some modern academics. Many have sought to explain his theories as a product of Thompson's particular upper-middle-class English background and the time in which he lived. It is said, for example, that he was greatly influenced by romantic Edwardian ideals of medieval life, of wise, benign churchmen like William of Wykeham, Bishop of Winchester, who founded the college where he went to school, and of sturdy, devout peasants building the great English cathedrals. He thus projected his own values and vision of the good life back onto the Maya. Indeed, his notions have been placed in the broader context of his experiences in the trenches and the climate of the end of the Second World War and the Nuremberg trials, the period when he was working on the books which conveyed his vision most clearly. When good had just triumphed over evil, when grey areas were not fashionable, the Maya became an archetypally benign race of people, defenders of culture and civilization, the equivalent of the Anglo-American alliance, contrasted with the dark cloud of evil that would later engulf ancient Mexico, the jack-booted Aztecs.

If judgements of Thompson's ideas have been critical, they are always qualified by the universal recognition of his greatness in his field and immensely important contribution to Maya studies, at a time when archaeology was far from what it is today. Until the 1960s it was still relatively amateurish as a scientific discipline, prone to broad assumption rather than reasoned hypothesis, and heavily personalized, in the sense that academic reputation was often of greater consequence in determining the shelf-life of a particular theory than pure scientific evidence. As the leading scholar of his day, Thompson's theories held almost total sway. Yet, for many of the ideas that he elaborated, there was indeed little evidence. The notion of Maya cities as vacant,

ceremonial centres was largely based on ethnographic studies of contemporary Maya towns and very little on surveys of what Maya cities
actually consisted of beyond the magnificent temples, pyramids and
inscribed monuments at their heart. The exclusive practice of slash-and-
burn agriculture in ancient times was also an inference founded on
observation of contemporary practice. But the greatest obstacle to
progress lay in the state of hieroglyphic decipherment, which by the
1950s had still advanced little beyond understanding of the astronomical
and calendrical content. This we now know to have completely skewed
interpretations of Maya society. 'I conceive the endless progress of time
as the supreme mystery of Maya religion', Thompson wrote,
'... a subject which pervaded Maya thought to an extent without parallel
in the history of Mankind. In such a setting there was no place for
personal records.'[78] Yet there was a place for those personal records. It
lay among the indecipherable glyphs in between the dates, which
Morley did not record and which many thought might remain for ever
unknowable.

NEW ARCHAEOLOGY

The ideas that Thompson and others of his day propounded were to be
most effectively demolished by more recent advances in decipherment,
which we shall consider more fully in Chapter 3. But by the 1960s the
practice of archaeology in the field was itself changing rapidly, advanc-
ing beyond a narrowly focused concern with chronology, the
description and comparison of archaeological remains and concentration on the most prominent centres of human occupation, to a broader
range of archaeological enquiry, asking a much more ambitious series of
questions about the past.

This fresh outlook, which turned into something of a theoretical
movement in American academic circles commonly known as the 'New
Archaeology', was positive and optimistic about what could be achieved
if the right approaches were adopted. Conclusions or theories about the
past could not simply be informed speculation. They must be scientifi-
cally grounded or tested by examination of all the available evidence: in
the Maya case, not simply the pyramids and temples, the intriguing
inscriptions and evidence of their intellectual life, but more mundane
and infinitely less romantic areas for consideration such as the broader

pattern of ancient settlement beyond the great cities, human adaptation to the environment, agriculture and other food-producing activities, technology, trade, all the independent variables or 'sub-systems' as they were defined, which when put together, once enough meaningful data had been obtained, would begin to create a picture of the organic, functioning whole of the ancient society. This demanded a rigorous methodology. Carefully conceived research designs introduced intensive survey techniques and programmes of targeted archaeological excavation within the precisely judged parameters of statistical sampling.

Much of this new approach, though not the explicit theory, was embodied in a project mounted by the University Museum of Pennsylvania at Tikal between 1956 and 1970. Until this time the site was still remote and difficult to reach, a matter of hiring mules and walking from Lake Petén Itzá, much as in Maudslay's day. But an airstrip was cleared and a large base-camp constructed close to the ruins. Some hundred scholars were to participate in the project over the years. It was the largest and most concerted investigation of a Maya city that had ever been undertaken and was to prove a landmark in Maya archaeology (see plate section). The results of the massive amount of work achieved in these years are still being published today.[79]

There were many different aspects to the project, and we shall return to them in the chapters that follow, but its underlying aim was to determine through survey and excavation what exactly Tikal had amounted to. It was the largest known Maya city, in the scale and spread of its monumental architecture, but was it in fact only a 'ceremonial centre', inhabited by priests, astronomers and their entourage?

Dramatic results were to come from intensive survey of the 16 square kilometres that formed the heart of the city. For over 3000 separate structures were recorded. The temples, palaces, ball-courts and other standing stone buildings were included in this figure, but the vast majority of the remains surveyed were 'house-mounds', features only detectable to the eye as bumps in the ground surface but which were in fact the remains of the earth and limestone platforms upon which perishable houses of vertical poles and thatch had been built. Estimating a population at any given time in the past from a count of house-mounds is obviously a complex and difficult matter, since not all the buildings will have been occupied simultaneously. But on a conservative estimate it was concluded that some 10,000 people had lived in this central part of Tikal when the city was at its height, towards the end of the Classic period. But this was not all. The survey was ultimately extended to cover 120 square kilometres. The abundant evidence of domestic occupation continued, and this wider area had supported perhaps another 50–60,000 inhabitants. Settlement was dispersed and haphazard, there was no regular grid-plan of streets, nevertheless this was a city in anyone's terms, with a very large, permanent population.

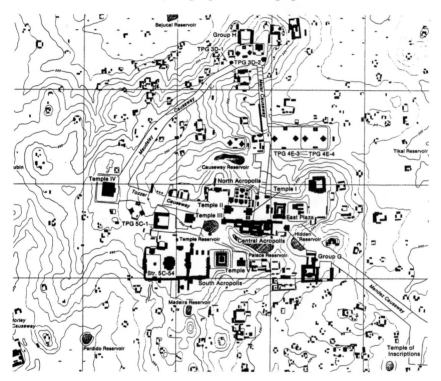

Plan of central portion of Tikal, each survey square 500m on a side, revealing the layout of the principal temples and palaces connected by causeways, with other groups of structures scattered around them.

The question that then arose was how such enormous numbers of people had been supported. Could they possibly have been sustained by slash-and-burn farming alone? It seemed inconceivable. The search was on for evidence of more intensive methods of Maya agriculture. This was soon to emerge, for aerial reconnaissance over Belize in the 1960s detected a lattice-work of curious lines crossing swampy areas close to some of the major rivers. In the following decade the US Space Agency, using a radar scanning device originally employed to monitor the surface

of Venus, detected further such anomalies over parts of both Belize and
Guatemala. Follow-up investigation on the ground proved that they
were networks of ditches or drainage channels, and that the excavated
earth had originally been piled up between them to produce elevated
planting platforms which came to be known as 'raised fields'.
Experimental reconstruction and planting demonstrated that they were
an extremely well-adapted and productive form of agriculture. The surviving evidence near Tikal was not so clear, but in ancient times there
had been large areas of seasonal swamp around the city which could well
have been cultivated in this manner. Besides raised fields, more evidence
would in due course emerge to demonstrate the complex array of
methods that Maya farmers used to sustain their cities.

The Tikal survey also revealed that the structures around the centre
varied greatly in size and configuration. Some were simple groups of a
few houses that gave onto a shared courtyard, others were arrangements
of much larger buildings around sizeable plaza areas that may have had
their own shrine or temple attached. Selective excavation indicated that
certain groups of houses were involved in specialized activities. For
example, the evidence of craft workshops was discovered, for the production of such things as chert axes or finer obsidian tools. Materials
such as these had often come into the site from distant places, indicating
some of the far-ranging trade connections that Tikal had possessed.
Differences in the quality of ceramics from burials, which were conventionally dug beneath the floor of a house or under the patio outside, and
the occasional presence of luxury goods such as small items of jade, also
indicated differences in status amongst the inhabitants of Tikal's
suburbs. Put together, all of this kind of evidence suggested a considerable complexity in urban society and further contradicted the older
image of the ceremonial precinct surrounded by the humble hamlets of
peasant farmers.

In other parts of the Maya lowlands broader studies of settlement
patterns, the manner in which the Maya had distributed themselves
across the landscape, were also underway. This kind of study had been
pioneered in Belize in the 1950s by the American archaeologist Gordon
Willey.[80] Down to the humblest hamlet, he had built up a picture of
Maya populations within a specific survey area. It had always been self-
evident that the major cities were the political focus of Maya society.
Thompson and others had talked of Maya 'city states', somewhat loosely
and often in comparison with those of Classical Greece, but to them

such an entity meant the city and an amorphous rural hinterland. From the work of Willey and those that followed him, a clearer though by no means uniform picture began to emerge. For beneath the city level, lesser centres were identified, what we might call small towns, and then perhaps a third rank or size of settlement, all surrounded by outlying villages and hamlets. What was suggested was a hierarchical political organization: the major city surrounded by dependent settlements of differing sizes. In due course decipherment, allied to the field archaeological recording, would elucidate further the political geography of the Maya world.

All in all, by the late 1970s work in the field had indicated a complexity in the social and political fabric of Maya society in the Classic period that had never been apparent before. Archaeologists could begin to talk about a rich and variegated society of kings and nobility, merchants, artists and craftsmen, the local lords of provincial towns as well as the Maya farmer and his family. The density of human occupation of the Southern Lowlands had become apparent, but so too had something of the versatility and potential productivity of Maya agriculture. No longer was the dazzling élite culture of Maya civilization the sole focus of scholarly attention. New approaches were combining to elucidate the underlying mechanics that had made it all possible. This was matched by an increasing awareness that before the Classic period there had been an impressive, formative prelude to Maya civilization. At Tikal, and in due course at other sites, formidable architecture, fine painted ceramics and other materials were identified that dated back to the early centuries BC. Largely disregarded in the previous era, the build-up to Maya civilization of the Classic period was to become an important new subject for research.

The Maya had thus begun to emerge from the romantic, mysterious shadows. It had not been an even progress from ignorance to enlightenment. Surveying the two centuries since the forests first began to yield up their secrets, it is easy to detect a broad movement from the naïve wonderment and curiosity of the early years through the more analytical, classificatory approach of the later nineteenth century to the better equipped, more scientific endeavours of modern times. But John Lloyd Stephens, somewhat paradoxically the man who had introduced the mysterious allure of the Maya in the first place, had come to some eminently sensible conclusions in the 1840s. For the next century, scholarship went backwards in many respects, pursuing the romantic image of the Maya as scholars wanted them to be.

Yet modern archaeologists, it must be said, do not necessarily possess a monopoly of virtue compared with their predecessors. By the 1980s, for example, some proponents of the 'New Archaeology' were being taken to task for a narrowness of approach and a kind of scientific exclusivity. Beneath the dense social-science jargon that some practitioners indulged in, of processes, systems simulations and sampling strategies, might there not be problems with their supposedly objective scientific perspective? It is a salutary truth that the material remains that archaeologists come upon will always be incomplete. They can only discover what has been left behind, survives in the ground and then happens to be encountered by the excavator. In today's archaeological approaches there are still unavoidable biases, as we shall see, and there remain thousands of square kilometres of forest out there, untouched by trowel or theodolite. In very many ways, for both field archaeologists and those who work at the decipherment of hieroglyphic inscriptions, the challenge of defining more precisely the nature of ancient Maya society, how it worked in all its parts and developed over time, is still a formidable one. Thus the possibilities, the controversies and indeed the romance of Maya archaeology live on.

CHAPTER TWO

The Origins of Maya Civilization

ARRIVAL

Amongst the welter of speculation about the native peoples of the New World that circulated in the sixteenth century, a few voices stand out as unusually clear-headed for their time. One of these is that of the Jesuit father José de Acosta who spent long periods as a missionary in both Peru and Mexico and whose great work, the *Natural and Moral History of the Indies*, was published in 1590. He looked dispassionately at the plants and the peoples of America and concluded that although both had striking individual characteristics, the product of many centuries of separate development, they were a part of the same overall world order, the same creation. As to the specific origins of the Americans, he believed that at some remote point in the past these particular sons of Adam had very probably walked into the continent via an unknown land connection, either to the south or the north. They were savage hunters, he thought, who had perhaps been driven from their own lands.

Today scientific opinion would agree with Acosta. Human life on the American continent began during the last Ice Age, when groups of hunters and gatherers crossed from Siberia into Alaska through or alongside what was then an icy land bridge. These people were not fleeing from anything; indeed, the reverse was true. They were pursuing the herds of mammoth and giant bison that fed on the grasses and shrubs of the windswept tundra. Once in Alaska it would not have dawned on them that they had arrived anywhere in particular. They and their descendants just kept on going, and in due course filtered slowly southwards and populated the whole of the Americas. From a range of genetic and other evidence, including such factors as the morphology of the teeth of different groups of native Americans, it now seems likely that there were three distinct migrations of Asian populations at different times, only one of which, the first wave, penetrated as far as Central and South America.

In outline, this is how the first peopling of the Americas occurred.[1] There is considerable disagreement about the nature of these migrations and when they took place. After about 8000 BC the ice began to recede, sea-levels rose, and very soon the land bridge was gone. It is hard to conceive of hunters and gatherers sailing across the Bering Straits after this time, though not impossible. But how much earlier could they have arrived? It used to be thought that an ice-free corridor would have been available from about 20,000 years ago, allowing hunting bands into Alaska across the Bering Straits' land bridge, up the Yukon valley and then down the eastern edge of the Rocky Mountains onto the Great Plains. More recently, however, this idea has been challenged. It would seem that between about 19,000 BC and 11,000 BC there was no such corridor. Humans either arrived before or after these dates, or they travelled some other way, perhaps in simple craft along the coastline. The waxing and waning of the northern ice-sheets in the late Pleistocene is the subject of intensive research, since it has implications for the understanding of global warming in our own time, and the matter of the route of arrival of early man in the Americas remains a fiercely contested one.

Even more vehemently contested, since it is the key to the whole peopling debate, is the dating of the earliest human occupations of the continent. Some more conservative dates have been established for many years. The so-called 'Clovis Horizon' refers to a certain category of fluted stone projectile points first identified at Clovis, New Mexico, in 1934, which were used in hunting mammoth and other large herbivores and have been found amongst the butchered bones at a number of 'kill sites'. The points are known from very many places across North and into Central America and have been securely dated as early as 9500 BC. Shortly after this time, however, hunters and gatherers had already reached as far as the southern tip of the continent. Stone tools, and the bones of extinct animals killed and eaten by man were discovered in 1937 in two caves close to the Straits of Magellan. These and comparable cave and rock shelter sites in Patagonia all have secure dates, some around 9000 BC. If humans were peering out towards Antarctica by this time, then it would be reasonable to assume that their ancestors entered Alaska at some point before the Clovis dates of about 9500 BC. Five hundred years would seem to represent a considerable sprint from one end of the continent to the other.

In recent years, widely accepted earlier dates have begun to appear. In North America the Meadowcroft rockshelter thirty miles from Pittsburgh provides evidence of human occupation that stretches back to at least 11,000 BC. The Meadowcroft dates still have their detractors, but a site in Chile is at last universally acknowledged by the academic community to have been occupied by about the same time. Monte Verde, on the banks of a small river amongst the temperate pine forests of south-central Chile, possesses a wide array of artefacts made of stone, wood and animal bone, the remnants of hearths and braziers, and even the remains of a dozen small structures made of logs and branches that were probably draped with mastodon skins. Rising water levels, which led to the abandonment of the site, and a fortuitous covering of peat have made the preservation here remarkably good.

The quality of surviving evidence at Monte Verde is a great rarity among hunter/gatherer sites. Elsewhere considerable controversy has been aroused by claims for very much earlier dates. The best known instance of this has been the rockshelter of Pedra Furada in Brazil. The archaeologists who excavated the site first announced that hearths and associated stone tools indicated a human occupation as early as 45,000 BC, which, if fully proven, would have been truly revolutionary in its implications. Most scholars, however, remained sceptical since it was not convincingly demonstrated that the carbon-dated hearths and the tools were the product of human activity. Forest fires and naturally flaking quartzite seemed a better explanation. More recently, other archaeologists have reviewed the evidence and concluded that the site does at least provide evidence of human occupation dating from about 15,000 BC. The peopling of the Americas debate is a live issue that will run for many more years. The odds would appear to be that much earlier dates will eventually be confirmed. The archaeologists at Monte Verde think that at a second site they have discovered, there are good indications of a human presence there by 30,000 BC.

As yet the Maya area has been untouched by such controversy. Indeed, very few hunter/gatherer sites have been found here. This must largely be a question of preservation. For the lowlands are an almost impossible environment in which to locate the remains of their temporary camps and in the volcanic highlands many of these are liable to have been covered by layers of ash. Rockshelters and cave sites exist, but to date few have yielded very early remains. One exception to this is Loltun cave in the Puuc Hills of northern Yucatán, where Mexican archaeologists have found the bones of a number of extinct animals and signs of human occupation that may date back to about 8000 BC. Along the coasts of northern Belize it would seem, from scatterings of stone tools, that groups of hunters may have arrived by a similar time and in the Quiché basin north-west of Guatemala City a large number of sites, yielding quantities of chipped basalt, appear to date back another thousand years. Thus, although the evidence is slim, we can assume that hunters and gatherers trod most parts of the Maya region in these distant centuries.

In the ninth millennium BC, when the great ice sheets still covered northern latitudes, the climate of the Maya lands was much cooler than that of today. The tropical forest would have been temperate forest of oak or pine and grasslands covered much of the highlands. Bands of humans would have roamed from place to place in a seasonal round of hunting and collecting. In leaner months they might split up into small family groups and then, when game and plant foods were abundant, come together in larger bands. The old, museum-diorama image of teams of shaggy hunters bringing down the fearsome 'megafauna' such as mammoth and giant bison is not inaccurate, but it was probably a rare occurrence. Smaller animals played more of a part in the diet, along with shellfish, fish, eggs, insects, snakes, fruits, nuts and a great number of plant foods. Broad-ranging forager would be a better description of how palaeolithic peoples actually operated, in most parts of the world. Indeed, as the idea of early man as big-game hunter has been superseded, so has our picture of what one might term his 'quality of life'. Primitive man as hunter always seemed a desperate character, permanently up against it, on the brink of starvation until the next large herbivore lumbered into view. More recently, some have suggested that the hunter/gatherer mode of life was in fact a rich and leisurely one, where the few humans about at this time wanted for very little. The 'first affluent society' was the phrase introduced about twenty years ago. There is the obvious danger here of veering from one romanticized image to another, but certainly hunting and gathering in the Maya region in the latter part of the Ice Age may indeed have been a successful and productive adaptation, with no obvious imperative or pressure for change. But change did come about, extremely slowly. Hunters and gatherers drifted into it, impelled by the lightest of evolutionary hands.

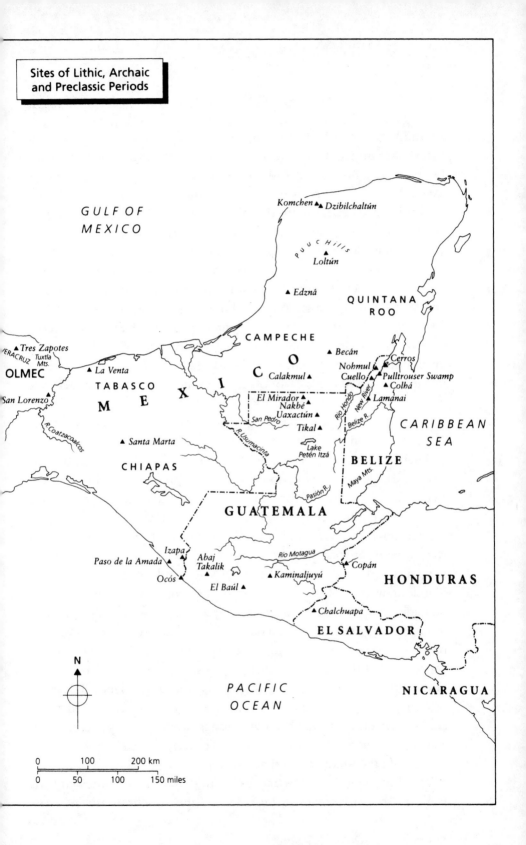

Sites of Lithic, Archaic
and Preclassic Periods

GULF OF
MEXICO

Komchen ▲• Dzibilchaltún

P U U C Hills
• Loltún

▲ Edzná

QUINTANA
ROO

CAMPECHE

Tres Zapotes
VERACRUZ ▲ Tuxtla
Mts.
OLMEC
San Lorenzo ▲

▲ La Venta

TABASCO

M E X I C O

C

▲ Becán

Calakmul ▲

Nohmul ▲•   ▲ Cerros
Cuello ▲• ▲• Pulltrouser Swamp
         ▲• Colhá

R. Coatzacoalcos

▲ Santa Marta

CHIAPAS

El Mirador ▲•
Nakbé ▲•
Uaxactún ▲
San Pedro
Tikal ▲•

R. Usumacinta

Lake
Petén Itzá

Rio Hondo

New River

Belize R.

▲• Lamanai

CARIBBEAN
SEA

BELIZE

Maya Mts.

Pasión R.

GUATEMALA

Rio Motagua

Izapa ▲•
Abaj
Takalik ▲•
Ocós ▲•

Paso de la Amada ▲•

El Baúl ▲

▲ Kaminaljuyú

▲ Copán

HONDURAS

• Chalchuapa ▲

EL SALVADOR

N

PACIFIC
OCEAN

NICARAGUA

0   100   200 km
0   50   100   150 miles

SETTLING DOWN

By the beginning of the Archaic Period (*c.* 6000–1800 BC), the climate had already turned. Once the northern ice-sheets had begun to retreat it became much hotter in the Maya region. The lowlands saw the gradual establishment of the rain-forest as we know it today, but the highlands appear to have become considerably drier. Certainly, in the highlands of Mexico, where the data are more complete, vast areas of what had been verdant grassland turned to scrub and to desert. At this time, too, the larger animals such as bison, mammoth, giant sloth and horse had been driven to extinction, perhaps a combination of change in their habitat and over-hunting by man. All life – human, plant and animal – began to adapt to different conditions. Hunter/gatherers had always relied heavily on plant foods, as we have seen. But now these were to become even more important as the peoples of Mesoamerica began to embark unwittingly on the road to plant domestication and ultimately the development of agriculture. By 1800 BC the first permanent village settlements had appeared, relying in large part upon the cultivation of plants such as maize, beans and squash.

There is, however, very little evidence for this process within the Maya area, also largely due to conditions of preservation. In Northern Belize the inventory of stone tools discovered here, perhaps spanning almost the entire Archaic Period, appears to include an increasingly greater percentage of grinding tools in later centuries; doubtless they were used to process plant foods. But no remains of the actual plants have survived. At the other end of the Maya world, at the cave of Santa Marta in western Chiapas, the evidence from the camps of semi-nomadic peoples dating from about 7000–3500 BC reveals the same intrusion of grinding implements in the tool-kit. A few charred remnants of plants in the refuse demonstrate that these were being consumed but there is not enough to provide any picture of the domestication process. To the west of the Maya area, in highland Mexico, persistently drier conditions into modern times have preserved much better indications of changing human adaptations over the Archaic millennia. Discoveries here offer some indication of what may have been going on in the Maya area at the same time.

The Tehuacan valley lies 200 kilometres south-east of Mexico City. Here, in the early 1960s, a team led by the American archaeologist

Richard MacNeish undertook a series of investigations which revealed how, over a period of about 10,000 years, hunters and gatherers in this region became settled farmers.[2] Their most dramatic discovery came in the excavation of dry caves where they found what at that time was the very earliest known corn. They managed to recover every part of the plant, including the cobs. They were tiny, only an inch or so in length, and at first it was thought they were wild. But in fact this miniature corn was planted and tended about 4500 BC, it was believed, and had already undergone a certain amount of genetic modification, which suggested that experimentation with the plant may have begun about two thousand years earlier. This initial experimentation is normally characterized as an unconscious, accidental process. Hunters and gatherers, as a matter of course, would tend to select the bigger, healthier seeds of the wild plants that they collected. Some would be consumed and some scattered by mistake amongst the garbage around a perenially visited camp-site. Here, in what was effectively a man-made environment, the seeds subsequently germinated and were able to grow without natural competition from other plants. This, in a very simple way, would have been the first stage in genetic interference. In due course the earliest cultivators would have started consciously to plant selected seeds and to weed around the shoots. The domestication process had begun. It is of course a very long way from this first tampering to the production of any sizeable crop. In the case of the corn at Tehuacan, the cobs were in the early stages of modification and they would have offered very little in the way of food. But by 2000 BC the cobs had become markedly more robust and eventually, by the time of Christ, maize produced in the Tehuacan valley was very similar to many strains still produced by Mexican farmers today. By 3000 BC beans, squash and peppers were also being cultivated at Tehuacan. Like the early types of maize, these too would not have been greatly productive. Even so, farming at this time, still combined with traditional forms of hunting and gathering, was able to support small hamlets of up to a dozen or so houses. It was not until about 1500 BC that far larger, permanent villages became established. By this time people were making pottery, weaving cloth from domesticated cotton and following most of the pursuits typical of sedentary life.

In the Valley of Mexico and the Oaxaca Valley, south-east towards the Maya region, archaeological excavation has revealed a similarly slow trajectory from hunting and gathering to settled village farming. In these areas permanent settlements came a little earlier, by about 2000 BC. In Oaxaca the earliest fully domesticated crop seems to have been squash, indicating the kinds of parallel processes going on, different plants domesticated at different rates depending on the nature of the local environment. In due course maize, the most productive and nutritionally beneficial of all plant foods, emerged as the dominant staple crop throughout Mesoamerica.

However, there are still many great uncertainties surrounding the emergence of agriculture in Mesoamerica. First, there is debate about the botanical origins of maize, whether it came from an ancestral, wild form of corn now extinct or is descended from an early variant of a wild grass known as teosinte. Second, exercising the minds of a number of researchers, is the question of the environment in which maize was first domesticated. For a long time, greatly influenced by MacNeish's pioneering work, most thought that the semi-arid conditions of highland Mexico were particularly conducive to its domestication there. From the highlands, maize agriculture had then spread to the tropical lowlands. This notion has recently been challenged, since evidence for the early cultivation of maize has been found in lowland Central American sites, for example in Panama, which would appear to date from about 5000 BC. Furthermore, it also seems now that the highland Mexican maize documented by MacNeish in fact dates to no earlier than about 3500 BC. So, like most of the American origins issues, this one too has a great deal of life in it yet.[3]

What more immediately concerns us here is that in the last few years, core samples through sediments from low-lying areas of northern Belize between the Hondo and New rivers, at places such as Cob swamp and the famously named Pulltrouser swamp, have revealed pollen and other evidence for the cultivation of both maize and the root crop manioc by about 2500 BC, also accompanied by the signs of a considerable amount of forest clearance.[4] No contemporary habitation sites have yet been found, and what this all means is still none too clear. Communication between the early peoples of Mesoamerica seems to have been surprisingly extensive. There is evidence, for example, that obsidian was exchanged across very long distances as early as 5000 BC. It may not be too fanciful to imagine seeds and 'gardening tips' being passed from one community to another throughout the region. What may be suggested is that hunter/gatherers operating along the Belize coast at the river mouths, who may already have settled into more permanent communities because of the rich and perennial food resources of the lagoons, swamps and estuaries, took up agriculture in a small way and then moved inland up-river as their dependence upon it increased. At the very least, what this new evidence would seem to challenge is the idea that Maya-speaking colonists from the highlands introduced maize agriculture to the lowlands at a later date. It was already there.

It remains the case, however, that the earliest well-documented signs of permanent human settlement in the Maya region come from the Pacific coasts of Chiapas and Guatemala. Here semi-nomadic groups had hunted and fished for at least a thousand years previously, but by about 1800 BC, the beginning of the so-called Early Preclassic period, large villages had been established a little inland from the coast.[5] Maize was being cultivated, and some have suggested manioc too, still combined with fishing and gathering. The most notable introduction was pottery, of surprisingly sophisticated form, including a range of jars and bowls, painted and modelled with abstract patterns, and also a lively variety of human figurines. By 1500 BC these populations along the coast had increased rapidly, some settlements had spread further inland and agriculture had become the mainstay of the diet. Significantly, too, there is evidence that village society was already becoming more complex. One or two villages are notably larger and appear to have dominated others, certain houses within villages are more impressive in scale and stand out from the rest and, during the 'Ocós phase' from 1500–1100 BC, settlements along the Pacific plains of Chiapas include for the first time what have been termed 'temple mounds'. These mark the first appearance in the Maya area of this enduring feature of Mesoamerican culture – literally a public platform for some kind of communal religious activity. At the site of Paso de la Amada, for example, archaeologist Gareth Lowe discovered a large mound three metres high, surrounded by arrangements of low platforms or house mounds that spread over a number acres. More recently, similar structures have been found which may date back even earlier.

Until now, the peoples of the Pacific coast have been regarded as precocious in their development compared with what is known about the Maya highlands and the lowlands to the north at this time. In the highlands there is very little indication of settled village life much before 1200 BC, and it is only during the Middle Preclassic period 1000–400 BC that, on present evidence, farming and pottery-using peoples became well established in the tropical forest heartland of later Classic Maya civilization. It has to be borne in mind, however, that this precocity may well prove to have been more apparent than real. Before following developments in the Maya lowlands, in order to examine the broader context of Maya emergence, we must now look at something truly precocious that was stirring by about 1200 BC just to the west of the Maya world, in the steamy swamps and plains of Tabasco and southern Veracruz, the homeland of a people known as the Olmec.

THE OLMEC IMPACT

The Olmec are often termed a phenomenon or an enigma. That they remain enigmatic is partly due to the fact that archaeologists have only been studying them since the 1920s, when their major sites began to be located. Even today much work remains to be done and many questions about them are still unanswered. They are a phenomenon because of the speed and force with which they appear on the Mesoamerican scene. Through their highly sophisticated art and their monuments they have left behind a powerful record of their rulers and gods and of a completely new order of society.

The Olmec began to congregate in permanent villages about the same time as and perhaps in a similar way to the peoples of the Pacific coast. They hunted and fished among the numerous slowly winding waterways that empty into the Gulf Coast and cultivated maize in the rich alluvial soils. Much of what is presently known about them is based on systematic excavations that have taken place at the sites of San Lorenzo and La Venta.[6]

San Lorenzo stands on a low hill above the Coatzacoalcos River in Veracruz. It was inhabited by 1700 BC, but in the space of two hundred years, between about 1100 and 900 BC, what had been a large village was transformed into something very different. The hill-top was completely levelled and large earth platforms to support buildings of perishable materials constructed on top. Beneath the complex an extraordinary subterranean system for drainage or water distribution was constructed, made out of U-shaped stones buried in trenches, which took water to different parts of the site, where it appeared in stone basins and even fountains. A series of stone monuments was set up in the shape of gods, animals and, most strikingly, colossal carved human heads of basalt, each weighing up to twenty tons and some standing more than two metres high. Ten such heads have been found to date (see plate section, p.7). In a remarkable display of concerted human effort, the basalt must have been dragged or floated on rafts from the Tuxtla mountains sixty kilometres away to the north-west, where an ancient quarry was discovered only a few years ago.

San Lorenzo appears to have been destroyed and abandoned soon after 900 BC. Many of the stone monuments were defaced, and sculptures systematically buried in a manner reminiscent of the way that in later centuries the Maya would ritually terminate or 'kill' monuments or buildings, sometimes after the death of a ruler, when their own life-span was deemed to have come to an end. We cannot know exactly what happened at San Lorenzo, but after this date another Olmec centre, La Venta, developed very rapidly.

La Venta covers a small island amongst swamp land along the Tonalá River, a hundred kilometres north-east of San Lorenzo. Here an even more remarkable programme of earth-moving and monument construction was undertaken between about 900 and 500 BC, although as at San Lorenzo, there had been an occupation here from much earlier times. The site covers two square kilometres and is made up of a series of earth platforms and mounds, also originally surmounted by buildings of pole and thatch. All of these earth monuments are aligned along the same roughly north-south axis, a pointer to the architectural design practices of the Maya, though at La Venta it is uncertain what astronomical or symbolic significance this might have had.

At the northernmost end of the site lies the most impressive arrangement of structures, known as Complex A, which formed a precinct all of its own. At the southern end of this complex the inhabitants of La Venta constructed a revolutionary architectural form – a mound of pyramid shape raised on an almost square base platform. The mound is about thirty metres high and, though much eroded, would appear to have had ten flutes or facets purposely cut out of its sides, which has led some to suggest that it was designed to mimic the form of a particular volcano, a sacred mountain for the Olmec, that lay amongst the Tuxtla mountains. There is no evidence of any stairway to gain access to the top and it is unclear whether it might originally have supported a temple-like structure. Beneath it is an open plaza area flanked on the east and west by two low parallel platforms about eighty metres long which lead north towards a smaller courtyard sunk about 8 metres into the ground. This is surrounded by further platforms and has a smaller pyramid mound directly to the north which originally had steps leading to the top. Complex A seems to have become the principal ceremonial or religious centre of La Venta and extraordinary efforts were made to embellish it. The sunken court was flanked by rows of two-metre-high basalt columns. Three elaborate mosaic pavements in the form of abstract masks, each consisting of nearly 500 blocks of serpentine, weighing about 900 metric tons, were laid out here. Two were positioned at the entrance to the sunken court and another just to the north of the pyramid. They were not left in the open but purposely buried and covered with layers of coloured clays. One of them also had twenty jade and serpentine celts – finely polished axes – laid out in a cruciform shape with a mirror of magnetite, a precious and magical item among both the Olmec and the Maya, at the centre.

Many other buried caches of granite, serpentine and jade have been found here, as have elaborate tombs with rich burial offerings. One particularly impressive tomb provides telling evidence of the nature of Olmec society by this time. A large chamber of basalt columns was constructed and within it were placed the bodies of two young children, accompanied by a beautiful array of jade objects. That two mere infants were given such a spectacular burial must mean that the Olmec were led by a hereditary ruling class, where noble birth was as significant as any achievement in life. La Venta, too, possesses colossal human heads of basalt. There were four of them here, set outside the arrangement of platforms and mounds as if to guard the monuments within. Very similar to those from San Lorenzo, they sport headgear like that of fighter pilots or American football players and each hat seems to display a different insignia of rank. There is little doubt in the minds of most researchers that each of these monumental heads represents an individual Olmec ruler.

Excavations at San Lorenzo and La Venta in recent years have shown that both were sizeable settlements, inhabited by many thousands of people. Spread around the centre, among the rivers and swamp land, were the households of ordinary farmers. At the core of both sites the major earth monuments were surrounded by the more prestigious residences of an élite group, the people who organized the construction of the ceremonial centres, co-ordinated the transport of massive amounts of basalt and the import of precious materials such as jade and serpentine from even greater distances.

But how had this new structure of society come about? The very earliest farming communities of the Pacific coast and amongst the Olmec themselves were, it is presumed, more egalitarian societies of autonomous villages roughly comparable to each other in scale and relative importance. Here social organization within villages would have been essentially tribal, the community probably organized through kin groups and lineages in whom land ownership or use was vested and among whom positions of authority and status within the community would perhaps have been rotated or shared, using the kinds of checking mechanisms which tribal societies that survive into modern times employ to prevent particular individuals or families from becoming inordinately powerful and breaking the social equilibrium. So why accept one lineage or group of people as above the rest of the population, in the way the Olmec did at some point before 1200 BC?

The concession of power to one particular group, the acknowledgement of a separation between rulers and ruled is, of course, the most fundamental leap that can be made in the development of human society. But to explain it in the case of a people such as the Olmec, or among the Maya, presents formidable difficulties. External factors can be discounted in the Olmec case. There is no evidence of invasion or of any outsiders imposing themselves upon the Olmec population. Certainly, more complex forms of society almost invariably appear where agriculture becomes productive enough to support large permanent populations. In the Olmec case, maize cultivation in this lowland environment would have proved highly successful. The alluvial soils of the Gulf Coast are very fertile and two crops a year could have been harvested with ease. Growing villages and the creation of new settlements may have led groups of these to aggregate under new forms of organization and managerial authority of a more coercive nature, to ensure the kind of social stability that benefited the bulk of the population within the larger territorial unit. Perhaps the possession of the best lands by a particular lineage enabled them to acquire the new, dominant role within their society. Alternatively, some suggest that population growth may have led to competition and conflict over certain lands, the ruling élite emerging as war leaders who united a number of villages by force and over whom they and their followers came to hold permanent sway. There is continued debate about these important questions, but definitive answers prove elusive since the surviving evidence for such factors as the incidence of warfare and of population growth is too insubstantial.

Today the majority of scholars, though not all, would conclude that the Olmec did not go blindly into a new order of society. They did not concede power to despots who forced them to level hillsides and drag colossal chunks of basalt from far-away mountains. The institution of rulership among the Olmec was a social adaptation, a necessary change to confront new realities. What this seems to have involved was welding the weaker, more decentralized powers of earlier village headmen to produce one pivotal authority to represent the new kind of enlarged community. The great construction projects were a co-operative endeavour, symbolizing political unity and creating the surroundings in which Olmec rulers could exercise the most significant power in such a society, which was indivisible from political power, namely religious leadership. Here, among the pyramids and platforms, they led religious observance and interceded with the gods on behalf of their people to bring prosperity and success in agriculture.

The religious role of the Olmec ruler has been suggested by analysis of Olmec art. Largely in the form of carved and polished stone, the art of the Olmec that comes down to us is one of the most astonishing achievements of pre-Columbian America. It seems to appear fully developed yet quite unheralded, without precedent anywhere else. Essentially naturalistic, both monumental free-standing sculpture and much smaller carvings of jade and serpentine reveal the same underlying simplicity, mastery of form and extraordinary sculptural power. Besides the human figure, there are a number of striking and often bizarre images that constantly recur. Most common are beings that are half-human and half-jaguar, commonly known as 'were-jaguars'. There are chubby, weeping babies that can also possess jaguar characteristics such as fangs and a snarling mouth. Sometimes such babies, wearing jaguar masks, appear cradled in the arms of human figures. Other powerful animals such as the cayman, harpy eagle or snake are represented individually or merged, often with human attributes, to produce powerful and disturbing supernatural beings.

Most of these images remain obscure and impenetrable. But researchers believe that they originally formed a pantheon of Olmec deities including gods of rain, earth and sky. They appear to represent a fascinating period of evolution, when ancient shamanic concepts, using the shifting symbolism of powerful animals, became codified into a more coherent religious system, the first that is identifiable in ancient Mesoamerica. A more formalized religion would inevitably have involved a body of priests or shamans, distinct from the curer or diviner of the local village and themselves members of the ruling élite, who would have interpreted and handled the new, more centralized religious messages. Most significant of all, perhaps, is the way that the ruler himself appears to be projected as both king and priest in one.

At San Lorenzo the ideal of rulership seems more exclusively represented by the fearsome colossal heads, unique to the Olmec. But at La Venta other forms develop, notably the setting in the ground of large, vertical carved stones or stelae. Here Olmec rulers appear holding sceptres, with elaborate head-dresses and with smaller supernatural figures with were-jaguar features floating in the air above them. On a few of these stelae two figures confront each other as if some specific event is being recorded. Another kind of stone monument is known as an 'altar', though they were more likely the thrones of Olmec rulers. Many of these depict a cross-legged human figure seated at the mouth of a cave, symbolizing, it would seem, the ruler's access to the powers of the Underworld and his position as mediator between human society and the supernatural (see plate section, p.7). The public art of La Venta, then, the monuments that the populace would have seen within the sacred precincts, the cathedrals of their society, included images of the king elevated above the rest of his people through his unique sacred qualities. What we witness here is a pattern for the kind of rulership that would develop among the Maya.

Indeed, in the 1930s and 1940s, when Olmec sites began to be investigated, many scholars thought that they must have been contemporaries of the Classic Maya. It was only in the 1950s that radiocarbon dates revealed the true age of Olmec civilization. From then on they were to be termed the 'mother culture' of Mesoamerica, the first to develop a complex political, religious and artistic tradition deserving the description 'civilization'. It was out of the cultural matrix that they helped to create that Maya civilization would emerge.

For Olmec influence is widespread after about 1000 BC, visible from Guerrero 800 kilometres to the west in Mexico to as far away as El Salvador. At some places in Mexico they appear to have established colonies of their own people. Since there is little to suggest Olmec military expansion, these people were probably traders, who forged a series of outposts and connections to secure their supplies of precious commodities. There is no evidence of direct Olmec contact with the Maya lowlands, but in the southern area their influence is seen across Chiapas and along the Pacific coastline. Here a series of Olmec-style rock-carvings are to be found, depicting figures with elaborate costumes and headdresses. The site of Abaj Takalik in Guatemala, a little inland from the Pacific coast, includes an Olmec-looking individual carved on a large boulder. Similar boulder carvings have been found at Chalchuapa in El Salvador. By 900 BC the early inhabitants of Copán, close to the important jade sources of the Motagua valley, were making imitations of Olmec ceramics and jade carvings that included certain Olmec religious motifs.

The more precise nature of the Olmec impact is still hard to define, but at the very least they introduced new ideas and images that were adopted by local rulers to reinforce their own emerging authority. For many of the societies of the southern Maya highlands seem to have been going through their own processes of social and political change quite independently. We have already seen the first stirrings of this along the Pacific coast during the Ocós phase. After about 800 BC the pace quickened and a whole series of chiefdom societies began to appear. The northern Maya highlands also display comparable developments at this time. Small towns grew up that, if they did not construct monuments on the Olmec scale and with such impressive and complex art styles, still included prominent platforms for the construction of temples or residences for the local chief and his family and the figure of the ruler himself carved in stone.

THE RISE OF CIVILIZATION IN THE MAYA LOWLANDS

The Middle Preclassic 1000–400 BC

While the Olmec were levelling the hillside at San Lorenzo at the turn of the first millennium BC, farming communities were establishing themselves in the forests of the Southern Lowlands. We must presume that there had been scattered groups of hunters and gatherers throughout the area for many millennia. How many remained, whether they were forced into marginal areas, wiped out, or integrated with the newcomers, there is no means of knowing. In northern Belize, as we have seen, there are good indications that such peoples may have eventually settled along the coasts, taken up agriculture and then moved slowly inland along the major river systems. But groups of Maya-speaking farmers undoubtedly descended north out of the highlands of Chiapas and Guatemala, keeping at first to the courses of the major rivers and along the lake shores where the most fertile soil for agriculture was to be found.

Archaeologists still know very little about this earliest period of lowland Maya development. One major practical problem is that the Maya of later centuries tended to build directly on top of the settlements and monuments of their predecessors. Thus any more humble remains from the Preclassic are liable to be completely obscured and may only appear in an occasional exploratory trench or as a handful of potsherds found amongst the architectural fill used in the construction of later buildings. But it is also the case that until the 1970s, as we noted in the previous chapter, very few archaeologists were inclined to focus their research on this period of Maya prehistory. Excavations at a number of sites had produced pottery sequences indicating occupations from at least 500 BC, but there was little more systematic investigation of the nature of Preclassic societies and how far back the roots of Maya civilization could be traced.

In more recent years a few significant advances have been made which have begun to fill in some of the picture. At Cuello in northern Belize in the 1970s and 1980s, Norman Hammond and his colleagues excavated a farming village whose settlement spans the whole of the first millennium BC.[7] The earliest occupation of the site, by a few hundred people, may date from as early as 1200 BC. But the maize they cultivated was already adapted to the tropical forest environment and they possessed a developed and distinctive pottery-making tradition. Where they might have come from is unknown. The river route from the Caribbean coast might seem the more likely, but this is by no means proven. They could just as well have come inland from the south. Intriguingly, maize pollen has also been detected in cores from lake-beds in the Petén dating from about 2000 BC, although, as in northern Belize, no evidence of actual human settlement this early has yet been found.

As the Cuello village became established, some families began to build their pole and thatch houses on low earth platforms coated with lime plaster. But this would not seem to denote any great differences of status within the community. Until about 400 BC, all the burials investigated at Cuello contain much the same kind of grave goods, namely a few pots and shell beads. Cuello thus seems to have been a simple, egalitarian and relatively insignificant village, no doubt typical of many hundreds of such communities at this time. As villages grew, small groups would have split off to found settlements elsewhere. The technique of building *chultunes* or underground cisterns cut into the limestone for the storage of water and crops seems to have developed, and this may have helped in the spread of people away from the rivers and lakes to populate the forested interior.

The horizons of communities such as Cuello were far from parochial. From earliest times it was trading in a few limited commodities. Some obsidian from the Guatemalan highlands appears after 800 BC and a tiny amount of jade from the Motagua valley and other greenstones began to be imported a couple of centuries later. Granite for grinding stones was brought in from the Maya Mountains of southern Belize. The kind of pottery produced in the early centuries at Cuello has been found at a number of other sites in northern Belize such as Santa Rita, Nohmul and Colhá. After about 900 BC, various other regional pottery styles are apparent, along the Rio Pasión in the Southern Lowlands for example, in the area around Tikal, where a Preclassic occupation at Tikal itself is first indicated about 800 BC, and at sites such as Dzibilchaltún in northern Yucatán. But from about 700 BC a type of pottery known as Mamom is found at a great number of Maya sites across the lowlands, suggesting considerably increased population and density of settlements, and communication between one region and another. Some specialized village centres emerged, such as Komchen on the northern Yucatán coast, which even at this early stage appears to have been involved in the manufacture and trade of salt, and Colhá, in northern Belize, which began the production of chert tools at about this time.

At a few sites of this period excavation has revealed some rudimentary forms of public architecture, such as low platforms that were perhaps intended for communal ceremonies. But on the whole it was thought, until a few years ago, that the Middle Preclassic in the lowlands was a period of steady colonization and consolidation by a society still largely made up of villages which produced little in the way of art, architecture or any of the more elaborate trappings of civilized life. In this way the Maya of the lowlands appeared to lag behind the Olmec or even the Maya of the Guatemalan highlands. Now, however, this picture has changed dramatically, due to recent discoveries in northern Guatemala.

Nakbé, and its sister site of El Mirador twelve kilometres away, lie deep in the forests of the northern Petén, close to the Mexican border, and are rarely visited by anyone other than archaeologists, chicle-gatherers and looters. The archaeologists working there in recent years cut an air-strip close to El Mirador, but otherwise it takes three days to get to the ruins by mule train through the jungle from the nearest road-head to the south. Both sets of ruins were sighted through aerial reconnaissance in 1930, but it was not until 1962 that they were first surveyed by Ian Graham. He thought that much of both Nakbé and El Mirador was Preclassic in date, but few at the time agreed with him as the kind of architecture he described seemed inconceivable before the Classic period. Now, however, a team from the University of California at Los Angeles led by Richard Hansen is discovering that Nakbé may well have been the very first of the great centres of the lowland Maya, which developed independently at the same time as the growth of La Venta among the Olmec.[8]

Between about 1000 and 700 BC the settlement at Nakbé was indeed little more than a large village, with a series of relatively inconspicuous pole-and-thatch buildings. But then, over the next 300 years, much more impressive and sophisticated structures were put up which would have necessitated a tremendous input of organized labour. Just like Maya cities of later periods, Nakbé developed a central core area of stone-faced platforms and pyramids around plaza areas. These are arranged in two groups to east and west, joined by a limestone causeway. From one end of the site centre to the other is a distance of about a kilometre. One platform built at this time in the east group is thirty-two metres high and a second to the west rises forty-five metres. They are surrounded by a series of other structures, some of them on large terraces. Sophisticated pottery from as early as 1000 BC has been encountered here, but the vast majority of sherds from excavations form part of the same Mamom complex that spread over the lowlands between 700 and 400 BC. By the end of this period, Nakbé probably had a population of many thousands and was functioning as a true city.

The most intriguing discovery of all, perhaps, in front of one smaller platform, was the damaged remnants of a carved stela. When the fragments were put together, they revealed two standing male figures in elaborate costume facing each other (see overleaf). They may represent Maya rulers, but certain details also suggest the earliest known depiction of the so-called 'Hero Twins', two key characters of Maya myth who appear in the Popol Vuh. This remarkable scupture seems to date from around 400 BC.

The results of the work at Nakbé, which is still continuing, have led to a major rethink about the origins of Maya civilization in the lowlands, pushing the start of the developmental trajectory way back in time. The

Stela 1, Nakbe.

most fundamental transformation in Maya society, which saw it on the road to the complex state societies of the Classic period, may have begun here, maybe as early as 800 BC, so Hansen believes. These recent discoveries may also indirectly suggest the likelihood of future revision of the present dates for the first settlement of the lowlands, that is from about 1200 BC. Archaeologists are still hampered by a fundamental lack of data, since Hammond's Cuello project is the only systematic survey of one community and its development throughout the Preclassic period that has ever been carried out. Cuello was an insignificant settlement, as he himself points out, and it was probably one among many hundreds, possibly even thousands, of others. As a speculative exercise it is also worth recalling the tantalizing pollen evidence for the presence of maize in the Petén about 2000 BC. Such a date for the arrival of the first farmers in this region would seem to square much better with the necessary build-up to the emergence of Nakbé.

The Late Preclassic 400 BC–AD 250

The people of Nakbé did not stop building in 400 BC. Further construction was carried out over the next hundred years, when a series of even bigger monuments were erected over the previous platforms. Four great stepped pyramids were built, which revealed the very first use of lime plaster or stucco as a decoration for the façades of buildings. A dozen gigantic modelled stucco panels have been discovered, some with the remains of the coloured washes of blues and reds with which they were originally painted. The most striking are five-metre-high relief masks of a fearsome vulture god, commonly known as the 'Principal Bird Deity' or the Vucub Caquix bird, another mythical protagonist who appears in the Popol Vuh.

Nakbé and El Mirador were linked together by a limestone causeway twelve kilometres long. Soon after 300 BC, for reasons still unclear, the focus shifted to El Mirador. Nakbé, if not deserted, saw little further building activity until the Late Classic period. El Mirador, on the other hand, over the next 450 years became a massive city covering about twenty square kilometres; its density and scale of ceremonial architecture compares with anything ever built by the Maya.

Like Nakbé, the major buildings at the centre of El Mirador are split into two principal groups, to the east and west. The western group is dominated by the so-called El Tigre temple complex on a levelled area of high ground overlooking a large *bajo* or area of swamp. The massive Tigre pyramid is constructed on a base platform some 125 x 135 metres and rises to 55 metres (see overleaf). At the very top of the pyramid, above a wide central stairway, are three stepped temple structures, one larger construction and two smaller ones beneath it which face each other. This triadic pattern of temples, one large and two small, is repeated in the construction of the whole complex; beneath the main pyramid upon the base platform are two further flanking temple structures. One of these has been thoroughly excavated, revealing monstrous jaguar masks and paws in stucco, their teeth and claws painted red. Beneath the El Tigre complex are a series of other platforms, plazas and pyramid structures, few of which have been investigated. Many may have been residences for the city's rulers.

Two kilometres east of El Tigre and connected to it by a causeway lies an even larger complex of buildings known as Danta. Taking advantage of a low hill, an enormous terrace was first laid out measuring about 300 metres square and 7 metres high. This supports a number of buildings including another trinity of temple pyramids to the south west. But a further great terrace to the east, built upon the first one, supports a triadic arrangement of temples that reach seventy metres above the forest floor. Here, too, the great masks of the gods have been discovered, including giant jaguars and vultures, which flank the temple stairways. Since these constructions are still largely enveloped in forest it is almost impossible to take in or convey photographically their truly vast scale. The surface area of the El Tigre pyramid is six times greater than that of the largest of the pyramids at Tikal, Pyramid IV, and the

The El Tigre Pyramid complex.

Danta complex must rank as the most massive construction project ever undertaken in the Maya world. Comparison with the great pyramids of Egypt is inescapable – vast monuments conceived at the very dawn of the Maya state which dwarf the constructions of later periods and involved the mobilization of enormous numbers of people by the ruling élite of society, who in the Maya case still remain anonymous.

The excavations carried out to date show that El Mirador was built on Middle Preclassic foundations but that most of the site was laid out during the Late Preclassic between about 200 BC and AD 150. Investigation of residential areas around the core of the site can as yet only offer a broad estimate of the population, but it must certainly have been in the tens of thousands. Furthermore, a series of limestone causeways radiating from the centre of the city lead not just to Nakbé but to other smaller towns in the area, such as Guido and Tintal to the south. Nakbé and El Mirador thus appear to be prototypes, not just for those cities with monumental constructions at their heart to be seen in Classic times, but also as political realms made up of dominant sites and subsidiary, dependent settlements that were to form the building blocks of the political landscape in later centuries.

No contemporary Maya centre in the lowlands can remotely match the scale and formidable power displayed at El Mirador. But populations seem to have been increasing rapidly at this time and it was to be a

crucial transitional period when kingdoms were forming and the monumental fabric of Maya centres taking shape. Tikal, for example, eighty
kilometres south-east of El Mirador, had been occupied since about
800 BC. For centuries it remained little more than a farming community
occupying higher ground amongst the swamps. There is little sign of
major construction at the time of the rise of Nakbé but in the second
century BC a large stepped pyramid was built, more than thirty metres
high and eighty metres square at its base with relief masks flanking its
stairways, much like those at El Mirador but on a smaller scale.
Commonly known as the 'Lost World' pyramid, it can still be seen in its
restored state. At about the same time, large paved plazas were laid out
and work began on the so-called North Acropolis, already a focus of
early settlement but soon to become the religious heart of Tikal. Temple
upon temple was to be constructed here in a continuous process of levelling and rebuilding over the next 900 years. At the bottom of this
superimposed construction, archaeologists in the 1960s found the
beginnings of such temple architecture, probably dating from late in the
first century BC. The outer wall of one of these first buildings retained
the traces of remarkable paintings, in shades of red, yellow and black,
depicting elaborately dressed human figures against a background of
billowing scrolls.

Several tombs were discovered here, too, in stone chambers spanned
by some of the earliest examples of the Maya corbel vault. In one of
these, the remains of a man were found without the head and with much
of his legs missing, the body trussed up in a cotton bundle. Whether he
lost his head and limbs in some engagement with enemies or the skull
and some of his bones were retained as relics among his family, a
practice on occasion in Classic times, no one can be sure. With him were
interred a large number of pots, a spondylus shell and a stingray spine,
the instrument employed in rituals of personal bloodletting. Lastly, sewn
on the top of the bundle, as if to substitute for the missing head, was a
portrait mask made out of green fuchsite, the teeth and eyes inlaid with
shell (see overleaf). Significantly, around the forehead of the mask
appears the sacred headband adorned with sprout-like, trefoil symbols,
the equivalent to the crown of Maya kings in later centuries. The mask
may well have been worn by the deceased in life as a pectoral ornament,
of a type often illustrated in later Maya art. Who this man was is still
uncertain. A radiocarbon date from charcoal found in the tomb places
his burial in the first century AD. Until now most scholars have assumed

A Greenstone mask from Burial 85, Tikal.

that he is one of the early, pre-dynastic rulers of Tikal. But, as we shall see in Chapter 4, a school of thought now believes that this may be the man recognized by later kings as the founder of the Classic period Tikal dynasty.

While the people of Tikal were raising their earliest monuments and taking the first steps towards future greatness, another city was emerging a short distance away to the north. As we saw in the previous chapter, Uaxactún was investigated by archaeologists from the Carnegie Institution of Washington in the 1930s. During their excavation of one particular concentration of buildings, they removed the superimposed burden of later construction to reveal a magnificently preserved temple, now known as Structure E-VII-sub (see plate section, p.7). At the time it seemed an anomaly, since no one thought that such architecture had existed before the Classic period. Compared with the monuments of El Mirador, it is a modest structure, in the form of a truncated pyramid eight metres high, which would have supported a small temple of perishable materials. Like a giant wedding cake, the pyramid rises on several tiers and is covered with a thick coating of lime-plaster that was still a brilliant white when the structure was first revealed. Steps lead to the top on all four sides, flanked by a series of stucco masks in the form of jaguar and serpent heads.

Modelled stucco became an exceptional Maya art form in Classic times, most famously at Palenque. But the origins of such stucco work go back to the Preclassic period, indeed stucco was the first great artistic medium in Maya lowland architecture. Lime plaster was easy to make anywhere as long as enough wood was available to burn the lime. It could be sculpted more readily than stone and it enabled massive images to be created. For the masks produced at El Mirador and at Uaxactún, stone armatures were first made that protruded from the walls of a structure. The plaster was then layered on top, carved and modelled, and finally painted in shades of red, yellow or blue, as were the surfaces of the buildings themselves. Originally these were astonishingly vivid and powerful monuments. What the Preclassic masks such as those at Uaxactún depicted was critically important. For they are the prototypes of enduring symbols in Classic period art. During the Preclassic such symbolism appears to be taking form and, as we have seen with the Olmec, is associated with the special powers of Maya rulers. On E-VII-sub at Uaxactún the jaguar masks stood for the Jaguar God of the Underworld or the Sun at night, the serpent-head the so-called 'Vision Serpent'. The Jaguar Sun was one of the principal tutelary deities later associated with Maya kings and the 'Vision Serpent' represented the path of communication between the human world and the supernatural. The effect of such images was to transform the architecture symbolically into a sacred setting for ritual led by members of the Maya ruling élite.

In the 1980s an even more impressive set of stucco masks and panels were unearthed at Uaxactún by the Guatemalan archaeologist Juan Antonio Valdés. Here, within what is known as Group H, he discovered an arrangement of six Late Preclassic temples on top of a broad platform. All these temples have remarkably well-preserved masks. The most striking are depictions of sacred mountains. They represent nothing less than the creation of the world, the original mountain of creation rising up out of the primordial ocean, the earth taking form. Such an image served to associate Uaxactún rulers with the most powerful processes in the world order, to furnish them with divine sanction. Figures of the ruler, or indeed rulers, are also depicted here in stucco panels. A number of these appear in profile, richly costumed, with large ear ornaments, elaborate headdress surmounted by the long-nosed head of a god and a belt from which dangle three stone plaques or axes and bifurcated plumes. All of these elements would endure as royal attire for many centuries. The figures are also completely encircled by volutes or scrolls that may symbolize both the smoke of incense and the blood of sacrifice burnt as an offering to the gods. One can compare these images with the painted human figures from the North Acropolis at Tikal and with the stone stela, with its two very similar profile figures, from Nakbé.

The Petén was not the only region where such elaborate temple-building is evident at this time. In Belize the Late Preclassic saw the emergence of the remarkable site of Lamanai, the longest lasting of all Maya cities. It was first settled about 1000 BC, the same time as Cuello, which is only fifty kilometres away to the north, and was continuously occupied into the early Colonial period, one of the few cities in the Southern Lowlands that was unaffected by the Maya 'Collapse' in the ninth century. A remote place, far away from the early centres of Spanish occupation, it did not receive Franciscan missionaries until the seventeenth century. Indeed, the name *Lamanai*, meaning 'submerged crocodile', was recorded by the Franciscans at that time and may well be its original Maya name. This is extremely rare. Most other Maya cities have acquired their names in more recent times. The name Tikal, for example, the 'place of the voices' in Itzá Maya, was adopted soon after it was discovered in the 1840s. 'El Mirador' , the 'look-out' in Spanish, was apparently so named by the *chicleros* who visited the site before archaeologists started working there and admired the magnificent view from the top of the pyramids.

In the Classic period, Lamanai became a formidable city. It lies on the banks of a lagoon on the New River, a haunt of crocodiles in ancient times, and indeed they feature large in Lamanai art. There is evidence of an ancient harbour to the north of the site, suggesting the importance of trade, in such commodities as the cotton or cacao produced in this region, as a foundation of Lamanai's prosperity. That prosperity had clearly begun by the Late Preclassic, since large stepped and richly stuccoed pyramids discovered here date from about 100 BC, one of them rising thirty-three metres and which, before the confirmation of El Mirador's early date, was the largest Preclassic pyramid known. Here, too, in a comparable format to the Petén temples, giant stucco masks of jaguar gods flank the stairways leading to the top of the pyramid.

Down the New River, at its mouth overlooking Chetumal Bay, stands the smaller Preclassic site of Cerros. It flourished only briefly and was abandoned for unknown reasons at the end of the Preclassic period. This gave its team of excavators, headed by David Freidel, the opportunity to study the architectural development of a Preclassic centre without having to cope with the overburden of later buildings. What they were able to document here was the abrupt transformation of a relatively simple village of fishermen, farmers and coastal traders into an impressive town with a remarkable series of ceremonial buildings. These buildings signified the arrival of what Freidel and his co-author Linda Schele term 'divine kingship' among the inhabitants of Cerros.[10]

It was in about 50 BC that the old village was levelled. From then on monumental platforms to support temples were constructed overlooking the bay, along with other shrines, houses, a number of ball-courts and an area of raised fields, all enclosed within a large semi-circular canal which fed water to houses and fields and also effectively cut off the town from the mainland, and thus very probably served a defensive function.

Five principal temples were laid out here. The first to be built, known as Structure 5C-2nd, was placed at the northernmost point of the town with its back to the bay and faced due south through the heart of the settlement towards one particular ball-court, the very last monument in this direction within the encircling canal. To Freidel and Schele, this placement of the temple was of great significance. We know that in Maya cosmology north was seen as upwards, the position of the sun at its zenith and the direction of the heavens, the abode of the gods. South was similarly conflated as down, the direction of the Underworld, where the sun in jaguar form battled at night against the forces of darkness before being reborn. So, positioned to the north, the temple, the religious expression of the power of the ruler, was symbolically connected to the heavenly realms.

Structure 5C-2nd was on two terrace levels, originally surmounted by a thatched building open at the front but with an inner sanctum at the rear (see plate section, p.8). A south-facing central stairway and two landings on the way up were highly visible to members of the community who would have gathered in the plaza below to watch rituals that Schele and Freidel suggest were carried out by the ruler himself. Flanking the stairway as he made his ascent were four large painted stucco masks that represented two of the most powerful forces of the heavens. On a lower level to the east of the stairway was a mask symbolizing the rising sun. At the centre of this mask is the snarling face of a jaguar, the night sun rising from the underworld at dawn. On the jaguar's cheek is a sign in the shape of four petals that in Classic Maya writing would represent *kin*, the sun. To the left of the jaguar's face is the sign *yax* or 'first', meaning the first sun on the horizon at dawn, the moment at which the sun is reborn. In the first century BC the appearance of the fully developed Maya writing system was still some two centuries away. But here, it seems, was one way in which writing in the lowlands began, as symbolic tags or labels which in time would take their place as Maya hieroglyphs.

To the west of the stairway another jaguar mask represents the setting sun, on the point of descending on its nightly journey through the Underworld, the abode of death. On the upper terrace to the east, Venus is depicted in mask form, Venus as morning star which appears before dawn and heralds the sun's arrival. On the west side Venus reappears as the evening star that follows the sun into the earth after sunset.

The inhabitants of Cerros in the plaza below were potentially confronted by both cosmic reality and cosmic image. From the promontory here they could witness Venus and the sun rising from the sea to the east and descending into the waters to the west. The symbolic manifestation of these natural forces flanked the ruler as he ascended the stairway. As he did so, and as he stood at the temple top, at the northernmost point, the direction of the heavens, he would appear as the central, pivotal force around which the cosmos itself turned. His ritual activities within the inner sanctum of the temple, involving blood-letting and sacrifice, were carried out to maintain both the cosmic and the social order.

There is a further, intriguing set of symbols believed to be represented here. We have already briefly encountered the so-called 'Hero Twins' or 'Ancestral Twins' of the Popol Vuh. These two characters are known as Hun Ahau and Yax Balam in Yucatec Mayan and Hunahpu and Xbalanque in Quiché Mayan. In the myths of Maya creation, they are portrayed as semi-divine culture heroes or proto-humans who, at the time just before creation, are put through a series of deadly trials by the Lords of the Underworld. Surmounting all these challenges, they finally defeat the Lords of Death, emerge from the Underworld and are permanently reborn as Venus and the Sun respectively.

At Cerros, the Venus masks on the upper landing bear the headband with the three-pointed motif, the symbol of Maya royalty that we saw on the greenstone mask from the tomb at Tikal. But this headband is also an emblem of the Hero Twin Hun Ahau, the elder of the twins, who as Venus precedes his brother out of the Underworld. Similarly, the *kin* sign and jaguar characteristics are emblematic of Yax Balam ('First Jaguar'), the younger brother, the Sun. Significantly, the Hero Twins came to be regarded in the Classic period as the prototypes and ancestors of Maya rulers. Like them, the Maya king represented his society in dealings with the supernatural. Through the successful practice of ritual, which involved entering the world of the spirits, he too would always emerge victorious, guaranteeing the maintenance of earthly order, the coming of rains, the cycle of maize and the prosperity of Maya people. There is thus a second layer to the symbolism of the masks. The ruler on the steps was flanked by representations of his divine ancestors, the very originals of Maya rulership, who could thus be seen as giving sacred legitimacy to his position in the social order.

The abrupt transformation of Cerros leads Freidel and Schele to a certain amount of speculative reconstruction. They suggest that its inhabitants deliberately chose to adopt the institution of rulership. They did so because they were forced to confront the reality of developing social inequality within their society. Instead of allowing this to lead to conflict, to the break-up of the social fabric, they sought not to deny such inequality but to embrace it, to institutionalize it by creating one central force so powerful and given such extraordinary symbolic legitimacy that it overrode all others. What is suggested here is a kind of social contract of rights and obligations. Humbler members of the community had to pay tribute to maintain the ruler and his lineage or followers, to participate in the building of temples and other communal constructions. But in return the ruler provided security, managerial authority to resolve disputes and organize public works and above all, as we have seen, he provided a religious focus – he took care of the spiritual matters of so fundamental an importance to such a society. In this way, as Freidel and Schele would have us believe, the Maya here were making the same social leap as the Olmec centuries before.

In truth, we have no way of knowing why or how the transformation at Cerros came about, whether it was indeed the result of a form of community decision-making or whether the new system was imposed in some way, either internally or externally. Indeed, it has been suggested that Cerros, as a key trading post and entrepôt for goods from Lamanai, was taken over by the latter, who installed a ruler who set about creating a new town. But whatever happened in detail at this one site, there is no doubt that profound changes are visible across the lowlands from at least 300 BC. The evidence from El Mirador, Tikal, Uaxactún, Lamanai and Cerros points to a different kind of society, where the very existence of hierarchy, of rulership, is proclaimed in art and architecture and is made to seem, literally, the most natural thing in the world.

The process seems not to have been a uniform one and may best be seen as a local response to particular social and economic pressures. The growth of population appears to have been particularly rapid during the Late Preclassic. Maya communities were expanding and settling into every favourable niche in the landscape, confronting each other in the process. Evidence for warfare is slim, as it is indeed for most periods of Maya history. There are some signs of defensive walls at El Mirador and a kind of moated, island fortress, for example, at the Late Preclassic city of Edzná in Campeche. The only site with clear evidence of fortifications constructed in this period is Becán, to the north of the Petén in the centre of the Yucatán peninsula. Here a great ditch nearly 2000 metres in circumference encircles the settlement, whose purpose can only have been a defensive one. However limited the evidence, few would deny the role of conflict over land and conflict to establish territories and aggregations of populations as a major cause of the social changes evident at this time.

With the increase in population came the need to secure and expand agricultural production. During earlier Preclassic times raised fields had already begun to be created along the rivers of northern Belize, notably the Rio Hondo and in the lower reaches of the New River at places such as Pulltrouser Swamp. But the Late Preclassic would have seen considerable expansion of such systems. Major canal building projects were undertaken at developing cities at this time. At Edzná massive waterworks have been documented, including a twelve-kilometre canal running between the city and the nearby Champotón River and a series of shorter ones that provided water for the city centre, fed outlying reservoirs and irrigated surrounding fields. It has been calculated that they provided themselves with a total capacity of 2,225,000 cubic metres of water storage, essential in an area drier than the Petén, and that the construction of this hydraulic system would have needed some 1.7 million man-days of labour. A staggering total, it illustrates again the remarkable capacity of societies at this time for sheer organization of manpower, which must have been directed by a strong centralized authority.

The most impressive manifestation of such organization is, of course, the great city of El Mirador. One of the persistent questions, indeed mysteries, about this and other sites in the Petén at this time, such as Nakbé, Tikal and Uaxactún, is why they were built where they were – right in the heart of the peninsula, away from major rivers and in what seem extremely inhospitable areas. Recent environmental studies around Nakbé and El Mirador seem to have provided the answer. During the centuries of their expansion, the climate appears to have been considerably wetter than it is today. Enormous *bajos*, or areas of swampland, would have surrounded these sites, in particular the so-called El Mirador basin, and they offered tremendous potential for raised field agriculture. Thus it would appear that El Mirador was a flourishing agricultural society which, through the production of size-able surpluses, was able to attract and organize very large populations within the political territory it controlled. The same would have been true for the other great cities of the region.

Trade has been cited as a reason for the growth and prosperity of such cities. They were well positioned, it is suggested, to control the portage routes for trade commodities between the upper reaches of the northern Belize waterways, such as the Rio Hondo, and the headwaters of rivers such as the San Pedro, which flow west out of the Petén to the Gulf Coast. Thus they controlled all the trade crossing the Yucatán peninsula. There may be some force to this argument in later centuries, especially in the case of Tikal, but even then there is little actual evidence for it. There is no reason to believe that trade would account either for the precocious emergence of Nakbé or the sheer scale of El Mirador.

This is not to deny the importance of trade connections. Those with the highlands appear to have been strong. Such commodities as obsidian, volcanic stone for grinding implements and jade were imported into the lowlands from early times. At El Mirador, volcanic ash was even acquired from the highlands to use in the temper to make pottery. In return, the lowland cities would have exported such things as feathers, animal skins, hardwood and fibres. Indeed, constant interaction between these two geographical areas would appear to have been a key factor in the development of the particular characteristics of lowland Maya civilization. To developments in the highlands we shall now briefly turn.

We have seen how Olmec influence seems to have been a spur to the rapid growth of small chiefdoms in the highlands before about 400 BC. After this date, Olmec civilization faded rapidly and had collapsed by 100 BC. But during the Late Preclassic the Maya highlands enjoyed a great period of prosperity. The greatest power in the region during these centuries was the city of Kaminaljuyú. It lay in the valley of Guatemala, where Guatemala City now stands, and today most of it is buried beneath the city's suburbs. But originally Kaminaljuyú covered nearly eight square kilometres and some two hundred great earth platforms have been recorded here. One has to bear in mind that, in contrast to the lowlands with their ready availability of easily workable limestone, the dense basalts of the highlands were extremely difficult to quarry and transport. Thus the bulk of architecture here was of earth, or mud brick. Today most of this kind of architecture has dissolved into amorphous mounds, making it difficult to imagine how impressive many of these sites must have looked originally. Kaminaljuyú would have been the highland equivalent of El Mirador. It was situated on the edge of a large lagoon and a series of formidable canals served the city with water. Kaminaljuyú became a great market centre, linking highland Mexico with lower Central America, and, lying only twelve kilometres from the quarries of El Chayal, became a purveyor of obsidian to places far and wide. At El Mirador, for example, an obsidian workshop was discovered during excavation and trace-element analysis proved that all the material they were working came from El Chayal.

Beneath one large platform mound at Kaminaljuyú, two magnificent and what can only be termed royal tombs have been found. The individuals were accompanied by spectacular jades and other prestigious items, surrounded by great quantities of ceramics and by attendants who were sacrificed to accompany their lord to the Underworld. So far, no such lavish burials of this date have been found in the Maya lowlands. Another characteristic of the highlands at this time is the way that individual rulers were memorialized on stone stelae and other monuments, the convention first introduced by the Olmec. Stela 11 from Kaminaljuyú, for example (see plate section, p.8), displays the warlike figure of a ruler standing in profile with a sceptre in one hand and a large flint axe that appears to be dripping blood in the other. He wears an enormous bird-headed mask and stands between two smoking incense-burners. His feet rest on what may well be a sign representing the earth, with a second framing device, a deity floating above him, standing for the sky. Another monument, a fragmentary altar, depicts a similar richly dressed individual holding up an almost identical axe, often termed a 'decapitator'. To the right is the fantastic, fanged head of a deity, while a second figure below appears to be kneeling in a gesture of supplication, his arms outstretched.

Besides Kaminaljuyú, other sites in the highlands possess comparable monuments that display the political and ritual authority of local rulers, scenes related to warfare and the taking of captives along with a great variety of mythological subject matter. Izapa, for example, is a large site some thirty kilometres from the Pacific in Chiapas, close to the Guatemalan border. Sculpture in characteristic Izapa style is found over a wide area. The majority of monuments from the site itself, where thirty-eight carved stelae have been recorded, date from 300–100 BC. Much of the imagery of these stelae is still not well understood, but there are certain identifiable themes that appear at a later date in lowland Maya art. A god with a protruding lip or snout seems an early manifestation of the Maya rain-god Chak, and one richly complex scene illustrates a number of human and supernatural figures surrounding a central tree which appears to be a prototype for the great 'World Tree' or central axis of the world depicted in Classic Maya art, in particular at Palenque. There are also at Izapa clear references to some of the stories in the Popol Vuh – to the vulture-headed god Vucub Caquix and the adventures of the Hero Twins. We have already seen iconographic allusions to the Hero Twins in the lowlands. What seems to be apparent in this period is that a body of religious ideas and images were exchanged across the highlands and lowlands, many of which would eventually become fully crystalized in the lowland art of the Classic period.

One of the most significant developments in the highlands during the Late Preclassic is the spread of hieroglyphic writing and of dates in both the Calendar Round and the Long Count. We shall look more fully at the nature of the Maya script in the next chapter, but the Maya themselves did not invent writing in Mesoamerica nor, for that matter, were they the first to devise calendrical systems. The evidence for Olmec writing is limited to one or two very simple notations. More sophisticated forms of definable early script only began to appear after their decline, around 400 BC. This occurs among the Zapotec of Oaxaca and one can also see the spread of different glyphic systems across Veracruz, Chiapas and into the Maya highlands. None of these are understood, nor is it known with any certainty what languages they express.

By the first century BC, texts – many with dates – are to be found in the Southern Highlands and at sites above the Pacific coast. At Abaj Takalik, where we saw carved boulders of Olmec style at an earlier date, stelae were erected which bear two figures on either side of a central text. One of these carries a date which is damaged but must lie in the first century BC, and a second shows two similar human figures and between them a text and an identifiable Long Count date of AD 126. What this form of stela may be demonstrating is the transference of power from one ruler to another, the text providing an historical gloss. Slightly different in style, an impressive stela from El Baúl, a hundred kilometres south-east of Abaj Takalik, depicts the lone figure of a ruler grasping a long staff or spear flanking a vertical inscription, much of it erased but with a Long Count date of AD 36 (see below). Nothing from these texts has been deciphered, apart from the dates, and some of them may not be in Maya languages but in forms of Mixe-Zoquean, a language family stretching from the Gulf Coast across the western fringes of the Maya area; it may indeed have been spoken by the Olmec. In Veracruz in 1986 the dramatic discovery was made of an enormous basalt stela which bears the impressive image of an elaborately dressed ruler. Above the figure and facing him are vertical columns of glyphs, some 400 in all. Within the text are two Long Count dates, for AD 143 and 156. That this is a historical text describing the doings and prowess of the depicted king there is little doubt, but few would claim that this text, in a script which has been called 'Isthmian', is near to being decipherable. Superficially it may appear similar to lowland Maya texts of a later date, but very few glyphs have been identified that are at all comparable.[11]

Although the non-calendrical parts of the various texts mentioned above cannot be understood, it is clear that these early scripts developed as a political tool, part of an overall imagery of power. There thus appears to be a marked contrast between these monuments and what is visible in the Maya lowlands at this time. In the highlands and across to

Stela 1, El Baul.

the Gulf Coast, carved stelae publicly advertise the ruler as a warrior, a religious leader and seemingly as a dynast who hands on power to his successor. In the lowlands, such forceful images, along with dates and hieroglyphic texts, are absent until the very end of the period. Large and complex political and religious messages are presented in stucco on the façades of temples, but the stelae discovered to date are either plain (they may have been painted, but there is no scientific evidence of this), fragmentary or portray images, such as the two figures facing each other at Nakbé, that are equivocal. Are these representations of individual rulers, or more abstract symbols of authority? At Uaxactún and Tikal there are multiple stucco images of figures in royal regalia. But as yet no single representations of lowland kings have been found prominently displayed at sites during the Late Preclassic. There is still no satisfactory answer to this. Some suggest that it reflects the nature of political authority, which in the lowlands at this stage may have been more collective, shared perhaps amongst powerful lineages.

However, by the time of Christ, in both highlands and lowlands, Maya civilization had taken form in most of its essentials. Towns and cities had emerged, stratified societies had developed composed of rulers and ruled, among whom many had specialist or semi-specialist occupations such as craftsmen, traders or priests. Intensive forms of agriculture were practised and great schemes of canal building and monument construction had been initiated. Religion had become increasingly codified and organized to support what one can legitimately begin to call the power of the state. Certainly at cities such as El Mirador, with a population in the tens of thousands and control over an extensive hinterland and smaller dependent towns, the model for the city state of the Classic period was in place.

But in the second and third centuries AD disruptions and catastrophe hit the Maya world. About AD 150, El Mirador seems to have collapsed quite suddenly. Until very recently, it was a mystery why this had occurred. Archaeologists had found signs of violence in the city centre. Many monuments and most of the stelae recovered here were found smashed. Were they invaded by their enemies? Yet the signs of abandonment were almost total and it seemed extraordinary that such a great power should fold so completely. Today the findings of climatologists and soil scientists are suggesting environmental reasons for El Mirador's demise.[12] For the tens of thousands of people congregated in the area would very quickly have destroyed the forest cover for miles around.

They cut down trees to cook, to fire pottery and above all to burn the lime to produce ton after ton of lime plaster for endless construction projects and repairs to buildings and reservoirs. As they did this, the climate began to change. After about AD 100 it became drier across this part of the lowlands, a cyclical phenomenon which was to last for about four hundred years. This increased aridity may well have been enhanced locally by the scale of deforestation. And when it did rain, the water ran soil and sediment from the denuded landscape into the once-fertile swamps. In due course they dried up. Here may have occurred, in microcosm, a rehearsal for the greater Maya collapse at the end of the Classic period. It illustrates, at an early date, the vulnerability of Maya society.

By AD 150 people were on the move in the northern Petén. The destruction seen at El Mirador may have been carried out by the inhabitants as they left, a ritual farewell, a termination of the powers of the great city, as the Olmec perhaps did at San Lorenzo and as the Maya would continue to do to monuments and indeed whole cities whose cycles of power and prosperity were finished. A plausible reconstruction now being developed is that the inhabitants of El Mirador moved north and swelled the population of a city called Calakmul. In due course, in the Classic period, Calakmul was to take over El Mirador's mantle and become one of the two most formidable powers of the Maya world.

The smaller cities of the Petén, such as Tikal and Uaxactún, seem not to have been affected by any climatic changes at the end of the Late Preclassic. But some feel that indirectly, in their forms of political organization, they may have been. One hypothesis is that more complex water-management systems became necessary in a drier environment and that this in turn led to the greater concentration of political power. Another interpretation suggests an increased incidence of warfare, due to the disruptions caused by the fall of El Mirador, the resultant nucleation of population for defensive purposes around Maya cities and the emergence of new, more centralized political institutions.[13]

In the Maya highlands, after about AD 250, events appear to have been more dramatic. Many towns and cities seem to have been abandoned; some, like Kaminaljuyú, declined for a period but at a later date recovered. Here, too, natural disaster may have played a part. The Llopango volcano in central El Salvador erupted around this time and caused catastrophe in the immediate area and disruption far and wide. Populations may have been forced to migrate, and many of the old trade

An Indian look-out observes the arrival of Spanish ships off the coast of Mexico.

View of the ruins of Uxmal by Frederick Catherwood.

Yllmo. Sr. D. Fr. Diego de Landa, natural de Cifuentes
ana, Obispo de Yucatan. Siendo Guardian de este
vento de S. Antonio, 1553, fabrico el primitivo claustro y esta
esia y Santuario de la Inmaculada Concepcion Nra. Sra. de
nal, cuya milagrosa imagen inauguro trayendola de Gua
ala, costeada por el Pueblo Izamalense, año de 1559. Trajo a
rez otra igual que dejo en Merida, y habiendose aburado lo
despues de 389 años en el incendio de esta Yglesia el 17
... otra.

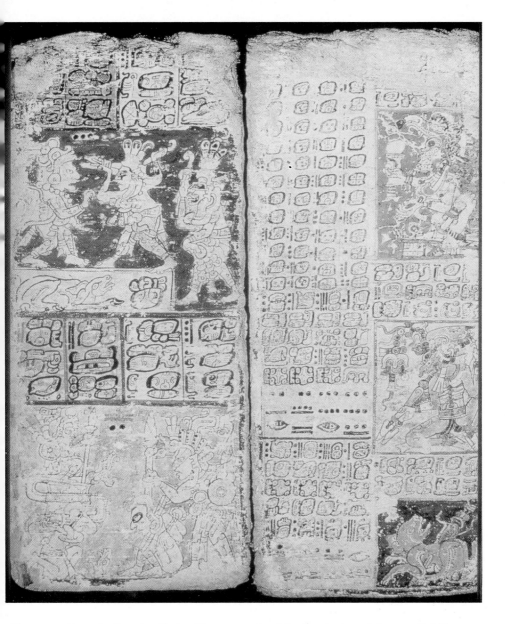

Two pages from the Dresden Codex. Page 47, to the right, is a section of the so-called Venus Table. The text includes the dates of different stations or appearances of Venus in the sky and lists of presiding Venus deities, two of which are depicted here.

FACING PAGE (clockwise from top left)

Diego de Landa. One of the few known portraits, from the church at Izamal.

Jean Frédéric Waldeck in later years.

John Lloyd Stephens.

Colonel Juan Galindo. A portrait miniature.

Alfred Maudslay at work in one of the buildings of Chichén Itzá. This photograph by
his assistant Henry Sweet shows the typical outline of the Maya corbel vault, thick walls
built up with overlapping blocks of masonry that each project slightly inwards until the
walls are bridged at the top by capstones.

ABOVE Tikal in
1881. A photograph
taken by Alfred
Maudslay from the
top of Temple I,
facing west across
the Great Plaza and
showing Temples II,
III and IV cleared
of vegetation by his
workers.

RIGHT The
Bonampak murals.
Room One.

ABOVE Desiré Charnay in search of lost cities.

LEFT J. Eric Thompson with a group of Lacandón Indians in 1946.

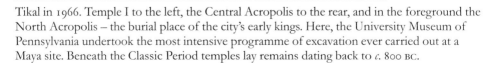

Tikal in 1966. Temple I to the left, the Central Acropolis to the rear, and in the foreground the North Acropolis – the burial place of the city's early kings. Here, the University Museum of Pennsylvania undertook the most intensive programme of excavation ever carried out at a Maya site. Beneath the Classic Period temples lay remains dating back to *c.* 800 BC.

ABOVE LEFT An Olmec colossal head of basalt, more than 1.5 metres high, one of ten such heads from the site of San Lorenzo. 1200–900 BC.

ABOVE RIGHT Altar A from La Venta. In his right hand the figure of an Olmec ruler grasps a rope attached to a captive carved on the side of the monument.

Uaxactún. The Late Preclassic Temple E-VII-sub after excavation by the Carnegie Institution in the 1930s and displaying well-preserved stucco masks.

Cerros. Structure 5c-2nd partly excavated, revealing two of the four masks that flanked the central stairway.

LEFT Stela 11 from Kaminaljuyú. One of the city's Late Preclassic rulers wears an elaborate headdress and bird mask and grasps a flint 'decapitator' in his left hand.

BELOW Yuri Knorosov.

8

routes between Central America and Mexico were perhaps severed for many years, affecting the wealth of towns and cities in the Guatemalan highlands and along the Pacific Coast. Much of the trade that had once flowed through the highlands may have been diverted to other routes across the lowlands, to the benefit of cities like Tikal.[14]

The two regions had been bound together for centuries. Indeed the ancestors of most lowland peoples, way back in the collective memory, had descended from the highlands to open up the tropical forest, no doubt taking with them enduring concepts of the creation and order of the world, the powers of mighty planets, images of sacred mountains formed by the volcanoes of the Cordillera. Highlands and lowlands continued to trade and to exchange new ideas and religious concepts. The early developmental stages of the Maya writing system that emerged in the Classic period are still a mystery. If it had some indigenous roots in the lowlands, much of its origins must lie in those glyphic systems originally developed in the highlands. The chain of events there in the third century AD is as yet unclear and archaeological investigation of this region still has much ground to make up. What is evident is that the highlands became politically debilitated. They no longer created monuments to their lords with hieroglyphic inscriptions. Instead, it was the Maya of the lowlands who took up the stelae, the texts, the elaborate images of individual rulership, that 'divine kingship' whose pattern had been laid down by the Olmec, and over the next seven centuries brought Maya civilization to its greatest heights.

Any civilization passes through a formative or preparatory phase when the elements that define it come together. For a very long time, one of the mysteries of the Maya was that the great achievements of the Classic period seemed to appear in fully developed form from nowhere, from humble village farming communities. The archaeological work of recent years has revealed how complex and surprising a process the emergence of Maya civilization was. But the threshold around AD 250, the beginning of the 'Classic' period, is still a valid marker. For it is at about this time that the Maya themselves tell us that their great ruling dynasties began. The parallel has been drawn with ancient Egypt and Shang dynasty China.[15] For we move from a shadowy pre-dynastic period to the dynastic era of the Maya story. We begin to encounter real individuals and 'history' itself. Now we must turn to how that history has been retrieved.

CHAPTER THREE

Cracking the Code

'Hieroglyphics explaining all but perfectly unintelligible... Who shall read them?' At long last, after more than a century and a half, John Lloyd Stephens' challenge has been triumphantly met. Today the decipherment of Maya writing has reached an exhilarating pitch of almost constant revelation. Professional epigraphers are all busy people, deep in the translation and analysis of texts in museums and university departments, or out in the field alongside their archaeologist colleagues. For new inscriptions are still appearing frequently in excavations. An epigrapher of note will commonly be associated with an archaeological project or loosely attached to a number of them. He or she will visit the archaeologists on site in the dry season months and may indeed be present when an inscribed monument is unearthed. This will be a moment of great excitement. The chances are that much of the text can be translated verbatim. The information could be of singular importance. It may record the victory in battle of one Maya city over another, the capture and sacrifice of a Maya lord. A political alliance could be commemorated between two cities previously thought to be enemies, or the identity revealed of the mysterious occupant of a newly discovered tomb.

Complete decipherment of this complex, intractable writing system will almost certainly never be achieved. But the process is still unfolding, the understanding of a phrase in one context leading to a chain reaction and a flurry of decipherments among other inscriptions. Even a small advance leads the epigrapher back to reinterpret known texts, to those recorded by Maudslay for example, or to the more recent work of Ian Graham and his colleagues. It may even demand examination of dusty casts in the basements of museums to double-check key glyphs whose original outlines may be preserved there. The rapid progress of recent years is due in no small part to the collaboration and sense of scholarly community among most epigraphers. Colleagues often work away together at the same texts and researchers constantly exchange insights with each other, e-mailing their progress across the globe. Seminars and conferences are frequent and workshops in Maya writing are held annually, where professional academics mix with the burgeoning fraternity of amateur enthusiasts to share the discoveries of the previous year.[1]

Only a few decades ago, however, the situation could not have been more different. The picture one has is of frustrated Mayanists shuffling drawings of inscriptions across their desks and staring at the wall. The rich seam of decipherment mined by Forstemann and others at the turn of the century had long been worked out. Occasionally a small nugget of fresh enlightenment appeared but fast piling up was a slag heap of unsubstantiated theories and wishful thinking. Maya calendrical and astronomical inscriptions were well enough known by the 1950s; the 'non-calendrical' glyphs still appeared quite impenetrable.[2]

Examination of a sample Maya text, Lintel 21 from Yaxchilán (see below), will serve to explore the workings of the script and as a demonstration of the impasse that had been reached by mid-century.[3] For those unfamiliar with Maya inscriptions it is difficult to know where to start with this dense slab of alien writing. One can rapidly make out a number of elements that seem realistic or pictorial: human and animal

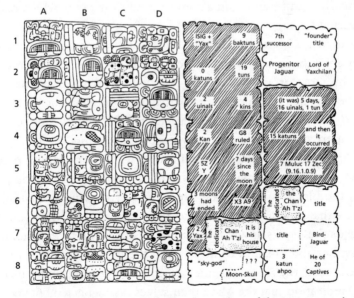

Lintel 21 from Yaxchilán. In the translation, the sections of the text concerning the calendar are shaded. The unshaded areas represent the 'non-calendrical' content only deciphered in more recent years.

heads, skulls, a pair of crossed legs, a hand with the palm open, the small figure of a bird. Yet there are so many other odd shapes, and what to us might seem arbitrary doodles, that the eye rapidly shifts from one seemingly more intelligible image to another. This must have been the way that early explorers like Del Río or Galindo would have reacted to the inscriptions, scanning the mysterious signs and searching for anything familiar, anything that might offer a meaning. It is easy to understand how those with madcap theories about the ruins – like Waldeck – could see elephants, marimbas or many other things that were simply not there.

The basic elements of Maya writing are individual signs or glyphs, the two terms being interchangeable. They are found together in glyph groups, commonly known as 'blocks' on the stone monuments where they are of a regular square or rectangular appearance, as here. The reading order of the blocks is left to right, top to bottom in pairs of columns. A grid with co-ordinates is conventionally imposed by epigraphers upon their drawings of inscriptions as an easy frame of reference. Thus, this text is read A1, B1, A2, B2 and so on down to B8. Then you begin again at the top of the next section and proceed C1, D1, C2, D2 as far as D8. Other texts, however, are of a more irregular form and some inscriptions – on pottery, jade or bone for example – may read left to right in a single horizontal line, top to bottom in a vertical column or, particularly with ceramics, in a combination of the two, which results in an inverted L-shape.

To impose a somewhat artificial order upon texts, glyphs are classified by epigraphers according to their size and position within the block. Thus the most prominent and largest signs are known as 'main signs' and the smaller glyphic elements arranged around them are called 'affixes'. Moving clockwise these affixes are defined as prefixes (to the left), superfixes (above), postfixes (to the right) and subfixes (below). Very rarely is a main sign accompanied by a full complement of affixes and on occasion one main sign will fill a whole block. Reading order within the block is most often prefix, superfix, main sign, subfix and postfix – that is, left to right, and top to bottom in the same manner that one reads the blocks as a whole. But this can vary greatly, depending on the number and position of affixes and the personal style of the Maya scribe. Indeed, the above scheme can only be a general guide since there is little indication that the Maya themselves distinguished between main signs and affixes. This will be quite evident in some of the glyph blocks on Lintel 21.

The outline workings of the script were well enough known fifty years ago. We will proceed through the text to see what they were able to translate at that time. It begins at A1 with the so-called 'Initial Series Introductory Glyph', which always serves to introduce a date in the Long Count calendar. The Long Count date then proceeds from B1 to B3. It corresponds to 16 October AD 454. Here it can be seen that the glyphs representing the divisions of the Long Count, the *baktuns*, *katuns*, *tuns* and so on, are the main signs in their blocks, and the bars and dots of the numbers and the shell denoting *o katuns* appear in the form of prefixes. In A4 comes the first part of the Calendar Round date, 2 Kan. Its companion, 2 Yax, does not turn up until the first part of the block A7. In between is a curious set of glyphs. B4 represents one of the so-called 'Lords of the Night', which were first defined by Eric Thompson. Each of these nine deities of the Underworld was, in turn, a patron of each day in the Maya calendar. Thus a glyphic expression for one of them appears after every single date expressed in the Long Count. The next glyph block A5 remains undeciphered, followed in B5–B6 by three expressions of the so-called 'Lunar Series'. These glyphs refer to the appearance of the moon for this particular day in the Long Count. They were first deciphered in the 1930s by John Teeple, a great friend of Thompson, who studied the glyphs as a hobby. Thus B5 states that it was seven days since the last new moon, A6 indicates that 3 moons had ended in a cycle of six lunar months and B6 says that the particular lunar month in question contained 29 (rather than 30) days. This is all dense, complex stuff, testimony to the constant Maya pursuit of calendrical exactitude, and such intricacies kept Teeple occupied for many years.

We now enter the first section of those 'non-calendrical' glyphs which could not be fathomed half a century ago, from the second half of A7 to D2. With C3, Maya time intrudes once more. There are more dates within the next six glyph blocks, C3 to D5. This involves a count forward from the first Long Count date, at the beginning of the inscription, to a second date expressed in the Calendar Round as 7 Muluc 17 Zec, at C5 and D5, the equivalent of 12 May AD 752. It was Thompson who recognized that D4 was what he called a 'Posterior Date Indicator', a glyph which told you that you had to count forward, in this case 5 *kins*, 16 *uinals*, 1 *tun* and 15 *katuns*, to the second Calendar Round date. These numbers, C3 to C4, came to be called 'Distance Numbers' since they defined the gap between one date and another. But what did the dates and references to the state of the moon actually mean, and why make the connection between these two particular dates, which are almost three hundred years apart? Sometimes a second date such as this might be an obvious anniversary of the first one, or mark the completion of a particular calendrical cycle. But this was not the case here. The short answer is that no one knew what these dates signified.

The rest of the inscription, C6 to D8, could not be understood in the 1950s. This meant that in total about two-thirds was decipherable and one third not. In retrospect, we know that the unknown third makes sense of the whole inscription. We will return to Lintel 21 below. But here we must make an attempt to understand the predicament that people like Thompson and Teeple were in. The preponderance of glyphs in a text such as this was concerned with calendrical matters. In many longer inscriptions, expressions of time recur over and over again, connected by one Distance Number after another. It was this which gave the clear impression that concern with the passing of time was somehow at the heart of Maya thought. As for the non-calendrical sections, Thompson was convinced that just as the main signs in temporal expressions (such as the signs for *katuns*, *tuns* and so on) expressed 'concepts' of periods of time, so the undeciphered glyphs very probably represented ideas or abstract concepts to do with Maya religion, prophecy or ritual practices linked to their obsessive time reckoning. But how could the meaning of all this be retrieved if, as he put it, after the Spanish conquest 'most Maya ritual terms and religious imagery unrecorded in Maya-Spanish dictionaries, were lost with the disappearance of the Maya hierarchy'?[4]

This leads us to the fundamental question of what kind of script this was, and how 'meaning' was conveyed. One way of approaching writing systems, commonly adopted earlier in the century, was to use an evolutionary scheme that placed them in broad categories running from the simplest to the supposedly most sophisticated. Sylvanus Morley followed such a scheme in his own assessment of the Maya script in the *Ancient Maya* of 1946.[5] Firstly, he wrote, there came *pictographic* writing, the most primitive of all. Thus a simple depiction of a man, a bird, a house or a mountain largely meant just that, a sense directly or indirectly connected with the pictorial representation. The next stage was *ideographic* writing. Here a sign stood for an idea, a whole word or unit of meaning. Some signs might appear pictographic, a hangover perhaps from the earlier evolutionary stage, but what they looked like had no necessary connection at all with the meaning conveyed. Lastly there were *phonetic* writing systems which could be divided into two: *syllabic,* where signs represented whole syllables, and *alphabetic,* regarded as the most advanced of all, where signs stood for the most basic 'phonemes' or units of sound in language.

Where did Maya writing fit into this? Thompson published a catalogue of individual Maya hieroglyphic signs, one of his great achievements and still used to this day, in which he recorded some 800 glyphs in all, including both main signs and affixes.[6] This very number helped him and Morley in their definition of Maya writing: 800 individual glyphs meant that the system could not have been alphabetic, since only 25–30 would have been needed. Likewise, a syllabic script would have required little more than 100 individual signs. The conclusion had to be that, as Morley wrote, 'The Maya hieroglyphic writing belongs to Class II (ideographic)... its characters represent ideas rather than pictures – or sounds'.[7] Thus, in a text such as Lintel 21 from Yaxchilán, the ideas would be represented by the main signs and the affixes were there to elaborate (or in more technical terms act as grammatical 'modifiers') of the meaning inherent in those main signs. One objection to this conclusion might be that 800, or nearer 700 if the affixes are subtracted, did not represent a very large number of words or 'ideas'. Surely the Maya had more to think or write about than this? The answer that Thompson and Morley gave was that Maya writing only concerned itself with a very limited and abstruse range of subject matter – not mundane, earthly concerns, but religious ritual and the majestic passing of time.

So, the lack of progress in Maya decipherment by the 1950s was explained by what seemed to be very cogent, mutually reinforcing arguments. By its very nature the Maya script was barely penetrable since, aside from the calendrical references, it largely represented 'ideas'. And these ideas were so esoteric and complex, known only to long-dead Maya priests, that they would probably remain permanently baffling.

In the later 1950s and 1960s, however, this entrenched, pessimistic view began to be dismantled systematically. The modern revolution in Maya decipherment was about to begin. Advances by linguists and epigraphers would establish the true nature of Maya writing and, quite independently, some remarkable detective work was to reveal what most Maya texts were actually talking about.

THE CONTENT OF MAYA WRITING

The first hint that there might be rather more to the subject matter of the inscriptions came with the work of Heinrich Berlin, a German-born businessman who lived in Mexico City and had begun to undertake his own independent study of the texts of Palenque and of a number of other sites. His greatest achievement was to isolate what he referred to in 1958 as 'emblem glyphs' (see below).[8] He had noticed that at cities such as Palenque, Tikal, Copán and Yaxchilán a particular kind of glyph block was very common. The affixes remained largely constant but the main sign to the bottom right of the block would vary from place to place and seemed to belong to or represent a specific city. Thus at Tikal the main sign looked like a knotted bundle, or as many now believe a head of hair knotted at the back, and at Copán it was a bat's head. He thought that such signs might be either a place name or stand for a ruling dynasty or lineage. What is more, he discovered that an emblem glyph that seemed to pertain to one particular site might occasionally appear at others, suggesting relationships of some sort between Maya cities.

Berlin made another important advance. In 1952 the Mexican archaeologist Alberto Ruz had made a spectacular and momentous discovery beneath the Temple of the Inscriptions at Palenque. He located the magnificent tomb of a Maya ruler, who had been buried in a lidded stone sarcophagus placed in a large crypt within the heart of the Temple (see plate section, p.18). Finding the tomb of an identifiably real, royal individual – the first such discovery to be made by archaeologists – was

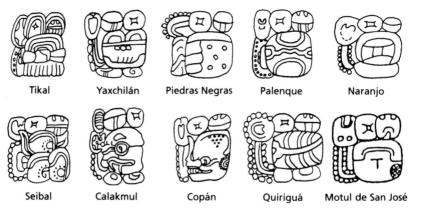

Tikal   Yaxchilán   Piedras Negras   Palenque   Naranjo

Seibal   Calakmul   Copán   Quiriguá   Motul de San José

Emblem Glyphs.

to lead to concerted efforts to decipher the texts related to it. We will see the dramatic outcome of this in due course. But, as a hint of what was to follow, Berlin noticed that the sarcophagus bore a series of portraits, coupled with brief glyphic notations, along its sides. He managed to demonstrate that these portraits were almost certainly those of the royal ancestors of the buried ruler and that the glyphs represented their names.[9] In sum, then, what Berlin's work suggested was that Maya inscriptions were not simply the sacred writ of priests or philosophers of time, but that they might contain documentary information about places and real people.

The truly revolutionary breakthrough was to be made by the formidable scholar Tatiana Proskouriakoff in her study of the monuments of Piedras Negras. Proskouriakoff was from an emigré family that had settled in the USA at the time of the Russian Revolution. She studied architecture at the University of Pennsylvania and soon after graduating in 1930 began working as an archaeological draughtsman for the University Museum. She first visited Piedras Negras to make reconstruction drawings of the architecture there and went on to do similar work at Copán and other sites, producing in 1946 *An Album of Maya Architecture*, impressive wash drawings of the way Maya sites might originally have looked, though singularly empty of population or of many other structures surrounding the major architecture (see plate section, pp.11, 16). In this way her drawings reflected the prevailing view of the largely vacant Maya ceremonial centre. But her later work would far from tow the conventional line. In 1950 she produced a classic study of style in Maya sculpture, and this was the interest that took her back to Piedras Negras in 1959.

Discovered by Teobert Maler on the northern banks of the Usumacinta, some forty kilometres downriver from Yaxchilán, Piedras Negras possessed impressive groups of stone stelae, all with well-preserved inscriptions and dates, which had been purposely set up in distinctive rows in front of different temples. The first stela in each of these groups bore the carved figure of a man in a niche. He was in elaborate costume, seated cross-legged on a throne. Above the niche were sky symbols and an image of the so-called celestial bird. Such imagery placed the figure symbolically close to the heavens and the supernatural realms. Thompson thought the figures represented priests, at the very least, and most probably gods. Each niche was elevated, often with a ladder leading up to it carved with footprints. Some of these initial stelae also had the figure of a woman below, looking upwards at the man in the niche. The conventional view at the time, however, was that these were not women but male priests in special ceremonial garb. One particularly fine stela also depicted a sacrificial victim at the bottom of the ladder, stretched on his back with his chest ripped open.

Proskouriakoff's aims were certainly art-historical to begin with, the well-preserved dates roughly spanning AD 600–800 offering a good chronological control for stylistic analysis of the sculpture. But her research took a very different direction. 'My first thought was that the "niche" motif represented the dedication of a new temple, and that the ladder marked with footsteps ascending to the niche symbolized the rise to the sky of the victim of sacrifice, whose body was sometimes shown at the foot of the ladder.' She had hoped that she could perhaps identify a hieroglyphic expression to represent human sacrifice, but 'what I found instead started an entirely new train of thought and led to surprising conclusions'.[10]

Firstly, and most telling of all, she noticed that within each discrete group of stelae the span of dates was never more than that of a single human lifetime. Second, it was clear that one particular glyph, termed the 'upended frog' glyph by Thompson, always followed the very earliest of all the dates within each group. Invariably, the next earliest date had following it the so-called 'toothache glyph', which looked like the bandaged jaw of a vulture. The date associated with this came between twelve and thirty-one years after the first one. Following the first 'niche' stela, subsequent monuments were each set up every five tuns, or roughly five years, after the previous one and on these stelae the 'toothache glyph' and its associated date would often reappear, apparently commemorating the anniversary of the original date. Finally, the very latest date within a set of stelae was also accompanied by one recurring sign.

The patterns of dates on the Piedras Negras stelae and the repeated hieroglyphic expressions associated with many of them led her to some deceptively simple but brilliant conclusions. Each separate group of stelae must have been erected to commemorate events in the life of a Maya ruler. The 'upended frog', which she first termed the 'initial event', had to stand for birth and the 'toothache glyph' for accession to the throne. The sign associated with the latest date within each group represented death. On this basis she worked out a sequence of six rulers who reigned for thirty-five, forty-seven, forty-two, twenty-eight, five and

'Dynastic Event' glyphs
a) Birth   b) Accession   c) Death

seventeen years respectively. Upon the death of one king, his successor would begin to erect his own cluster of stelae in front of a different temple. Indeed, each of the buildings may have been constructed, or at least renewed, by a different individual.

As to the specific imagery of the more elaborate first stela in each group, the figure in the niche, not unlike the Olmec image of the lord at the mouth of a cave, depicted the ruler at his enthronement. The ladder and footprints symbolized his ascent to power, 'the seating on high of the lord', as the Maya books put it. Here what crossed her mind was a reference in the post-Conquest Books of Chilam Balam to the enthronement of a Yucatán lord called Hunac Ceel, not long before the Spanish Conquest. 'Then they began to set aloft the house on high for the ruler. Then they began the construction of the stairway. Then he was set in the house on high.'[11]

This was far from the sum of the information that Proskouriakoff managed to tease out from the texts. Their very structure, their seemingly repetitive format, suggested that she might be able to predict where different kinds of information came. She was beginning to get a tentative grip on Maya grammar, following the work of the American linguist Benjamin Whorf, who in the 1930s had proposed the word order of verb followed by subject through his studies of the Dresden Codex. The patterns observable at Piedras Negras appeared to fill this out, suggesting a sequence of date, verb, subject and then a short series of glyphs representing the honorific titles of the subject – in other words, the Maya ruler:

It seems safe to say that glyphs which immediately follow dates ... make reference to actions, events or ceremonies and are essentially predicate glyphs. Following them we can expect to find substantives referring to the protagonists of the events, and if the representations are historical, some of these should be appellatives identifying the persons involved.[12]

She not only predicted correctly where references to the rulers of Piedras Negras should come in the texts but also pinpointed glyphs which referred to the figures of the women on the stelae. She identified their birth dates, followed by name glyphs. And each of these was prefixed by a female head in profile with a knot of hair attached to the forehead, signifying that a woman was being described (see below). On one stela an adult woman was depicted and next to her a smaller female figure. There were references to two females in the texts and their birth dates almost certainly proved that they were the wife and daughter of the ruler who appeared in the niche.

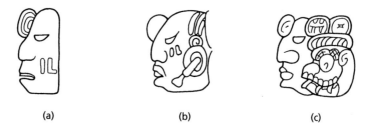

(a)   (b)   (c)

The Female Prefix
a and b are the prefix alone. Note the elaborate 'ear flare assemblage' of b.
c is the prefix combined with the emblem glyph of Calakmul, part of the
titles of Lady Evening Star, a princess from that city who became one of the
wives of Shield Jaguar of Yaxchilán.

Proskouriakoff's study of Piedras Negras was published in 1960 in the journal *American Antiquity* under the modest title 'Historical Implications of a Pattern of Dates at Piedras Negras, Guatemala'. All her conclusions have been borne out since and it has proved to be one of the truly seminal publications in the history of Maya archaeology. She did not stop there, but rapidly followed it up with a study of the inscriptions of Yaxchilán.[13] The stelae and stone lintels there had been well-recorded by Alfred Maudslay and, photographically, by Teobert Maler. The famous Yaxchilán lintels in particular have proved remarkably informative, since many of them depict detailed and extremely beautiful narrative scenes which provide a graphic illustration of the contents of the texts. To some degree Proskouriakoff had already proved the close relationship of text and image at Piedras Negras, but at

Yaxchilán the association was clearer and enabled her 'translation' or structural analysis of the texts to be even more convincing, although she did not have the benefit of such a helpful arrangement of dated stelae as at Piedras Negras.

At Yaxchilán she produced an outline dynastic history for a period of just over one hundred years, from the seventh well into the eighth century AD. This was evidently a time of great expansion and prosperity in the city, a period dominated by two powerful rulers. Unlike at Piedras Negras, the name glyphs of these rulers were so 'pictographic' and easily identified that she gave them nicknames. The earlier individual she called 'Shield Jaguar' since his personal sign combined the head of a jaguar with a smaller glyph that resembled a shield. He appeared to have reigned for a very long time and died in his nineties, in AD 742. He was eventually succeeded, after an intriguing gap of ten years, by a man, probably his son, whom she called Bird Jaguar, whose name glyph combined a similar jaguar head prefixed by the figure of a bird.

Shield
Jaguar

Bird
Jaguar

The Yaxchilán texts spoke, in similar terms to those of Piedras Negras, of accession to rulership, of birth, death and the celebration of important events and anniversaries within the career of the ruler. But here she was able to document some different kinds of information. Firstly, far from wanting to project themselves as high-minded pacifists and calendar priests, it seemed that both Shield Jaguar and his son were keen to commemorate victories in war and their taking of prominent captives. The best-known example of this is Lintel 8 (see overleaf), whose text is brief and the imagery so graphic that she was able to work out the meaning of the bulk of the inscription. The scene on the monument depicts Bird Jaguar, in elaborate costume and with a spear in his left hand, and a secondary lord taking two captives. Both of these doomed individuals, destined ultimately for sacrifice, wear little but loincloths

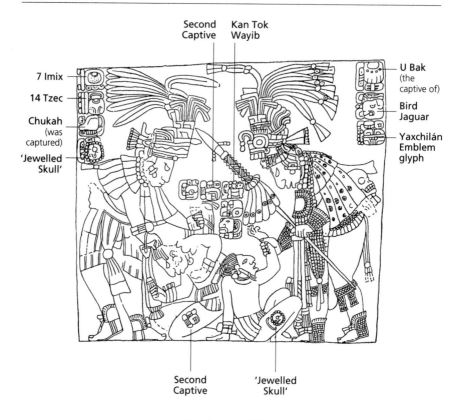

Lintel 8, Yaxchilán

and appear in attitudes of subjection. One is being grabbed by the arm and the other by the hair, a classic Maya image of captive-taking. The text begins with the Calendar Round date '7 Imix 14 Tzec', corresponding to 9 May 755. There then follows a glyph block that Proskouriakoff interpreted as the past tense 'was captured'. The next glyph is identical to the one that appears on the thigh of the individual grasped by Bird Jaguar. She took this to be the name of the person who 'was captured', whom she called 'Jewelled Skull' as the glyph seems to represent a skull fringed with jewels. The next series of glyphs, above the figure of Bird Jaguar, begins with a glyph block now known to mean 'the captive of'. It was followed by Bird Jaguar's name glyph and finally the emblem glyph for Yaxchilán. Here of course Proskouriakoff was incorporating Berlin's pioneering work within her own study. So, the text can be translated as 'On 9 May 755 Jewelled Skull was captured, the prisoner of Bird Jaguar, Lord of Yaxchilán'.

The second captive also has a glyph on his thigh, which reappears in the text above him, where reference is made to his capture by the lesser lord or *sahal*, known as Kan Tok Wayib. Proskouriakoff went on to demonstrate that the names of famous captives, from the ruling families of other towns and cities, were regularly identified and came to constitute a part of a ruler's elaborate, if not bombastic, titles. Thus, we know today that Bird Jaguar had earlier called himself 'Captor' of one 'Ah Uk'. After AD 755 he was replaced with a regular reference to 'Jewelled Skull', who was presumably a more notable prize.

At Piedras Negras, Proskouriakoff had already revealed the importance to the Maya of recording the role of women in dynastic affairs, notably in the way their participation had been physically represented in those first, more elaborate 'niche' stelae commemorating accession to the throne. On a number of lintels at Yaxchilán there were arresting images of women taking part in ritual activities. The most graphic of these Maudslay had removed and are now in the British Museum. Their more precise content and meaning we will return to in Chapter 5, but the texts on these monuments are also short and very much to the point and already, by the mid 1960s, through analysing image and text in tandem, Proskouriakoff had demonstrated that certain glyphs must refer to ritual bloodletting and that both Maya rulers and their consorts participated together in such rites at Yaxchilán.

'In retrospect, the idea that Maya texts record history, naming the rulers as lords of the towns seems so natural that it is strange it has not been thoroughly explored before.'[14] In this disarmingly wide-eyed way, Proskouriakoff referred to the outcome of her initial work at Piedras Negras. It was indeed very strange. John Lloyd Stephens had suggested it more than a hundred years previously. The Maya had 'published a record of themselves', as he put it. It was as simple as that. The characters depicted on the stelae and lintels were not gods or priests, but Maya rulers. Today Mayanists find it almost impossible to understand the suspension of critical faculties that overcame their predecessors earlier this century, when eminent scholars – not journalists or crackpot speculators – were prepared to believe that the Maya, possessed of an evidently sophisticated writing system, had used it not to record the power and status of ruling dynasties and their foreign conquests, the worldly things that the rulers of all other ancient civilizations sought to advertise, but in benign intellectual speculations and the search for religious truth.

Almost overnight, Proskouriakoff had changed the direction of Maya scholarship. To Thompson, the results of her work must have come as a cruel shock. So much of what he had believed in was now revealed as a myth, largely of his own construction. To his great credit, he admitted that he had been wrong. Those who knew him imagine that earlier in life he would have embraced the new discoveries and incorporated them into his own work. But by the 1960s it was too late. For the rest of his years, until he died in 1975, he devoted most of his time to the codices and to the less contentious realm of Maya religion with which he was most comfortable. But Thompson did remain active in an area not directly concerned with the contents of the inscriptions. It was the debate about what kind of writing system this was.

The Nature of the Maya Script

The discovery of Landa's *Relación* by Brasseur de Bourbourg a hundred years earlier had first opened the question of how phonetic the Maya script might be. Brasseur had naïvely applied the 'alphabet' to the codices and signally failed. Despite the opinion of De Rosny, who remained a believer in the underlying phonetic nature of the system, the more widely accepted view, propounded by the likes of Forstemann and maintained by Thompson, was that the script was 'ideographic', or in more modern parlance 'logographic', and that in essence each main sign represented a word or an idea. Brave but ultimately thwarted individuals, notably the American Cyrus Thomas who came up with some astonishingly modern ideas about the script in the 1880s and 1890s, proposed phonetic theories but were never able to convince the wider academic world. In the 1930s Benjamin Whorf attempted to open once more the 'phonetic question' as it had become known. He thought that 'Landa's list of characters has certain earmarks of being genuine and also of being the reflex of a phonetic system'.[15] He felt that even the tiniest elements of Maya signs might represent units of sound. Yet he, too, could not prove it satisfactorily and his arguments were rebutted with ease by Thompson.

Thompson's own work on the script was an immensely impressive scholarly achievement. He produced a great many important technical books and papers concerning the calendar and on Maya religion as expressed in the texts. He also demonstrated the complexity of Maya writing and its seeming flexibility. For example, he showed that certain Maya signs could function grammatically in different ways. He himself had deciphered the sign *te*, for tree, which he had noted repeatedly under illustrations of trees in the codices. But he also showed that the same sign could appear in other contexts where it had a quite different meaning or function. *Te* could be used, for instance, as a 'numerical classifier', a necessary term placed between a number and the object being numbered. Thus, to say 'three stones' in Yucatec, you cannot say *ox tun* but have to express it as *ox-te-tun* or 'three te stones'. The same was true in ancient times. What Thompson could not accept was the idea that any sign could act on its own as a single syllable or unit of sound which might be combined with others to make up words, that is, that the system might be truly phonetic. To him, no Maya hieroglyphic sign could be anything less than an individual 'morpheme' having its own specific meaning or grammatical function.

The crucial breakthrough in defining how the Maya writing system worked came in the end from a direction that no one could have anticipated, not from within western academic circles but from a lone linguist working in Stalinist Russia at the height of the Cold War, a man who had never been within a thousand miles of a Maya ruin and who first came upon their writing in the most extraordinary way. Yuri Knorosov, Michael Coe relates, was in the Red Army in Berlin in 1945, where he came upon the great edifice of the German National Library going up in flames (see plate section, p.8).[16] Oblivious, it seems, to any danger from the burning building, he found his way to the section which most interested him. There he perhaps took off his helmet and browsed for a while. Before leaving, he pocketed a volume which had caught his eye and took it with him all the way back to Moscow. It was a facsimile edition of the Dresden, Paris and Madrid codices.

At the end of the war Knorosov resumed his studies at Moscow University, where his main interest had previously been in Egyptian hieroglyphs. But his improbable find led him in a new direction. His doctoral thesis was to involve a translation and study of Landa's *Relación de las Cosas de Yucatán*. He now turned a young, fresh mind, in awe of no one else in the field, to Landa's mysterious 'alphabet'.

Knorosov concluded, as everyone else had by now, that the 'alphabet' was no such thing. Yet he felt that the list of signs was not baffling or meaningless. It was the result of a problem of communication or cultural confusion between the Spanish friar and his Maya informant. One day in the mid-sixteenth century, during that calmer period of optimism in his mission before he had turned to burning books and attempting to stamp out Maya culture with a vengeance, Landa had settled down with

Gaspar Antonio Chi, one of his principal Maya friends and informants, to talk about Maya writing and to see if he could record some of it for posterity. He went about it in a rather curious way. In essence, since there were a number of more complex elements to his procedure, Landa must have pronounced out loud each letter of the Spanish alphabet and then asked Chi to write down the Maya hieroglyphic equivalent. What Chi wrote could not have been an alphabet. He simply did his best to represent in hieroglyphs the sounds that he heard for the names of the Spanish letters. In Spanish the alphabet is pronounced Ah, Bay, Say, Day and so on, which are in fact largely syllables. Knorosov believed that the so-called alphabet was thus a partial syllabary.[17]

So, when the syllable signs were put together, they might spell words phonetically. It was evident from contemporary Mayan languages that many words were in the form consonant–vowel–consonant or CVC. Very few ended in vowels. What Knorosov suggested was that in Maya texts the initial syllable of a CVC word would be represented by a CV sign, like those in Landa's list. The final letter would also be a CV sign, which began with the requisite consonant and whose vowel was the same as that in the first CV syllable. But, this vowel would be dropped in speaking the word. Thus, the word for a *quetzal* would be written *kuku*, but pronounced *kuk*. Knorosov gave the term 'synharmony' to this principle of consonance between the initial and final vowels.

Knorosov tested his ideas in the codices, which were the natural vehicle for such an exercise. Firstly, they were believed to have been written in Yucatec Mayan in the centuries not long before the Spanish Conquest, and there were a few good early dictionaries of Yucatec which might provide the meanings and sounds of words not far removed from the time when the codices had been written. Above all, the codex format was such that depictions of gods, animals and other images appeared to be closely related to sections of text. In many instances, specific glyphs had evidently acted as labels identifying certain of the images. We will proceed here, in a simplified way, to follow something of Knorosov's procedure. One of his key labelled images was that of a turkey in the Madrid codex. The word for turkey in sixteenth-century Yucatec was *cutz* (see overleaf). Looking at Landa's list, he saw that one of the signs on the list, marked *cu*, was the same as the first of two glyphs in the codex representing turkey. Following his principle of synharmony, the second glyph should thus be *tzu*. He then looked in the Dresden Codex at two glyphs that were thought to represent 'dog'. The

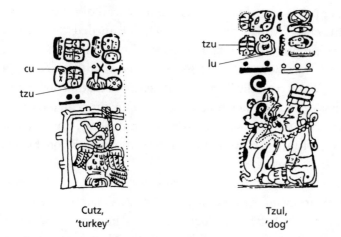

Cutz,
'turkey'

Tzul,
'dog'

first glyph was the same sign as the second syllable of turkey, the hypo-
thetical *tzu*, and the second was identifiable from Landa's list as *lu*. *Tzul*,
or *tzu-lu* as the ancient Mayan would have written it, was an old word for
dog in the Yucatec Maya dictionaries. Thus he had translated two words
phonetically: *cutz* – turkey and *tzul* – dog.

The way Knorosov worked naturally led on to new hypotheses. Thus,
knowing the sign for *cu* in the codices meant that seeing the same *cu* sign
plus an unknown one above an image of a goddess carrying a burden
must represent *cuch(u)*, the Yucatec for 'burden'. The unknown sign
must then be *chu*. So he proceeded. The last syllable of 'burden', *chu*, he
found represented the first syllable of *chu-ka-ah*, 'captured', seen over the
image of a captive god. It was indeed this very reading of *chu-ka-ah* as
'capture' that Proskouriakoff used to confirm her reading of the capture
glyph at Yaxchilán.

This may all sound very easy, and prompts the question why
Knorosov did not then go ahead *ad infinitum*, build up a complete
syllabary and thus translate the glyphs? In fact this is broadly the way
that Maya phonetic decipherments are worked out today, going from
the known to the unknown, glyph by glyph, and using the early Colonial
dictionaries as an essential reference. But the script cannot be cracked so
simply. Firstly, Landa only recorded a certain number of the syllables –
those, relatively few of them, which approximated to the sounds of the
Spanish alphabet. There are many Maya signs for syllables that still
remain unknown. Secondly, Knorosov realized that the Maya script was
not a purely syllabic system. He looked at Maya writing from a

comparative perspective, as a linguist familiar with other ancient scripts such as ancient Egyptian or Chinese. The claim that the system was 'ideographic', representing a cryptic code of pure ideas known only to Maya priests, was nonsense. He felt that Maya writing, like Egyptian hieroglyphs, was a typically 'logosyllabic' script in that it combined logographic signs, representing whole words or units of meaning, with other signs that were purely phonetic or syllabic. In this way, the total number of signs, in fact rather more than 800, was about right for this kind of 'mixed' writing system.

Knorosov published his work throughout the 1950s, beginning in 1952 with an article in the journal *Sovietskaya Etnografiya*. This first paper was prefaced by a brief introduction, which he did not write, which scoffed at the previous failure of imperialist academics and trumpeted a great triumph of Soviet scholarship. This did not of course go down too well in the West in the early years of the Cold War, and contributed to the hostility with which his ideas were received. Knorosov also left himself open to criticism by making certain claims for phonetic decipherments that could not be substantiated. His principle of synharmony, for example, seemed open to doubt. In those simple instances that we followed above, it works. But, as his critics demonstrated, Knorosov himself violated the principle in some of his readings. It was Eric Thompson who was most active in picking holes in the details of his arguments, conveniently presuming that Knorosov was proposing a completely phonetic system, which was quite inaccurate. Knorosov's approach took a very long time to be widely accepted. But, unlike previous attempts to establish the idea of phoneticism, the broader propositions he was putting forward were taken up by a few key supporters in western academic circles, notably Michael Coe, whose wife translated Knorosov's work, the linguist Floyd Lounsbury and the epigrapher David Kelley.

The next stage along the road of decipherment was to be the integration of Proskouriakoff's and Knorosov's work. It was achieved by a coming together of people as much as methodologies, of personal chemistry among a group of enthusiasts with diverse backgrounds who began to put their minds to the writing system at a series of seminars and conferences. The turning point was the first 'Mesa Redonda' or Round Table at Palenque in 1973, where the main protagonists were to be Lounsbury, Peter Mathews and Linda Schele, who have led much of the recent progress in decipherment among younger scholars. The

Proskouriakoff approach, as we have seen, was a purely structural one. Working within the established frame of knowledge of the calendar and studying very carefully the relationship between glyphic phrases and the images on the monuments, she managed to work out what certain glyphs *had* to mean and to come to some simple conclusions about the word order of Maya texts. Lounsbury argued, on the basis of Knorosov's work, that the method adopted by Proskouriakoff should be taken further. The presumption should be that the glyphs reflected a spoken language with a grammar and syntax which could be established and paraphrased, even if individual words could not be read.

Mathews and Schele had already worked individually on the Palenque inscriptions and the iconography of the relief sculpture. In late 1973, at the Mesa Redonda, they sat down together with Lounsbury and, pooling their expertise, worked out in paraphrase form, in the space of only a few hours, the last 200 years of Palenque's Classic period dynastic history, beginning with a ruler whom they first called 'Shield', since that was what his name glyph depicted. That first session they broke the inscriptions down roughly into the word order of date, verb, object and subject, incorporating all the 'verbs' that were known from birth through accession to death. The copious dates, linked together by Thompson's Distance Numbers, acted as a handy frame, almost a kind of punctuation. After 'Shield' they defined five separate successors, the whole sequence running until the end of recorded history at Palenque, at the turn of the ninth century AD.[18] The following year, at another mini-conference at Dumbarton Oaks in the USA, the same group plus David Kelley, by a similar process of brain-storming, added all the Palenque kings for the first two hundred years. They did not succeed in translating all the texts in the early days, but by the end of the 1970s the greater part of the dynastic history of Palenque was known from its temple walls, chronicles that connected Palenque's earthly rulers back thousands of years to remote ancestors in the mythological past.

The collaborative work on the Palenque texts in the 1970s is widely regarded as the true dawn of modern decipherment. Once phonetic decipherments began to be fed into the structure of grammar and syntax, the fluid and complex nature of the script was revealed. For example, the ruler known originally as 'Shield', who was in fact the man buried in the stone sarcophagus beneath the Temple of the Inscriptions, was soon given a phonetic Maya name, 'Pakal', by David Kelley, who had earlier deciphered a very similar title at Chichén Itzá. This name was written at Palenque in different ways and is a good example of the 'mixed' nature of the writing system. Firstly, it could be represented by a logograph, a sign standing for a whole word. This was a pictorial sign, a small shield of a kind known from depictions of Maya warriors. It was also written on occasion purely phonetically *pa-ka-l(a)*, the last vowel dropped following Knorosov's principle of synharmony. There was a third way of doing it as well. This was to add a syllabic sign to the logograph as a so-called 'phonetic complement', used to remove any ambiguity as to what the shield sign meant. This use of the phonetic complement and alternative phonetic spellings has been of great assistance to epigraphers in helping them to work out the meaning of logographic signs, many of which are not as obviously pictorial as 'Pakal', or 'Balam', the Maya word for 'Jaguar' (see overleaf).

In many other respects, however, Maya scribes have proved not to have been so helpful to modern-day decipherers. Some syllabic signs, for example, can have more than one sound value. They are what is called 'polyvalent'. What is more, different signs can also express the same sound. Only very painstaking work of textual analysis can pick these up. The same-sounding Maya word can also mean different things. Thus the word *kan* means either 'snake', 'sky' or 'four' in the way that in English 'game', as a noun alone, can mean an amusement or pastime, a wild animal that is hunted or the flesh of such an animal. Each different sense of *kan* will be expressed by a different logograph, but the sound being always the same gave the more teasing of scribes the chance for word play, the substitution of one logograph for another and a form of Maya punning.

Signs could also be combined or conflated. Thus the successor to Pakal at Palenque was a man named 'Kan Balam' or Snake Jaguar. His name glyph was on occasion combined, a snake and jaguar head merged together. In this example it is easy enough to detect the conflated elements, but on other occasions it is not. Knorosov's principle of 'synharmony' is another area of inconsistency. Knorosov was in fact broadly right in this theory, but a large number of instances demonstrate that the convention was often flouted.

Writing systems that evolve over many, many centuries cannot be expected to follow neat rules. An organically developing script will build up a host of exceptions, anomalies and downright eccentricities over time. This is especially the case when the writing system was the exclusive preserve of an élite class of scribes, keen to maintain the

Different ways of writing PAKAL and BALAM:
a) As a logograph.
b) Phonetically.
c) Logograph plus 'a phonetic complement'.

mystique and exclusivity of writing and to display their virtuosity. With
its beautifully sinuous, calligraphic quality, the Maya script was an art
form as much as a means of communication. Experienced epigraphers
become accustomed to the different styles and 'schools' of writing in the
great Maya cities. Thus the florid and adventurous forms of expression
used at Copán and Quiriguá, and the magnificent, more three-dimen-
sional stone carving on stelae and other monuments there, contrast with
the conservative style of writing and of sculptural representation found
at Tikal.

DECIPHERMENT TODAY

Despite the host of complexities that face the modern epigrapher, understanding of Maya writing has advanced at a pace unthinkable even in the 1970s. But how much of the Maya script can now be deciphered? Linda Schele put it in the following way:

> I must always answer that it depends on what you mean by deciphered. Some glyphs can be translated exactly; we know the original word or its syllabic value. For other glyphs, we have the meaning (for example, we have evidence that a glyph means 'to hold or grasp'), but we do not yet know the Maya words. There are other glyphs for which we know the general meaning, but we haven't found the original word; for example, we may know it involves war, marriage, or perhaps that the event always occurs before age 13, but we cannot associate the glyph with a precise action. For others, we can only recover their syntactical function; for example, we may know a glyph occurs in the position of a verb, but we have no other information. To me the most frustrating state is to have a glyph with known phonetic signs, so that we can pronounce the glyph, but we cannot find the word in any of the Maya languages. If a glyph is unique or occurs in only a few texts, we have little chance of translating it.[19]

About 50 per cent of Maya inscriptions can now be deciphered phonetically, where the meaning of the Maya words is known. Overall understanding of the contents of the texts now stands at more than 80 per cent. The result is that in city after city, where inscriptions are sufficiently well preserved, scholars are now able to follow the fortunes of individual Maya rulers and build up an outline history for many parts of the Classic Maya world. Heinrich Berlin's emblem glyph has been fully deciphered. The constant affixes read k'ul ahaw, meaning 'holy lord'. Thus each individual Maya king – and there were dozens of them – regarded himself as divine. The variable main sign of the emblem glyph represents a place-name, confirmed in recent years by the epigraphers Stuart Houston and David Stuart, so that the glyph as a whole reads 'holy lord of Palenque', 'holy lord of Tikal' and so on (see overleaf). Some forty different emblem glyphs are now known, serving as a primary source for understanding Maya political geography during the Classic period. The signs probably refer to a territory, to the city-state or

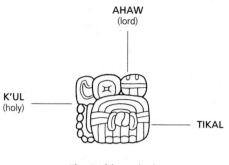

AHAW
(lord)

K'UL
(holy)

TIKAL

The Emblem glyph

kingdom as a whole rather than the individual city. Thus Palenque as a kingdom was known as 'Bak' or 'bone', the main sign of the emblem glyph, whereas the city itself appears to have been called 'Lakam-Ha', which translates as 'Big Water' and must refer to the fast-flowing Otolum and other streams which pour down the hillside through the city. Many other more localized place-names have now been identified, including mountains, lakes and caves and within sites, at Tikal, Palenque, Copán and Yaxchilán in particular, we now know that specific buildings and monuments were given names.

Proskouriakoff first identified the glyphs for such events as birth, accession, death, capture and the titles of rulers and their wives. More recent decipherments have demonstrated ever more precisely that the major concerns of the 'holy lords', as expressed on their monuments, were to proclaim their political power and dynastic authority. Warfare, which seems to have increased in intensity towards the end of the Classic period, was a major preoccupation. Texts often refer to war between cities by placing a certain glyph, known as the 'shell-star' glyph, associated with Venus (the Maya Mars) over the main sign of the emblem glyph of a city under attack (see overleaf). The aim of warfare, in part, was to capture prominent individuals from an enemy state, put them to torture and finally to sacrifice them, normally by beheading, for which an appropriate glyph was used, depicting an axe. But this was the ritual, symbolic side. Particular glyphic expressions also talk of laying waste another city, of the demolition and 'throwing down' of monuments. A glyph for 'tribute' describes the probable outcome of the defeat of one city by another.

War, sacrifice and bloodshed figured large in the Maya scheme of things. But blood also meant descent, bloodline. Dynasticism is the

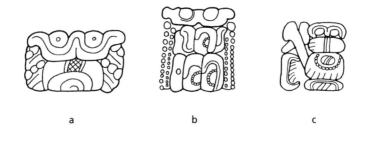

a   b   c

Warfare glyphs
a) 'Shell-star' glyph, representing war
b) 'Star over Seibal', to denote the city of Seibal under attack
c) an 'axe event'

most prominent theme of all in the monumental inscriptions. Certain glyphs clarify family relationships amongst members of a royal dynasty. Thus there are phrases which distinguish 'child of man', 'child of woman', 'child of parent' and also refer to siblings. A glyph for the 'founder' of royal lineages has been defined and another helps the epigrapher to work out the numerical position of a ruler in the order of succession, a succession that in normal circumstances would pass from father to son. Other signs suggest marriage alliances and refer to the visits of members of one royal family to those of another friendly city. Here again the emblem glyphs come into play, helping to explain who is forming a diplomatic relationship with whom. The concern with lineage, with dynastic politics as a major element of both the domestic and foreign affairs of the Maya world, seem to have been much the same as amongst the royal houses of Europe.

With this in mind, we can return to Lintel 21 at Yaxchilán to see what can be made of it today, following Linda Schele's reading of the text (see p. 149). The initial expression of time, the reference to the 'Lord of the Night' in B4, the age of the moon expressed in B5–B6, mean exactly what they did back in the 1950s. The more recently discovered sense is that on this date in AD 454, something happened. For the second, right-hand half of block A7 is a verb 'he dedicated'. It is followed in B7 by *chan ah t'zi* and 'it is his house'. This can be paraphrased as 'he dedicated the 4–bat place; it was his house'. *Chan ah t'zi*, 4–bat place, is a successful phonetic decipherment of a localized place-name. We have thus had an expression of time, followed by a verbal expression and an object, the house that was dedicated. In the conventional Maya word order we can now expect a subject. This is prefaced by a still imperfectly understood title 'sky-god', taking up A8 and some of

B8. Then follows the name of the subject, a ruler called 'Moon Skull' represented by the bottom two glyphs of B8 – the logographic sign for moon followed by a more pictorial logograph, a skull.

Moon Skull is known to be a ruler of Yaxchilán from other textual evidence. C1–D2 then tell us in more detail who he is. He was the seventh successor (C1) to the founder, for D1 is the now well-known 'founder' title. The name of the founder of the Yaxchilán ruling dynasty then follows in C2 – a man known as 'Progenitor Jaguar'. D2 provides two variants of the Yaxchilán emblem glyph, thus describing Progenitor Jaguar as the original 'Holy Lord of Yaxchilán'. So far, then, the sense of the text is that on 16 October 454 the ruler Moon Skull, seventh successor to the founder of the Yaxchilán Dynasty, Progenitor Jaguar, dedicated the house called '4–bat place'. The following section C3–D5 we have already translated. It takes us forward, using Thompson's Distance Numbers and 'Posterior Date Indicator', now glossed as 'and then it occurred', to the Calendar Round date 7 Muluc 17 Zec, or 12 May 752. C6 represents what Schele believed to be an equivalent phrase to A7–B7, 'he dedicated the *chan ah t'zi*'. D6 is still unclear, related perhaps to a deity. C7 is the same 'sky-god' title observed in A8–B8. Then follows a glyph we have come upon before, that of 'Bird Jaguar', the jaguar head and the small bird that rests on top of it. C8 reads '3 Katun Ahaw' rendered here as *ahpo*. This glyph, originally worked out by Proskouriakoff, means that Bird Jaguar had entered his third *katun* or period of twenty years. He was thus aged between forty and sixty. Finally, in D8, he is described, as so often, as 'He of twenty captives'.

Lintel 21 spanned the central doorway of a building at Yaxchilán known as 'Temple 22'. This '4–bat place', was rededicated by Bird Jaguar on 12 May 752, known from other textual references to have been nine days after his accession to the throne. In the lintel text he is linking his own dedication of a new building to the very same act by his predecessor Moon Skull, almost 300 years before. Temple 22 had just been rebuilt on the same '4–bat place' site. The dates that so transfixed Thompson and Teeple we might thus see as secondary to the other information that Bird Jaguar wants to convey. At a point very early in his reign, he is seeking to connect himself symbolically with his ancestors, both to Moon Skull and ultimately to the founder of the Yaxchilán royal line, Progenitor Jaguar. In this way, Lintel 21 commemorates a historical event and its central concerns are descent, legitimacy and the continuity of the royal line of Yaxchilán.

The dates and astronomical references, recorded here in such detail and with such care, were still of critical importance. For Maya rulers were always concerned to fix their actions precisely within the divinely ordained cycles of time. At Palenque, for example, royal history was very often expressed through a continuous 'count of the *katuns*'. After the Spanish Conquest histories in *katun* form continued to be recorded in the northern Yucatán in the native Books of Chilam Balam. By this time such records were a quite explicit basis for prophecy. Each individual *katun* in an independent cycle of thirteen, or approximately 260 years, was believed to possess its own prognosticatory complexion. Thus the nature or general texture of events played out within a particular *katun* in one cycle were liable to recur in an equivalent *katun* in the following one. The meticulous recording of the past thus served to predict the future.

When Bird Jaguar dedicated the house, the '4-bat place' at Yaxchilán, his actions would no doubt have been accompanied by elaborate ceremony. The word broadly translated as 'dedicated' in the Lintel 21 text has the more precise meaning of 'to enter with smoke', in other words to accompany the ceremonial with the burning of copal incense. On this occasion the text does not provide us with any more detail. But other inscriptions have greatly increased scholars' awareness of the religious, ritual role of the Maya ruler. For example, glyphic expressions refer to so-called 'period ending' ceremonies, at the completion of the *katuns* or the endings of other important calendrical cycles, and to special 'scattering rites', commonly depicted by a hand from which droplets of liquid fall (see overleaf). This liquid would often be a blood offering from the ruler himself, shed as part of the process of ritual communication between the divine lord, his ancestors, considered equally divine, and the gods. A very significant recent discovery, made simultaneously by the epigraphers Stephen Houston, David Stuart and Nikolai Grube, has been the so-called *uay* glyph, which depicts a human face half-covered with a jaguar pelt (see overleaf).[20] It stands for the lord's spirit companion, or a kind of supernatural alter ego, represented in the form of a powerful animal. Most often these seem to be bizarre composites with strong jaguar elements. A number of images of such *uay* spirits have now been identified on fine painted ceramics. Even today, traditional Maya communities in the highlands of Chiapas preserve a similar concept of a spirit companion or animal counterpart, though in this case of one individual species, who shares a part of the human soul. Another connotation of *uay* is to sleep or dream, the dreaming of visionary experience. Put together, the evidence suggests the central role of shamanistic transformation in Maya religion, the ruler as leader of religious ritual, king and shaman in one, able to transform into his spiritual alter ego and directly enter the realm of the supernatural.

scattering   'uay' glyph

On a seemingly more mundane level, decipherment has provided us with some more personal touches. This includes what has been defined by Peter Mathews as 'name-tagging', or the labelling of objects with the names of their owners. This hinges on knowledge of the use of 'u' as the possessive pronoun, initially deciphered, through a piece of inspired guess-work, by Brasseur de Bourbourg in the mid-nineteenth century. But it was Mathews who first read *u tup* or 'his ear spool' followed by the name of the owner on an inscribed obsidian ear ornament found at the city of Altun Ha in Belize. Since then, many other objects discovered in prestigious graves have revealed the same custom, most famously some carved bones from the tomb of the Tikal ruler Hasaw Chan K'awil beneath the great Temple I at Tikal. These read *u bak* ('his bone') followed by the ruler's name. The very name Hasaw Chan K'awil is itself a good example of the advance of phonetic decipherment. Many years ago he was simply known by archaeologists as 'Ruler A' from tomb 116 beneath Temple I. Then he was referred to as 'Ah Cacao', translated as 'he of the cocoa bean', because of what some saw as a resemblance between his name glyph and an opened-out cacao or chocolate pod. The present lengthy title is an accurate phonetic rendering of his name glyph. However, to date it has proved to be one of Linda Schele's examples where a successful phonetic decipherment has not been matched by understanding of what the Maya words actually mean.

The name-tagging custom extends in more elaborate form into the inscriptions on Maya ceramics, where formulaic texts often refer to 'his' or 'her' drinking vessel, bowl or tripod plate, followed by the name of the owner and by identification of the kind of maize food or chocolate

A rabbit as scribe, painting in a codex covered in jaguar pelt. Detail from a ceramic vessel.

Hand holding a paintbrush. An incised bone from the tomb of King Hasaw Chan K'awil of Tikal.

beverage for which the container was used. An even more direct personal imprint, and unique in pre-Columbian America, are the signatures of artists and scribes. The very finest pottery was occasionally signed, and on one celebrated vessel for chocolate drinking a man named 'Ah Maxam' describes himself as 'the son of the ruler of Naranjo and the Lady of Yaxhá'. Signatures also appear on sculpture. David Stuart first discovered these, including some on the Yaxchilán lintels, and identified the glyphic phrase *yuxul*, 'the carving of', to be followed by the artist's name.[22] *Yuxul* has also been found on some ceramics, but only where pots have been carved rather than painted, which has served as confirmation of the word's meaning. On some sculptures more than one name has been distinguished, suggesting workshop production with perhaps certain specialists carving particular sections (the Maya equivalent of the 'drapery man'), with the more recognized artist stepping in to complete the main details of the scene and the inscriptions. This area of decipherment is still in its infancy, and many of these personal titles remain obscure. The vast bulk of Maya works of art were not signed, so it is unlikely that in years to come we will find ourselves becoming familiar with the Praxiteles and Michelangelos of the Maya world. Nonetheless, the existence of Maya art that was signed self-consciously by individuals represents a considerable challenge to traditional Western concepts of the essentially anonymous, 'ethnographic' nature of pre-Hispanic art in the Americas.

MAYA HISTORY AND ARCHAEOLOGY

We now possess a Maya history, and what is more, a spoken language has been retrieved. We can now speak the names of Maya kings and members of their families – Pakal and Kan Balam of Palenque, Hasaw Chan K'awil from Tikal, the royal artist Ah Maxam from Naranjo – names that have not been uttered for more than a thousand years. And, dwelling on the meaning of Maya words, better equipped to understand the intricate symbolism of Maya art, which is so often a visual re-statement or even an elaboration of the meaning of an accompanying text, some scholars have begun to penetrate the subtleties of the Maya mind and see their world as they saw it themselves.

There are, however, very real deficiencies and shortcomings in the kind of documentary evidence we now possess. Firstly, it is limited in scope. The inscriptions shed very little direct light on the everyday lives of the vast majority of the Maya population. Records of economics, trade, administration, the kind of mundane information that would help to build up a picture of the more material functioning of the Maya world, do not exist. Some believe that Maya bark-paper books might have served for such record-keeping. But if they did play anything like the role of the clay tablets of ancient Mesopotamia, as repositories for government archives, accounts, even codes of law, they have all long since perished. Thus large areas of ancient Maya life remain, in effect, pre-historic. They can only be reconstructed through the techniques of archaeology, combined with judicious use of early Colonial accounts of Maya society, such as that of Diego de Landa, and some equally cautious analogy with traditional practices among Maya communities today.

The texts which have come down to us, from massive stone monuments to tiny inscribed jades found in tombs, reflect the interests of only a tiny minority – the topmost stratum of Maya society. The inscriptions were composed, and probably executed as well, by members of the ruling élite. They concern the things they wanted to write about. They are formal in tone and follow accepted, traditional modes of expression. The list of the doings of Maya rulers is recounted relentlessly in the third person. There are few negatives and little hint of failure. The achievements of Maya 'Holy Lords' are celebrated as formally and reverently, if not as fulsomely, as the deeds of those other gods in their own lifetime, the pharaohs of ancient Egypt.

As we saw in the previous chapter, Maya writing first emerged at the very time that Maya kingdoms were forming, at the end of the Preclassic period. There can be little doubt about the connection. Along with certain esoteric religious ideas, artistic images and the Long Count calendar, writing developed as a political tool used by the ruler to justify and maintain his position at the apex of society. Full literacy, the ability both to read and write, would always have been the preserve of a very small group among the élite. The cultivated exclusivity of this must have been daunting, suggesting the possession of unseen, sacred powers.

The degree of partial literacy – how far the wider population was able read the inscriptions – is impossible to calculate. It is commonly presumed that this was extremely limited. However, many ordinary Maya farmers, visitors to the major cities, would have become familiar with the texts on stelae and other more public monuments. If they were unable to read the bulk of them, some signs, especially the more pictographic ones, would have been perfectly understandable and often explained by the accompanying sculptural imagery – explained also, many now believe, by oral performance which used the inscribed monuments as props or prompts to help convey in song and pageant the stories behind the stones. Those stories concerned war and peace, the role of the gods in the Maya world, shared concerns of all Maya people. But, while style and emphasis might vary from city to city, the central focus was always the cult of the Maya ruler and his ancestors.

This brings us to what proved a divisive issue amongst Maya scholars for many years. If writing served, from its very beginnings, as a form of royal propaganda, how far did this go? In fact, could the texts be trusted at all? The initial reaction of some field archaeologists to the rapid advances of decipherment appears to have been ungenerous, to say the least. This was largely prompted, Michael Coe suggests, by feelings of envy and academic pique.[23] After years spent poring over potsherds or researching the niceties of Maya agricultural techniques in the swamps of Belize, the archaeologists found that all of a sudden smart young epigraphers were turning up with Maya 'history', receiving a great deal of media attention and making their own painstaking methods look decidedly dull and unproductive. The temptation was to deny the value of the epigraphers' work. Firstly, since their purpose was so obviously propagandist, what use were these writings? How could one separate truth from falsehood, history from self-serving myth? And, what is more, even if there was some truth to them, what they talked about – narrow dynastic concerns, the recording of religious rituals – was quite marginal to the broader study of Maya society, its economy and material infrastructure, those things with which 'dirt' archaeologists were concerned and which, in a more fundamental and important way, determined the nature of Maya civilization as a whole. Thus, having disposed of one erroneous thesis which paid too much attention to Maya élite culture, that of Thompson and Morley, it became easy to characterize epigraphy as another equally unbalanced preoccupation with the same section of society. Only the obsession this time was not with peaceful, star-gazing theologians but with blood-letting, sacrifice and Maya kings as trancing shamans.

Today, although some residual animosity lingers between a few epigraphers and archaeologists, and may still add a compelling edge to conferences where both are gathered together, the dust has largely settled. In truth, the archaeologists had valid cautionary points to make. Epigraphers now recognize that the texts with which they work, though extraordinarily rich about certain areas of Maya life, are partial and have to be rigorously tested and augmented by other kinds of evidence. Certain themes, such as elaborate stories linking Maya rulers to the gods and to ancestors thousands of years in the past, are quite clearly mythological. But such material can be separated from the narrative histories that speak of a ruler's earthly deeds. Here we are on different ground. Epigraphers have to approach these with due care, like any historian. Blind faith in one version of events is obviously misplaced. Yet the continuing progress of decipherment has meant that in certain instances a ruler's claims can be assessed critically by cross-checking against accounts of the same events given by a different city. The course and outcome of a war, for example, can on occasion be viewed from different perspectives. As we shall see in the following chapters, Maya 'historical' records appear to stand up well under this scrutiny. A certain cosmetic economy with the truth for domestic consumption is evident, the kind of bias that historians the world over have to deal with, but of sustained campaigns of official lies there is, to date at least, little evidence.

Ironically, perhaps, it is field archaeologists themselves who are now beginning to prove the veracity of many of the ancient texts. Some lengthy dynastic histories were once thought to be fictional, the invention of Maya kings short of a pedigree and seeking to legitimize their right to rule. Yet recently, as we shall see in the next chapter, archaeologists have discovered key ancestral bodies, along with confirmation of their identities amongst accompanying texts and images, thus proving such genealogical texts to have been accurate all along.

The disciplines of field archaeology and epigraphy obviously need each other, since neither approach can tell the whole story. One cannot expect to gain a complete picture of Maya society from the inscriptions, any more than you can find out what ancient life was like along the Nile valley from the texts of ancient Egypt alone. Thus today, while analysis of Maya hieroglyphic inscriptions goes on, archaeological research within a Maya city and its surrounding region deals with those remains that do not speak, testing out on the ground the histories we now possess and putting the recorded doings of Maya lords into a wider context and a critical perspective. The era of a truly 'historical archaeology', as a number of scholars now term it, is underway in the Maya world. It is this integrated approach that we shall now follow in charting the rise and fall of Maya cities in the Classic period.

CHAPTER FOUR

The Early Classic

The term 'Classic Period' was introduced earlier this century to describe the Maya at the height of their powers and prosperity. It was perceived as a period of extraordinarily original achievement, of intellectual and artistic accomplishment unmatched in any other part of Mesoamerica, all seemingly contained within a period of six centuries between about AD 300 and AD 900. Today the lustre of that Golden Age remains undimmed. Yet we now know the tenor of those times to have been very different from the arcadian image that scholars once contrived. Competition and conflict, burgeoning populations stretching agricultural ingenuity and the carrying capacity of the forest environment – such were the pressures, ultimately to become the stresses, that formed the background to the brilliance and creativity of the period.

It is also apparent today, as we saw in Chapter 2, that many of the essential ingredients of Maya civilization were already in place by the beginning of the Classic period: urban centres, great building projects, intensive agriculture, the emergence of a powerful ruling élite, such details as the use of the corbel vault in architecture and fine painted ceramics. The difference, which still justifies the use of the term, is that during the Classic period all these elements came together throughout the Southern Lowlands. In particular, the anonymous rulers of the Preclassic became *k'ul ahaws* or Holy Lords. The Classic was, supremely, the time of kings in Maya society, individuals who assumed power over their city state through that institutionalized royal succession advertised in the inscriptions on their monuments.

In this and the following chapter we will be concerned with reconstructing the course of events and tracing, as best we can in the present state of knowledge, the story of the major participants in lowland Maya civilization. For the Late Classic period, from about AD 600–900, this becomes an easier task, since the evidence from archaeology and

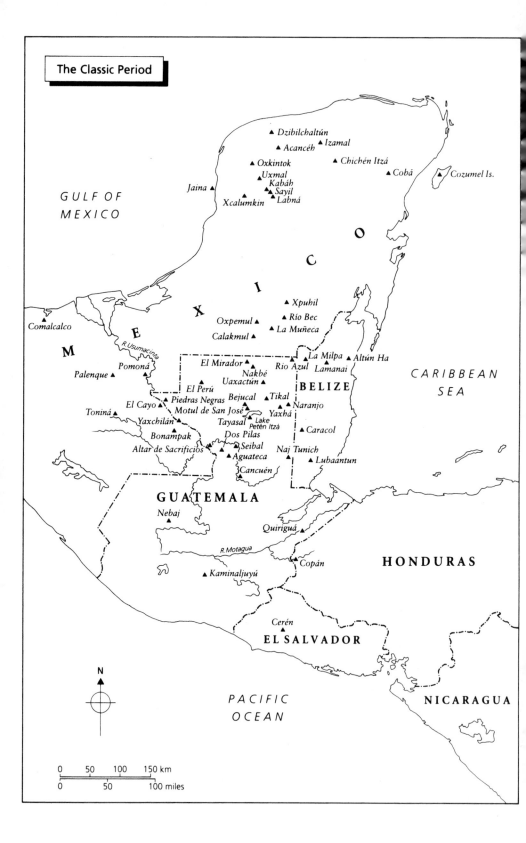

The Classic Period

Dzibilchaltún
Acancéh Izamal
Oxkintok
Uxmal Chichén Itzá Cobá
Kabáh Cozumel Is.
Jaina Sayil
Xcalumkin Labná

GULF OF
MEXICO

Comalcalco

M E X I C O

R. Usumacinta

Xpuhil
Oxpemul Río Bec
Calakmul La Muñeca

El Mirador La Milpa Altún Ha
Pomoná Nakbé Rio Azul Lamanai
Palenque Uaxactún BELIZE
El Perú CARIBBEAN
El Cayo Piedras Negras Bejucal Tikal SEA
Toniná Motul de San José Yaxhá Naranjo
Yaxchilán Tayasal Lake
Bonampak Petén Itzá
Altar de Sacrificios Dos Pilas Caracol
Seibal Naj Tunich
Aguateca Lubaántun
Cancuén

GUATEMALA

Nebaj
Quiriguá

R. Motagua

Copán HONDURAS

Kaminaljuyú

Cerén

EL SALVADOR NICARAGUA

N

PACIFIC
OCEAN

0 50 100 150 km
0 50 100 miles

hieroglyphic inscriptions is much more abundant. For the Early Classic however, *c.* AD 250–600, the problems are formidable. So many Maya sites have not been excavated at all, and at those which have been, remains from these centuries are still often buried under the temples and palaces of later rulers. The epigraphic record is very limited. Although a number of cities, in later inscriptions, trace the foundation of royal dynasties to this time, until the sixth century surviving contemporary texts are few and restricted to a very small number of sites. The value of the information they provide is also poor, compared with the more revealing records of later times.

Nevertheless, research into the Early Classic has made some dramatic strides in recent years. It has introduced important new players, and personalities, onto the stage of Maya history and succeeded in pointing up in much more detail certain characteristics of the period long identified by Maya scholars, serving to distinguish it from the Late Classic. The first is the profound impact upon the Maya world of the great civilization of Teotihuacan in central Mexico; the second the dominant role of sites in the north-eastern Petén of Guatemala and southern Campeche in Mexico, cities that had already become firmly established in the Preclassic and had survived, and indeed become strengthened, after the fall of the Preclassic giant, El Mirador. It was in this region that dynastic rule among the lowland Maya first took root. The best known city of all, whose emergence has traditionally defined the onset of the Early Classic period, is Tikal.

THE RISE OF TIKAL

The Pennsylvania University Museum project in the 1950s and 1960s first revealed the full extent and nature of Tikal as it developed during the Classic period. It grew into a dispersed garden city, some sixty square kilometres of residences with kitchen gardens and cultivated plots in between, supporting a population in the tens of thousands. At its heart lay the magnificent nucleus of fine limestone buildings, the palaces and temple pyramids presided over by the Tikal royal line, the nobility and their retainers. The focal point of the city is the 'Great Plaza', bounded to the east and west by the famous pyramids, Temples I and II (see plate section, pp. 5–6, 9 and plan on p. 107). To the north lies the so-called North Acropolis, with its ranks of smaller temples and in the plaza at its feet a series of stelae and altars, some of them plain lime-stone slabs, others bearing hieroglyphic texts and carved with the now much-weathered images of Tikal's kings.[1]

For the visitor who might have come from the more modest ruins of Palenque or Copán, the sheer scale of Tikal's principal monuments is awe-inspiring, with their great masses of masonry, vertigo-inducing stairways scaling the principal temples and vast roofcombs, now amor-phous crests of eroded limestone rearing up out of the forest canopy but which once bore gigantic, multi-coloured stucco figures of Tikal's rulers. From the tops of Temples I and II, from the platforms in front of their tiny summit rooms, one can see the roofcombs of the other great temple pyramids. Temple V rises to the south and Temples III and IV away to the west. Temple IV is the very tallest of all, some sixty metres high, and forms the western boundary of the city centre. On the evidence of the one burial so far discovered beneath Temple I, all of the great pyramids were intended as mortuary shrines to Tikal royalty. As artificial moun-tains soaring heavenwards, they were a means of communication with the gods and deified ancestors. But they are also statements, in our terms, of more wordly power, in that northern Petén tradition of unalloyed architectural size established in the Late Preclassic period by Nakbé and El Mirador.

To the south of the Great Plaza, beyond a disproportionately tiny ballcourt hemmed in alongside Temple I, lies the Central Acropolis, a large complex of forty-five buildings arranged around a series of interior courtyards. These structures, some of two or three storeys, have mul-tiple entrances and contain what are today dark, damp and generally very small rooms with extremely thick walls, as prepossessing as the dun-geons in a Norman castle. Tikal never achieved that airy spaciousness due to their greater technical command of the corbel vault, displayed by the architects of Palenque. These buildings are still commonly known as palaces, the presumption being (and it has to remain largely a presump-tion, since the archaeological evidence is equivocal) that they were residential and administrative buildings used by successive rulers and their entourage. Many of the chambers have built-in stone ledges that probably served as beds and upon which mats or skins were draped. Indeed, once fires were lit to dry them out and persuade the bats to depart, these buildings were used by Maudslay and Maler as their lodgings.

Beyond the Central Acropolis, next to Temple V, is the expanse of the South Acropolis, still unexcavated and rising from an enormous base platform covering more than 20,000 square metres. To the west lies the 'Plaza of the Seven Temples', the temples themselves set in a row on its eastern side, with 'palace' structures to the south and west and a curious 'triple ball-court' to the north. Further in this direction one enters the complex of the so-called 'Mundo Perdido' or Lost World, centred on the great flat-topped pyramid with stairways on all four sides flanked by masks of the Sun God that was first raised in the Late Preclassic period.

Exploring the ruins of the city today, wandering through the forest from one group of buildings and spacious plazas to another, some of these a considerable distance apart, the lack of any more concentrated urban plan as we would know it is all too apparent. This is true of all Maya sites. But at Tikal, as in most cities of the Petén, the scattered layout was largely dictated by the topography, which consists of parallel series of limestone ridges that rise above low-lying, swampy areas. The major architecture thus formed discrete clusters of construction upon levelled areas of the higher ground. Raised causeways or *sacbes* were constructed to bridge the swamps and link the different complexes of buildings. Here at Tikal the causeways, made of packed and plastered limestone, are particularly broad and impressive. Given the names of some of the early explorers and archaeologists, the Maler, Maudslay and Méndez causeways connect the Great Plaza and Temple IV with residential groups to the north and to Temple VI, also known as the Temple of the Inscriptions, some distance from the centre to the south-east. These great urban arteries facilitated day-to-day traffic during the months of heavy rains and doubled as dams. On a less practical level, no doubt they also served to underline the importance of the powerful, sacred places they connected and they are best imagined as ceremonial ways, which at the time of major celebrations would have been thronged with people and borne colourful processions of musicians and dancers, and Maya lords carried on elaborate litters between the temples and palaces.

Of course, one also has to envisage the centre of Tikal in ancient times without forest. The vast majority of trees would have been cut down to burn the limestone to produce mortar and plaster. Some woods were used for construction, in particular the dense, extremely hard and termite-resistant sapodilla which was employed for the lintels of temple doorways and the beams to help support the enormous burden of

Tikal's corbel vaults. At times of major building activity, which in the later Classic would have been almost continuous, thousands of labourers would have been drafted in. The limestone was immediately available and quarried on-site. The large man-made depressions this formed, along with some natural ones, were plastered in order to seal them and used as reservoirs. Water storage was a matter of critical importance and its collection and distribution required centralized planning and hydraulic engineering of a high order. The principal plazas, paved with brilliant white stucco, were laid out with a finely calculated gradient so that in the rainy season they drained water through a system of canals into the reservoirs, from which in the dry-season months it would be distributed to the surrounding population.

Most of the fabric of Tikal that one sees today dates from the Late Classic period. But there are two areas of the city which were occupied in the Preclassic, considerably embellished and extended in the Early Classic, yet which escaped being submerged by later building activity. The most important of these is the North Acropolis (see plate section, pp. 6, 9). From before the time of Christ it was the burial ground of the city's earliest, more shadowy rulers and it became the most revered, sacred spot within Tikal. Successive temples and shrines to royal ancestors were constructed here, one on top of the other. Around AD 250 it seems that all earlier structures were levelled and a fresh start made. Three hundred years later, eight individual temple pyramids, each with a tall, elaborate roofcomb and a central stairway flanked by masks of the gods that led to a small sanctuary at the summit, had been laid out on a great artificial platform a hundred metres long by eighty metres across. Little further construction was carried out on the North Acropolis after this time, and it was significantly remodelled only once more in the Late Classic. The Tikal Project excavated here for many years, sinking a massive trench straight through it and painstakingly unravelling the daunting complexities of its repeated construction and reconstruction.

The second area to reveal signifcant remains from the Early Classic is the 'Lost World' complex, where Guatemalan archaeologists have made major discoveries since the late 1970s. In the Early Classic the central Preclassic pyramid was enlarged, formal plazas laid out at its base and a series of structures built around it. This included three temples positioned on a raised platform to the east. Almost identical to a well-known and thoroughly surveyed arrangement of buildings at Uaxactún, it seems that this formed an astronomical observatory, the east-facing stairway of the pyramid being the observation point and the temples on the platform providing fixed lines of sight from which to plot the rising of the sun on equinoxes and solstices. Thus, if the North Acropolis in the Early Classic was the hallowed home of royal ancestors, the stage for the accession of kings and where successive rulers set up their stelae and altars, the Lost World appears to have been the focus for public rituals to observe the movements of planets and stars and mark the passage of time.

Combining the results of archaeological investigation of these two key areas with evidence from Tikal's monumental inscriptions enables one to build up a still incomplete outline of the city's early dynastic history. Here we will follow the dynastic sequence as revised very recently by the epigraphers Nikolai Grube and Simon Martin (see Appendix 2).[2] The founder of the Tikal royal line was a man named Yax Moch Xok, translated as 'First Scaffold Shark'. Inscribed monuments from his own time are unknown but he is referred to as lineage founder in a number of later texts. None of these references is accompanied by a date, but today it is felt that he may have reigned as early as the first century AD. His name is thus linked with Burial 85, the tomb from this period located deep in the very heart of the North Acropolis and which, as we saw in Chapter 2, contained the headless body of a man accompanied, amongst other grave goods, by a greenstone mask bearing the three-pointed royal headband. Even if hard evidence emerges to prove the connection between Burial 85 and Yax Moch Xok, we know that he was not the very first ruler of Tikal. There were many powerful men before him. But due to his particular achievements, perhaps in warfare, perhaps in uniting diverse Tikal lineages, he was the charismatic individual chosen by later kings to be commemorated as their revered founding father.

Of any immediate successors to Yax Moch Xok, nothing is known. The first, very obscure character, whose position in the sequence is unclear, is a man who has been called Scroll Ahau Jaguar and who was once thought to be represented on Stela 29, the oldest surviving dated stela from Tikal, which was set up in AD 292. This is still the earliest complete Long Count date recorded in the Maya lowlands. The face of the much-damaged monument, broken in antiquity like so many of Tikal's stelae and found not in the North Acropolis but in a rubbish-dump close to Temple III, bears a portrait of a king dressed in royal regalia and carrying some of the most powerful symbols of rulership, including the double-headed serpent bar. The knotted bundle, the main

sign of the Tikal emblem glyph, appears here for the first time, surmounting a head of the jaguar sun-god attached to his chest. Floating in
the air above the king and looking directly downwards at him is the head
of an ancestor, possibly Scroll Ahau Jaguar's father, or maybe even Yax
Moch Xok himself. The reverse of the monument carries the Long
Count date, which is the only part of the inscription that survives. What
remains of this stela is magnificently carved, the confident command of
the medium suggesting a long and rich tradition of such sculpture, of
which we possess tragically few examples today.

The first well-documented Tikal king is known as Great Jaguar Paw,
who was the fourteenth in line after Yax Moch Xok. He ruled, it would
seem, from AD 317 to 378. It is to Great Jaguar Paw's reign that the
Guatemalan archaeologist Juan Pedro Laporte attributes much of the
rebuilding of the Lost World complex. The Central Acropolis would
also appear to have been developed during this period, since a ceramic
vessel discovered beneath one of the buildings bears a text which refers
to the dedication of the 'Sacred House' of Jaguar Paw, suggesting that he
had his palace there.

Other extant references to Great Jaguar Paw, like those to Yax Moch
Xok, are almost entirely retrospective and very brief. We have no knowledge of any of the events of his long reign until two years before its
close. It was then that the now fragmentary Stela 39 (see overleaf) was
erected in front of a building in the Lost World complex. On one side
are the lower body and legs of the ruler, trampling on the prostrate and
richly attired figure of a bound captive and holding in his left hand a
large flint decapitating axe in the form of a jaguar paw. There is no
doubt that the bound individual, with a goatee beard, many ornaments
around his head and all the signs of being a noble individual, was destined for sacrifice. The inscription on the reverse says that Jaguar Paw
celebrated the completion of the seventeenth *katun*, which being in
Baktun 8 corresponds to a date of AD 376, and that he let his own blood
from his tongue as part of the ceremony. There is also mention of a particular location, a 'sky place' within Tikal, where these events took place.
Many believe this is a reference to the Lost World pyramid and that the
sacrificial victim met his end there. However, less than two years after all
these celebrations, we now know that the dynasty of Great Jaguar Paw
was to come to an abrupt and violent end. Momentous events took
place in this year, which epigraphers have only begun to piece together
very recently. They involved other major players beyond the city itself.

Stela 39, Tikal.

TIKAL, UAXACTÚN AND STRANGERS FROM THE WEST

Following the shady path through the forest that leads visitors to the ruins of Tikal, a sign appears that points the way to the site of Uaxactún. Few go that way. The track is rough and winding and even in the dry season you need a four-wheel drive. The journey can take up to three hours. But the distance in a straight line from Tikal to Uaxactún is little more than twenty-five kilometres, for the Maya an easy morning's walk.

From Preclassic times these two cities grew up in parallel. Like the early villagers of Tikal, the first farmers of Uaxactún congregated around the ridge-tops of the undulating Petén terrain. Over time, they also levelled some of the hills and constructed platforms to support brightly painted and roof-combed temples and funerary monuments to royal ancestors. Both cities built impressive stepped pyramids, ornamented with giant masks of the jaguar sun-god from which they marked the turning of the years. By the fourth century AD at least, Uaxactún also possessed a royal dynasty memorialized on stone stelae set up in front of their temples. But very few Uaxactún stelae survive. Those that do are much eroded, their texts barely legible, and the names of the Uaxactún kings still elude epigraphers. The iconography of these fourth-century stelae, the earliest dating from AD 328, is much the same as at Tikal: the standing figure of the ruler adorned with the appurtenances of kingship and at his feet a cowering prisoner who, to heighten the dramatic effect, is invariably depicted on a much smaller scale.

In both of these cities the humiliated captive destined for sacrifice was the symbolic expression of royal prestige and authority, an early manifestation of what was to become a recurring Classic-period image. In later centuries we know that such representations were more than empty metaphor. These trampled people were real individuals. But here, in the first part of the Early Classic, it is impossible to know who these prisoners were, where they came from and the kind of war in which Tikal or Uaxactún might have been engaged. Texts from these times provide very little direct information about such things or political matters in general, being almost exclusively concerned with ritual events, the celebration of period endings and the accessions of kings. It is only in the Late Classic period that bellicose encounters begin to be referred to more regularly and the names and origin of captives recorded. Even then, some cities are less forthcoming than others in their references to martial events.

The notion of the pacifist Maya may be long gone, but the nature and level of warfare over the centuries remains one of the most debated issues in Maya archaeology.[3] A decade or so ago, an influential school of thought argued that Maya war, at least in the Early Classic, was of low intensity, largely involving raiding and skirmishes, since its fundamental objective was not the conquest of territory but the acquisition of captives for sacrifice. In effect it was a ritualized war, with a prescribed set of rules, a kind of chivalric code adhered to by the participants, who were not ordinary farmers but strictly the élite of Maya society. Once the requisite number of prisoners had been obtained, the victors would withdraw with their prizes and the previous territorial *status quo* would be maintained. The blood of the noble captive would be shed as an offering to the gods and such ritual sacrifice would serve to perpetuate the charisma of the ruler and his royal line.

Many who once held this view have changed their minds. For example, close examination of some of the old reports from archaeological excavation at Uaxactún and the North Acropolis of Tikal has led to a reassessment of the extensive evidence of burning and destruction of many of their monuments in the Late Preclassic and Early Classic. It is now felt that much of this evidence suggests not simply the ritual destruction of buildings prior to the construction of new temples on the same site, but purposeful desecration perpetrated in all likelihood by aggressive enemies. Such a conclusion ties in with what others have long thought, that powerful and successful cities such as Tikal and Uaxactún were forged by war. The pressure of increasing populations and competition over agricultural land during the Late Preclassic contributed to the emergence of war-lords and royal dynasties in the first place.

Whether Tikal and Uaxactún were periodically at war with each other by the fourth century AD no one can say. But it would seem impossible for two such close and potent neighbours to have remained independent powers for long. What occurred in AD 378 led to the final elimination of any threat to Tikal from Uaxactún. The sequence of events involved not these two cities alone, but people who were foreigners, who came from way beyond the boundaries of the Maya world.

More than a thousand kilometres from Tikal, just to the north-east of the urban sprawl of modern Mexico City, lie the ruins of an ancient metropolis without equal anywhere in the ancient Americas. The later Aztecs who wandered its by then deserted streets, in awe of the city's staggering scale and the sacred power that it retained in the minds of Mesoamerican peoples, called it Teotihuacan or, in a recent translation, 'the place of those who possess the road to the gods'.

Already settled by about 300 BC, Teotihuacan grew with astonishing speed in the two centuries after Christ and by 500 had a population approaching a quarter of a million, making it one of the largest cities in the world at that time. Covering more than twenty square kilometres, the city was constructed along a north–south axis with a great central avenue, known as the Street of the Dead, running for five kilometres at its heart (see plate section, p. 10). On either side, 2000 residential compounds or apartment blocks were put up, made of stone and mud-brick, modules for urban life, each with its own shrines and communal platform for religious ritual. There was a grid plan of streets, a market area, sections of the city devoted to particular crafts such as the production of obsidian tools, and special districts set aside where groups of foreigners seem to have been congregated.

Six hundred individual pyramids have been counted here, two of quite exceptional scale. At the northern end of the Street of the Dead lies the Pyramid of the Moon, set beneath a venerated sacred mountain, an extinct volcano known as 'Cerro Gordo'. To the east of the main street and facing the setting sun stands the Pyramid of the Sun, rising on five squat stepped levels to a height of over sixty metres. It is a plain yet spectacularly vast monument, one of the most imposing structures ever built in the New World. In the size of some of their individual pyramids the great Maya cities of El Mirador, Tikal and Calakmul bear comparison. Yet in its ambitious grand design and centralized planning – most of Teotihuacan seems to have been built in one burst of creative energy, employing tens of thousands of labourers over little more than a century – it is unlike anything ever built by the Maya.[4]

Teotihuacan sustained itself through efficient agriculture. The valley was rich, with large areas of land that could be cultivated under irrigation fed by local springs. But its power grew immensely through trade. Nearby was the source of a distinctive green obsidian of exceptional quality, which was in demand all over Mesoamerica. The city also sat at a key intersection of long-established trade routes for many other valuable commodities travelling both north and south. It became the hub of a commercial empire unmatched until the time of the Aztecs.

Archaeologists have made detailed surveys and excavated many parts of Teotihuacan, but mystery still surrounds the people who built it. Where they came from, their ethnic identity and the language they spoke is unknown. They left no written records that have survived, only a few indecipherable symbols or notations. They had no divine kings or ruling dynasties that are as yet easily definable. It was once believed that Teotihuacan, too, was a pacifist theocracy. But this has gone the way of similar theories about the Maya. The regime that ran Teotihuacan was authoritarian and militaristic. It seems that the city was so rich that, unlike any other contemporary people, they could even afford a standing army. And at the heart of the success of this supremely efficient and ambitious civilization was a state ideology of war and sacrifice, and the belief that Teotihuacan was the very place where life on earth began.

The city's most important religious precinct, known as the Ciudadela, was constructed at its precise geographical centre. Within it stands the Temple of the Feathered Serpent. At the dedication of the temple in about AD 225, great numbers of warriors, their hands tied behind their backs, were sacrificed. They were then buried in groups precisely positioned corresponding to the cardinal directions. The archaeologists who excavated the temple suggest that the total number of victims interred here was 260, which is the same as the number of days in the sacred calendar observed throughout Mesoamerica. Indeed, Clemency Coggins believed that this temple served to commemorate the birth of the calendar and the creation of humankind at Teotihuacan.[5] For the image of the feathered serpent, known to the Aztecs as Quetzalcoatl, is an ancient and enduring one in Mesoamerican thought and closely associated with concepts of human origins. In the highland Maya myths of the Popol Vuh, for example, it was the feathered serpent, called Gucumatz in Quiché Maya, who lived in the great primordial ocean in the darkness before creation. Through its word the earth and the first animate beings took form. In this way the feathered serpent can be related to that moment when time itself began. And to keep time on its course and maintain the workings of the cosmos, what was demanded above all else, among the people of Teotihuacan as among the Maya, was the blood of human sacrifice.

There is another, even more sacred place in Teotihuacan. Beneath the Pyramid of the Sun is a series of caves. These were venerated and used for rituals in very ancient times and were almost certainly the first focus for religious worship in the city, over which the Pyramid was later constructed. Caves, offering access to the Underworld and the supernatural realms, were viewed as extremely powerful locations and commonly linked with ideas of human emergence. The concept of this uniquely impressive city amongst the mountains of central Mexico as a place of origins seems to have been assiduously promoted by her rulers. Given Teotihuacan's conspicuous success, it is hardly surprising that the belief was to gain credence through much of Mesoamerica. It endured long after the violent destruction of much of Teotihuacan in the seventh century and its decline thereafter. The site remained a holy centre of pilgrimage until the Spanish Conquest and the Aztecs believed that the era in which they lived, the fifth great cycle of time, began when the gods met at Teotihuacan and sacrificed themselves to ensure the rising of the sun and moon.

Besides the Feathered Serpent, two other highly important but still poorly understood deities presided at Teotihuacan, depicted in sculpture and brightly painted murals which covered the plastered walls of buildings. The first was a 'Great Goddess', associated with rain and fertility and depicted in wall paintings as an Earth-Motherly provider of all the bounties of nature, perhaps linked in some way with a vision of Teotihuacan as both place of creation and earthly paradise. The second was a Storm God, to be known by the Aztecs as Tlaloc, who was also a god of war and particularly related, it would seem, to the rulers of the city. Tlaloc is instantly recognizable by his goggle eyes and sometimes protruding set of teeth.

The artists of Teotihuacan also portrayed people besides the representations of the gods in their murals. Yet these are no more than archetypes from their seemingly regimented society. There are warriors who bear spear-throwers and darts, and are often associated with the characteristics of Tlaloc, and figures who appear to be priests, carrying ceremonial bags that perhaps contained ritual objects. Such figures, and indeed Teotihuacan society as a whole, are often characterized as missionaries. For Teotihuacan influence spread far and wide. They were a power that no one in Mesoamerica could ignore, who established faraway outposts and connections and meddled in the affairs of their neighbours – militarily, commercially and as religious evangelists – in a shadowy way that is often hard to define. It is hard to resist the comparison with the influence of the USA in Central America in more recent times.

Teotihuacan established a particularly powerful presence in the Maya highlands. Kaminaljuyú, the greatest of the highland cities, had gone into a rapid decline around AD 250. But its equally swift recovery a century or so later is undoubtedly linked to the presence, in one form or another, of Teotihuacan. The burials of Kaminaljuyú's rulers contain much green obsidian and characteristic Teotihuacan pottery, including lidded vessels of ample, slightly flaring cylindrical form on tripod feet which were stuccoed and brightly painted with images often comparable to those on Teotihuacan murals. Much of the centre of Kaminaljuyú was reconstructed in the distinctive architectural style of Teotihuacan. Like the Temple of the Feathered Serpent, façades were built in the so-called *talud–tablero* style, the *tablero* being a rectangular, horizontal framed section projecting from the façade and often decorated with paintings or sculpture, and the *talud* or *talus*, a sloping wall in between. From the base of their associate Kaminaljuyú, Teotihuacan was also to monopolize most of the Mesoamerican obsidian trade and gain privileged access to commodities such as jade, quetzal feathers, cacao and other products, including those from the Maya lowlands.

With the rise of this new imperial power, it should come as no surprise to find central Mexican goods and certain stylistic influences in lowland Maya cities. Green obsidian, for example, and Teotihuacan-style ceramic vessels are found at a number of southern lowland sites by the beginning of the fourth century AD. At Tikal a *talud–tablero* façade was applied to a temple in the Lost World group between AD 250 and 300. But this particular stylistic intrusion presaged a very special relationship between these two cities. For quite suddenly, at the end of the fourth century, Teotihuacan influence increases dramatically in the archaeological record. Fine quality tripod vessels with painted stucco decoration appear in prestigious Tikal tombs and not just one building but a whole plaza full of temples in the Lost World complex was to be covered in *talud–tablero* façades.

Stela 31, Tikal.

The most striking evidence for the impact of Teotihuacan comes from stone sculpture, in particular from the most beautiful and historically significant of all Tikal's surviving inscribed monuments, Stela 31. The Tikal Project discovered it buried in the North Acropolis, and although the base of the stela and part of the inscription is missing, it is otherwise in remarkably good condition. The monument was set up in AD 445 by a Tikal ruler named 'Stormy Sky' to mark the completion of the first *katun* since his accession to the throne. The front of this rough-hewn shaft of limestone – Early Classic stelae at Tikal always being of such robust, unfinished form – shows Stormy Sky in the act of crowning himself with an elaborate version of the Maya headband of rulership, which also contains the hieroglyph for his own name. Above him, in by now conventional fashion, his father is depicted as an ancestral deity. The details of Stormy Sky's costume and other ceremonial attributes are also of traditional Maya form. However, on the sides of the monument, flanking and seemingly protecting him, are two figures that are not Maya at all (see below). They are dressed as Teotihuacan warriors. Their costume is distinctively Central Mexican and they hold the lethal spear-thrower and darts always carried by Teotihuacan soldiers and which the Maya, it seems, had not adopted. They also carry shields bearing one of the most characteristic Teotihuacan images, the leering, goggle-eyed face of the god Tlaloc.

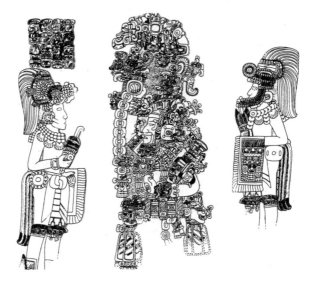

The reverse of Stela 31 bears a very lengthy inscription, unusually long for the Early Classic period, which would suggest that to the Maya themselves this was a highly important document. It has proved an extremely difficult text to understand, due not so much to the preservation of the hieroglyphs as to the obscurity of the glyphic phraseology. Little by little, key information has been teased from it, a fascinating case-study of the emergence of Maya history. By the late 1970s a broad understanding of the contents of the text had been reached. It presented epigraphers with an incomplete but priceless king-list, upon which most of the early dynastic history of Tikal has come to be based. The inscription refers to Yax Moch Xoc as the founder of the dynasty and goes on to name Great Jaguar Paw. Then in a slightly later, more easily decipherable section, it mentions the following ruler, the fifteenth successor. This was a man called Curl Nose, who succeeded to the throne in AD 379 and was the father of Stormy Sky.

Much attention came to be paid to Curl Nose. His tomb, identifiable from a small jade carved with his name glyph, was very rich and contained some magnificent pottery. There was an incense-burner in the form of an aged god of the Underworld seated on a stool made from human bones and holding a severed head in his cupped hands. This uniquely fearsome piece of work was accompanied by a series of cylindrical fresco-painted chocolate pots and other vessels which were clearly of Teotihuacan derivation. Such grave goods were very like material from the tombs of Kaminaljuyú. Curl Nose's tomb, Burial 10, was discovered in the North Acropolis and above it were two stelae that he had dedicated. Both represent him front on, an unusual pose for a Tikal ruler in the Early Classic, and dressed in very Teotihuacan style.

It seemed evident, then, that Tikal and Teotihuacan had formed some kind of relationship immediately following the reign of Great Jaguar Paw. It had lasted into the reign of Stormy Sky, but then appeared to have waned, for Stormy Sky had represented himself on Stela 31 as a traditionally Maya king. But what had the nature of that relationship been? Some scholars, such as Clemency Coggins, who did much of the early work linking the inscriptions and the archaeology of Tikal, believed that foreign influence had been imposed in some way, very probably via Kaminaljuyú. Curl Nose himself may have been a Mexicanized Maya from that highland city who perhaps married into the Jaguar Paw dynasty. Others thought that Tikal might even have been conquered or taken over more directly by Teotihuacan, or that at the very least Mexican warriors had been hired to weigh the balance in factional fights among Tikal lineages.

During the 1980s, however, the idea of such more overt Teotihuacan interference came to be discounted by the majority of scholars. Almost certainly there had been Teotihuacan merchants in the city, a kind of chamber of commerce or 'embassy', as it was termed, in the way that excavations at Teotihuacan revealed that groups of lowland Maya may have been established there. They would have been accompanied by contingents of Mexican warriors, since this was how Teotihuacan commercial expeditions seem to have operated, soldiers riding shotgun, as it were, with the cargo. But it was felt most likely that Tikal rulers had merely adopted something of the iconography, the religious ideology, in general terms the formidable aura of the distant great power. In truth, the limits of the evidence meant that a whole range of possibilities remained open.

Stela 31, however, had still not been fully deciphered and this, coupled with understanding of a few other key monuments, was where progress was made. Above all, it emerged that there was another character, a man given the memorable name 'Smoking Frog', who had to be taken into account, especially in the short space of time in AD 378–9, before Curl Nose came to the throne. He was mentioned on Stela 31 and also, significantly, on Stela 5 from Uaxactún. Here Smoking Frog was depicted in Teotihuacan military costume, holding a spear-thrower and a war-club set with obsidian blades. In the inscription on the reverse he seemed to be identified as a lord of Tikal, accompanied by a date of 16 January 378. Many eminent epigraphers had been studying the inscriptions of Tikal and Uaxactún for this period, but it was Linda Schele who now took the lead.[6] On Stela 31 she saw a reference to this same date coupled with the name of Smoking Frog and a phrase she interpreted as 'he warred'. She acknowledged that the 4–glyph phrase in question was still a little uncertain, but she was convinced that Smoking Frog 'demolished and threw down the buildings of Uaxactún'. Furthermore, another phrase suggested that Great Jaguar Paw had 'let blood from his genitals to sanctify the victory of his warriors'.

Schele and her colleague David Freidel thus proposed that Smoking Frog was a younger brother of the ageing Great Jaguar Paw. By AD 378 relations with Uaxactún had come to a head. Led by Smoking Frog, Tikal embarked on the conquest of Uaxactún, and in doing so they adopted the full military paraphernalia and a completely new ideology of all-out war derived from Teotihuacan. It was astronomically driven, so-called 'Tlaloc–Venus' war, and they believed that from this time on, as was certainly evident in the Late Classic, the Maya timed their battles and went to war following the movements of Venus, geared particularly to the planet's appearance as Evening Star. Smoking Frog then became ruler of Uaxactún and Curl Nose, a son of Jaguar Paw, acceded as Lord of Tikal soon after the elderly ruler's death in 379. Thus the rulers of Tikal had indeed absorbed a good deal of an ideological nature from Teotihuacan, they may even have had 'military advisers', but in essence the conquest of Uaxactún had been achieved by Tikal itself.

This reconstruction appeared to fit with much of the evidence and, persuasively championed by Schele and Freidel, was widely accepted. Until, in 1997, first David Stuart and then Nikolai Grube and Simon Martin looked very hard once more at the Stela 31 text and found that some key details had been overlooked. The critical passage spoke not of war, but of something very different. It announced the appearance of a foreigner. On 16 January 378 Smoking Frog, whose phonetic name 'Ciak K'ak' is better translated as 'Born of Fire', 'arrived' at Tikal. Furthermore, he is said to have arrived 'from the west' and is indeed called 'Lord of the West'. The west, of course, is the direction of Teotihuacan. Smoking Frog was not the brother of Great Jaguar Paw, which Schele had already by this time recognized. He came from somewhere else, very probably from central Mexico. David Stuart also found some remarkable supplementary evidence. A text from the nearby site of El Peru, west of Tikal, stated that the same Smoking Frog had 'arrived' there eight days previously, on 8 January. Thus his very progress across country towards Tikal could be charted.[7]

A very different scenario now emerges. Great Jaguar Paw did not 'let blood from his genitals' to celebrate victory at Uaxactún. Instead, the Stela 31 inscription says that he 'died', on the very day of Smoking Frog's arrival. The phraseology is still a little obscure, but the probability must be that he was put to death. What seems to have taken place, in effect, was a military coup and the key player in these events at Tikal was the outsider, Smoking Frog. But what of any war against Uaxactún? Smoking Frog did indeed become established as ruler there and a

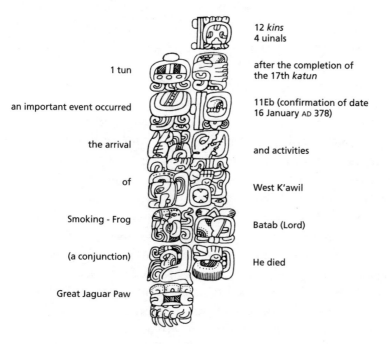

	12 *kins* 4 uinals
1 tun	after the completion of the 17th *katun*
an important event occurred	11Eb (confirmation of date 16 January AD 378)
the arrival	and activities
of	West K'awil
Smoking - Frog	Batab (Lord)
(a conjunction)	He died
Great Jaguar Paw	

Smoking Frog at Tikal. A section of the Stela 31 text.

further stela from Uaxactún, Stela 4, indicates that he ruled until at least AD 396. However, the circumstances of the takeover of the city are still unclear. There is little archaeological evidence of any violent confrontation, apart from an isolated discovery made many years ago. In the 1930s a tomb was found under a temple at Uaxactún. It contained the bodies of two women, one of whom was pregnant, and two children. All appeared to have been killed. Stela 5, Smoking Frog's earliest monument which records his takeover at Uaxactún, was erected outside this temple at the very time when the tomb was dug and the temple above it constructed. The 'conquest' of Uaxactún may then have been a bloodless victory, save for the elimination of the most important women and children of the Uaxactún royal line, the ruler himself and any male heirs being taken back to Tikal for sacrifice.

After some delay, Curl Nose took the throne of Tikal on 13 September AD 379. He reigned for forty-seven years. Yet, while Smoking Frog was still alive he remained his subordinate. For Curl Nose is referred to in Tikal inscriptions by the significant hieroglyphic phrase *y ahaw* meaning 'the lord of' or 'his lord'. In other words he was the vassal of Smoking Frog. But he was more than that. He was certainly not a son of Jaguar Paw. Instead, he is referred to in the Stela 31 text as the son of the 'spearthrower-owl-shield person', a name which involves a cluster of peculiarly central Mexican images. But this 'spearthrower' individual, who also appears to have been in Tikal at the time, is in turn called the 'brother' of Smoking Frog. If we take it literally, Curl Nose was thus Smoking Frog's nephew. Either way, however, Curl Nose's origins can also be associated with Teotihuacan.[8]

Such are the complexities that have emerged from the reinterpretation of Stela 31. It presents us with a picture of dramatic events and changes at Tikal. Yet, just as important, the stela goes out of its way to stress – or at least pretend to – continuity. Nowhere in the text does it say that there has been a change of dynasty. Far from it. Briefly, and somewhat vaguely, Jaguar Paw is said to have passed away. Curl Nose is then integrated seamlessly as the next successor to the founder Yax Moch Xoc. The likelihood is that he took as a wife a member of the old Jaguar Paw lineage. His son, Stormy Sky, could then, through the matriline, claim a rather more substantial Maya legitimacy. And, as we have seen, Stormy Sky represents himself on Stela 31 as a traditional Tikal ruler, with none of the accoutrements of central Mexico.

Future work and the discovery of new inscriptions will undoubtedly clarify much that can still only be conjectured about the events of these years. At the time of the 'takeover', there is some archaeological evidence of a group of Teotihuacan people living in a residential area close to the Lost World complex (see below). But how far Teotihuacan warriors may have occupied the city, in what number and how long they stayed is impossible to say. There is certainly little evidence of what we might term a conquest, or that Tikal became an out and out satellite of Teotihuacan. All that is detectable at present is the installation of a new regime, headed at first by foreigners, but whose offspring rapidly became Mayanized. What seems to have been achieved, and what Stormy Sky may be announcing symbolically on Stela 31 (the Maya ruler flanked by protective, guiding images of Teotihuacan), was a new, dynamic synthesis. The more centralized state efficiency of Teotihuacan, with its distinctive modes of warfare and war gods were grafted onto the emerging Maya concept of divine kingship. In an arrangement that suited both parties, what was still an essentially Maya Tikal became the pivotal ally and trade connection of Teotihuacan in the Maya lowlands.

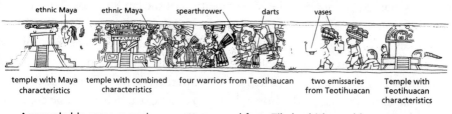

A remarkable scene carved on a pottery vessel from Tikal, which would seem to show people from Teotihuacan, carrying spear throwers, darts and pots of typical central Mexican form, arriving at a Maya city, quite possibly Tikal itself. To the right is a temple in Teotihuacan *talud-tablero* style and, far-left, a stepped pyramid of lowland Maya form.

The galvanizing effect of this new relationship appears to have been immediate. For Tikal swiftly achieved dominance over much of the northern and eastern Petén. Uaxactún had effectively been absorbed into a combined kingdom and many smaller towns close to Tikal became dependent from this time onwards, and cities such as Bejucal and Motul de San José, close to Lake Petén Itzá, begin to express their relationship through texts which use the *y ahaw* phrase to indicate subordination to their powerful neighbour. By the mid-fifth century it appears that Tikal had achieved a solid territorial domain, at least twenty-five kilometres in radius.

The Tikal sphere of influence became much wider than this. The city of Río Azul, a hundred kilometres to the north-east, occupies the banks of the

Azul River, which flows into the Rio Hondo and thence to the Caribbean. Only discovered in the 1960s, much of the site was systematically looted, trenches and tunnels dug right through the principal temples, before the Guatemalan authorities were alerted. What were to all intents and purposes belated rescue excavations were undertaken here in the 1980s.

Río Azul dates back to the Middle Preclassic, but, significantly, the greatest period of growth at the site came between about AD 390 and 540. The most dramatic and informative feature of Río Azul are its tombs. A number had already been stripped by the time the archaeologists began work, their magnificent jades and fine pottery, some in Teotihuacan style, appearing on the art market and in private collections over the ensuing years. But two were excavated intact, and even those that had been plundered had much to reveal. For they were dug into the limestone bedrock and the walls painted in vivid red and black with inscriptions. The evidence of these mortuary texts, combined with Río Azul's few stone monuments, indicates that the city was taken over by Tikal in the time of Curl Nose. An important ruler of Río Azul in the early fifth century was a man named Six Sky and the most beautiful of the city's tombs, Tomb 1, painted in an earthy red hematite pigment with broad, confident brushstrokes provides glyphic references to Curl Nose. Some feel that this ruler was the son of Stormy Sky of Tikal (see plate section, p. 10).

Río Azul thus became a Tikal outpost, perhaps a military one against hostile cities further to the north, but also as an extremely valuable trade link, a central concern to the new Tikal–Teotihuacan alliance. The city was in a good position to control the flow of commodities up from the Caribbean and thence across country to Tikal, and perhaps on to central Mexico. These could have included any number of things, many of which – such as feathers, animal skins, salt, cotton textiles and other fibres, wooden objects – have long ago perished in the tropical climate. A major trade item was almost certainly cacao, from nearby Belize or western Honduras. Thus the limited evidence so far available suggests that Tikal was spreading tentacles of influence to strategic locations far from its territorial nucleus in the Petén. Indeed, Tikal's reach may have been very considerable indeed.

COPÁN IN THE EARLY CLASSIC

Some 300 kilometres from Tikal, on the south-eastern edge of the Maya world, Copán lies amongst the gentle uplands of western Honduras, an environment very different from that of the great jungle cities of the Petén. The climate is relatively mild and pleasant, the altitude being some 600 metres above sea level. The surrounding hills are dotted with stands of pine and oak and it is only in the valley bottom that small patches of tropical forest are to be found, such as the Spanish cedars and giant Ceiba trees that have been left to shade the ruins. In the time of Stephens and Catherwood, the remains of the city and much of the bottom land was covered in forest. But this had grown back since pre-Hispanic times and the landscape today, cultivation extending up the slopes of most of the hills, probably looks much as it did at the height of Copán's prosperity in the eighth century AD.

The Copán River, which runs northwards into the Motagua, winds picturesquely through the valley and over the centuries has deposited extremely rich alluvial soils, the greatest extent of them surrounding the city, which is positioned immediately overlooking the river. Copán was not only blessed with dependable water supplies and good agricultural land. There were outcrops of fine-quality building stone close by, a volcanic tuff of a distinctive pink and pale-greenish colour well resistant to erosion; beds of limestone to make stucco; pottery clay was plentiful; obsidian was brought from the nearby Guatemalan highlands; and the only source of jade in the whole Maya region, found in boulder and river-worn pebble form in the middle Motagua valley, was also only a few days journey away. Copán was thus a place of abundance, initially at least, for those who raised one of the truly great Maya cities here.

Following the common Maya pattern, the Copán kingdom, as it became established, included a central urban zone, its more immediate rural population and smaller dependent centres and settlements in other pockets of fertile land within the Copán River drainage. It was of middling size compared with great city-states such as Tikal and Calakmul, and the total population was probably never more than about 25,000 people. But what it lacked in overall scale it made up for through the astonishing creative endeavour, expressed in magnificent relief sculpture and elaborate architectural ornament, that was lavished on the civic and ceremonial buildings at its heart. Detailed investigation of the growth of Copán and patterns of ancient settlement in the valley began in the 1970s and a series of major projects has focused on both the city centre and its hinterland ever since. Areas of considerable uncertainty remain, but today Copán must rank as the best understood of all Maya cities.[9]

The valley was occupied by 1000 BC, by pioneering farmers whose ceramics suggest connections with the Guatemalan highlands and other regions to the south-west, which in fact continue throughout Copán's history. These first people built insubstantial dwellings, little more than temporary camps, cut the first clearings for the planting of maize, beans and squash and hunted for deer, peccary, rabbits and turtles. By 800 BC settlements had become permanent and extensive and beneath a few of their houses some rich burials have been found. These included quantities of finely worked jade ornaments and ceramics that displayed clear Olmec influence. This signals the early emergence of a ruling élite connected in some way, as we saw in Chapter 2, with the Olmec sphere. Very probably this was a trading relationship centred on the Motagua jade source. Curiously, however, these early developments seem not to have been sustained. At Copán there is very little surviving evidence from the Late Preclassic period, the time when cities such as Tikal, Uaxactún and many others in the lowlands to the north and west were growing rapidly. The population may even have declined at this time. But by the third century AD it had picked up again and there was a series of settlements spaced out along the bottom of the Copán valley, each perhaps the base of a particular Maya kin group ruled by a lineage lord. In the middle of the fifth century came the most significant change. One of these settlements grew rapidly, acquiring fine masonry buildings, plastered with stucco and ornamented with complex religious and political iconography. Monuments with hieroglyphic inscriptions began to be set up. Dynastic rule had arrived at Copán and was to last for 400 years.

Originally surrounded on every side by residential areas, the civic and ceremonial heart of the city that one sees today, all of which dates from the Late Classic period, is aligned along a north-south axis and covers a rectangular area roughly 500 × 300 metres (see plate section, p. 11). It is easily divided into two discrete sections. To the north is a series of open public spaces or plazas. In the Middle Plaza two roads converged, coming from the east and west. Entering the city centre in this way, visitors in ancient times had two choices. They could move north and enter the Plaza of the Stelae. This contains many of the finest stelae and so-called altars, most of them set up by the early eighth-century ruler known as 18 Rabbit. This area is enclosed on three sides by a series of steps from which ceremonies amongst these monuments could be witnessed.

To the south the Middle Plaza leads to the magnificent Copán ballcourt, the largest and most beautiful of all Classic Maya ballcourts, which is given a prominent place in the city lay-out. Its south-east corner abuts Temple 26, better known as the Temple of the Hieroglyphic Stairway (see plate section, pp. 14, 16). Here, on some seventy steps rising to the Temple Summit, were carved more than 2200 glyphs, the largest single Maya stone inscription known. Over the centuries many of the carved blocks tumbled from their positions. But extraordinarily painstaking work of study and reconstruction in recent times has restored much of this astonishing monument to its original state. Whole sections are too eroded to read and other parts of the text are so elaborate and complex – Copán inscriptions being notoriously challenging to epigraphers – that little more than half of the complete inscription will ever be deciphered. But what is evident is that this was once a grand statement of the dynastic history of Copán, illustrated by life-size sculptures of some of the city's greatest rulers, placed at intervals up the steps.

The Hieroglyphic Stairway faces west onto an open court that connects with the main plazas to the north. Thus the populace in the eighth century would have been able to approach the base of the stairs and view the glorious images and stone chronicle of their city's royal past. This, it seems, was the limit of more 'public' access to the heart of the city by this date. For rising steeply to the south are steps that only the chosen few would have climbed. They afforded the sole access to the inner sanctum of Copán royalty, the Acropolis.

The awesome mass of the Acropolis rises to some thirty metres at its highest point. There was no hill or topographic relief of any sort here originally. We now know that this is a completely man-made artifact, an accumulation of royal palaces and temples stacked up one on top of another over four centuries. Visible on the summit today is a series of ruined Late Classic structures around two sunken plazas, known as the East and West courts. Remains from earlier periods lie below the visitors' feet, wrapped in an embrace of rubble and constructional fill.

The North Acropolis at Tikal had presented archaeologists with an extraordinary complexity of superimposed buildings. There it was the Preclassic levels that were deeply buried. At least the Early Classic architecture was accessible, since by the mid-sixth century most construction, apart from one singular later embellishment, had ceased. Thereafter Tikal's lords moved on to other building sites nearby. But here at Copán they had doggedly continued, onward and upward on the same spot. At least, that had to be the presumption little more than a decade ago. For at that time, before archaeologists began to probe the Acropolis, there was very little physical evidence from which to gauge how the city had developed and functioned in earlier centuries. Indeed, maybe Copán had amounted to very little until the Late Classic period. All there was to go on were Copán's later monuments and inscriptions.

In 1839, in their wanderings on top of the forest-shrouded Acropolis, Stephens and Catherwood came upon that extraordinary Altar, which presented 'as curious a subject of speculation as any monument in Copán'. This was Altar Q, which lay in the west court at the foot of a stairway leading to the summit of what is now known as Temple 16, the central and most imposing structure on the Acropolis. To Stephens, the sixteen seated figures around its sides represented noble 'personages' and the thirty-six blocks of hieroglyphs on top of the stone probably recorded some event in the history of the mysterious people who once inhabited the city. This modest opinion came to be considerably elaborated in the early twentieth century. It was Herbert Spinden who first suggested that they were Maya astronomers, who had met up to discuss a correction to the 365-day solar calendar, to bring it into line with the true 'tropical year' of 365.242 days. Certainly the Maya would have had trouble keeping their solar calendar in step with the seasons over long periods of time, and maybe groups of concerned 'astronomers' did meet up on occasion to talk about the matter. But, however delightful the notion may be, the 'astronomical hypothesis' has long been rejected as an explanation of Altar Q.

The sixteen figures are in fact rulers of Copán. This unrivalled stone depicts the complete Copán royal line and is of priceless documentary importance. The key men represented here are the two central figures on the west side of the monument (see plate section, p. 11). Between them is a date in the Calendar Round, 6 Caban 10 Mol, which corresponds to 2 July 763. This was the accession date of the figure to the right, known as Yax Pac. He was the sixteenth and the last ruler of Copán. The individual opposite him is the founder of the dynasty, a man called Yax K'uk Mo, who is symbolically handing Yax Pac his sceptre of office. Between them, along the other sides of the monument, the intervening fourteen rulers (see Appendix 2) are depicted in order of succession and each of them, as Stephens first suggested, sits on a cushion which bears a glyphic representation of his name, though some are worn and indecipherable. The exception is the founder, who is seated on an *ahaw* glyph, meaning lord, and whose name appears in the elements of his headdress. One might also note here two unusual features of Yax K'uk Mo's appearance. He possesses pronounced goggles around his eyes and bears on his right forearm a small shield of unusual form.

The unique feature of Altar Q is that it bears not just one royal predecessor hovering protectively above the ruler, as seen for example on the stelae of Tikal, but a whole ancestral portrait gallery represented in an extraordinarily realistic and almost intimate manner. These are not remote, deified images. Each character is individualized, with his own style of dress and ornaments. Yax Pac has represented himself convening a whole family gathering, what looks like a council of the long-deceased, to witness the most important moment in his royal life. And the central message conveyed here is his direct lineal relationship to Yax K'uk Mo, the founder.

This is not in fact an 'altar', the word is a misnomer. Such monuments are most probably thrones, as are all the other 'altars' coupled with stelae. The Maya themselves refer to a number of them as 'throne stones'. The ruler would have sat on top of them on an animal skin or a cushion stuffed with kapok from the Ceiba or silk cotton tree. On the top of Altar Q, where Yax Pac would have been seated, lies a critical inscription for the interpretation of Copán's early history. For it refers to Yax K'uk Mo's display of his sceptre of office in the year AD 426, in effect the date of his accession and the very beginning of the Copán dynasty.

Thus Altar Q appears to present us with an anchoring date for the foundation of the Copán royal house, and indeed Yax K'uk Mo's name and the same date appear in other Copán inscriptions. However, these are all retrospective references. They cannot serve as proof that Yax K'uk Mo and the other individuals depicted on Altar Q were real people. As late as the 1980s there were some archaeologists who felt that the first ten rulers of Copán were very probably mythological, the figment of later royal imagination. In fact, without good contemporary evidence attesting to the existence of these early rulers, it was legitimate enough to regard them, to use the word employed at the time, as 'putative' kings. Since the late 1980s, however, some remarkably skilful and imaginative excavation within the heart of the Acropolis, led by archaeologists William Fash, Ricardo Agurcia, Robert Sharer and David Sedat, has produced dramatic and momentous discoveries. Copán's early kings are no longer so putative.[10]

The initial breakthrough was made in 1988 by Fash's team during excavations way beneath Temple 26, the temple on top of the

Hieroglyphic Stairway. There they discovered the remains of an Early Classic temple, to which they gave the name 'Papagayo'. From radio-carbon dates and the evidence of associated ceramics there was no doubt that it was constructed in the fifth century AD. A stela was found, known as Stela 63, broken into three pieces but whose base was still in place where it had been set up inside the building. It contained text alone, and no other imagery, but the inscription was explicit. It said that the stela had been erected there by Yax K'uk Mo's son, a man known as Popol Hol or 'Mat Head', from the mat-weave appearing in details of the headgear on his portrait-head name glyph. But the stela commemor-ated an extremely important event in his father's reign, the completion of the ninth *baktun* in the Long Count. In Maya notation the date was expressed as 9.0.0.0.0. It meant that a full nine cycles of approximately 400 years had passed since the theoretical beginning of recorded time in 3114 BC The completion of the *baktun* marked the end of one era and the start of a whole new epoch, much like our own turning of the mil-lenium. This had taken place on 11 December AD 435, and, fittingly, the founder Yax K'uk Mo had led the ceremonial at this new dawn for Copán.

Beneath Papagayo an even earlier building was found in 1992 and given another ornithological working title, 'Motmot'. In front of Motmot was a stone of quatrefoil shape set into the floor. Upon it appear the seated figures of Yax K'uk Mo and his son. Here celebration of the 9.0.0.0.0 period ending was mentioned once more. Although neither Stela 63 nor the Motmot floor-marker were monuments set up by Yax K'uk Mo himself, their texts and archaeological contexts prove beyond any reasonable doubt that he was in place as king of Copán by AD 435. One can also take it at face value that he had been installed as founder of the dynasty nine years previously, as recounted on Altar Q.

Excavation under the Temple of the Hieroglyphic Stairway had also provided some physical evidence of the early growth of the city. Papagayo and Motmot were not well preserved. Both had been 'termi-nated' – comprehensively dismantled and ritually put to sleep before other constructions were built on top of them. But they were evidently among the initial building blocks of the Acropolis that we see today. Furthermore, alongside Motmot, clearly extending beneath the latest, surviving structure, the outlines of the very first Copán ballcourt were discovered.

These first productive excavations provided the impetus for further probing beneath the Acropolis. The Honduran archaeologist Ricardo Agurcia decided to focus his attentions on what might lie buried within Temple 16, the tallest monument of all and which, before the Copán River removed part of the eastern section of the site, had stood at the very centre of the Acropolis, between the East and West Courts. The sixteenth ruler, Yax Pac, completed the last stage of Temple 16 and it was then, at the temple's dedication in 775, that he placed Altar Q beneath it as a monument to his own accession twelve years previously.

We can imagine today the richness of ceremonial that would have attended this event: the clouds of smoke that billowed from countless ceramic incense-burners; musicians banging drums and producing an unearthly wailing from conch-shell trumpets; the lord, his family and the Copán nobility dripping with jade ornaments, their turbaned head-dresses cascading with plumes of brilliant feathers. Such pageantry can be conjured up from the narrative scenes on fine painted Maya ceramics and the courtly spectacle displayed in the Bonampak murals. To guess at the meaning of the symbolic drama that unfolded is, of course, a very different matter. The impermanent elements – the words of solemn oration, the steps of the dance, the ritualistic detail – are quite irretriev-able. But there are a few more tangible clues. Firstly there is Altar Q itself, the ancestral theme encapsulated by the central image of Yax Pac receiving the sceptre of office from the founding father. There is another fascinating survival. Fifteen jaguars were sacrificed here and buried in a small crypt next to the stone, evidently one of these sacred animals for each of Yax Pac's ancestors. The jaguar was the animal counterpart of Maya royalty. Both possessed equivalent supernatural powers and acted as intermediaries between the natural world and the divine, between the living and the dead. The jaguar was equated with the sun, in particular the sun at night as it journeyed through the Underworld. The Maya lord was also commonly identified with the sun, as one of the Hero Twins who, victorious in his struggles with the Death Gods, himself emerged from the Underworld to bring light to humanity. At Copán the very first Lord of all was named in full K'inich Yax K'uk Mo. He was the 'Sun-faced Blue-Green Quetzal Macaw'. In this way the Copán dynasty was itself proclaimed as born of the sun.

One particular question would have been in Agurcia's mind as he and his colleagues tunnelled into the depths of Temple 16. If such powerful ancestral symbolism had surrounded Altar Q, at the foot of the temple stairway, might such concerns also be reflected in earlier remains within the temple? For among the many things that archaeologists have learnt about the thinking behind Maya architecture in recent years, two principles stand out. Firstly, the buildings themselves seem to have been viewed as living beings with a birth, life-span and death all of their own. Hence the trouble taken to ritually terminate them before a new structure was born, or in a sense re-born, on top. For the second axiom was that once a building was established and devoted to a particular activity – be it a temple to the dead, a ballcourt or an astronomical observatory – all succeeding buildings in that location would continue to serve the same purpose, recapitulating the same underlying theme.

Within Temple 16 Agurcia first encountered the outlines of a previous stepped pyramid, similar in form to the very latest structure, but completely destroyed. Then, however, on the same central axis but slightly further to the north, they came upon the painted stucco façade of a much earlier temple. Their tunnels followed this façade and over the succeeding field seasons, as the fill from immediately around the buried temple was carefully removed to form tall access galleries, it became apparent that Agurcia and his team had made a quite spectacular discovery. What was truly remarkable was the temple's state of preservation. Instead of the decoration being destroyed, stucco reliefs hacked off, the upper portion of the building smashed and rooms filled with the rubble (the normal practice), the whole structure had been covered in a protective layer of plaster and very gently interred, intentionally left intact. Why was this? The only answer seemed to be that this was an especially sacred building.

The temple was given the nickname Rosalila (see plate section, p. 12). It is about thirteen metres tall, twelve by eighteen metres in ground plan and of two storeys, topped by a large roof-comb. The lower storey contains three rooms running north to south and a fourth east to west. The principal façade faces west, with a central entrance approached by a broad stairway. In excavating these stairs, which revealed the shallow pyramidal substructure upon which the temple had been built, a short hieroglyphic inscription was revealed on one of the steps. It included the date AD 571, almost certainly the time when the building had been dedicated.

The whole temple was originally painted red and the stucco ornament picked out in blue, green and yellow. The iconography of the relief ornament is complex and its finer points still much debated, but there is little doubt about the underlying ideas expressed here. On the façades of the lower storey appear striking polychrome birds with a central humanoid mask. Beneath the mask are large talons and fanning out above it a glorious array of feathers. The reliefs were given fresh coats of stucco many times, a practical necessity to seal the building and avoid damage from the rains. But there is evidence that these feathers were repainted on occasion in different colours – for a period they would be green, like the plumage of the quetzal, and then for a number of years red, to represent the brilliant feathers of the macaw. These composite birds were nothing less than portraits of the dynastic founder, 'Kuk' and 'Mo', quetzal and macaw in one. On the next level of the façade appears a central mask of the sun personified, K'inich Ahaw, with serpent wings which extend to the corners of the building, framing further images of the sun. At the base of the roof-comb is a massive monster mask, a so-called 'wits' monster representing both a sacred mountain, seen as the home of the ancestors, and the very fabric of the earth itself. To either side of this mountain rise the bodies of two serpents which join above to form the arc of the heavens. K'inich Yax Kuk Mo is thus portrayed here as a prime mover among the very forces of the cosmos. Indeed, in supernatural bird form, at the base of the temple, he is in effect supporting the world.

Maya temples were never neutral locations in which to perform religious ceremonies. They were symbolically loaded. As early as the Preclassic, as we have seen at Cerros or at Uaxactún, pyramids were adorned with images that represented great natural forces combined with more muted emblems of rulership, such as jaguar masks, references to Venus and the Hero Twins. During the Early Classic, however, as the more personalized cult of the dynastic ruler became established, Maya leaders themselves began to be incorporated more directly into the iconography, as Rosalila reveals, a demonstration to ordinary Maya people that rulers possessed powers that no one else could dream of emulating. In the Late Classic this would be taken even further. At Tikal or Yaxchilán for example, the monumental stucco statues of kings perched upon the roof-combs of temple-pyramids, like so many King Kongs above Manhattan, represent unashamedly overt hoardings to advertise royal power.

Today, the demands of conservation mean that the visitor is rarely able to enter the tunnels under Temple 16 and see the remains of Rosalila *in situ*. But a full-size replica of the temple, left open to the elements and soaring skywards level with the roof over the surrounding galleries, forms the brilliant centrepiece of the Copán site museum. Much like the realization that the Parthenon was once garishly painted, a technicolour recreation such as this comes as a considerable shock to those accustomed to Maya buildings as tastefully weather-worn stone. But this was how Maya architecture actually looked. Most city-scapes, it would appear, were studies in scarlet or strawberry pink.

Rosalila was constructed about AD 570 by the little-known tenth ruler, Moon Jaguar, and may have been used for as much as a century, further testimony to the reverence in which it was held. At the turn of the seventh century it dominated the growing Acropolis. The embodiment of the deified founder and focus for ancestor veneration, it would have been the very heart and soul of the Copán city-state. But what of buildings prior to Rosalila, from the time of the founder himself?

In 1991 Robert Sharer and David Sedat started to probe the depths of the Acropolis from a different direction, the great *corte* or cut on the eastern side where the river had previously undercut and destroyed part of the site. This was the sheer drop that Galindo and Stephens, initially at least, had imagined was a large retaining wall. Galindo had dug into the *corte* and found a vaulted tomb containing human bones, pottery, obsidian and jade all lying on a plastered slab. In the 1930s the course of the river was diverted and it no longer threatens the ruins. The *corte* has been shored up and stabilized, and in recent years has proved of immense help to archaeologists. For it provides a complete stratigraphic sequence of building activity, walls and floors revealed in cross-section from the time when the very first structures were raised here about AD 400.

Sharer and Sedat aimed to tunnel in at different levels and piece together in more detail the earlier constructional sequence. Working in strength-sapping conditions, in the dust and humidity of a maze of narrow tunnels, they were to plot an array of different kinds of buildings – palace-type structures, temples and tombs. By 1993 they had burrowed their way into the heart of the Acropolis, on the central axis well below both Temple 16 and Rosalila. Here it was that they discovered another wonderfully well-preserved façade, that of a smaller temple which had been buried in a soft earth to keep it from harm. The symbolism was even more unmistakeable than that displayed on Rosalila. Between two framing, ornamental bands representing the earth and the sky were a green quetzal and a red macaw, their heads intertwined and the visage of the sun-god emerging from their beaks: K'inich Yax K'uk Mo was rendered in its totality.

In a vaulted chamber within this building, which they called Margarita, they encountered a large stone slab or step at the base of a wall, one face with a well-preserved panel of hieroglyphs. It bore a date of AD 437, the names of both Yax K'uk Mo and his son, and what seemed a reference to the 'death house of the lord of Copán'. The rest of the inscription has proved very difficult to interpret, but now at least the founder himself seemed to be getting very close. Beneath this chamber within Margarita, and connected by a staircase, they then encountered a tomb. The remains were found lying on an immensely heavy stone within a small, well-constructed room. The contents of the burial were astonishing. The bones were surrounded by a vast quantity of jade objects including many thousands of beads, carved jade pieces across the individual's chest, bracelets and ear ornaments of jade and a shell collar. The burial and the whole chamber had also been plastered with an enormous amount of bright red cinnabar or mercury sulphide, a compound so poisonous that it had initially delayed entry into the tomb, but which to the Maya represented sacred blood and resurrection.

Who was this evidently royal individual? At first the only two candidates were thought to be Popol K'inich, Yax K'uk Mo's son, or even perhaps Yax K'uk Mo himself. But then examination of the bones told a different story. This was no Maya lord but a lady. The woman had been tiny, only about one and a half metres tall, and was fifty-five or maybe a little older at the time of her death. From the wear on her pelvis it appeared that she had had at least three children. There were clear signs that the chamber had been left accessible for some time after her death and had been turned into a shrine. The question of the identity of this elderly, revered and richly endowed woman could not, as yet, be answered.

Excavating deeper beneath the Margarita building the archaeological picture began to get more complex. Within Margarita were the remains of the substructure of another smaller building, named Yehnal, which preserved a fine stucco panel of the sun-god on its façade, comparable to those that adorned Rosalila many metres above. Inside Yehnal was yet another earlier stepped platform, which they called Hunal. Cut into this was a second tomb, which lay beneath and very close to that of the royal woman. The design of the tomb was similar: a corbel-vaulted masonry chamber, originally plastered (though all of this had peeled off), with a plain stone platform within held up at each corner by four large supports. Lying face up on the slab were the remains of a man (see plate section, p. 12). Analysis of the bones showed that he, too, had probably died at some time in his fifties, and that his body had suffered considerable wear and tear. He had had arthritis, there were signs that his left shoulder had been dislocated and that at some point many of his teeth had been knocked out. His right forearm had been fractured and had never healed properly.

The quantity of grave goods did not match that of the woman and there were indeed few material indications of his royal status. A fine jade bead carved with a mat motif, an emblem of rulership, had been placed in his mouth at the time of burial and he had an anklet of jaguar canines and a large bar pectoral of jade, further accoutrements of royalty. But there were no inscriptions, little else to advertise directly who he was. Yet there are good reasons to believe that these are the remains of Yax K'uk Mo. Firstly there is the position of the tomb, lying directly beneath all the succeeding temples and memorials to the founder and cut into the Hunal structure, which is one of the earliest, if not the earliest, of all the Acropolis buildings. Before AD 400 a series of artificial platforms had been built here close to the Copán River. These Sharer and Sedat have identified right on top of the ancient ground surface. But they were unsophisticated earth structures. Hunal marks the beginning of concerted construction in stone and seems the initial seed from which the Acropolis grew.

There are also certain telling details which would seem to link the burial with the portrayal of Yax K'uk Mo on Altar Q. The jade bar pectoral found in the tomb is almost identical to that which he wears in his portrait sculpture. The small shield – too small, it would seem, to be very effective in combat – he wears on his right arm. Does this suggest that Yax K'uk Mo was left-handed? Or could it be that a man with a fractured and permanently incapacitated arm needed something to protect and maybe even to disguise it? The shield is worn on the forearm, exactly where the fracture is located.

Other distinguishing characteristics of Yax K'uk Mo on Altar Q take us in a rather different direction. The tiny shield he wears is unusual in another way. For it is central Mexican in style, likewise the pronounced goggle that we see around his eye. These are the goggles of the Teotihuacan storm god Tlaloc. Moving from his portrait to the text on the top of the Altar, there are also extraordinary parallels between this text and that on Stela 31 at Tikal. The very first section of the Altar Q inscription refers to Yax K'uk Mo's 'arrival' at Copán, the same phrase used to describe Smoking Frog's appearance at Tikal. Furthermore, Yax K'uk Mo, like Smoking Frog, is referred to as a 'Lord of the West'. Does this mean that Yax K'uk Mo was also an outsider with a link to Teotihuacan?

There is further persuasive archaeological evidence that suggests he was. Hunal, that first building at the base of the Acropolis, was put up in Yax K'uk Mo's time and it also contains his tomb, dug into the structure by his son. What is remarkable about this building is the *talud–tablero* form of its substructure. It is in pure Teotihuacan-style. Hunal is quite unique at Copán. No other building discovered to date is like it. The founder's house, the location of his tomb, is distinctly foreign in appearance. What is more, the grave goods of both Yax K'uk Mo and the royal woman, whom all the evidence now suggests was his wife, contain large quantities of Teotihuacan-style ceramics. One astonishing fresco-painted tripod vessel found with other grave goods in the associated chamber above the lady's tomb, seems to tell the story on its own. It is brightly painted in red and green with a goggle-eyed Tlaloc head peering out from the doorway of a temple: it has a *talud–tablero* substructure and could even be Hunal, with Yax K'uk Mo himself inside.

It would appear that Yax K'uk Mo was indeed an outsider who managed to impose himself on the people of Copán. Before his arrival, around AD 420, a string of different settlements existed along the valley. In much later texts there are rather obscure references to events and 'rulers' as early as the second century AD. This suggests that powerful chiefs, the heads of local kin groups, were well established and that perhaps one paramount lineage was in place at the time of his appearance. Yet there is also some evidence, such as a number of defensible hill-top sites dating from this period, which might indicate an unstable political situation. Perhaps, then, Yax K'uk Mo had the opportunity to attach himself to a competing faction, or he may have been expressly invited in to help resolve local conflict. The extent of his wounds – the broken forearm, dislocated shoulder and smashed teeth – could also be made to paint a colourful picture of a battle-hardened mercenary. If he was a warrior with Teotihuacan connections, he was also no doubt able to establish those trade connections that any Teotihuacan affiliation would have offered. And one of the prerequisites of effective rulership was the ability to reward followers with rare and prestigious goods. Large quantities of green obsidian from Teotihuacan found in buildings of Yax K'uk Mo's time and the immense amount of jade in his wife's tomb (women, it seems, often being the repository of material wealth), would suggest that he was more than able to fulfil this responsibility.

A plausible reconstruction is that Yax K'uk Mo married into one of the local lineages and established his power base at a pre-existing settlement where the Acropolis now stands. Taking the sceptre of office in 426, he reigned for little more than ten years, meeting his death in 437. In that brief period he established the bare outlines of Copán the dynastic centre. But the major expansion took place in the time of his son and immediate successors, whose personal histories and the whereabouts of whose tombs remain unknown. By AD 500, plastered stone buildings, a range of residential, administrative and religious complexes, probably covered the whole extent of the present Acropolis. The functional and ideological template for later architectural development had been established. In the early sixth century a ruler named Waterlily Jaguar, the seventh ruler in line, built a palace which lies under the present Temple 11, atop the great stairway leading to the Acropolis from the plaza of the ballcourt. He called it the 'House of K'inich Yax Kuk Mo'. This appears to have been a special lineage house where the royal archives may well have been kept, bark-paper books recording genealogical history and the sacred lore that surrounded the dynasty.

The powerful legend of the Copán founder was, of course, the creation of his heirs, and the two immediate image-makers were no doubt Yax Kuk Mo's son, Popol K'inich, and his wife, who appears to have survived him by a decade. Yet, in their nurturing of the personality cult of the first dynast the most striking feature is the complete lack of explicit reference to Teotihuacan. The Hunal building, with its *talud–tablero* façade, had no successor. Yehnal and the Margarita structure, with its magnificent entwined birds, are pure Maya in style. Other patterns in material culture, such as ceramics, return rapidly to their indigenous forms. Domestic political circumstances, a certain reaction to foreign ways, may have necessitated a swift adjustment of this kind after his death. By the time of the Rosalila temple there is little in the building's iconography to dispute Yax K'uk Mo's essential Mayaness.

To date, no tomb that can confidently be said to be that of a dynastic founder has been discovered at any other Maya site. What is also unique is the Russian-doll structure of temple after temple, so many of which survive intact, all set up in the same spot in memory of the first dynast. It provides an unparalleled insight into the public relations of Maya kingship, the transmogrification over time of a toothless, one-armed warrior into a god. And if Yax K'uk Mo's Teotihuacan connection appears to have been publicly glossed over after his death, it was never forgotten but maintained in oral tradition, perhaps committed in detail to bark-paper in the 'House of Yax K'uk Mo'. Later kings, on occasion, make discreet artistic reference. And then, in the eighth century, came a spate of Teotihuacan revivalism which climaxed in Yax Pac's Altar Q and the decoration of Temple 16 where, in a central room at the summit, whose sculpture has recently been reassembled, the founder is portrayed with Tlaloc-goggle eyes emerging from the gaping mouth of a 'Vision serpent', the conventional way of conveying the supernatural, visionary manifestation of a long-dead ancestor. So it was that hundreds of years on, when Teotihuacan itself had fallen by the wayside, the great city in the mountains of Central Mexico still retained among the Maya of Copán a powerful mythic importance.

Trace-element analysis of Yax K'uk Mo's bones may very soon yield information about the diet and physical environment of his youth, which could help archaeologists to pin down his more precise origins.[12] There are some who would already suggest Tikal as the place of his birth. Indeed, years ago scholars such as Sylvanus Morley and Tatiana Proskouriakoff believed, largely on stylistic, art-historical grounds, that the royal line of both Copán and its neighbour Quiriguá had been founded by colonists from Tikal.

Yax K'uk Mo took the Copán throne in AD 426. This was the same year that Stormy Sky succeeded Curl Nose at Tikal, by which time, on the evidence from Río Azul, Tikal's influence had already spread rapidly across the Petén. Copán is very much further away, but for any Tikal/Teotihuacan trading alliance it would have been a key location on the frontier with lower Central America. Without doubt the greatest power in the Southern Lowlands at this time, Tikal's very reputation perhaps acted as a catalyst to persuade other cities to emulate its system of dynastic rule. But during these years of political fluidity, Tikal also had the ability to support freebooting individuals, men from the combined Tikal/Uaxactún power-base who could gain their own wealth and power by opening up new trade routes, colonizing new lands and founding royal dynasties at newly emerging cities. In other words, Tikal now perhaps had its own missionaries, its own Smoking Frogs.

At Tikal there exists something of a curiosity which, though it may well be pure coincidence, just happens to fall in with this line of thought. In the sculpture museum is the headless statue, in the round, of a corpulent man, bereft of clothing and ornament, seated cross-legged and

Buddha-like, his hands on his knees, one palm facing up, the other down. Quite anomalous in style, the sculpture has been known for years simply as 'Hombre de Tikal', the 'Man from Tikal'. On the back it bears an incomplete and complex text, not all of which has been deciphered. The figure is unique at Tikal in that the individual depicted is not a member of the ruling line. He is called an *ahaw*, simply a lord, perhaps the head of one of the city's powerful but subordinate lineages. Indeed, the sculpture was found in a complex of outlying residential structures that probably housed just such a group. The man's name, intriguingly, is 'K'uk Mo' and the sculpture appears to date from around AD 406. The evidence is purely circumstantial, but some scholars have been prepared to speculate that this might be the same man who, twenty years later, took the throne of Copán, who 'arrived' from the west – in this case from the direction of Tikal – bringing with him the acquired cultural baggage of Central Mexico.

Speculation, in this still extremely cloudy period of Maya history (the above being only a minor example), is inevitable as part of the rearrangement of scholars' mental furniture after notable epigraphic advances have been made. With the appearance of a few fresh pieces in the jigsaw, enticing new possibilities spring into view. It is at such moments that archaeologists are liable to step in with a few cautionary words to restrain the enthusiasm of some of their more imaginative epigrapher colleagues, who have been known to pick up the ball of conjecture and run with it way beyond the court of credibility.

Mayanists have been well aware for many years of the influence of Teotihuacan within the Maya world during the Early Classic period. The difference now is that epigraphy is able to provide extraordinarily detailed information about events, dates and times of 'arrival' of named personalities, who suddenly appear very tangible. There remain, however, considerable uncertainties. Much of the evidence scholars are dealing with – styles and symbols in architecture and pottery, the particular iconographic details of stone sculpture – are open to different interpretations. The textual record is also often insubstantial and enigmatic. We are told of men 'from the west' who 'arrive'. We have to draw our own conclusions as to what these phrases actually mean, bearing in mind that Maya discourse, down to the present day, is well known to be highly metaphorical. None the less, the present combination of evidence suggests that, at Tikal in particular, the Teotihuacan impact was a very real and direct one.

What occurred at Copán must remain an open question for the time being. On the face of it, however, at both cities by the mid-fifth century, what had been a powerful injection of influence from outside appears to have been absorbed and a 'Maya' normality restored.

After the events recorded on Stela 31 the history of Tikal becomes much more difficult to follow. Stormy Sky died in 456 and was laid to rest in the North Acropolis. The walls of his rock-cut tomb were painted, much like those at Río Azul, with his name glyph and the date of his death. Stela 31 was set up above the place of burial. He was followed on the throne by a man known as Kan Boar. He and his immediate successors are called the 'Staff Kings' from the way that they represented themselves on their few surviving stelae in relatively simple costume, bereft of more overt military or captive-taking imagery, holding decorated staffs in rituals marking period endings in the Maya calendar. The inscriptions on these stelae provide nothing in the way of 'historical' information. A particular fascination of the early sixth century is the first documented appearance of a royal woman in Maya texts, mentioned on one extremely damaged stela, Stela 23. Born in 504, her name is unknown and she is simply referred to as 'Lady of Tikal'. What is now thought to have been her palace has been identified near the centre of Tikal. During a period which appears to have seen serious problems with the dynastic succession, she may even have taken the throne herself for a short time.

If the very slim epigraphic evidence suggests a climate of political uncertainty, the archaeological picture indicates that Tikal continued to prosper. There was a considerable amount of construction activity, particularly on the North Acropolis, where a splendid new temple was put up above Stormy Sky's tomb facing onto the Great Plaza. We know nothing of the 'foreign affairs' of this period, although the appearance of a Tikal emissary recorded at Yaxchilán in 508 might suggest that the city maintained – and was perhaps even attempting to expand – an axis of allies and trade connections, all keyed in to what most would presume was a continuing relationship with Teotihuacan.

The mysterious 'Lady of Tikal' may well have been the mother of a man called 'Double Bird', the twenty-first ruler, who came to the throne in 537. It is with the ill-fated Double Bird that the mists begin to lift slightly over the history of this period. What we can now make out is unprecedented disaster for Tikal. For the power and prominence it had gained in the Maya world was to be challenged by another force, a shadowy and still little-known Maya city to the north which had been gathering strength for centuries.

KINGDOM OF THE SNAKE

The greatest extent of tropical forest remaining today in the whole of Central America straddles the Guatemala/Mexico border and includes two vast, contiguous and officially designated conservation areas: the 3 million acre Maya Biosphere Reserve covering the Petén north of Tikal, and the Calakmul Biosphere Reserve, some 1.8 million acres of Southern Campeche. The long-term protection of these areas is still in the wishful-thinking stage of grand public pronouncements and dotted lines on maps, since the terrain in question is enormous and governmental resources severely limited. But for the time being, most of this green heartland of the lowland Maya world remains as it has been for centuries, sheltering a host of Maya ruins. Besides those recently investigated early giants such as El Mirador and Nakbé, there are still dozens of jungle-clad towns and cities in this remote region. A number have by now been explored, but the true scale of many may still not be apparent and others undoubtedly lie waiting to be discovered.

About 30 kilometres north of the Guatemalan border lies the city of Calakmul. It was first discovered in 1931 and initial surveys of its buildings and monuments were carried out in the next few years. But it is only since the early 1980s that the true scale of this great city has begun to be appreciated, due to the work of two Mexican archaeological projects led by William Folan and Ramon Carrasco. A dirt road now leads to Calakmul from the main trans-Campeche highway, and although much of it is still covered by vegetation, visitors can begin to appreciate what is now acknowledged to be the largest of all Classic Maya cities, bigger even than Tikal. Well over 6000 individual structures have now been recorded within an inner residential area of some twenty-two square kilometres. Here there are more buildings, more densely packed than at Tikal, including the greatest known concentration of well-built stone 'palaces', which would have given Calakmul the look of a Maya metropolis.[13]

The city was surrounded by a sophisticated system of canals and reservoirs, thirteen of the latter providing a quite staggering storage capacity of some 200 million litres of water to see the city's 60,000 or so inhabitants through the months of the dry season. Much like El Mirador or Tikal, Calakmul was laid out on higher ground flanked by large seasonal swamps or *bajos*, in particular a vast area to the west, thirty-four by eight kilometres, known as 'El Laberinto', its margins providing great potential for raised field agriculture. At Tikal, broad limestone *sacbes* were constructed to connect different sections of the city. Survey on the ground and from the air, using satellite imaging, has detected sections of a much more extensive system at Calakmul – not just city-centre causeways but long-distance limestone roads. Their date is still uncertain, but by the Late Classic period at least, Calakmul possessed an efficient transport network, essential in this region in the rainy season, which served to connect a number of towns, such as Oxpemul to the north or Naachtun to the south, with the great city itself. Folan and his colleague Joyce Marcus, who first proposed the term in the early 1970s, describe Calakmul as a very large 'regional state', with a lattice-work of secondary and tertiary centres subservient to the major power. Indeed the area over which it had direct territorial control may have been more permanent and much greater than Tikal's, even stretching, Simon Martin suggests, into Quintana Roo to the north.

At the very centre of Calakmul is a great plaza, with the major groups of palaces and public buildings extending to the east and west. Folan's team has delimited a core area here of 1.75 square kilometres with 975 structures; 300 have vaulted stone masonry and 92 buildings were laid out on sizeable pyramidal platforms around courts and plazas. The most impressive structure of all, to the south of the central plaza, is Structure II, a pyramid 140 metres square at its base and rising some 55 metres high (see plate section, p. 13). Dating from the Late Preclassic period, it is comparable in scale and construction to the gigantic 'El Tigre' pyramid at El Mirador. Structure VII, twenty-four metres high, also Preclassic in origins and with a Late Classic temple on top, is the main temple pyramid to the north. Clustered at its foot and beneath the other main buildings were groups of the stelae erected by Calakmul's kings. On the east side of the plaza stand a group of three buildings in a row, Structure IVa, b and c, and facing them to the west is a higher, flat-topped pyramid. These almost certainly functioned as the kind of astronomical observatory we have seen at both Uaxactún and Tikal.

To the south-east, a short distance from the plaza, lies an impressive palace known as Structure III, originally surmounted by three hollow roofcombs, with a wide access stairway leading to three principal entrances. The labyrinthine interior contains twelve separate rooms where grinding-stones, hearths and the remains of cooking-pots suggest that a good deal of domestic activity went on here. Chert implements also seem to have been worked in one of them. But it was here, too, that beneath Room 6 Folan's team found a very rich and intact Early Classic burial, known as Tomb 1, dating from the fifth century AD. The deceased, a male at least thirty years old, had been laid on a woven mat within a lidded masonry cavity and was accompanied to the afterlife by elaborate pottery in traditional Maya style, a sting-ray spine of the kind used in personal bloodletting, shell beads and ear ornaments and a number of shells carved in the shape of human skulls. Three beautiful jade mosaic masks had been placed on his face and chest and originally attached to his belt, along with other jade jewellery. The whole burial, like that of Yax K'uk Mo at Copán, was covered in copious quantities of red cinnabar. The most interesting items were three jade plaques, which would have hung from one of the masks. Each is incised with a pair of glyphs, one of which seems to record the name of the occupant of the tomb, whom Joyce Marcus has provisionally called 'Long-lipped Jaw-Bone'. The identity of this man, however, whether he was a ruler of Calakmul or merely a member of the aristocracy, is still unknown. The pottery indicates a fifth-century date, but it is impossible to be any more precise.

The earliest decipherable hieroglyphic evidence for a fifth-century date at Calakmul comes from Stela 114, set up by an Early Classic ruler in 431. So we know that a Calakmul royal dynasty was in place at the same time that Stormy Sky and Yax K'uk Mo were on the throne. How much earlier it might have been established remains an important question. On Stela 114 little is legible apart from the date, which introduces the major problem at Calakmul, and the reason why the city's importance has been almost universally underestimated over the years: the state of preservation of its monuments. Calakmul possesses the largest number of stelae of any Maya city, presently totalling 116. Some of these are very large and imposing and there seems to have been the unusual tradition here of producing pairs of monuments depicting both Calakmul rulers and their wives. But the local limestone is of poor quality and erosion has been severe. The vast bulk of Calakmul's inscriptions are totally illegible.

We saw in the previous chapter how, since their discovery by

Heinrich Berlin in the 1950s, 'emblem glyphs' have proved a vital tool in reconstructing the political geography of the Classic period and the relationships between individual cities. Coupled with the name of a Maya ruler, they refer to the 'Holy Lord' of a particular political entity. They are specific to one territory and found both at the 'home' site itself and at other cities with which it had particular connections. There are still a few documented emblem glyphs that are not attached to a known site. In other words, we know about them from their appearance in a 'foreign' context, or sometimes on looted monuments, but the towns or cities they refer to have still not been positively identified. In the Usumacinta valley region, for example, not far from Yaxchilán, the sites of Sak Tz'i and Man are known because their emblem glyphs are cited by their neighbours. But their ruins must be lurking somewhere in the forest, unrecognized or, less likely, still undiscovered.

In the 1970s scholars noticed that one particular emblem glyph, with the main sign of a snake's head, was to be found distributed over many parts of the Maya lowlands. Indeed it was the most commonly named 'foreign' city mentioned in the records of others. The city's importance and influence by the Late Classic was clearly considerable, but for a long time no one knew to whom the mysterious snake's head belonged. In 1973 Joyce Marcus suggested that it might be connected with Calakmul. Proof, however, was long in coming, principally because, although the snake's head could be defined on some Calakmul monuments, the inscriptions were so worn that the context in which it appeared was unclear. The reference could have been to another foreign city. Other candidates were put forward as potential owners of the snake's head emblem besides Calakmul, and then for many years, pending positive identification, researchers agreed to refer to the snake's head city by the appropriately mysterious title 'Site Q', invented by Peter Mathews, the 'Q' standing for 'Que?' in Spanish. Newly discovered texts at Calakmul now demonstrate beyond reasonable doubt that it was Calakmul's rulers who referred to themselves as *K'ul Kan Ahaw* or 'Holy Lord of the Snake'.[14]

If the matter of the Calakmul emblem glyph has been resolved, the inscriptions from the city still yield very little information, especially about its history during the Early Classic period. Simon Martin has pieced together some of the frustratingly fragmentary clues and devised a provisional dynastic chronology, but many uncertainties remain. There are also some intriguing possibilities, or perhaps diversions. Martin has recently analysed the texts from an extraordinary series of painted ceramic vessels known as 'Dynasty Vases'.[15] These form a small group of very similar pots, all of which were found by looters and are thus devoid of any archaeological context. The best that can be said at present is that they originate from the broad northern Petén / southern Campeche area and date from the seventh or eighth centuries. They are all vessels of similar cylindrical form, of the kind commonly used for chocolate drinking, and are painted in a variant of what Michael Coe has termed the 'Codex Style', pots decorated with marvellous calligraphic assurance and freedom, normally depicting narrative, mythological scenes accompanied by sections of text, and framed in such a manner, within formal lined borders on a page-like buff or cream ground, that they offer one a vivid idea of what a Classic period codex might have looked like. In fact, Maya vase painters were almost certainly codex painters as well.

The Dynasty Vases are a distinctive sub-group in that they are all text, completely covered in columns of glyphs painted in black with certain details picked out in red. The most impressive example of all apparently provides a king-list for maybe 400 years of Calakmul's early history, noting the names and dates of accession of nineteen 'rulers', accompanied by repetition of the Calakmul emblem glyph (see plate section, p. 13). However, the dates are not anchorable to the Long Count, given only in the fifty-two-year cycle of the Calendar Round, and there are many scribal errors and omissions. The list of kings throws up names that are the same as those of a few known Calakmul rulers, but none can be directly connected to documented individuals since none of the accession dates on the pots match those which have survived in the monumental inscriptions. All in all, it seems unlikely at present that the Dynasty Vases will offer a meaningful royal history for the Classic period. One also has to remember, Martin cautions, that these are pots rather than stone monuments, and painted ceramics, buried with the dead and destined for the Underworld, are conventionally more inclined to record supernatural and mythological subject-matter. Thus what is phrased as history may mean something of a different, mythic nature. But, in the same way that the inscriptions of Palenque provide a dynastic chronology that, as one goes back in time, moves from the verifiably accurate to the seemingly legendary and the plainly mythological, so these ceramic texts may represent either a list of very early Calakmul rulers, from whom later kings took some of their names, or of legendary figures from the Preclassic past of Calakmul, or even El Mirador. For, as Martin suggests, Calakmul may have gloried in a distant inheritance of political authority from its great Preclassic neighbour.

On a clear day, you can see the great pyramids of El Mirador thirty-five kilometres to the south from the top of Structure II at Calakmul. Recent work here has shown that the city was well-established in the Late Preclassic period and shared architectural styles and ceramic traditions with El Mirador. Their relationship at this time, whether they were allies or competitors, is still unclear. There is no doubt however, that after El Mirador's downfall around AD 150, Calakmul began to develop into one of the great cities of the Maya world. What remains of its architecture, as eroded as its stelae, has none of the beauty of other, better-preserved Maya cities. Yet the sheer scale of Calakmul is formidable. It appears that the city may have taken in considerable numbers of people migrating north, away from the local environmental problems that crippled El Mirador. During the Early Classic it formed a successor power bloc, founded on direct overlordship of much of the northern Petén and southern Campeche. Once Tikal had overcome Uaxactún and, fortified by the association with Teotihuacan, was spreading its sphere of influence across the central Petén and as far north as Río Azul, less than a hundred kilometres south-east of Calakmul, one might imagine that these two great cities would soon come into direct confrontation. Establishing convincingly that this was indeed the case, and that enmity between Tikal and Calakmul was to be played out across the Southern Lowlands throughout much of the Classic period, represents one of the major recent breakthroughs in our understanding of Maya political history.

The evidence for their developing rivalry in the Early Classic does not come from the hieroglyphic inscriptions of the protagonists themselves, Calakmul's own records being lamentably unreadable and few inscriptions surviving from Tikal for the later part of the Early Classic, for reasons that will become apparent. The key texts are those of other, emerging cities, just beginning to write their own histories, who seem to have been caught up and forced to take sides as the two great powers jostled for supremacy and sought to form alliances against each other. In charting this developing clash, Martin and Grube focused on precise hieroglyphic phrases which convey relationships of domination and subordination between Maya cities.[16] One of these, *y-ahaw*, 'the lord of' or in effect 'his vassal' we have already come across in relation to

Tikal. Curl Nose referred to himself as the subordinate of Smoking Frog in this way and, as Tikal's influence around Lake Petén Itzá grew, rulers of lesser towns in the area began to concede that they were vassals of Tikal. A second critical phrase occasionally appears in texts that speak of the accession of kings. This is *u-kahiy*, which translated literally would mean 'it was done by him' but which can also be interpreted as 'under the auspices of'. Combined with the name and emblem glyph of a foreign lord, it conveys the clear idea of a patron–client relationship – the ruler of a lesser kingdom coming to the throne with the approval of the leader of a more powerful city.

The *u-kahiy* phrase is used at the accession of new kings at cities to the east of Tikal in the middle of the sixth century. A stela at Naranjo records a ruler taking the throne in 546 under the auspices of the king of Calakmul. Seven years later, a man known as 'Lord Water' accedes at the city of Caracol in Belize. This time the *u-kahiy* agency term is coupled with the name of Double Bird of Tikal. Thus these two cities each had a different patron, seemingly pulling the strings in the background. At Caracol the situation becomes extremely interesting. For if it was Tikal's ally in 553, relations changed rapidly. This is recorded by an inscription, sections of it extremely worn, on what is known as Altar 21 at Caracol – in fact a circular stone marker or monument from one of Caracol's ball-courts, often a location where incidents of warfare or sacrifice are commemorated. After recalling Lord Water's coming to the throne, at the nod of Double Bird, the text goes on to state that three years later, in 556, Tikal carried out an 'Axe War' or a 'Decapitation Event' (as Martin and Grube phrase it) against its former associate. A prominent individual from Caracol was captured and sacrificed by Double Bird. Thus the Caracol–Tikal relationship had turned abruptly from co-operation to antagonism. The following year we know that Double Bird celebrated the *katun* anniversary of his accession by raising Stela 17 at Tikal. This was to be the last cause for celebration at Tikal for a very long time.

Sometimes a Maya city will publicly admit to a defeat. Almost invariably however, this only serves as preamble to a confident affirmation that the reverse was eventually put right. Such is the case with the inscription on Altar 21 at Caracol. For it proudly proclaims that, five years after their man was sacrificed by Tikal, a terrible revenge was exacted. According to Altar 21, in 562 a victorious 'Star War' was carried out against Tikal, a term only used when the loser suffers a decisive defeat. This war was indeed a catastrophe for the great city. Its effects were profound and long-lasting and they explain what for many years was known as the Tikal 'Hiatus', a period of well over a century, between 557 and 692, when some serious malaise had clearly affected Tikal and not one inscribed monument was erected.

Today we can reconstruct in outline what very probably happened. In 562 Tikal's enemies overran the city. They smashed and burnt monuments and shrines, uprooted stone stelae and broke them to pieces, discarding or burying the fragments. One can see today the tell-tale signs on those monuments that survive: the rubbed surfaces, the faces of sculptures obliterated, their heads and hands lopped off, the pecking marks from frenzied attacks with stone tools. Archaeologists have found human bones, jade ornaments, caches of obsidian and fine pottery from temples and tombs on the North Acropolis scattered about and stuffed into nearby *chultunes* or underground storage chambers.

The perpetrators of this iconoclasm set out to humiliate Tikal, to insult the memory of the royal dynasty they had defeated and very probably to take away in triumph some of its portable and holiest images, a practice well-attested from later times. Yet this was not a war of conquest, as we would understand it. Tikal may have been occupied for a short period, but the victors had no desire to take it over on any permanent basis. Their aim, which proved extremely successful, was to keep the city subdued and crippled. The archaeological record reveals that for the next century Tikal's population stopped growing, and may even have declined. People from the outskirts moved closer to the centre, perhaps for greater security. There were no stelae or great public monuments erected, but they still had rulers. The precise fate of Double Bird is unknown, though we may presume that he was taken away and sacrificed on top of an unfamiliar pyramid. Another man, called Animal Skull, became ruler in his stead and on his death around 600 he was buried in the North Acropolis in a well-furnished tomb. Accompanying him was a ceramic plate with an inscription which described him as the twenty-second successor to the Tikal throne, Double Bird having been the twenty-first. The pretence of normality was thus maintained. But the text goes on to name his father. It was not Double Bird. Where Animal Skull came from is unknown. He may have been from a foreign city, but it seems more likely that he was a collaborator from within. For the next century, Tikal's quisling rulers or appointees did not live in the centre of the city, but were relegated, it seems, to an area in the southern suburbs.

Tikal's trade and its wealth declined dramatically in these years. The quality of grave goods became uniformly poor and the production of painted ceramics at Tikal almost ground to a halt. In contrast, those who had defeated Tikal prospered. The work of Arlen and Diane Chase at Caracol since the mid-1980s has demonstrated this very clearly.[17] Caracol lies in a favourable location at the foot of the Maya Mountains in Belize. It dates back to the Late Preclassic period, and the city's early growth is probably connected in part to its control of a valuable nearby source of rock for grinding-stones, which were distributed over much of the lowlands. But Caracol remained a middle-ranking Maya town until the defeat of Tikal, after which its growth was spectacular. The population is thought to have increased more than 300 per cent in a very short space of time and was eventually the equivalent of Tikal's at its height. For decades the city was an ongoing building site, with impressive temple pyramids and a large residential area. Causeways up to ten kilometres long stretched to outlying settlements, and large expanses of terraced fields were laid out on neighbouring hill-slopes, one of the best examples of such terracing in the Maya area, to feed the mushrooming population. Especially striking are the richness of Caracol's tombs, even among those who were not of the topmost élite and who lived far away from the city centre. Prosperity seems to have filtered down through the whole fabric of the society, also evidenced, the Chases suggest, by the greatly increased amount of ritual activity, the most common way of displaying wealth in Maya society, carried out not just among the governing class but by the more humble inhabitants of Caracol. It thus appears that Caracol's expansion was a direct material consequence of Tikal's defeat. The Chases believe that the city received tribute from Tikal and that much of this was in people, large numbers of Tikal's inhabitants being taken to work on the construction and embellishment of the victorious city.

A key question is whether Caracol was working alone against Tikal in 562, for on the vital text on Altar 21, the phrase that would indicate who prosecuted the war is illegible. After Tikal's fall there is increasing evidence in other hieroglyphic inscriptions of a close relationship between Caracol and Calakmul, including *u-kahiy* expressions which clearly indicate that Calakmul was the dominant partner.[18] By the early seventh century, by which time the two cities were allies in campaigns against Naranjo, Caracol's monuments directly cite Calakmul as the prime mover in these encounters. Increasingly, scholars are coming to agree that the principal agent behind the downfall of Tikal was the menacing force of Calakmul, which for years had quietly been building up a formidable alliance and eliminating Tikal's more vulnerable allies. Tikal's old outpost of Río Azul, for example, seems to have been sacked around 530, and the city largely abandoned for the rest of the century. La Milpa, the second largest Classic Maya site in Belize and not far to the east of Río Azul, suffered a similar abandonment a little later and did not revive until the end of the seventh century. Both may well have been taken out by Calakmul.

The Early Classic remains an extremely cloudy epoch. Little is known about many cities undoubtedly developing at this time. Until the end of the period, very few were keeping substantial records in stone and much archaeological investigation remains to be done of the buried Early Classic levels of Maya cities. But the large-scale projects at Copán, Caracol and Calakmul in particular, coupled with ongoing work at Tikal, have succeeded in radically modifying previous ideas. Something of a pattern is detectable through these centuries. During the first part of the Early Classic, Tikal was the pre-eminent power in the Southern Lowlands, immeasurably fortified by its relationship with Teotihuacan. From Tikal the institution of dynastic rule and the carving of monuments with inscriptions and dates, the so-called 'stela cult', spread throughout the region. But Tikal did not have the field to itself, as was once thought. Out of the forests of Campeche, Calakmul has arisen dramatically in the last decade to claim a central though still enigmatic place in the history of the Classic Maya. Very little is known about Calakmul before the sixth century. We cannot say when the rivalry with Tikal began in earnest, though the arrival of Smoking Frog at Tikal may well have precipitated it. In due course two power blocs emerged: a more 'internationalist' alliance, as some would term it, gathered around Tikal and its connections with central Mexico, and perhaps a more 'conservative' Maya axis headed by Calakmul. By the middle of the sixth century, encircled by enemies who had fallen to the threats and blandishments of Calakmul, Tikal was vulnerable. This vulnerability may have been increased by the declining power of the empire of Teotihuacan, already overstretched and on the wane, withdrawn perhaps from its trading connections with Tikal and unable to offer any support to its faraway Maya ally. Thus it was that Tikal confronted defeat and a kind of suspended animation for over a century. But it was not to be the end of the story of rivalry between the two 'superpowers' of the Maya world.

CHAPTER FIVE

The Late Classic

If one were to compare the different stages of Maya civilization to the growth of the maize plant – appropriate enough, since to the Maya maize was not only the staff of life but also the stuff of which humans were formed and its life-cycle the supreme metaphor for existence on this earth – the Late Classic would be the swelling time of fruitfulness just prior to harvest, before the cob is lopped and left hanging from the stalk. The two centuries between about 600 and 800 AD were the unsurpassed heyday of the Maya and an extraordinary period of creativity in art, architecture and the elaboration of religious beliefs. Our familiar vision of the ancient Maya today is largely formed by the enduring images of temple pyramids, relief sculpture and fine painted ceramics from this era.

These years were a time of unparalleled growth in a more literal sense, namely a dramatic increase in the population of the Southern Lowlands. Established cities greatly expanded and new ones sprang up as colonists began to fill in areas that before had only been sparsely settled. The vast majority of Maya people still tilled the fields, but urban society became more and more complex, made up of a growing body of permanent city-dwellers, the relations or retainers of a now proliferating ruling élite. Many of these people were necessary for the arts, sciences and religion, the administration of trade and tribute, the whole more elaborate superstructure of Maya society to function efficiently.

During the course of the seventh century, while Tikal was temporarily removed from the scene as a major force, other cities began to emerge, to make their presence felt within their own particular area of the Maya lowlands and to advertise the doings of their rulers. In the Late Classic period emblem glyphs identify some forty cities who all claimed independence under their own royal dynasty. They may have claimed as much but for many this was a boast with little basis in fact. For there were great differences in scale, population and relative power between Maya city-states and, as we began to see in the previous chapter, patron–client relationships grew up between the stronger cities and their weaker neighbours. The most powerful states of all, Calakmul and Tikal, were capable of interfering in the affairs of other realms hundreds of kilometres away.

If one examines a more complete archaeological map of the area for the Late Classic period, triangles or dots, representing hundreds of ancient sites, blanket the Southern Lowlands. Here we restrict ourselves to those better-known sites where the progress of both archaeology and the study of Maya texts allows us to get closer to the triumphs and failures of Maya cities and their rulers.

COPÁN AND QUIRIGUÁ: THE ART OF KINGSHIP

John Lloyd Stephens first came face to face with the magnificence of Maya civilization at Copán. Yet the city he found was in a truly ruinous state. It was the very romance of that fallen grandeur which evoked such a sense of mystery and loss in his writings. Many of the great stelae were still standing where they had been set up more than a thousand years before, but the bulk of the city's architecture had tumbled. Fragments of sculpture and inscriptions and block upon block of cut stone were heaped up on the forest floor. Not until he reached Palenque could he imagine what ancient Maya buildings actually looked like. Stephens was certainly correct in his assessment of the relative merits of the two cities' architects, or more precisely, their masons. Copán's buildings were all covered originally in stucco. Once the city was deserted, the rains eventually washed this away. The interior of the walls being mud, without any admixture of lime to bind it together, as in most other cities, the inevitable result was that tree roots, clinging vines and further rains prized the stones apart and the fabric of Copán swiftly crumbled.

Putting parts of the city back together again has been one of the great achievements of the intensive work that has gone on here in recent years. Now we can begin to appreciate the extraordinarily rich artistic legacy of the city from the Late Classic period, and to connect particular rulers to the monuments that they created, although the extensive but extremely difficult texts at Copán provide much less in the way of narrative 'history' than many other Maya sites.

It was the tenth ruler of Copán, known as Moon Jaguar, who constructed the marvellously preserved Rosalila temple. He died in 578 and was succeeded by two long-lived and successful rulers. These were Butz Chan, or Smoke Serpent, who ruled for fifty years, and about whom very little is known, followed in 628 by the twelfth Copán king, called Smoke Jaguar, whose impact is better documented and who is regarded by archaeologists today as the single most important ruler of Copán after Yax K'uk Mo. By the end of his sixty-seven-year reign, the longest of any Copán king, there is clearer evidence of political expansion and greatly increased prosperity.

Smoke Jaguar is best remembered for erecting stelae a few kilometres beyond the confines of the city at both the eastern and western entrances to the valley. Five such stelae were set up in 652, an important period-ending in the Maya calendar. Their texts have only been partially deciphered and the precise purpose of such widely distributed monuments is still not clear. But one symbolic effect they must have had was to demarcate the more immediate territorial domain of the city and to advertise to any visitors that they were entering the sacred province of the lords of Copán. Studies of local settlement patterns have shown that by the middle of the seventh century the valley's population was steadily growing. It had still not reached much more than about 10,000 people in what is known as the 'Copán Pocket', the area of prime agricultural land surrounding the city that stretched some seven kilometres along the river. Likewise, the four other more distant 'pockets' that Copán dominated, covering about twenty-five kilometres of the valley, were also only lightly settled compared with a markedly steep climb in population during the eighth century. Thus the end of Smoke Jaguar's reign probably saw a peak in agricultural self-sufficiency and relative productivity, when most inhabitants of the area had access to good valley-bottom land.[1]

Copán's trade also appears to have flourished. Before about 650 its main external links had been with regions to the west and south, namely the upper Motagua valley and the Guatemalan highlands as far as Kaminaljuyú. Such commerce may well have been built up through Yax K'uk Mo's Teotihuacan connections. But after Teotihuacan's fall and the dislocation of many long-established networks, the main focus of Copán's interests shifted. A few rare, high-status items were always imported from the lowland Maya area to the north-west, but by the end of the seventh century the bulk of trade was with the south-eastern periphery of the Maya world. At this time, using the locally available clay sources, the Copán valley became the centre for the manufacture of a fine polychrome pottery known as 'Copador' ware which was exchanged far and wide into Honduras and El Salvador. In turn, large quantities of so-called 'Ulua Polychrome' ceramics from central Honduras were imported into Copán and are found in the rubbish dumps of houses throughout the valley. Doubtless many other perishable commodities were regularly exchanged in this way. Copán thus became a major power in trade with non-Maya peoples, and there is even some evidence of small groups from central Honduras settled in the Copán valley as dependent clients, almost the personal servants, of powerful Copán lineages.[2] During Smoke Jaguar's reign, we know that Copán dominated her Maya neighbour Quiriguá, sixty kilometres to the north. In that same period ending in 652, he erected an inscribed altar there which talks of the 'joining' of the two cities, a connection which almost certainly dates back to much earlier times. What this meant was that Copán held sway over a strategically situated city along the Motagua valley which controlled the jade sources up-river.

Thus it was that in 695 Smoke Jaguar handed over an expanding and cosmopolitan city state to his son – a man known some years ago by the rather curious name of '18 Jog', given him by Eric Thompson, who felt that the animal in his name glyph, which he couldn't identify, looked like a cross between a jaguar and a dog. Some call it a gopher, but there is now more general agreement that he should be known as '18 Rabbit'. His reign was to be a famous time, a truly great period in the cultural history of Copán, when art and architecture reached its greatest heights.

If Smoke Jaguar had spread his monuments around the valley, 18 Rabbit focused on the remodelling and beautification of the city centre, beginning a programme of monumental construction whose primary concern seems to have been to glorify his own role as the Divine Lord at the centre of the Copán world. The Acropolis had achieved its present form in outline by this time, with two spacious courtyards to the east and west. To the north of the East Court, on the edge of the Acropolis, remote though visible from the open, more public plazas below, 18 Rabbit had his masons and sculptors devise a wonderfully imposing temple, known as Temple 22. In earlier times buildings such as Rosalila were decorated in modelled stucco, thick layers of lime plaster built up over stone armatures and then carved and richly painted. By 18 Rabbit's reign, architecture was still stuccoed but in much thinner layers of lime-wash. The accent now was to be on direct carving of the malleable volcanic stone. One reason for the change in technique may have been the realization by the seventh century that the production of unlimited quantities of plaster, made by burning lime in wood-fired kilns (an example of which has recently been excavated), was contributing heavily to the depredation of the valley's forests. Practical necessity – one might call it environmental awareness – led to artistic triumph. For the switch in emphasis from stucco to stone had the effect of liberating Copán's sculptors, who developed their unique school of elaborate high relief carving and produced some of the finest of all Maya works of art.[3]

Much like Rosalila, Temple 22 was conceived as embodying some of the most elemental forces of the universe. The exterior corners of the building and the cornice running around it display the fearsome masks of *wits* monsters, *wits* being the Maya word for hill, deciphered by David Stuart which announce that the structure is, in effect, a personified mountain. The central doorway above a flight of steps was in the form of a gaping monster mouth. Passing the threshold across the protruding teeth of its lower jaw, led inside the mountain. Anyone entering here in ancient times, and (few would have done so) would have found themselves in a fantastic torch-lit cave, faced by an even more extraordinary inner doorway framed by relief scupture that was bewilderingly alive (see overleaf). To either side of this entrance are the figures of two *bacabs*, also known as *Pauahtuns*, the sky-bearer gods, holding up the earth to the east and west. Above and between them, writhing over the doorway, is a celestial 'serpent monster' representing the heavens and the daily path of the sun as it moves across the sky. Beneath the *bacabs'* feet are two large human skulls, denoting the realm of the Underworld beneath the plane of the earth. Further skulls are to be found interspersed in an inscription below the threshold, which records the dedication of the temple at the completion of the first katun of 18 Rabbit's reign. Beyond this doorway is a small, elevated inner sanctum where 18 Rabbit and his acolytes would have been at the very heart of the mountain. Here he would have come to sanctify his kingship and give offerings of human blood, his own and that of noble captives, to nourish the forces of the earth and to celebrate the time of creation itself. For throughout this temple were personified images of maize, the material from which the Maya believed people were fashioned and which was first located and brought forth by the gods from within the heart of a sacred mountain. The Maize God was thus characterized as 'First Father', the father of creation, and from Temple 22

Reconstruction drawing of interior doorway leading to the inner chamber of Temple 22, Copán, prepared for Alfred Maudslay by Annie Hunter.

survive the most beautiful of all Maya sculptural representations of him as a young man.

It is to the north, however, amongst the more public plazas, that one witnesses today 18 Rabbit's greatest material impact upon the city. Immediately beneath the Acropolis lies the Copán ballcourt, in a beautiful position with the cleft hills to the north of the valley mirroring the form of the court itself (see plate section, p. 14). 18 Rabbit undertook the last remodelling of one of the most impressive ball-courts in the Maya world, which had been reconstructed a number of times since it was first laid out in the time of Yax K'uk Mo.

Stephens had connected what he called the 'gymnasium' at Chichén Itzá with the ball-game described by Spanish chroniclers at the time of the Conquest. To the Spaniards, whose previous experience of playing ball may have amounted to little more than kicking a pig's bladder around town back in Extremadura, the ritualized formality of the Aztec game, the athleticism of the players, and the fervour which surrounded it as a public spectacle were quite astonishing. Cortés despatched a troupe of Mexican ball-players across the Atlantic in 1528 to feed European curiosity. Different versions of a ball-game were played in Mesoamerica from very early times and the earth embankments of what may be one of the most ancient courts of all, dating back to about 1800 BC, have recently been discovered at Paso de la Amada along the Pacific coast of Chiapas. The Olmec played the game and ancient balls, boiled and solidified spheres of black latex, have been found preserved at Olmec sites. Indeed the name Olmec, which was given to the people of the Gulf Coast by the Aztecs, means in Nahuatl 'the people from the land of rubber' and appropriately, from this steamy Dunlop county of the Aztec empire, the annual tribute sent to Tenochtitlan consisted of 16,000 rubber balls.[4]

Local variation in the layout of ballcourts was considerable, but by Aztec times the playing alley, flanked by two parallel walls, was on average eight to ten metres wide, up to forty metres long and opened out into two end zones that gave the court an I-shape. As recorded by the chroniclers, the game was played by two teams of no more than four players. The idea was to keep the ball in the air by striking it with the hips, thighs or upper arms and bouncing it off the side walls. Use of hands or feet was forbidden. The solid rubber ball was little more than ten to fifteen centimetres in diameter and extremely hard. Serious injuries were commonplace. The players wore only loincloths but protected themselves with gloves to soften the impact from wall or ground as they flung themselves about, pads on the knees and upper arms, and a very large protector for the hips and waist known as a 'yoke', made of animal skins, wood or perhaps of fibre padding within a wicker frame. Stone yokes are known from some parts of Mesoamerica but there is still debate about whether these may have been ceremonial attire, or perhaps the moulds around which protectors of perishable materials were formed.[5]

There is also much uncertainty about the rules of the game and the system of point scoring, since the Spanish accounts do not mention such things in any detail. By the time of the Conquest stone rings had come to be sunk vertically into the centre of each of the side walls, and anyone who succeeded in passing the ball through them was immediately declared the winner. But the holes in the rings are little bigger than the diameter of the ball and such a winning score must have been a freakish rarity, no doubt turning the player responsible into an instant hero. Simply making contact with the rings seems also to have been an element in scoring, as was propelling the ball far into the end zone of the opposition. Allowing the ball to touch the ground, however, led to penalty points and even to the loss of the whole match. The Aztec game drew passionate and often wild popular support from enormous, partying crowds and the Spaniards, themselves inveterate gamblers, were amazed at the level of betting. People lost their clothes, consignments of agricultural produce, and even sold themselves into slavery on the outcome of a game. The Spanish eventually banned it, not simply because of crowd trouble and the threat to public safety, but because the important events were much more than just a game. Here idolatry and abomination festered. For the ballcourt was a place of sacrifice, an arena where death often awaited the loser, whose head would then be impaled on a skull-rack adjoining the court.

Among the Maya of the Classic period, there were probably significant differences in the way the game was played. Scenes of the ball-game illustrated in Maya sculpture and painted ceramics suggest that the ball may have been much larger. The court, however, was smaller than in later times, that at Copán being the largest Classic court known, and the walls invariably had sloping sides, 'benches', off which the ball was perhaps more easily bounced and kept in play. Solid stone 'markers' were set into the walls rather than rings, and at Copán these are in the form of macaw heads, three to each side, one at each end of the court and one in the middle, positioned at the top of the inclined benches. Flat stone markers were also evenly placed along the middle of the playing alley, though their role in the game is unknown. Three beautiful carved examples from Copán, produced early in 18 Rabbit's reign, depict pairs of supernaturals playing the game (see below).

The Copán ball-court is a magnificent arena. In ancient times it could be viewed by the élite of Copán society from the steps of the surrounding temples. In the plazas below there no doubt milled the bulk of ordinary ball-game goers, those groundlings who may not have been able to see much of the game but could hear the thud of rubber ball on stone, hip or thigh and the whoops and cries of more privileged viewers

Ball-court marker Copán. The player to the left, wearing a large, padded 'yoke' or protector around his waist, may be Hunahpu, one of the Hero Twins, his opponent a lord of the Underworld.

that told them how the match was progressing. It was once thought that, compared with the barbarity that accompanied the Aztec version, the Maya played a more benign and elegant game of skill. But it is now evident enough, from the many depictions that survive and from what is revealed in hieroglyphic texts, that the Classic Maya ball-game, though probably played on a number of different levels, was of central importance in the religious life of the community, above all in its connection with the rites of kingship. And the outcome of the Maya game could be just as deadly as it was among the Aztecs. For the ballcourt was a magical threshold between the everyday world and the supernatural. On a simple level, the very act of keeping the ball in the air may have represented maintaining the sun and the planets on their course. Letting it fall to earth risked incurring the wrath of the gods of the Underworld, only separated by a thin symbolic membrane beneath the court. But the ball-game was at its most significant and potent when Maya rulers sponsored a game or participated themselves. Then it was that a man such as 18 Rabbit, through the ritual re-enactment of Maya origin myths, was seen to defeat the lords of the Underworld and keep human life on its course, ensuring the continuing cycles of regeneration and fertility. The climax of such rituals was the sacrifice of a captured nobleman, ideally a king, whose blood was deemed to be especially powerful. As in a Roman gladiatorial contest, the victim would be doomed to play a part, go through the motions of a game he could not win, and finally be despatched.

As a great ceremonial focus, the principal ballcourts at Maya sites were often given a central place in the layout of a city. At Copán the court forms the bridge between the Acropolis, the sacred precinct of kings, and the more mundane public plazas to the north. The latter area was laid out afresh by 18 Rabbit and was where he placed his most famous monuments, the astonishing stelae that have so overawed and perplexed visitors since the time of Stephens and Catherwood. One of these, a more modest example known as Stela J, was placed on its own at the eastern entrance to the Middle Plaza, at the point where a stone causeway leads into the centre of the city from one of Copán's main residential zones a kilometre away. Decorated in low relief with a simple mat-weave pattern on one face, it commemorates 18 Rabbit's accession in 695. But the main group, all planted in the northernmost 'Plaza of the Stelae', are very different. There are seven of them, known as Stelae A, B, C, D, F, H and 4. They are the ultimate expression of that flamboyant, baroque style of carving, almost in the round, peculiar to Copán. Once thought to have been gods, priests, women or men in skirts, they are now known to be portraits of 18 Rabbit in the guise of the gods.

Stela B represents him bearing many of the most typical symbols of office, comparable to the stelae at other sites such as Tikal. He supports with his two hands a 'sky serpent bar', the ruler symbolically holding up the sky. Jade plaques dangle from his belt, as do portrait masks of his ancestors, and two lancets for ritual blood-letting are tucked into it, encased in individual holsters. His turban-like headgear, seemingly unique to Copán and also to be seen on the figures around Altar Q, supports a headdress surmounted by a curious scene of human figures, almost certainly ancestors, among cloud scrolls on top of a sacred mountain. On either side of the mountain are the heads of two macaws with long, dangling beaks – Count Waldeck's elephant trunks. An ancient mythical name for Copán was Macaw Mountain, and the scene may represent 18 Rabbit communing with his ancestors at its summit.

Stela H is perhaps the most haunting of all the Copán stelae (see plate section). It represents the king wearing the apparel and symbolically transformed into the Maize God. Indeed, the face of 18 Rabbit here, eyes seemingly closed in contemplation, lips slightly apart, has much of the stylized, tranquil air visible on the sculptures of the god from Temple 22. The figure wears the net skirt common to representations of the deity and his 'back-rack' (a wooden or fibre frame fitted into the back of the belt to support the towering layers of ornament that rulers carried above and around the head in ceremonial) cascades with corn foliage, out of which tiny individual figures of the Maize God appear, clinging on with their hands. The likelihood is that 18 Rabbit, dressed in something like this extraordinary garb, would have descended from his maize mountain of Temple 22 to officiate in elaborate ritual here on the plaza.

The panels of hieroglyphic inscriptions upon these stelae are works of art in their own right, and so many sophisticated and idiosyncratic scribal devices have been employed that epigraphers still find the texts extremely hard to understand. They certainly commemorate period-endings in 18 Rabbit's reign and much of the content appears to be made up of ritual formulae and references which perhaps connect the dates of the erection of the monuments with particularly important and unusual alignments of planets and stars. Indeed, it may be that the original performance that went on around some of them took place at night.[6]

A section of the inscriptions on Stela A has become a famous text. It seems to promise much, for it brings together, in a most unusual way, the emblem glyphs of Copán, Tikal, Palenque and Calakmul, each associated with one of the signs for the 'four skies' or cardinal directions. Was this a reference to these cities as particularly sacred sites or did it mean, as a few scholars thought some years ago, that by this point in the Late Classic period the Maya lowlands were divided up politically into powerful territorial states controlled by these four 'capital cities'?[7] Today this latter interpretation seems unlikely, but exactly what the text is saying remains none too clear. At the very least it would indicate that 18 Rabbit saw his city, and doubtless himself, as amongst the major players in the Maya world. Such haughty presumption did not save him from a most unfortunate fate. For, having presided over forty-three of the most glittering years in Copán's history, 18 Rabbit was to be dramatically cut down to size.

In 725 he had installed a man named Cauac Sky as ruler of Quiriguá. At the time this would have been little more than confirmation of the *status quo*, the traditional subordination of Quiriguá to its more powerful southern neighbour. But in 738 the tables were turned in a lightning coup, the news of which one can imagine spreading rapidly around the Maya world. Cauac Sky captured 18 Rabbit, took him back to Quiriguá, and sacrificed him. How this came about, no one can say. Only a few months previously, 18 Rabbit had dedicated his new ball-court. Some imagine that he may then have been on the look-out for prestigious captives to sacrifice there. The ruler was ageing, not as agile as he once was and maybe he took unnecessary risks in his quest for prisoners. He might have strayed into Quiriguá territory and been ambushed. Such scenarios are not impossible, but Maya texts tell us little. The monumental inscriptions of Quiriguá, where the event was to be repeatedly and triumphantly recalled, simply tell us, with brutal brevity, that the Copán king was 'chopped'.

Today's archaeologists can at least suggest the likely background to these events. Quiriguá, though still only a small city within the sphere of Copán, was, potentially at least, extremely wealthy in its own right. It was agriculturally rich, controlled the Motagua jade sources and the flow of other commodities such as cacao up and down the valley between the Gulf of Honduras and the Guatemalan highlands. But because of his city's political dependency, Cauac Sky would have seen much of this wealth siphoned off as tribute to Copán, a state of affairs that Quiriguá had probably had to live with for many years. It seems that he patiently laid the ground to challenge Copán's overlordship. In 734, for the first time in the city's history, Cauac Sky began to use his own Quiriguá emblem glyph and to call himself a *k'ul ahaw*, a holy lord, rather than a mere *ahaw* or subordinate lord. This cosmetic, preliminary assertion of independence must have been backed up, it is thought, by the formation of an alliance, quite possibly with non-Maya peoples from the lower Motagua valley, an alignment that, when the time came four years later, Copán could not resist. So, from Quiriguá's point of view, there was much more to the capture of 18 Rabbit than merely the acquisition of a prized royal head to be parted from its body. Behind it all lay hard-nosed political calculation, motivated by the prospect of increased power and material gain. Yet the success of any such strategy was immeasurably enhanced by the sacrifice itself. The offering to the gods of the blood of such a powerful *k'ul ahaw* would have vastly increased the prestige of Quiriguá and the authority of its fledgling royal line among both its own and neighbouring peoples. Cauac Sky seems to have achieved all those things, both sacred and secular in our terms, that were required of a Maya ruler. He had been successful in warfare, proved his supernatural power and relationship with the gods by a quite spectacular sacrifice, and very soon drew material wealth and people to his kingdom. Thus, much as Caracol had prospered and expanded markedly in the wake of the defeat of Tikal, so did Quiriguá, though in a more modest way. In the afterglow of his triumph, Cauac Sky turned his attentions to the design of a city commensurate with his new status. He decided to look no further than Copán itself as a model. The architecture that one sees today at Quiriguá, though it follows something of the same layout, is unimpressive. But what is immediately striking is the scale of the plaza and the monuments he set up there. They are enormous, far bigger than those at Copán, a deliberate attempt, it would seem, to outdo 18 Rabbit. Seven formidable stelae date from Cauac Sky's reign, vast blocks of reddish sandstone that were dragged to the site from quarries about 5 kilometres away. These are the biggest single stone monuments ever carved by the Maya. Stela E, for example, weighs more than sixty tons and is over ten metres high. Almost square in cross-section and decorated on all four sides, many of these stelae possess two images of the ruler, back and front, depicting him in a somewhat lower-relief style than that of Copán.

The intricate ornament is picked out with extraordinary precision, the quality of the stone enabling the sculptor to achieve a finish of almost metallic sharpness which has survived well down the years. The long panels of glyphic text are some of the most complex and beautifully executed of all Maya stone inscriptions, virtuoso performances by scribal sculptors, exemplified by the use, as at Copán, of so-called 'full-figure' glyphs, the substitution of the normal bar and dot numbers and hieroglyphs for the cycles of time by representations of the gods, which are as exquisitely, playfully carved as the miniature beings on medieval corbels or misericords.

Alongside its startling new stela tradition, Quiriguá developed another quite unique monumental style, the carving of large, irregularly shaped boulders with extraordinary composite creatures – elements of toads, birds of prey, crocodiles and jaguars that often surround the figure of the ruler, emerging from a monstrous mouth. It is the kind of fantastic, shamanistic jumble of powerful symbols from the natural world that takes one back to Olmec times. These famous 'zoomorphs' were completed by Quiriguá's two later kings after Cauac Sky's death in 784. For Quiriguá continued to flourish, and apparently to retain its independence, until the turn of the ninth century.

If Quiriguá thrived, Copán must have been stunned. The material effects were not catastrophic. There is no evidence of the occupation of the city by hostile forces or of damage to her monuments. Copán did not suffer like Tikal in the wake of her defeat by Calakmul and Caracol. She lost her economic connections with the lower Motagua. But the Copán population remained stable, the city was not drained of human and material resources, disabled by the demands of tribute. There was no great influx of Copán goods into Quiriguá and in both places the styles of ceramics and other artifacts remained quite distinct and much the same as before. But the more psychological blow, extremely hard for us to understand, to both the community as a whole and, above all, to the prestige of the royal dynasty, must have been severe. It would have seemed that the favour of the gods had been withdrawn, that the city's destiny was in the balance. It was vital, then, that the royal line should regroup and revive the confidence of the population. What is particularly interesting at Copán is that we can now appreciate both the public relations exercise that the ruling dynasty embarked upon in order to regain its authority and the extent to which that authority became in reality much diminished.

Tikal. Temple II, nearly 40m high, on the west side of the Great Plaza. The broad central stairway, now restored, leads to the funerary temple surmounted by a large decorative masonry crest or 'roof-comb'. Temple II may be the burial place of Lady Twelve Macaw, wife of Tikal's greatest Late Classic ruler Hasaw Chan K'awil, though to date no tomb has been discovered here.

The North Acropolis at Tikal in its restored state today following the excavations of the Tikal Project. By around AD 550, by which time construction on this site had almost come to an end, eight major temples were clustered together on a huge artificial platform. In the Great Plaza below stand the ranks of stelae that recorded the careers of the rulers buried here.

Teotihuacan. The heart of the city, looking south from the Pyramid of the Moon along the 'Street of the Dead'.

Rio Azul. Tomb 1. The painted inscription here on the rock-cut wall at the rear of the tomb begins with a date of 8.19.1.9.13 in the Long Count, or 29 September AD 417. It is followed by a glyph normally signifying birth, but which in this context may well mean 're-birth' in the after-life – in other words the death of the ruler buried here. The elaborate image on the right includes glyphic references to Curl Nose, king of Tikal, evidence of the connection between the two cities. This tomb had been stripped bare by looters by the time Ian Graham entered here and took this photograph in 1981.

Copán. Watercolour reconstruction by Tatiana Proskouriakoff of how the centre of the city would have looked towards the end of the Late Classic period.

1. Middle Plaza
2. Ball Court
3. Hieroglyphic Stairway
4. Temple 22
5. Temple 16
6. Plaza of the Stelae

Altar Q at Copán. The west side of the monument shows the founder of the royal dynasty Yax K'uk Mo handing the sceptre of office to Yax Pac, the 16th ruler.

The remains of Yax K'uk Mo in his tomb chamber way beneath the Acropolis at Copán are examined by archaeologist Robert Sharer. Amongst the bones lie small items of jade, including a bar pectoral much like that worn by the king on Altar Q.

Copán. A reconstruction drawing reveals the location of the buried Rosalila Temple and the structures and tombs beneath it.

1. Temple 16
2. Rosalila
3. Quetzal Macaw Panel
4. Margarita
5. Royal Female Burial
6. Yax K'uk Mo Burial
7. Yehnal
8. Sun God Panel
9. Hunal

The best example of the 'Calakmul Dynasty Vases'. The continuous text lists nineteen Calakmul 'rulers', dates and events to do with their accession to the throne and includes repeated versions of the city's emblem glyph. Standing on three small feet and with a rattling device in a false bottom, this pot is an unusual version of the form of vessel used for drinking a variety of chocolate beverages.

The north face of Structure II at Calakmul. Standing some 55 metres high, larger than any of the pyramids of Tikal, it is the most imposing structure at the heart of this great city. Dating from the Late Preclassic, it compares with the architecture of El Mirador, both in scale and the 'triadic' arrangement of temples that it supported.

The Ballcourt at Copán, in the distance the rolling hills that surround the valley.

Stela H at Copán. Dedicated by 18 Rabbit in AD 730 and representing the ruler wearing the netted skirt and other attributes of the Maize God. This stela still bears traces of original red paint.

The Popol Na, or Council House at Copán, distinguished by the pattern of mat-weave in stone mosaic on the façade of the building. The carving of a fish here is an emblem of one of the powerful families who would have been represented on the Council.

Temple 33, one of Yaxchilán's most impressive buildings, dedicated by the ruler Bird Jaguar in AD 756, four years after his accession. The remarkable pierced roof comb is a characteristic feature of the city's architecture. The remains of a large seated stucco figure of Bird Jaguar can be made out in the recess at the centre of it.

Tatiana Proskouriakoff's watercolour reconstruction of the Hieroglyphic Stairway, the history in stone of the Copán kingdom. It was completed around AD 755 by the ruler Smoke Shell, who erected the stela at the foot of the stairs.

For nineteen years, as far as the royal textual record is concerned, everything went very quiet. No more stelae were erected. We are told in later inscriptions that a certain Smoke Monkey was inaugurated soon after 18 Rabbit's death. He ruled for ten years and was followed in 749 by a man called Smoke Shell. By this time work had begun on the Hieroglyphic Stairway, that extraordinary monument which was designed to symbolize Copán's revival (see plate section, p.16).

Hieroglyphic stairs were the triumphal arches of the Maya world, commemorating victories in war and the sacrifice of important individuals. Usually, however, they advertise the successes of one particular ruler, and never on such an ambitious scale as at Copán. For this is the stairway to a complete pyramid which climbs twenty metres from the plaza lying to the south of the ball-court. The massive text of some 2200 recorded glyphs was carved on the risers of more than seventy steps that led originally to a platform and temple structure on the top. Today it appears that a first stairway was in fact begun by 18 Rabbit. Smoke Shell elaborated and completed it and constructed the shrine on the top. When it was finished, it provided nothing less than an official public history of the dynasty from the time of its foundation by Yax K'uk Mo. Large sections of the text are now lost, eroded or still indecipherable. But originally the inscriptions provided the birth and accession dates of rulers, the most important rituals they performed and the dates of their death. Seated sculptures of the last five successors before Smoke Shell were placed centrally at intervals on the way up.

Amongst these figures is a statue of 18 Rabbit, and a reference to his passing, an expression translated by David Stuart as 'his breath expired in war'. Although this phrase contrasts somewhat with the cruder, matter-of-fact word 'chopped' employed by those responsible for his death, there is no real distortion here or attempt to avoid confronting the fact. Indeed, there are a number of unarticulated blocks from the stairway that bear 18 Rabbit's name and there may well have been a longer section of text which perhaps said more about the Quiriguá episode. It is probably significant, too, that all his major monuments were to remain untouched, enduring witness to his greatness; he was to be venerated as a martyr who had given his life for his country in this latest chapter of the Copán story. For the essential message of the stairway was that 18 Rabbit's heroic end should be seen merely as one brief, unfortunate episode in the glorious 300-year march of Copán history. In the service of patriotic revivalism, the roll-call of royal ancestors, successful in war, successful in their dealings with the gods, was invoked as a rallying cry for the future.

Logically enough, the imagery that surrounded the figures on the stairway and in the temple at the summit was almost exclusively that of warfare and sacrifice. The seated sculptures bear shields and other martial emblems, some have captives at their feet and, ascending the stairs (that is, following dynastic history back in time), Tlaloc symbolism, that iconography of war adopted originally from Teotihuacan, becomes stronger until, at the summit, the façade of the temple was covered with huge Tlaloc masks. For this shrine was dedicated to the memory of that first great ancestral warrior king, Yax K'uk Mo. Thus it was that, in a time of uncertainty, the re-establishment of the founder's name and all that it stood for, began to be taken even further by the next ruler of Copán, Yax Pac.

At the base of the stairway is a stela that commemorates Smoke Shell, who dedicated the finished monument in 755. To crown dynastic rehabilitation he arranged a prestigious marriage for himself, to a royal lady from Palenque. By the time that Yax Pac came to the throne twelve years later, Copán was prospering once more and its population dramatically on the increase. He began his own major programme of building on the Acropolis. Thus, outwardly at least, normality had returned to the city. But the seeming re-establishment of the authority of the dynasty came at a price.

'Las Sepulturas', so named after the large number of tombs found in the area, was one of the principal residential zones just to the east of the city centre. Within it was a large family compound belonging to one long-established lineage, which in Yax Pac's day was headed by a man known as Mac Chanil. There he had quarters for his family members and more humble dwellings for a large contingent of retainers. It was this lineage who seem to have been host to a group of foreigners from central Honduras. Amongst the many things that extensive and extremely important excavations have revealed here is Mac Chanil's own palace, where he held court. It possessed a magnificent stone bench where he would have sat to receive visitors.[8] The bench was carved with six beautiful figures of Pauahtuns supporting it and bore an elaborate inscription made up of sixteen 'full-figure' glyphs, mentioning his mother and father and describing the lord as something like a 'courtier' of Yax Pac. It goes on to say that Yax Pac himself came to attend the dedication of the house, bringing with him a ceramic offering of some kind.

Maya rulers wielded their authority with the support of an aristocracy of powerful noble families, often linked by blood-line or marriage, whose allegiance was secured by royal largesse and patronage. But for the greater part of Maya history these people remain anonymous. That Mac Chanil should commemorate himself on his own monument is extremely rare. Not only that, but he used the same kind of cosmic imagery, the Pauahtuns and various other details, normally reserved for royalty; above all, we observe Yax Pac, the ruler, not receiving his courtiers at the time of his choosing in his own palace, but going off to participate in religious ritual in the house of a subordinate. In fact, in the inscription, the two men involved are accorded almost equal status. This is not an isolated example. By Yax Pac's reign the heads of other lineages were erecting their own monuments and asserting their individual status in this way. A brother and half-brother of the king were even employing the Copán emblem glyph in inscriptions alongside their names and one of them appears to have played the role of something like a chief minister.

The only building known to have been constructed immediately after 18 Rabbit's death, in the reign of Smoke Monkey, is the 'Popol Na', the 'Mat House', which we know from the use of the phrase among the Maya in more recent times to have been a Council House, the place where the most eminent community members came to debate public affairs, seated on mats. The Popol Na at Copán, Structure 22A, much of which has been brilliantly reassembled through the combined efforts of art historians, archaeologists and epigraphers, lies on the Acropolis just to the west of 18 Rabbit's Temple 22. There is a large patio outside the building where the members of the council may have congregated. The façade of the Popol Na is decorated with large woven mat or 'pop' designs (see plate section, p.15) and between them appear individual hieroglyphs which identify the members of the council and where in the Copán realm they came from. Above the glyphs were statues which appear to have represented the various local lords. Very recently, archaeologists have been able to connect the names of the powerful families appearing on the façade, such as the 'Fish' lineage, with their residential compounds in the valley below. All Maya kings in the Classic period appear to have ruled formally 'in council'. But nowhere else do we find such direct evidence, as displayed both in the Popol Na and their outlying residences, of the seeming devolution of power to the noble élite of a community. Yax Pac appears to have been forced into this to maintain their allegiance.

One of the greatest problems in the understanding of the Maya political system is to get beyond the rhetoric and display, the elaborate 'propaganda' of kingship, to the reality which lay behind it. The awesome stelae of 18 Rabbit convey the impression that power was highly centralized in the exalted semi-divine person of the ruler. There is little to suggest otherwise in the seventh and earlier eighth centuries. But after 18 Rabbit's death, major changes seem to have occurred which can be put down not only to the uncertainty of the times, when perhaps the nobility stepped in to fill something of a power vacuum, but also to other growing pressures within Maya society, to which we shall return in Chapter 7.

WARRIOR LORDS OF THE USUMACINTA

Apart from the debacle of the Quiriguá episode, mention of other smaller towns in its orbit and certain very rare references to diplomatic relations, such as the marriage alliance with a lady from Palenque, little is known about the external affairs of Copán. If those rulers whose memory was invoked on the Hieroglyphic Stairway were indeed great warriors and sacrificers of men, we don't know who they were fighting or where their captives might have come from. Copán's kings choose not to tell us, heightening the impression, which may well be an accurate one, that the city ploughed its own furrow on the eastern fringes of the Maya region in glorious and relatively peaceful isolation.

Along the banks of the Usumacinta River, 300 kilometres to the north-west, it was a very different world. The Usumacinta is formed from tributaries in the Guatemala and Chiapas highlands. One of these, the Rio Chixoy runs north out of the highlands and joins the Rio Pasión at the site of Altar de Sacrificios, a city that is not well preserved today but, given its position, must have been of considerable importance during the Classic period. Beneath it the Usumacinta flows majestically on towards the Gulf Coast, forming the greatest of all the Maya highways for canoe-borne trade and communication. Along it there are scores of Maya sites, great and small. The best known and the most formidable were Piedras Negras and Yaxchilán, both located at strategic points on the river itself, and Bonampak to the south of Yaxchilán, close to a looping tributary. The alluvial soils along the Usumacinta here are very productive, another reason why this region should have been densely populated. But exactly how dense is not known, since this is still a wild, jungle-clad, frontier region. It is in these forests, for example, that there still lie, somewhere between Piedras Negras and Yaxchilán, those presumably substantial sites such as Sak Tz'i, Witz or Man, which possessed their own emblem glyphs and are known from the inscriptions at other cities but which have not to date been identified on the ground.

A major new project is presently beginning at Piedras Negras, but concerted archaeological investigation of the sites in this region has been limited, apart from previous excavations at Piedras Negras in the 1930s and work carried out by Mexican archaeologists at Yaxchilán and at Bonampak in more recent years. Thus we have little of that extensive material context of the kind that now exists for Copán or Tikal. But the corpus of beautiful inscribed monuments, including stelae, 'altars', lintels, stone panels set into walls and hieroglyphic stairs, many of them well preserved, represents the most historically informative group of such monuments extant. For they treat of many different themes. Firstly, of course, as Tatiana Proskouriakoff began to unravel, they set down the dynastic records of ruling families. But they go beyond this, as she realized at Yaxchilán. Instead of the formal poses and terse, almost formulaic texts of many other cities, they provide a richer, more directly personalized history, often accompanied by narrative depictions of rulers playing the ball-game, for example, dancing or involved in bloodletting rituals. And besides the ruler himself other individuals are often mentioned, such as royal women, visitors from neighbouring cities and lesser lords.[9]

The most striking feature of the Usumacinta sites is the preoccupation of their monuments and inscriptions with warfare, more so than in any other part of the Maya world.[10] The most famous example is the Bonampak murals, with their graphic scenes of battle, capture and sacrifice. But many of the stone monuments exhibit comparable images: lords outfitted for war, standing over bound captives or grasping them by the arm or hair, pitiful compositions of prisoners awaiting sacifice, often accompanied by the 'count' of captives and the naming in a ruler's titles of his most famous prisoners. The clear impression is that warfare was more prevalent here among the Maya than anywhere else. This may well be true, particularly during the latter part of the eighth century, when the number of references to attacks and captures increases markedly. But it is very difficult to be sure that the Usumacinta was necessarily so different from other parts of the Maya world. Further north – in the Petén, for example – the situation may have been similar, only they chose not to write about it so much in stone.

Bonampak will be examined in more detail in Chapter 7. Here we will concentrate on what is known about Piedras Negras and Yaxchilán, only a day's canoe journey apart along the Usumacinta. For the history of these two cities during the Early Classic period, epigraphers have been able to piece together only a limited amount from references in later texts and, at Yaxchilán, early stone inscriptions remounted in Late Classic buildings. Thus we can trace Yaxchilán's foundation to Progenitor Jaguar, who came to the throne in 319, and we know the names of the city's first kings. The origin and most of the early history of Piedras Negras is still obscure, but by the sixth century it seems to have become the more dominant of the two. Indeed, the ninth ruler of Yaxchilán is depicted as a captive at Piedras Negras in 514. What is interesting and perhaps significant in this context is that in 508, Yaxchilán had received an emissary from Tikal, while there are indications in the inscriptions that Piedras Negras was already aligned with Calakmul. Thus, it may well be that the long-distance power-play between the two greatest Maya cities had already begun to manifest itself in this region. In 537 a Calakmul delegation, perhaps bearing the kind of offer that was hard to refuse, appeared at Yaxchilán. The immediate outcome of this visit is unknown. After this date there are very few references to events at Yaxchilán until the second half of the seventh century. Then it was, in 681, that Shield Jaguar II, better known as Shield Jaguar the Great, came to the throne. It was during his sixty-one-year rule and that of his son, Bird Jaguar IV, whose histories were first recorded by Proskouriakoff, that Yaxchilán was to reach its peak.

Shield Jaguar began the construction of the beautiful riverside city as we see it today, its buildings ranged on successive terraces and natural hills within the horse-shoe shaped bend in the Usumacinta. Much of the city's wealth must have been based on the control of commercial traffic, and signs of what, if not a bridge, was perhaps a control point or a kind of toll house have been found in the silt. Like some moated medieval castle, Yaxchilán would have been an impressive and intimidating sight for flotillas of canoes passing by, especially if, as some imagine, headless sacrificial victims were suspended on occasion from the roofcombs of the city's main temples, looking much like the dummies of Judas Iscariot that dangle from the towers of Chiapas churches during Easter today.

Yaxchilán's temples are similar in many respects to those at Palenque, with their mansard roofs and broad, pierced roofcombs. The majority of the buildings have multiple (normally three) entrances, and the distinctive feature here is that the doorways were spanned not with lintels of sapodilla wood, the more conventional practice, but of stone. In the hands of Yaxchilán's artists they became a magnificent and now famous form of architectural sculpture. Some, such as Lintel 21 which we examined in Chapter 3, were covered in hieroglyphic inscriptions. But Shield Jaguar gathered together a group of quite exceptional sculptors to found a new tradition, subordinating text to dynamic narrative scenes. These lintels have proved of great documentary importance and are a fascinating source for the history of his reign. He commissioned two major sets of lintels, each with a different thematic focus. The first was designed for Temple 44, on what is known as the West Acropolis. Here the emphasis is upon Shield Jaguar as a warrior, the same kind of images that appear on the face of his stelae. The second set was placed above the three doorways of Temple 23, which stands on the southern side of Yaxchilán's main plaza facing the river. These are very different in narrative content, for the theme is that of ritual blood-letting and the principal actor is a woman.

As one faces Temple 23, what is known as Lintel 24, removed by Maudslay and now in the British Museum, spanned the left hand doorway (see overleaf). It depicts Shield Jaguar standing to the left holding a large flaming torch above the kneeling figure of his principal wife, known as Lady Xoc. The action must have taken place either within the darkness of a temple interior or possibly at night. The arresting drama of the composition, the torch thrust diagonally across the frame, directs the eye immediately to Lady Xoc's face where we see her engaged in one of the most startlingly gruesome of all Maya acts of auto-sacrifice or personal blood-letting. She is passing a cord spiked with thorns, in effect much like barbed wire, through her tongue. The rope trails onto a woven basket containing strips of bark-paper, which were used to catch the blood and would be burnt as an offering. On her cheek are dotted lines which, though they resemble tattoos, a well-documented form of body ornament, are generally held to represent the fluid spurting from her tongue. This extraordinary work of art is now one of the best known masterpieces of Maya sculpture, in part because of its chilling content, which so encapsulates the new, more sanguinary vision of the Classic Maya. The lintel's preservation is remarkably good, bearing considerable traces of its original red, blue and yellow paint, and

Lintel 24

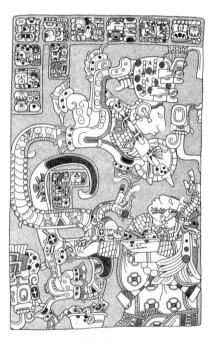

Lintel 25

the relief of the figures and accompanying text, deeply separated from the background of the panel, retains much fine surface detail, in particular of the figures' clothing. Shield Jaguar wears a tasselled cape, two fine woven belts and jaguar-skin sandals; his long, bound hair is surmounted by what may be the shrunken head of a sacrificial victim. The marvel, however, is the precise representation of Lady Xoc's magnificent 'huipil', a kind of shift still worn by Maya women today who, in the highlands of Chiapas, weave much the same diamond design that appears here. Only fragments of ancient weavings have survived and Lintel 24 provides a glimpse of the fine quality and great beauty of Classic period textiles, one of those many perishable art forms that we have lost.

In Lintel 25 (see above), from the central door of Temple 23, Shield Jaguar has disappeared from the scene. Lady Xoc is in a similar kneeling position, her left hand holding a bowl of blood-spattered paper and piercing instruments, including a sting-ray spine and a lancet of obsidian. On the ground is another bowl of bloodied paper. We have proceeded a stage further in the blood-letting rite. Now she looks upwards at the product of her piety and pain, a visionary manifestation of an ancestor, almost certainly Progenitor Jaguar, the founder of the royal line in the guise of a warrior, holding a lance and shield and emerging from the wide-open jaws of a rearing snake or 'Vision Serpent'. Shield Jaguar returns once more to join his wife in Lintel 26, the last of the series (see overleaf). Here both figures are standing. Lady Xoc, bearing smears on her cheeks from blood-letting, presents Shield Jaguar with his battle dress, including a helmet in the form of a jaguar's head.

These three scenes appear to follow a natural sequence: the act of blood-letting followed by the resultant vision of the warrior founder and then the preparation of the lord to follow his ancestor's example and go in search of captives for sacrifice. Yet, curiously, the accompanying texts tell us that they commemorate three different events widely separated in time. The blood-letting on Lintel 24 happened during the ritual celebrating the birth of Shield Jaguar's son Bird Jaguar in 709; the vision scene of Lintel 25 forms part of the rites surrounding Shield Jaguar's accession back in 681, and the final lintel, number 26, represents an event that took place around the time of the dedication of the temple in 726.

A second unusual feature is the central role that Lady Xoc plays in the narrative. This is not to suggest that royal women do not figure prominently in Maya art. In cities such as Copán and Tikal their appearance is indeed rare, but at others, as wives and particularly as mothers involved

Lintel 26

in the rites of heir designation and accession, they are depicted with some frequency in the Late Classic period, most notably on the accession stelae of Piedras Negras. On occasion, in very special circumstances, they come to the fore. At Palenque, as we shall see, women became regents and even ruled for a time, and at the city of Naranjo, 'Lady Six Sky', the foreign mother of the famous 'Smoking Squirrel' who came to the throne at the age of five, is represented assuming royal duties and even, on one stela, trampling in time-honoured fashion upon a bound captive. Yet, such high-profile careers tended to be brief and when men were ready to take over power once more the women resumed their subsidiary roles. Thus the appearance of Lady Xoc centre stage demands an explanation. There is a further riddle. Despite all the attention paid to her here as Shield Jaguar's wife, involved in some of the most important events of his reign, Bird Jaguar – the son and heir whose birth is referred to in the text of Lintel 24 – was not in fact her son. When he came to the throne he proclaimed repeatedly, stridently even, that his mother was another woman, called Lady Evening Star.

A very plausible answer to this was first put forward by Linda Schele and David Friedel.[11] Shield Jaguar did indeed have two principal wives that we know about (he may of course have had many more): Lady Xoc and Lady Evening Star. He married them, it would appear, for very different reasons. Lady Xoc was evidently a local lady, from a powerful Yaxchilán lineage whose support may well have been critical at the time he came to the throne. Lady Evening Star, whom he married later, represented a very different kind of alliance. For she was a woman from Calakmul. In much earlier times, as we have seen, Yaxchilán may have had friendly relations with Tikal. But by the seventh century at least, with Piedras Negras already in the Calakmul camp, it seems that Yaxchilán, too, had felt it advisable to align itself with the other distant great power. The marriage with Lady Evening Star would have cemented that connection.

Looking to the succession upon his death and having to choose whom he was to designate as heir, Shield Jaguar, with his two powerful wives and the political constituencies or concerns they represented, faced something of a problem. He had to square the need to ensure domestic support and stability with that of maintaining an important foreign alliance. By 726, the time of the dedication of Temple 23, in the forty-fifth year of his reign, he had decided on the strategy, the delicate balancing act that he had to perform. He designated Bird Jaguar, the son by the Lady from Calakmul, as his heir. But, although her son was to be the next king, Lady Evening Star herself was given little public credit for this. Not one reference was made to her on any of the monuments of Shield Jaguar's time and we only know about her from the monuments of her son. Instead, the woman who was accorded extraordinary respect and was depicted by the artists of the Temple 23 lintels as so central to royal life and the rites of kingship, was Lady Xoc.

This compromise of fêting the local lady, and by association her family, while treating the mother of the heir, more publicly at least, as a non-person succeeded until Shield Jaguar died in 742. But then things must have gone very wrong, for Bird Jaguar did not come to the throne until ten years later. What went on during this interregnum is unknown. No inscriptions survive from the period and there are no later references, not surprisingly perhaps, to anything untoward at this time. Yet there must have been a serious struggle, quite possibly bloody battles, over the succession. We do not know whether Lady Xoc had any surviving children, or whether she had any children at all for that matter. If she had sons of her own, that would clearly have provided the reason for conflict. But even if she did not, there may have been elements within Yaxchilán that did not want the son of a foreign woman to be king.

Whatever the answers, this episode provides an illustration of the domestic pressures that Maya kings could face. Shield Jaguar was a very successful ruler and he lived for a long time. This provided the stability for impressive growth in the wealth of Yaxchilán and its power in the Usumacinta region. But his very longevity meant that he acquired numerous wives and quite possibly a number of fractious, competing children. It was for this reason that heir-designation was such an important event in the political life of a Maya city. Many Maya monuments depict the presentation of the heir to the throne, well before time, in an attempt to ensure the orderly transfer of power. The murals of Bonampak, for example, record battle, sacrifice, courtly pageant, a great many things, but essentially all these are elements in a very elaborate heir-designation ceremonial spread over a number of months. The little heir to the throne may seem peripheral to the action, held in the arms of a bored-looking court attendant, but he and the dynastic continuity he represents form the underlying theme of the paintings.

Bird Jaguar, who seems to have been as dynamic and effective a character as his father, eventually came out on top. He married another important local lady and they produced a child shortly before his formal accession. He was forty-three when he became king and was to rule for sixteen years. Though his reign was short compared to his father's, he was a successful ruler who, according to his monuments, gained many captives in raids against neighbouring kingdoms. He quotes their names, though unhelpfully he doesn't often say where they came from, and it is he who is apt to brag about the sheer number he has supposedly taken: 'He of twenty captives'. One of his most famous monuments, as we saw in Chapter 3, is Lintel 8, where he is shown taking 'Jewelled Skull' prisoner, accompanied by a Yaxchilán lord called Kan Tok Wayib, who is grabbing his own captive by the hair. This lintel is significant in many ways. The themes of Bird Jaguar's monuments very much reflect the problems he faced before he came to the throne. Thus his lintels go out of their way to celebrate and justify his mother as of great importance to Shield Jaguar, they underline the right to rule of his own son and heir, and they depict him involved in military or in ritual activity with members of the Yaxchilán nobility. This sharing of status, a new departure at Yaxchilán, is comparable to what we have seen occurring at Copán about the same time. Yaxchilán nobles did not set up their own monuments and inscriptions in the residential areas around the city itself, they did not hold court and receive the ruler at the dedication of their own palaces, as far as is known. But they were depicted on monuments of state in the company of the lord. Thus, like Yax Pac, Bird Jaguar evidently found it necessary to involve the heads of powerful families publicly in the affairs of his realm, no doubt the price he had to pay for the support of those who had seen him through the crisis of the interregnum.

Bird Jaguar presided over a major programme of urban expansion at Yaxchilán. One of his finest buildings, and probably the most impressive of all in ancient times, is Temple 33, perched on a hill and facing north across the ranks of other buildings and plazas towards the river (see plate section). Here it was that Maudslay stayed and where he found a mass of pots for the burning of copal incense left behind by the Lacandon, who until recent times treated a headless statue of Bird Jaguar inside the building as an object of veneration. Remnants of a giant seated figure of the ruler can also still be seen set into the centre of the roofcomb. Temple 33 was designed as the memorial to his accession and was perhaps meant to symbolize the prosperity and political stability that he had managed to return to his kingdom. The three lintels from above its doorways display Bird Jaguar in all his finery accompanied by his wife, Lady Great Skull, the mother of his heir, Shield Jaguar III; the king and little Shield Jaguar engaged together in religious ritual; and Bird Jaguar appearing at a period-ending ceremony with another of his most prominent lords. The upper steps of Temple 33 were cleared twenty-five years ago to reveal some remarkable scenes of the ball-game. Amongst them is the image of a captive trussed up as a ball, whom Bird Jaguar is seen bouncing down the stairs to his death. The man is named as 'Jewelled Skull', none other than the captive that we saw being taken on Lintel 8. Jewelled Skull may indeed have been killed on these very stairs, after a hopeless encounter in the Yaxchilán ball-court.

Bird Jaguar tells us that he continued in bellicose vein for the rest of his life. He seems to have avoided major confrontations, registering the captures of lords from minor and often unidentifiable sites and maintaining good relations with Piedras Negras. His son also went on to play a prominent regional role. He appears in the Bonampak murals, where he joins up with the local ruler, Chan Muwan (his brother-in-law), to go to war and return with sacrificial victims for the ceremonies that surrounded the designation of Chan Muwan's heir.

On the northern, Guatemalan bank of the Usumacinta, forty kilometres downriver from Yaxchilán, lies Piedras Negras. Until very recently
it remained remote and little-visited. Yet it was a formidable city, its buildings not dispersed over terraces and hilltops as at the smaller Yaxchilán
but massed into impressive complexes or Acropoli, more comparable to
some of the architecture at Tikal but with open, galleried palaces, and its
roofcombed temples more like those of Palenque. Covered for many
years in jungle, plagued by its inaccessibility and the use of the area as a
bolt-hole by guerilla groups and a variety of fugitives, Piedras Negras may
have much to reveal to archaeologists in the near future.

For now our knowledge of its history is still largely founded on that
array of formidable stelae that Proskouriakoff studied here, a monument erected every five years in an extraordinary unbroken sequence
from 608 to 810. This in itself says a lot for the independence and political stability that Piedras Negras' rulers maintained. Given how close the
city was to Yaxchilán, and the generally friendly relations they seem to
have forged after some initial hostilities, it is surprising how different
Piedras Negras' artistic traditions are. The imposing sculptural style of
its stelae, in particular those accession monuments where the ruler is
modelled three-dimensionally inside his 'niche', is quite distinctive.
Piedras Negras did not follow the same lintel tradition as Yaxchilán.
Instead there are other unusual forms, such as intricately carved thrones
and relief panels commonly called 'lintels' but which were made to be
set vertically into walls. These are amongst the most striking of all Maya
sculptures and two of them display very unusual scenes.

In the first, known today as Wall Panel 2, the king is standing in military costume, holding a lance in one hand and a square shield in the
other. In front of him six figures kneel in a row, wearing feathered war
bonnets, padded armour and also holding spears. Behind the ruler is a
smaller figure in similar though more ornate dress. The glyphic texts that
surround the group tell us that the six figures are all men or, judging by
their scale, youths of noble status that have been sent by their respective
kingdoms – Lacanhá, Bonampak and Yaxchilán – to participate in an
event which appears to be connected with the putting on and display of
helmets. The main protagonist is 'Ruler 2' of Piedras Negras and the
date of the event is 658. The small figure behind him is almost certainly
his son, who is perhaps donning the full regalia of a warrior for the first
time in what may be defined as an initiation rite. It would seem that the
six kneeling figures are expressing their support, or to put it more

strongly, their allegiance to the king and to the younger man, in this way expressing the relationship between the cities involved. There is also a reference in the text to an earlier event in which both a Piedras Negras ruler and a Calakmul lord participated.

'Wall Panel 3' is an outstanding piece of relief sculpture, even though sections of it are now badly damaged (see below). Framed by a glyphic commentary, it also has an interior architectural frame, clearly indicating that the action is going on within a palace building. What appear to be curtains are drawn back above the figures. The central, commanding presence is the ruler, sitting on a carved throne, leaning energetically outwards over seven lesser Piedras Negras lords seated cross-legged on the floor, between them a large ceramic vessel of the kind used in chocolate-drinking. To the right of the lord are a standing group of four: three children or adolescents, and an adult figure whom Michael Coe believes to be a scribe of high-standing who may be acting as a kind of master-of-ceremonies.[12] To the left of the throne appear three further standing males. These people, the text tells us, are from Yaxchilán and they have come to visit by canoe. One of them is the Yaxchilán lord Bird Jaguar. The panel was commissioned at the very end of the eighth century, but it recalls the event seen here which took place in 757. It was the time when 'Ruler 4' of Piedras Negras designated his heir, one of the youths to the right, and evidently Bird Jaguar was considered a prestigious enough ally to witness the ceremony. This is a graphic and very rare depiction of that 'royal visiting' that commonly went on between friendly powers.

Piedras Negras Wall Panel 3

Such inscribed monuments, along with some of the surviving accounts of wars and captures, help to suggest something of the political hierarchy amongst the cities of the Usumacinta.[13] Thus Piedras Negras would seem to have been the major regional power for most of the Late Classic period, with Yaxchilán, certainly by the time of Bird Jaguar, its nearest competitor, although as we have seen relations between the two appear to have been peacable from at least the mid-seventh century. This relationship may have been further bolstered by both having established ties with Calakmul. We shall return to the rivalry between Tikal and Calakmul and the broader political picture across the Southern Lowlands at the end of this chapter, but Calakmul's policy of forming a confederacy against Tikal seems to have spread successfully to the Usumacinta region. Here, in the Late Classic, Tikal had no allies at all.

If Piedras Negras and Yaxchilán were the two predominant cities, there were others, nominally independent and with their own emblem glyphs, but which in reality occupied a subsidiary level. Bonampak, for example, appears to have been an effective subordinate of Yaxchilán for most of the Late Classic, demonstrated late in the period by the Bonampak murals where decipherable sections of painted text indicate that the ceremonial and warlike activity depicted here went on with what might be termed the official approval of Yaxchilán.

As in other parts of the Maya world, the larger and more stable cities appear to have possessed a more or less constant core territory within which were secondary and even tertiary sites dependent on the main centre. Some inscriptions provide glimpses of how this worked.[14] Yaxchilán, for example, controlled the two secondary sites of Laxtunich and La Pasadita. In charge of each of them was a category of nobility known as *sahal.* So far we have only come upon the word *ahaw* or 'lord' when referring to the powerful families that ran a Maya city-state. All kings were of this rank and defined themselves more precisely as *k'ul ahaw* or 'holy lord'. But *ahaw* on its own is also used to describe members of the immediate royal family and heads of other major lineages. The distinction between the two is often hard to make in practice, but along the Usumacinta, *sahal* appears to refer to a slightly lower level amongst the aristocracy, often translated as 'governor' when it describes an individual who ran a dependent settlement on behalf of the king. La Pasadita, for example, on the opposite, northern bank of the Usumacinta not far from Yaxchilán, had no emblem glyph but it produced monuments with inscriptions which name the *sahal* in the time of

Bird Jaguar as a man called Tilot, who was evidently regarded as a man of substance since he is depicted in the company of Bird Jaguar on stone lintels from the site.

Within the Piedras Negras orbit examples of a more elaborate chain of political dependency can be discerned. For example, in 763 the town of El Cayo, south of the Usumacinta between Piedras Negras and Yaxchilán, saw the installation of a new local ruler, of the rank of *sahal*. Like La Pasadita, El Cayo has its own inscriptions, but no emblem glyph. A lintel from here talks of the man who came to power as acceding under the auspices of the larger town of Sak Tz'i. In turn the *ahaw* from Sak Tz'i who presided at the event did so on behalf of Piedras Negras. Thus at this particular point in the mid-eighth century a three-tier political set-up seems evident. How enduring such arrangements were is not at all clear. For although extensive compared with other parts of the Maya world, the historical record in this region remains fragmentary, making it very hard for scholars to plot the local alliances and shifting political relationships within this densely populated and volatile pocket of Maya civilization, which archaeologically is still so little known.

THE PRIME OF PALENQUE

The high point of any visit to Palenque is a descent to the tomb chamber of Pakal beneath the Temple of the Inscriptions. By mid-morning queues have formed. It is much like waiting to enter the tomb of a Rameses or a Seti in the Valley of the Kings. Indeed, on returning up the uneven, slippery stairs, young and old alike puffing and sweating profusely from the humidity, the common judgement is that this tomb, with its plunging descent and hints here and there of false doors and dummy passageways, ranks alongside those of the Egyptians. It is a real tomb, a tomb of the imagination. In recent years Maya archaeologists have become somewhat blasé about royal burials, which have begun to turn up regularly. But nothing like Pakal's mausoleum has been found to date. In scale and conception it is unique.

Yet for more than 150 years explorers and archaeologists had no idea of its existence. In 1949, the Mexican archaeologist Alberto Rúz was closely examining the inner chamber of the temple above. He noticed that the rear wall did not end at the level of the floor but appeared to continue beneath it. He also saw that there was a double row of curious holes, with stone stoppers, in one of the large limestone floor slabs. The Danish archaeologist Frans Blom had noticed these some years before, but had done nothing about it. Blom was fated to be an unlucky explorer, for he missed out on the two greatest Maya discoveries of modern times. In 1943, three years before Giles Healey came on the scene, he had been a mile away from Bonampak and its murals only to suffer a serious bout of malaria and be evacuated out of the area. Rúz persevered in his initial curiosity, believing that the holes had originally been used to lift the slab with ropes. Sure enough, it proved to be much like a trap-door. Beneath was a corbel-vaulted flight of stairs which had been completely filled with rubble and earth. It took him and his team three years to clear this away. Half way down, the staircase reached a landing, doubled back on itself and continued on down. At the bottom of this second flight they found a stone box or small chamber that contained the remains of five sacrificial victims. Just beneath this, they then came upon an enormous triangular slab that seemed to be blocking an entrance. Removing it, a Howard Carter moment of great expectation, they found themselves in a vaulted chamber or crypt some ten by four metres and seven metres high. Filling much of this space was a rectangular block of limestone, lying horizontally north to south. Its surface was magnificently carved with what has become one of the most famous of all ancient Maya images: Pakal at the very moment of his death, tumbling like the setting sun into the open jaws of the Underworld, with the cruciform 'World Tree' that supported the Maya heavens rising above him (see p.317). At first Rúz thought that the slab was a large altar of some kind. It was not until they brought lifting gear and winched the great stone upwards that a solid sarcophagus was revealed beneath, the sides decorated with hieroglyphs and portraits of Maya royalty with elaborate headdresses. A further, much thinner, lid covered the interior. This was hollowed out into a womb-like shape to fit the body, which had been placed on its back, head to the north. The man's bones were covered in cinnabar and a variety of fine jade and shell objects. These included an enormous collar made up of hundreds of jade beads, ear ornaments, two small statues of gods, jade rings on each finger and a simple sphere of jade by his left hand and a cube in the right, both of which have so far defied explanation. To the side of the skull were the remains of a remarkably fine mosaic portrait mask of jade, which had originally covered the dead man's face. The eyes were inset with shell and obsidian, and the arresting gaze lends formidable power to the visage of the greatest of Palenque's kings.

In 1952 Rúz had no idea who this individual was, of course. It was not until the dramatic breakthroughs in decipherment of the 1970s that we came to know him as Pakal. He came to the throne of Palenque in 615 when he was twelve years old and ruled until 683. Some time before he died, uniquely it would seem among the Maya, he began the design and construction of his tomb and the temple pyramid above it. Linda Schele believed that, mindful of his mortality, he directed work to begin around 675.[15] First they excavated the tomb chamber and placed the sarcophagus and covering slab in the centre, the slab itself precisely at the ancient ground level, in effect at the division between the world of the living and of the dead. The pyramid was then constructed above it on nine terrace levels, the same as the number of layers in the Maya Underworld. There are signs that the tomb was kept open for some years after his death, and then eventually the door was sealed. Scores of labourers emptied the rubble into the stairs and the slab in the temple floor was closed for the last time. But there was still a means whereby the Palenque royal family could communicate with their departed lord. For running out of the tomb chamber and up the stairs to the floor of the temple above is a strange stone tube, still visible today, known by Mayanists as a 'psychoduct'. This was not, it would seem, a means of ventilation, more a kind of spiritual wiring. By this means Pakal's descendants could feel close to their great royal predecessor, and through the performance of ritual and the shedding of their blood in the temple interior conjure up his presence in the form of a 'Vision Serpent', much as Lady Xoc had achieved her ancestral vision at Yaxchilán.

Observing the rapid and somewhat clumsy treatment of some of the final inscriptions in the tomb, Schele concluded that Pakal may have died suddenly, leading to the hasty preparation of the chamber before his funeral rites and interment. Likewise, she felt that the Temple was not completed quite as he had planned. The building faces directly north, with five entrances in its front wall. Originally there would have been a large, pierced roofcomb above, but little of this remains today. The interior is made up of two high, parallel galleries, running east to west, each spanned by a corbel vault. The rear gallery was divided into three and on either side of the doorway into the central chamber and into its back wall were inset three very large panels of hieroglyphic inscriptions. These texts were composed under Pakal's direction and form his account of Palenque's dynastic history. The six piers between the building's principal entrances were expropriated by Pakal's son Kan Balam. The two outer piers were covered in inscriptions on their exterior face that are now barely legible. But the four others bore designs in stucco relief, two of which can be partially made out. Here Kan Balam began to tell his own story. Each one depicted him when he was six years old, at the time of his designation as heir, being publicly presented, cradled symbolically in the arms of his ancestors (see plate section, p.17). There are some distinctive features to these images of the young Kan Balam. Firstly, he has an extra toe on one of his feet, a deformity that is evident in representations of him as an adult. His other leg is transformed into a serpent and, very difficult to detect today, a smoking axe protrudes from his forehead. Both of these are attributes of a god known as K'awil, the patron of rulers. Thus Kan Balam portrayed himself, even at this early age, as divine.

Once he had completed the Temple of the Inscriptions, he quickly set to work on his own monuments, not just a single structure but that group of three buildings known as the Cross Group to the east of the Temple of the Inscriptions across the Otolum river (see plate section, p.18). All face inwards onto a small plaza, the Temple of the Sun to the west, that of the Foliated Cross to the east and the largest, the Temple of the Cross itself, to the north. It is widely thought that Kan Balam's own tomb must lie beneath one of them, most probably the Temple of the Cross, but despite recent excavation and the use of ground-penetrating radar no sign of any burial chamber has yet been detected.

These buildings are exquisite examples of Maya architecture and of that particular grace and proportion achieved at Palenque. Set against the green backdrop of the forested hills, gleaming white in the sun, they look from a distance like lodges or summer-houses in a European landscaped garden. All three are of very similar design, standing upon terraced platforms above a single frontal stairway. Each has the sloping mansard roof so characteristic of Palenque, surmounted originally by fine pierced roofcombs. That on the Temple of the Sun is the best preserved today and faint traces of an original seated stucco figure of the ruler can be seen in a central position at the very top. The remains of reliefs of 'wits' monsters on the outer façades of these buildings, most visible on the Temple of the Cross, proclaim that these temples, too, were viewed as sacred, living mountains.

Like the Temple of the Inscriptions, each building is made up of two parallel galleries topped by corbel vaults. But here entrances running at right angles to the galleries from the stairway lead to an enclosed inner sanctuary referred to in the inscriptions as a *Pib Na* or 'Underworld House', further supporting the notion of these buildings as powerful locations where contact with the supernatural was made. Into the rear wall of the Pib Na were set large limestone panels, bearing similar scenes of two figures facing each other on either side of an elaborate central motif. It is these remarkable low-relief sculptures that have given the temples their individual names and which so impressed the earliest visitors to Palenque.

From study of the extensive inscriptions in the temples of the Cross Group we now know that the larger figure in all of the scenes is Kan Balam. He is very simply dressed, in effect in his underclothes, with a cotton cloth around his waist and another cloth binding his hair in readiness for a headdress to be placed upon it (see below). The smaller figure opposite him is his father Pakal, who is already dead and in the Underworld. The twisted cloth in which he is enveloped may even represent the cotton wrappings in which he was laid to rest in his tomb. Kan Balam has thus entered Xibalbá (the Underworld) to receive the trappings and costume of royalty from his father. On the piers outside the Pib Na, Kan Balam appears as if he has returned from the land of the dead, now fully dressed in royal regalia and holding the symbols of office with which he has been entrusted. Placed between the two figures in each Pib Na are some of the most powerful symbols of the Maya

Central tablet and two outer piers from the Temple of the Cross, Palenque. The pier to the left represents Kan Balam in royal attire, that to the right one of the lords of the Underworld.

cosmos. In the Temple of the Cross this is the World Tree, that extraordinary cruciform image we have already referred to on Pakal's sarcophagus. In the Temple of the Sun the central image is a shield covered with a mask of the Jaguar God of the Underworld. There are emblems of war and sacrifice here: crossed spears behind the shield, and a throne, bearing a jaguar head and two serpents, which is supported by Underworld gods in the guise of captives. In the Temple of the Foliated Cross, the shrine to the east in the direction of the rising sun, the great tree that supports the world is given another aspect, sprouting corn foliage and providing sustenance for humankind. We will return to the meaning of some of the Cross Group images in the following chapter, but the overt intent of the iconography, explained by the texts which accompany them, is to commemorate the orderly handing over of royal authority and divine sanction from Pakal to Kan Balam. And the location in which this is taking place is the home of the gods.

In the 1970s it was the decipherment of the very lengthy texts from the Cross Group and the Temple of the Inscriptions, the panels from the latter containing 617 glyphs in all, which was to provide the most detailed and unusual written history for any city in the Maya world. For these texts did not just recount a dynastic sequence from a founding ancestor, but linked the story of Palenque's kings with the mythological past, indeed back to the very time of creation itself. Interestingly, it is the more straightforward dynastic history, now generally accepted to be a reliable record of Classic-period rulers, which may reveal why both Pakal and Kan Balam should be so concerned to connect themselves to the time when the gods established the human order.[16] As we have seen at other cities, the right to rule was determined by lineage, more precisely by patrilineage, descent from revered ancestors through the male line. However at Palenque, in the years before Pakal came to the throne, there had been two clear ruptures to this sequence.

Combining both Pakal and Kan Balam's inscriptions, the recognized founder of the Palenque royal line can be identified as a man called K'uk' Balam, or Jaguar Quetzal, who took the throne in 431.[17] The following six rulers (see Palenque family tree overleaf), all came from his patrilineage, down to the time of Kan Balam I, who died in 583. He was succeeded – presumably he did not father a son or none survived – by his daughter, Lady Ol Ik'nal, who reigned for twenty years. Aside perhaps from the mysterious 'Lady of Tikal' of the early sixth century, she is the first recorded female ruler in Maya history. She herself, of

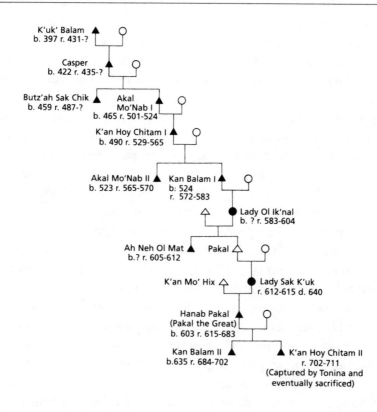

course, was a member of the ruling patrilineage that went back to K'uk' Balam, but since the Maya were barred from marrying members of the same lineage, by the time of the accession of her son Ah Neh Ol Mat, the conventional patrilineal sequence was broken. Ah Neh Ol Mat, through his father, who is not known, then began a new patrilineage. He only ruled for seven years, and when he died in 612 there was another crisis. Again there was no male heir, so the throne was occupied by another woman, Ah Neh Ol Mat's brother's daughter, Lady Sak K'uk, or 'Resplendent Quetzal'. She also had to marry outside her own lineage, to a man called K'an Mo' Hix. So, patrilineal descent was broken a second time when, after she had ruled for three years, she was followed by the twelve-year-old Pakal.

Although other ruling dynasties must have faced similar difficulties, Palenque's problems were particularly severe. As members of a lineage which, on the face of it, had no right to claim the throne, both Pakal and Kan Balam felt vulnerable, many scholars now believe, and anxious to prove their right to rule. If their legitimacy was hard to substantiate in the more conventional manner, the only answer was to prove an overriding supernatural authority. Put more crudely, it meant manipulating religion for political ends. The main plank of the ingenious argument they devised was that Pakal's mother, Lady Sak K'uk, was a reincarnation of 'First Mother', the mother of all creation, the birth of whose three sons, in the Palenque version of the creation story, had founded the present world order. Many elaborate devices were employed to prove some remarkable parallels between First Mother and her three sons and Lady Sak K'uk and Pakal, including such things as calendrically connected birthdays which suggested that all were of the same divine 'essence'. And, as the three gods had in effect 'succeeded' First Mother at the time of creation, so both Pakal and Kan Balam claimed an exactly parallel divine legitimacy, as descendants of Lady Sak K'uk, 'First Mother' on earth. The three temples of the Cross Group were in part shrines to each of this original triad of gods, and Kan Balam depicted himself here as an incarnation of aspects of these deities.

Thus it was that father and son deftly switched the focus away from mere earthly precedent. How could anyone dispute what was clearly a re-enactment of creation and so evidently ordained by the gods? The end product of their mythological contortions is some of the most complex and fascinating evidence for Maya myth and religion that has come down to us. And there is no doubt of Pakal and Kan Balam's propagandist success, for their reigns were to be the high point of the Classic period at Palenque.

Evidence from the Early Classic is beginning to appear in greater abundance and to offer some proof of the accuracy of Pakal and Kan Balam's king-lists. In 1985 David Stuart identified the name glyph of the second ruler in the dynasty on an onyx bowl from Palenque. This was a man familiarly known as 'Casper', who acceded to the throne in 435. More recently, a limestone tablet was discovered that dates from the Late Classic, probably from the reign of Kan Balam, but which refers to an event in the time of the fourth ruler, known as Akal Mo' Nab I. He was one of the sons of Casper who ruled from 501 to 524. The panel shows the king standing imperiously above a kneeling captive and the accompanying inscription refers to him taking the 'white headband' of rulership on his accession on 6 May 501. This impressive relief was found in Temple XVII, just to the south of the Temple of the Foliated Cross.

Further south, beneath Temple XVIIIA, an Early Classic tomb was discovered by Alberto Rúz in the late 1950s, after Heinrich Berlin had encountered the top of an early prototype 'psychoduct' just beneath the temple's floor.[18] The corbel-vaulted chamber was originally accessible via a stairway but was simple compared to Pakal's and with no stone sarcophagus. The tomb contained the body of a man of about twenty, and the accompanying ceramic offerings dated the burial to *c.* 500. There is still uncertainty as to who this individual might be. The presence of cinnabar on the bones, some impressive jade offerings including a small mosaic mask, and traces of paintings on the walls of the tomb, suggest that he must at least have been a member of the Early Classic royal family. The flesh had gone or been removed from the bones before interment and then they had been coated with the cinnabar. The unusual evidence for this is provided by a second occupant to the chamber, a woman of some twenty-five years of age who was evidently alive when she entered the tomb, for she had sealed the door with plaster from the inside. Her hand prints were found both on the door and in a bowl of plaster on the floor. Then, at some point during the contemplation of her inevitable fate, this extraordinary sacrificial victim, conceivably one of the young man's wives, had picked up his right tibia and lain down with it to die.

Pottery of Early Classic date has been found in surface collections over a wide area and in the fill of many later buildings. There is little doubt that the remains of structures and tombs from this period lie in considerable quantity beneath later constructions. No complete map of Palenque has yet been published and no one can estimate the full extent of the city or the size of its Classic-period population. Anyone who ventures away from the cleared area of the site up the Otolum valley to the south will come upon many ruins still shrouded in forest and appreciate the scale of the task, and the immense possibilities, that still await Palenque's archaeologists.

We know a great deal, however, about the impact of Pakal upon the heart of Palenque.[19] It developed considerably in scale and beauty, though not, for reasons that will become clear below, until later in his reign. His earliest building may well have been the so-called 'Templo Olvidado' or 'Forgotten Temple' some 800 metres to the west of the Palace, which was dedicated in 647. Then he constructed the Temple of the Count to the north and began to lavish attention on the courts, galleries and subterranean chambers of the marvellous Palace, work that was followed up by Kan Balam and Pakal's second son, K'an Hoy Chitam.

In the Palace the uniquely delicate architectural style of Palenque reached its fullest expression. As in Pakal's and Kan Balam's individual temples, here too corbel vaults were aligned parallel to each other. Unlike in the Petén, at Tikal for example, where vertical façades, solid flat roofs and bulky roofcombs meant that supporting walls had to be massive and interior spaces could only be tiny, at Palenque the upper part of façades angled inwards, following the slope of the interior vault to form the distinctive mansard roof line. The centre of the roof was supported by the interior wall between the two parallel galleries and above it rose the lightweight roofcomb. The effect of this was to considerably reduce the weight that had to be borne by the exterior walls, which did not have to be so thick. Vaults could thus be higher, airier and indeed ornamental in their form, best exemplified by that trefoil vault which since the eighteenth century visitors to the city have found so attractively Moorish in style. Further structural ornament was provided by the niches in many walls and T-shaped windows, the shape corresponding appropriately to the *ik* glyph, the Maya word for 'wind'. Stucco reliefs were to be found everywhere in the Palace and enough remains of them today, particularly on the outer piers of House D, facing onto the plaza to the west of the Palace, to appreciate that ornamental stucco, one of the oldest of all Maya art forms, was here brought to perfection. At Palenque there are no stelae. Tablets – sometimes quite massive panels of limestone – were the medium for the chronicling of dynastic history. For the limestone here, so finely grained that it has been likened to a lithographer's stone, was perfect for the production of remarkably crisp low-relief sculpture.

The plastered walls of the Palace, like Palenque's other temples, were originally all painted. The overall ground colour was red, with details picked out in what seems to have been a common Maya colour-coding: precious blue-green for the images of gods and attributes of the divine, yellow for other forms of architectural ornament, and further red for the flesh tones of humans. One particular building in the Palace, House E beneath the Palenque Tower, was described by the Maya themselves as the 'Zac Tun Na' or the 'White Stone House'. This was decorated in a very different style, painted with flowers, in brilliant hues, over a plain white plaster background, in places giving the walls a remarkably Spanish Colonial appearance. It is fortunate that Merle Greene Robertson, the great recorder of Palenque's monuments and the city's modern Maudslay, copied and photographed these paintings in detail in the 1970s. Today, with increasing atmospheric pollution and the flood of tourists, they are fast deteriorating.

The name 'Palace' was first bestowed upon these buildings by José Calderón in the eighteenth century. Subsequent visitors adopted it readily enough since, through European eyes, it is easy to imagine the royal family occupying this elegant and compact precinct at the centre of their city. It seems probable that the Palace was a more strictly ceremonial place and a centre of government, rather than a residential area. At present the buildings most likely to have served as the royal domestic quarters are those that Mexican archaeologists have excavated and restored to the east of the main, canalized branch of the Otolum River. Groups of well-built, serviceable structures extend down the hillside, quite beautifully positioned amongst streams of clear water that tumble as picturesque waterfalls across the eroded limestone. The extended families that lived here would also have had a magnificent view across the great floodplain to the north, where the wood-smoke rose from the compounds of farming families scattered amongst their maize fields.

The 'White Stone House' in the Palace appears to have been one of the focal points for exercising the more formal rites of kingship. It is here that the famous 'Oval Palace Tablet' is set into the wall, commemorating Pakal's accession and showing Lady Sak K'uk presenting her son with the crown (see below). Below are the traces of where a throne was once positioned against the wall. Many believe that the open court beneath the

OVAL BAS RELIEF IN STONE
in the Wall of one of the Apartments of the Palace Palenque

Frederick Catherwood's drawing of the Oval Palace Tablet, Palenque.

Tower may have been a 'Popol Na', where the ruler sat in council with his nobles. As for the remarkable, pagoda-like Tower itself, some have noticed that from the top on the winter solstice the sun can be seen setting directly above the Temple of the Inscriptions. No one has yet proved that its major purpose was as an astronomical observatory. It would also have served as a more practical observation point to survey activity, perhaps hostile movements, across the plain to the north. For Palenque, no less than other Maya cities, participated in many wars.

The East Court of the Palace is the arena where warfare and sacrifice were commemorated. On one side of the sunken court, flanking a central stairway, are nine roughly hewn limestone slabs carved with large and somewhat grotesque images of semi-naked captives, some with hieroglyphic inscriptions on their loincloths and one, to the extreme right, with a distended and scarified penis. The stairway between these figures would probably have been the entrance to the court for visitors, including those intended for sacrifice. The steps are unusually broad and steep. Anyone descending them today, even long-legged non-Maya people, instantly feel unsteady and slightly flustered. One wonders whether that was the original intent. For if victims did not necessarily confront their death in this part of the Palace, they may well have been brought here to be paraded and tortured, surrounded by the images of those who had suffered before them.

On the opposite, western side of the Court are a series of six smaller, more finished stone panels each bearing the head and upper torso of a further captive, one arm across the chest in a common attitude of subjection. Between them short inscriptions provide these individuals' names. The central stairs here, unlike those to the east, are carved with glyphs. Known as the Hieroglyphic Stairs of House C, they have proved extremely difficult to decipher. But recent studies by Schele, Grube and Martin have extracted fascinating historical details which, combined with evidence from the Temple of the Inscriptions and texts from other cities, cast a vivid light on the time surrounding Pakal's birth and the early decades of his reign. These appear to have been terrrible years of defeat in war and of destruction at Palenque.[20]

The first setback recorded on the Hieroglyphic Stairs came in 599, four years before Pakal was born and in the time of Lady Ol Ik'nal, Palenque's first female ruler. The city was attacked and a member of the royal lineage – it is not clear who – was sacrificed. The texts also suggest that many temples were desecrated and the treasured images of the local gods destroyed or taken away. The city responsible for this was Calakmul. In the next few years other assaults are mentioned, by Calakmul and then by smaller cities such as Pomoná, which lies thirty kilometres to the east of Palenque. Grube sees this as a common pattern in Maya wars – a major confrontation followed up by a cluster of raids carried out by lesser towns that pick off a larger, already weakened neighbour. In 603 there was an attack upon Palenque commemorated at Bonampak and in 610, when Pakal was seven, came another 'axe war' mounted by Pomoná, which again penetrated to the heart of the city. One can imagine little Pakal fleeing with his mother and their followers and perhaps hiding in the forested hills to the south.

The dynastic history commissioned by Pakal in the Temple of the Inscriptions is expressed in *katun* form. It bemoans the troubles of these times in an emotive manner that is quite unique amongst Maya texts. 'Lost are the gods; lost are the kings', they say, followed by a phrase Grube has translated as 'it is not adorned', meaning that due offerings could not be given to the gods because of all the disruption that had been caused.[21] The great significance of the catalogue of defeats and devastation is that it serves as a very probable explanation of the problems of dynastic succession in this period. Women ruled because their menfolk had been sacrificed by Palenque's enemies or had died on the battlefield.

A final reverse may have been suffered in 624, when a monument at Piedras Negras tells of the capture of a Palenque *ahaw*, a member of the nobility. But after this date, the city's fortunes were to change dramatically. Palenque enjoyed almost a century of success and prosperity. Its power expanded, not to the east or south where hostile cities such as Piedras Negras, Pomoná and Toniná blocked the way, but to the west. Here the smaller city of Tortuguero, led it would seem by a member of the Palenque royal dynasty who used the Palenque emblem glyph after his name, helped to bring Palenque's influence to bear across the northern foothills of Chiapas and perhaps as far away as Comalcalco, close to the Gulf Coast. The result was that by about 650 Palenque had carved out for itself a stable and formidable kingdom that was no longer easy prey for its enemies. It is thus no coincidence that Pakal's major building activities at the city should have begun at about this time.

Palenque's enhanced status was to be demonstrated by an intriguing series of events that took place in 659.[22] These are introduced on the Hieroglyphic Stairs of House C by that Maya phrase we have come across before – *huli*, 'he arrived'. The individual who arrived at Palenque was none other than the ruler of Tikal, a man known as 'Shield Skull'. The circumstances surrounding his appearance are still much debated, but what is well established is that two years previously, Calakmul had mounted another attack upon Tikal. It would seem that Shield Skull may have been forced into exile, eventually taking refuge at Palenque. For the two cities were evidently allies, whose relationship may have gone back a long way. Many scholars believe that Palenque, along with Copán, formed part of that Tikal-dominated axis of friendly powers linked in the Early Classic to Teotihuacan. By the Late Classic, Palenque represents Tikal's only well-documented supporter in this part of the Southern Lowlands.

Around the time of Shield Skull's arrival, Pakal took revenge against Palenque's nearby enemy Pomoná. The inscriptions from the Hieroglyphic Stairs tell us that he returned with captives, and indeed two of those six named prisoners whose images flank the stairway are identified as coming from that city. Then it was, the text goes on to say, that Pakal and Shield Skull appeared together formally at Palenque as 'companions'. What we can now envisage are the two friendly kings marking their solidarity against the power of Calakmul and its allies in a round of celebrations, culminating in the sacrifice of the men from Pomoná.

Crowned by the visit of the great lord of Tikal, the year 659 must have been the high point of Pakal's reign. But Palenque's success was to be sustained. The city's sphere of influence continued to enlarge, it would seem, under both Kan Balam and his brother K'an Hoy Chitam, who succeeded in 702. The turn-around in Palenque's fortunes from those dark days that surrounded Pakal's birth is remarkable. Indeed, one is tempted to put a different gloss on Pakal and Kan Balam's striving to number themselves among the gods and trace their mythological legitimacy. For the seventh century saw a new start, a glorious chapter for the dynasty. To compare Pakal's mother to the 'First Mother' of all creation was a way of celebrating symbolically the rebirth, the recreation of the city. The gods and kings were 'lost' no more, the temples were adorned. Palenque had entered a new auspicious cycle of time, when cosmic and earthly harmony had been restored.

Yet the roller-coaster of fate was to bring one more dramatic reverse. In the Palenque Site Museum there is a very large and magnificently carved limestone panel known as the 'Palace Tablet'. It depicts K'an Hoy Chitam seated on a throne between his parents. Pakal, on the left, is represented symbolically handing him that same crown or headdress covered with plaques of jade with which Pakal himself had been invested by his mother Lady Sak K'uk. On either side and beneath the three figures is one of the most beautiful monumental texts ever produced at Palenque, which recounts a series of auguries and tells of events in the careers of K'an Hoy Chitam and his father. The panel was to be set in the wall of a new building which K'an Hoy Chitam had designed at the northern end of the Palace. At the bottom of the text is a rectangular space, left blank, where a throne would have been placed. There is, however, something odd about the inscription. It becomes crowded towards the end, the glyphs smaller and more cramped, as if the scribal sculptor's planning had gone awry and he found that he had too much to say and too little space in which to say it.

The artist did indeed have rather more to include here than had been envisaged originally. For the text ends with a reference to another man called 'Xoc', who took charge of Palenque briefly, as a regent it seems, in 720. It was Xoc who finally dedicated the building and installed the panel. For something no one had bargained for had happened to K'an Hoy Chitam. He had been captured by the warlike city of Toniná in the foothills of Chiapas to the south. The Palenque texts tell us nothing. But at Toniná he is represented on a carved block of limestone, bound and half-naked (see overleaf). On his thigh a caption reads 'K'an Hoy Chitam Lord of Palenque'. The style of the carving is distinctive. It is that of Palenque, not of Toniná, and the strong possibility is that, as a form of tribute, artists were sent to Toniná to produce a monument to their own defeated king. He was captured in 711 but seems to have been kept hostage, waiting for his inevitable death, for many years. Only in 720 did the more normal workings of dynastic rule at Palenque resume. Xoc took control for little over a year and then handed on to a new ruler, Akal Mo' Nab III. However, the loss of K'an Hoy Chitam seems not to have greatly affected Palenque's fortunes. Although we can follow much less of her history, art of extraordinary quality continued to be produced at Palenque until the turn of the ninth century. Then no more monuments or inscriptions were created and our knowledge of the most beautiful of all Maya cities simply fades to nothing.

THE REVIVAL OF TIKAL

The appearance of Shield Skull at Palenque in 659 marks the sudden, yet

brief re-emergence of Tikal on the Maya political scene after a 'lost century' about which very little is known. The ruler Double Bird, eliminated by Calakmul and Caracol in 562, was followed by the usurper Animal Skull. His tomb has been identified on the North Acropolis and he is thought to have died around 600. Though from another lineage, or even perhaps a foreigner, Animal Skull called himself the twenty-second royal successor. We can deduce, from posthumous inscriptions, that Shield Skull was the twenty-fifth in line and so there were presumably two other Tikal kings in between. But nothing is known about them, not even their names. There is considerable evidence of building activity after Animal Skull's death, particularly the renewal of the public plazas around the centre of the city, and it seems that Tikal was slowly recovering, a process that archaeologists believe was eventually to accelerate under Shield Skull.[23] Despite the Calakmul attack of 657 and his flight to Palenque, he eventually returned to Tikal. But at the city itself there is no record of his activities. The practice of setting up inscribed stelae and altars had still not been resumed and Tikal was to remain mysteriously mute for another thirty years.

At some point during the early years of Shield Skull, or even perhaps in the time of his predecessors, since we do not know when he came to the throne, there must have been upheaval amongst those who governed Tikal. For a seemingly rebellious group, led by a man named Flint Sky, left Tikal to establish a new city known as Dos Pilas more than a hundred kilometres away to the south in an area called the Petexbatún, close to the Pasión River and to the east of the headwaters of the Usumacinta. Dos Pilas was founded in 645, at a site where there had been little previous occupation. Flint Sky fast established his own power base and, unlike his reticent, shadowy contemporaries at Tikal, recorded his career on a range of monuments, adopting the famous knotted bundle emblem glyph of the city of his birth as if to proclaim himself 'Holy Lord' of a new, alternative Tikal. Through warfare and strategic marriage alliances with other cities in the region, he and his successors carved out for themselves a small but extremely aggressive Petexbatún empire.[24] Flint Sky himself ruled for nearly fifty years, became a major player in the affairs of the Maya lowlands and, sponsored and manipulated by Calakmul, a fierce opponent of Tikal. He formed a close association with a Calakmul ruler known as Jaguar Paw. In his own inscriptions, Flint Sky defers to Jaguar Paw and acknowledges that he is *y-ahaw* or 'his vassal'. A second phrase used to describe their relationship, *y-itah*, means 'his companion' and is the same term used to describe relations between Pakal and Shield Skull at their meeting in Palenque. Flint Sky is known to have gone to Calakmul to witness Jaguar Paw's inauguration as king.

In 679 the co-ordinated hostilities of Calakmul and Dos Pilas against Tikal seem to have culminated in the capture and sacrifice of Shield Skull. Once more Tikal's fortunes appear to have reached a low ebb. Another of its rulers was dead and it was still surrounded by hostile powers, not just Calakmul and Dos Pilas but other cities such as Naranjo and El Perú, all part of an encircling confederacy that Calakmul had maintained for over a century. Yet, extraordinary as it may seem, in the aftermath of defeat Tikal was to be spectacularly reborn.

Hasaw Chan Ka'wil, the son of Shield Skull and the twenty-sixth ruler of Tikal, came to the throne three years after his father's death, in 682. He was soon to raise inscribed stelae and altars and to organize a programme of reconstruction in the Great Plaza and the North Acropolis. To restore the city's greatness he looked to the past. Indeed, in a very real sense he seems to have been convinced that with his accession the glories of the past were bound to repeat themselves. For time, quite literally, was on his side. He came to the throne in a calendrical era known as a 'Katun 8 Ahaw'. We will return to some of the intricacies of the *katuns* in the following chapters, but a Katun 8 Ahaw was one division, of almost twenty of our years, in a cycle of time, independent of the Long Count, that comprised thirteen individual *katuns* in all. Each was given the name Ahaw, prefaced by the number 1–13. The complete cycle thus spanned almost 260 years (in fact a little over 256). At the Spanish Conquest, by which time the Long Count had dropped out of use, this cycle, the 'Count of the Katuns', had become both the framework for the recording of history and the basis for prophecy, the belief that the complexion of events in a particular *katun* in one cycle were likely to repeat themselves when the same numbered *katun* came round again. There is now enough evidence to suggest that the *katuns* were already being used in this way during the Late Classic period. Clemency Coggins was the first to argue that Hasaw Chan Ka'wil sought to link his rule to the era presided over by the Early Classic ruler Stormy Sky, in whose day Tikal had reached its first great peak of power and prosperity. Thus, after the death of his father, Hasaw Chan Ka'wil seems purposely to have delayed formal assumption of the throne for three years in order to cue more precisely the forces of destiny and publicly project his reign as a restoration of Stormy Sky's. Subtracting 256 from 682, the date of Hasaw Chan Ka'wil's accession, the number you arrive at is 426, the year that Stormy Sky came to the throne. It would also seem no coincidence that the first major building project that he undertook was the construction of a magnificent new temple at the front of the North Acropolis, directly above Stormy Sky's tomb. He retrieved the latter's famous Stela 31, cast down in previous times of trouble, and replaced it with great honour in its original location within an earlier shrine above the tomb. Then the new Temple 33, as it is known, was raised directly on top. It was finally dedicated early in 695 and here again there was a direct reference to the past. For the ceremony was carried out exactly thirteen *katuns* or 256 years after the last date that Stormy Sky had recorded on Stela 31.

Very soon this symbolic declaration that Tikal would return to the glories of the past became a reality. For Hasaw Chan K'awil now went to war against Calakmul. One of the remarkably preserved wooden lintels from the shrine on top of Temple 1 in the Great Plaza tells us that on 5 August 695 he 'brought down the flint and shield' of Jaguar Paw. The Calakmul ruler and other enemy lords were brought back to Tikal in triumph. The excavated remains of stucco reliefs from a palace building in the Central Acropolis have revealed the figure of Hasaw Chan K'awil holding a rope attached to a bound captive, who may well be Jaguar Paw himself. The accompanying text explains that the prisoners were displayed in public thirteen days after they were taken in battle. Then Jaguar Paw and his companions were sacrificed in an event that almost certainly marked the full ceremonial inauguration of the new Temple 33. Revenge for the years of humiliation and suffering at the hands of Calakmul had now been achieved.

Temple 33 lay at the very front of the North Acropolis and its scale effectively ruled out any further architectural additions here, bringing an end to more than 1000 years of construction on this site. Plans for the redesign of the Great Plaza took many years to come to fruition. In the meantime Hasaw Chan Ka'wil revivified a traditional form of architecture at Tikal known as the 'Twin Pyramid Complex'. Placed a little beyond the immediate centre of the city, these were expressly designed for religious observance concerned, appropriately enough, with the passing of time – the end of one *katun* and the beginning of another. Each complex had four components. Two small, flat-topped pyramids were placed to the east and west, and to the south was a single building with nine entrances representing the levels of the Underworld. At the north stood a rectangular enclosure open to the skies, within which was placed a stone stela bearing an image of the ruler paired with an altar. From the pyramids the sun's passage across the sky from east to west would be tracked. But the main focus of ceremonial would have been the northern building. For this direction, conflated by the Maya with 'up', represented the heavens and the sun at its zenith. Here the king, symbolized by the planting of his stela, was linked with the power of the sun and the celestial realms, just as the North Acropolis, containing the shrines to deified royal ancestors, had always been the most potent, sacred spot at the heart of the city. The plaza area within each Twin Pyramid Complex could hold large numbers of people and celebrations would no doubt have gone on for many days, with the appropriate sacrifices and rituals undertaken and patterns in the past recalled, almost certainly from bark-paper books, in order to determine the auguries for the new cycle of time.

Hasaw Chan Ka'wil ruled for more than half a century and his defeat of Calakmul was followed by further successes against the great city to the north and her allies. It ensured Tikal and its people a final period of greatness. Temple 1 is his funerary monument and was probably designed by the ruler himself. Rising forty-seven metres above the Great Plaza, it is in effect a much larger version of Temple 33 on the North Acropolis. Unlike Pakal's Temple of the Inscriptions, it was not built during his reign. Hasaw Chan Ka'wil died around 734. He was buried in a vaulted limestone chamber and then his son Yikin Chan Kawil constructed the temple on top. In the 1960s, tunnelling through the bottom of the Temple stairway in search of evidence for earlier structures, the Tikal Project came upon it. The skeleton lay on the remains of a woven mat and was surrounded by a rich array of jades, including some strikingly large globular beads, pearls, spondylus shells and finely painted ceramics, many of these with vivid scenes of courtly life. The most extraordinary discovery, hardly noticed at first since they sat in a dusty pile near his right foot, was a collection of carved bones. Some of them, with pointed ends, looked as though they may have had a craft use. But when they were cleaned it appeared that their primary purpose may have been as ritual or even simply as decorative objects. These were in fact human bones. Whether they might have belonged to Jaguar Paw, his most famous sacrificial victim, we cannot say. But they appear to have been some of Hasaw Chan Ka'wil's most cherished possessions. Thirty-seven of them have incised designs. Some are covered in inscriptions, and one states that these were *u bak*, 'his bones'. Others display fine narrative scenes from Maya myth, including a beautifully engraved image of two gods paddling a canoe (see below). Their passengers are a lizard, monkey, parrot and a dog, all seemingly squawking, howling or wailing. In the middle of them appears a Maya individual in the guise of the Maize God, his hand to his face in his own gesture of lamentation. Such a scene was a way of portraying the dead Hasaw Chan Ka'wil on his journey into the afterlife. This was no Stygian crossing to a farther shore but a descent into the Underworld, and a second carving shows the canoe and all its occupants sinking under the waters.

A larger bone bears the moving image of a standing captive looking down at the ropes which bind him. The text upon it says that this man was a noble from Calakmul, taken not in 695 but on a later raid. Finally, a tiny carving which one might easily confuse with the most delicate of oriental ivories, depicts a hand holding a fine brush of the kind used for painting codices (see p.176). A ceramic inkpot in the form of a split conch shell was also found in the tomb close to his head. In the bottom of the bowl is a glyph which simply reads 'paint-pot'. So Hasaw Chan Ka'wil may have been an artist and man of letters as well as a warrior, a truly Renaissance Man of Tikal.

Yik'in Chan K'awil succeeded as the twenty-seventh ruler of Tikal and it was he who did most to transform the centre of the city into what we see today. Apart from Temple I, he also completed Temple II opposite his father's shrine, which may have commemorated his mother Lady Twelve Macaw, extended the causeways which connected the ceremonial complexes and went on to raise the largest monument of all at Tikal, the gigantic Temple IV. It is easy to forget that the great individual temple pyramids, those quintessential images of Tikal from every tourist brochure, were all constructed late in the city's history. The last of the pyramids, Temples III and VI, were put up by Yik'in Chan K'awil's little-known successors towards the end of the eighth century.

A SOCIETY AT WAR

For Maya scholars, in particular those who have been working in the field for decades and have witnessed the transformation in their discipline first hand, recent years have been ones of continuous and almost magical revelation. Frozen in time for more than a millennium, but now released from their spell by the kiss of decipherment, Maya kings and their consorts, individuals who were once little more to archaeologists than Rulers A or B from numbered burials, rise up and talk to us. We possess portraits and vivid representations in action of some of the most successful leaders and personalities of the Maya world such as Pakal, 18 Rabbit or Lady Xoc, who can be visualized today amongst the temples and palaces they built and where they acted in the seemingly constant round of ceremonial centuries ago. Taken together, both the wealth of detail provided by texts and the magnificently abundant sculptural and painted images of the Late Classic help initiate scholars into some of the mysteries of Maya religion and to understand much of the meaning behind the forbidding rituals that rulers performed to communicate with their gods and ancestors.

Yet, however profound in its effects the epigraphic revolution of the last few decades, there are, as we have seen, limits to what the surviving texts can tell us. Researchers are largely working with the descriptive, selective chronicle of those wars, sacrifices and rituals that served to glorify the achievements of rulers, prove their special relationship with the gods and justify the existence of a royal line to its own wider community. Because they reveal little about such things as economics, administration or the social structure below that of the topmost élite, we still have a very imperfect idea of how Maya cities and the territories they controlled actually functioned on a day-to-day basis. The courtly doings and deeds of Maya kings can thus tend to be viewed in glorious and somewhat unreal isolation, disarticulated from the rest of society. It is here that scholars lament the destruction or decay of the hundreds – perhaps thousands – of bark-paper books. If the much later codices of the Aztecs and other Mesoamerican peoples are anything to go by, these may have provided just the kind of information that is so lacking about trade, tribute, land tenure, the organization of agriculture and the government of a city-state which might have equipped scholars to define how the different elements of the economic and social fabric of a Maya city, the daily lives of farmers, traders and administrators as well as those of kings and the aristocracy, fitted together.

Another basic area of uncertainty, where emblem glyphs do not necessarily help us since they may be claiming an outdated or quite imaginary independence, is the definition of the individual units that made up the complex political mosaic of the Maya world. To use the phrase 'city-state', as we have employed it loosely in these pages, is often inappropriate. Mayanists tend to use the more neutral word 'polity', since one could be talking about a number of different arrangements – from a single city and the territory, including smaller settlements, which sustained it, to a great power controlling other substantial cities within a particular region, in the manner that Tikal and Calakmul evolved large 'territorial states' with cities such as Uaxactún directly under their sway. The geographical extent of individual territories and where the boundaries lay between the domain of one 'polity' and another are also very hard to establish. In many areas these must have fluctuated greatly as wars and alliances ebbed and flowed.

The only way to make up for the shortcomings of the inscriptions is through the combination of epigraphy with archaeology. At Caracol and Copán, where the amount of field archaeology carried out in recent years has been considerable and very precisely focused, archaeological data, providing evidence for such things as population levels, patterns of regional settlement, agricultural development and trade links with other areas, can be put together with the textual record to build up a clearer picture of the social and economic development of a centre over time and, for example, the domestic forces operating within the realm of Caracol after the defeat of Tikal in 562 or at Copán following the death of 18 Rabbit. At both cities we now have a greater understanding of the material consequences of important events recorded in the inscriptions. In an ideal world this is the future for Maya studies, integrated projects involving specialists from different sub-disciplines that each focus on a city and its region. In due course, one might imagine the dots of all this endeavour joined up to produce a panoramic reconstruction of ancient Maya society across the Southern Lowlands. In reality, the prospects are not so good. Aside from the fact that archaeology in the field is an extremely expensive and time-consuming business, many sites are much less manageable and conducive to archaeological excavation than others. The preservation and usefulness of inscriptions also varies greatly from site to site. For our purposes we have focused on those cities where surviving inscriptions are plentiful. In some, particularly in Belize, very few and sometimes no inscribed monuments at all were ever set up. Thus mysteries and anomalies will remain for many years to come. Above all, although we now possess a grasp of what happened in much of Classic period Maya history, understanding of why it happened is a different matter.

For example, one of the features common to the careers of so many cities is the boom and bust nature of their fortunes. Periods of florescence marked by energetic building activity are followed by disturbance or catastrophe and then by what often seems a surprisingly sudden renewal. Why was this so? How do we explain the magnificent flowering of Palenque under Pakal after the wave of attacks upon the city recorded around the time of his birth, or the seemingly miraculous reawakening of Tikal following the decline and silence of more than a century? In both cases we have little idea of the economic and political shape that these cities were in compared with their neighbours at the time. Any fuller, functional explanation of such great swings in fortune is a long way off. But, as the Maya themselves tell us, disasters in war brought these great cities low and successful wars restored them to prominence. Appreciation of what Maya war involved provides one of the keys to a fuller understanding of the Classic period, though this in itself is no easy task.

At the time of the initial exploration of Yucatán the Spaniards found Maya armies – they could field large numbers of fighters – fearlessly aggressive and indeed quite terrifying. The combatants were covered in tattoos and body paint, they bore war banners with 'abominable' images and their attacks were announced by the droning of conch-shell trumpets and a terrible whistling noise from the ranks of warriors which built up to a chilling crescendo before an assault was launched. They were also very well organized. In 1517, for example, Hernandez de Córdoba and his men found themselves engaged in a pitched battle against military units whose tactics clearly followed a practised series of moves: an opening barrage of slingstones and arrows, followed by a rapid, co-ordinated advance upon the Spaniards to engage in hand-to-hand fighting with lances, shields and stabbing knives of chipped, razor-sharp flint. On this and many later occasions during the eventual subjugation of Yucatán by the Montejos, the Spanish faced fierce resistance and took heavy casualties. Here, it seemed, was a particularly warlike people who must have become so through years of fighting each other. Of course one should be very cautious about projecting such a picture back into much earlier centuries. In the time of Eric Thompson, the fearsome reputation of the Conquest period Yucatec Maya was put down to outside influence, to invasions by the Toltecs from Central Mexico in the Postclassic era who had supposedly introduced the alien practices of militarism and wholesale human sacrifice to a previously peacable people. Such an idea is no longer tenable and the weight of evidence today suggests that to use Conquest-period analogies would not be so wide of the mark. In the Classic period the waging of war and the shedding of human blood was part of the fabric of Maya life and a religious obligation. The idea of a society that was not on a permanent war-footing would have been a quite alien concept. The important questions, however, concern the nature and motivation of wars.

Maya art is full of martial images. But what they depict on stone monuments and painted ceramics is limited. We almost invariably see warriors either preparing and setting off for war, with their helmets and headdresses, padded cotton armour, shields stretched with animal skin and lances tipped with flint (in the Late Classic they appear not to have used bows and arrows nor adopted the spear-thrower employed by Teotihuacan), or the end-product of hostilities, namely the grasping of the captive by the arm or hair and the display of the victim before sacrifice. Battle scenes as such, for example what might be the Maya equivalent of the pharaoh Rameses II's endlessly repeated excerpts from the Battle of Kadesh on the walls of his temples, were evidently not considered the kind of thing to be reproduced on Maya monuments, at least of stone. The most vivid image of Classic period combat, that provided by the Bonampak murals, is almost unique.

The war events documented by the inscriptions give the impression of troops marching about all over the Southern Lowlands and maybe élite corps of warriors, from Calakmul for example, deployed over long distances. But warfare has proved very difficult to document archaeologically until the end of the Late Classic period. There is some evidence of fortifications at a few Maya sites; Calakmul, for example, possessed a large canal that encircled the city centre and Tikal was surrounded by a series of earthworks in places where there were no swamps. Whether these were in fact for defensive purposes is much debated. It also cannot be presumed that a lack of obvious fortifications, of the kind with which we might be familiar, necessarily argues for any lack of warfare. There are some signs at Tikal of the destructive aftermath of the attack by Calakmul and Caracol in 562 and suggestions of sackings of the North Acropolis at an earlier period. At other cities, too, there is evidence of burning and destruction at certain times. But, to date, there has been little archaeological confirmation of those attacks upon particular cities at specific dates suggested in the texts, such as the supposed wave of assaults upon Palenque around the time of Pakal's birth. However, most of the key phrases related to war events have only been deciphered in recent years and previous field archaeologists may well not have been mentally attuned to war as an explanation for the evidence produced by excavation, attributing some of their findings to domestic burning or perhaps 'termination rituals' meted out to particular buildings rather than to destruction wrought by war. For this reason, a number of archaeologists are now busy going over old excavation reports. Certainly, the search for the physical evidence of documented wars is recognized as an important priority for the future, though technically it is difficult. Most weapons, for example, would have been the same as those used in hunting or in the fields.

There is, however, one striking example where archaeological excavation has revealed indisputable evidence of military conflict of a high intensity. This is in the Petexbatún area, where Dos Pilas, itself created by war in the mid-seventh century, met its end in an extremely violent manner about a hundred years later.[26] In what must have been an atmosphere of terrible insecurity and foreboding, building materials had clearly been torn hurriedly from the city's palaces and temples to construct a defensive wall around the very centre of the city. Within this first line of defence had been further walls, topped by wooden palisades, and the squatter settlements of the local population who had sought refuge here, their houses placed haphazardly among the pyramids and stelae. The occupation of Dos Pilas came to a sudden halt and confirmation of the city's downfall is given by the city of Tamarindito, which records the triumph over her Petexbatún rival in 761. The survivors from Dos Pilas then held out at two other fortified sites until these were eventually overcome. The final redoubt appears to have been Punta de Chimino, a peninsula stretching out into Lake Petexbatún. It was defended by two large moats, and at the bottom of one of them archaeologists discovered a large area of burning and a great quantity of chert spear-heads, some intact and others broken, left quite probably at the time of the last desperate struggle. The whole Petexbatún region was consumed by war in the second half of the eighth century, until nearly all the settlements of the Dos Pilas kingdom were finally abandoned. The level of conflict here may be anomalous; it may be an early sign of the increased intensity of warfare as the Classic period drew to a close, a harbinger of terrible times to come. Yet it also suggests that systematic excavation at other cities in the future may reveal comparable – though perhaps not such apocalyptic – evidence from earlier periods.

The Petexbatún example aside, the lack of useful images of war, the failure of the inscriptions to describe it in any technical detail, and the general paucity of material evidence means that such issues as tactics, the level of casualties and the overall scale of military hostilities remain open questions. But, on the assumption that warfare was a common pursuit throughout the Classic period, can we be clear as to what they were fighting about? Here more recently deciphered glyphic phrases that talk of war can be of more help, since they do suggest conflicts of differing intensity and with diverse goals.

It is obvious enough that the taking of captives was in itself one of the major aims of Maya war and essential to maintain the prestige of rulers. Before his accession to the throne, a future king had to prove himself by the capture of a noble prisoner. Among the Usumacinta sites it seems that the name of the prisoner involved in this royal rite of passage would remain amongst the king's titles for the rest of his career, along with the cumulative count of further captives. For he had to go on acquiring them on a regular basis in order to perform all the sacred, sacrificial obligations of kingship. Who the more run-of-the-mill victims were is unclear, since they are often not named or have no emblem glyphs attached to them. For all we know, some of them could even have been rebels or felons from the same city-state, though they were more likely the product of low-level raiding or kidnapping from neighbouring territories.

The tendency little more than a decade ago to attribute the motivation behind most wars to captive-taking for religious, ritualistic ends is not surprising when the recurring theme of so many Maya monuments is the display, sometimes striking and poignant, of doomed prisoners. But most scholars now agree that this artistic focus on the ritual outcome of war, images which seem to have been so important symbolically in the public display and legitimation of a king's authority, obscures the underlying motives behind many, if not the majority, of wars. The imposition of tribute upon a defeated city would have been the commonest goal of all. The evidence, though limited, suggests that it could take many different forms. At Caracol large numbers of people from the defeated realm of Tikal may well have been transported there after 562 to labour on the construction of the enlarged city. Indeed, this kind of impressed labour service may help to account not just for the extremely swift growth of Caracol, but for some of the rapid bursts of building activity visible in other successful cities. Whether this amounted to a form of slavery, such a loaded term in our own culture, is impossible to judge, though it is well-documented from the time of the Spanish Conquest, initially in that crew of chained canoe-paddlers which Columbus encountered in the Gulf of Honduras. An unusual dimension of tribute seems to have been the 'artistic' form visible at Toniná, where Palenque sculptors are thought to have been put to work to produce the image of their own captive ruler. Another example of this may be apparent at Piedras Negras, where the magnificent Stela 12, with a masterful and moving depiction of a group of prisoners at the feet of the victorious ruler, is carved very much in the style of Pomoná, where the captives came from. One can thus imagine that a range of different craftsmen such as potters and jade workers may have been transferred from one city to another as a consequence of war, to encourage or start up local traditions. Some have suggested that the touch of Copán's artists is visible on the stelae of Quiriguá.

More prevalent, perhaps, than the movement of people would have been tribute in kind. Foodstuffs, cotton cloth, feathers, cacao – the items involved would obviously have varied according to the natural resources or speciality in finished products of particular areas. Formal tribute-giving is depicted occasionally on Maya ceramics, although the specific contexts of such scenes are seldom clear; indeed the provenance of the pots is often unknown, given that the vast majority have been looted. Commodities, most commonly cloth, are seen being presented to enthroned lords by other dignitaries. A famous series of pots decorated by the same artist portray both captive-taking and the presentation of textiles and food, which might suggest that the latter is the end-product of the former.

Within the last few years the cleaning and computer-enhanced reconstruction of the Bonampak murals has brought to light many details that previously were very hard to discern. Amongst these are a number of bundles or sacks bearing glyphs which identify very precisely their contents. This was cacao or chocolate, and each bag, it is stated, contained 40,000 beans. This impressive amount of chocolate appears to have been delivered to the Bonampak court by a group of lords wearing white mantles. Since the discovery of the murals, successive interpretations have been put upon them and they have acted as a barometer of shifting scholarly attitudes to Classic Maya society as a whole. Now we appear to have another level of meaning to set alongside the evident concerns with dynastic continuity and the waging of war to procure sacrificial victims. Economics figures here. The message seems to be that war, a sacred obligation of kings, was also undertaken in unabashed pursuit of power and material wealth, visible not simply in the bags of beans delivered by the tribute-bearers but in the sumptuous costume, the bands of musicians and all the conspicuous consumption displayed in the elaborate ceremonial.

Such worldly considerations were present in the conflict between Quiriguá and Copán, a successful war of independence, it would seem, to gain sole control over lands and trade routes. In this case hostilities appear not to have touched either city, and Copán did not suffer any detectable imposition of tribute. The aims and effects of conflict were thus variable, although wars of conquest to absorb another city and its territory seem extremely rare, apart perhaps from the case of the Petexbatún. If Quiriguá managed to free itself from the overlordship of Copán, the opposite appears to have been the case in the initial wars of Dos Pilas to carve out a territory for itself by military means. The principal aim of the more powerful cities was to establish spheres of indirect dominance over the various regions of the lowlands, extracting tribute from subdued and weaker neighbours and maintaining the supply of sacrificial victims. Much of the instability, the ups and downs in the fortunes of individual cities, can be explained by the waxing and waning of local power structures, first one and then another city coming out on top.

Doubtless those who formed these mini-empires would have been keen to go on enlarging them, in emulation of Tikal and Calakmul. Simon Martin and Nikolai Grube have convincingly demonstrated that these two extraordinarily powerful cities exercised a level of influence right across the Southern Lowlands during the Classic period that operated on a quite different level from the more regional struggles for power.[27] Both these cities were ancient and enduring, with their roots deep in the Preclassic period. Each developed a home base of direct territorial control vastly greater than that established by any other city. Tikal's core area at its height stretched as far as Lake Petén Itzá to the south, to the borders with Naranjo and El Perú to the east and west, and beyond Uaxactún in the north. Within this region were other towns and cities whom we do not hear about for the most part, since they were not permitted to raise their own inscribed monuments. The overall population that Tikal controlled probably approached 500,000 people. Calakmul became an even bigger urban agglomeration and the populations and other centres it dominated, including sizeable but as yet little-known cities such as Naachtún, La Muñeca and Balakbal, were probably much greater still. In both cases the possession of a strong domestic power-base were the essential prerequisites for the spread of their influence. Another more intangible factor, but not to be underestimated, would have been the sacred power and reputation that these two centres of great antiquity possessed in the minds of others. Calakmul may have inherited this kind of leadership as a successor to El Mirador. Tikal undoubtedly acquired an extremely powerful ideological charter through its relationship with Teotihuacan.

Precipitated by that relationship with the greatest power in Mesoamerica at the time, which no doubt formed a model of informal empire for the Maya themselves to follow, based on the carrot and stick of trading advantages and military threat, Tikal rose to pre-eminence first. The full extent and nature of Tikal's power across the Southern Lowlands in the Early Classic is still not apparent. But Copán, Río Azul and almost certainly Palenque, her enduring ally in the Late Classic, seem to have been among the mainstays in a widespread network of associates, strongholds and trading partners. It was this that Calakmul sought to challenge and replace. By the middle of the sixth century, through the patient build-up of a counterweight alliance, she was ready to confront Tikal directly. Thus the war waged against Tikal in 562 was a pivotal moment in Classic period history, when the balance of power tipped dramatically in favour of Calakmul and her confederacy.

We know, of course, very little about the events or precise outcome of that war. The Tikal ruler was sacrificed, the centre of the city was desecrated, and it would seem probable that a level of tribute was fixed, involving the transfer of both labour and goods from the region, which considerably enriched her opponents. But there appears to have been no concerted occupation or administration of the city by foreigners. Another ruling line was installed, most probably a Tikal lineage prepared to collaborate. Local autonomy, in a formal sense, would thus have been maintained, though economically and politically it was severely restricted. The most powerful symbolic restriction seems to have been that Tikal was forbidden to erect inscribed monuments. In essence, the fate of Tikal followed a typical Maya pattern, writ large maybe. Calakmul doubtless did not possess the physical or bureaucratic resources to incorporate or take over the city directly. Indeed, the creation of large empires of territorial incorporation was simply never conceived as a viable strategy among the Maya. Martin and Grube draw wider Mesoamerican comparisons, in particular with the empire of the Aztecs. Although their control was more centralized than anything the Maya achieved, the power they exercised was in practice a similar hegemony over a range of other kingdoms and small, localized empires. Aztec conquests were followed not by occupation or administration from Tenochtitlan but by the imposition of tribute, maintained by the threat of force if the defeated did not continue to supply the consignments of goods demanded. Once they acknowledged their vassalage and complied, local rulers were by and large left in place and in peace.

Tikal was kept in submission, Calakmul securing its control through the encircling confederation of cities such as Caracol, El Perú, Naranjo, Cancuen and the traitorous kingdom of Dos Pilas. The relationships between these cities and Calakmul's effective overlordship can be deduced from those key glyphic phrases that speak of alliances in war, inter-dynastic marriages, royal visits between cities, and Calakmul's sponsorship of the accessions of kings. As we have seen, connections were also established with cities further afield such as Piedras Negras and Yaxchilán, the aim being, it seems, to convert or subdue Tikal's traditional associates such as Palenque. The ultimate prize would have been suzerainty over the whole of the Southern Lowlands.

The anthropologist Robert Carneiro has compared the political instability amongst the Maya with Anglo-Saxon England during the so-called Heptarchy, where from the sixth to eighth centuries kingdoms such as East Anglia, Mercia and Northumbria constantly fought each other, first one then another gaining the upper hand.[28] In fact, the inability of any one kingdom to unify the whole of England, Roman-style, by conquest was recognized, institutionalized almost in the title of 'Bretwalda', which meant 'wide-ruler', later taken to mean 'Britain-ruler'. In the seventh century the Northumbrians possessed the title, then in the following century lost it to the Mercians. With it came recognition of hegemony, that one particular kingdom sat on top of the pile, for a time. Others paid tribute, in coinage or cattle, attended the 'king of kings' court, fought with him and swore their life-long vassalage, until the precarious structure began to show signs of weakness; an outstanding ruler died, perhaps, or the convenience of particular alliances faded. Such an informal arrangement never had a hope of enduring in any particular configuration for long. Neither did the imperial protection-racket of the Aztecs, for that matter, whose dominance over reluctant and opportunist vassals collapsed like a house of cards at the arrival of the Spaniards.

Calakmul never achieved its ambition, for Tikal rose again. Once she had broken free, as Martin and Grube put it, 'the days of superstates and larger political groupings were numbered'. The inscriptions record further engagements between the two powers until the mid-740s. Neither succeeded in subduing the other and by the second half of the eighth century their more active rivalry seems to have been at an end. Then the historical record itself diminishes rapidly. It seems that the old alliances across the Southern Lowlands unravelled and many other competing local dynasties emerged. Anglo-Saxon England, faced by the external threat of the Vikings, was eventually unified. Among the Maya, the reverse was the case. The whole society disintegrated from within.

CHAPTER SIX

Gods and Men

THE SHAPE OF THE WORLD

So far we have approached the major Classic Maya cities individually and chronologically, charting the political relationships between them in the light of new understandings of Maya history. Here we will look broadly at some of the shared elements of Maya culture that made their civilization unique and at what is known of the social structure and the economic underpinnings of their society, which enabled royal dynasties, the brilliant aristocratic culture that surrounded them and the vast anonymous bulk of the Maya population to flourish, with what appears to have been little structural change in the system, for more than 500 years. We will begin with the beliefs of a society where religion and religious ritual dominated the lives of both kings and maize-farmers alike.

Many aspects of ancient Maya thought we shall no doubt never truly comprehend. But they have left behind a rich array of clues, in art and in inscriptions, which has led in recent years to a remarkably detailed understanding of many of the central aspects of Maya religion and the perceptions they had of their place in the world. It would be no exaggeration to say that we now know more about Classic Maya beliefs than we do about many of the more mundane aspects of their lives. To the wealth of surviving information from the Classic period can be added the Postclassic codices. Although they date from the time immediately preceding the Spanish Conquest and have to be approached with a certain amount of caution, as they reveal clear influences from Central Mexico, they are evidently based on centuries of accumulated, traditional Maya knowledge of the calendar, astrology, the practice of ritual and the nature of certain gods. Spanish and native writings of the early Colonial period provide considerable evidence of beliefs and practices which illuminate those of earlier centuries, and finally, evidence from the past can be combined with what is observed among the Maya of today who, despite the changes wrought since the Conquest, have maintained some of the most fundamental of ancient beliefs.

Put together, all the evidence demonstrates that Maya religion was founded on a perception of the world fundamentally different from our own. For they saw no real distinction between an everyday 'natural' world in which humans lived and a 'supernatural' world of gods and spirits. Indeed the universe as a whole appears to have been conceived in ancient times as one continuous existence in which all things, animate and inanimate, visible and invisible, were charged to a greater or lesser extent with what is commonly defined as a kind of sacred 'essence' or energy. Such energies were most clearly and powerfully manifested in the skies and possessed by the dark, unseen forces of the Underworld. But every person, animal or object on earth also commanded a degree of this spiritual potency, conveyed by the word *k'ulel* or *ch'ulel,* best translated as 'holiness' or 'sacredness'.[1] Expressed adjectivally it is the same *k'ul* as in the ancient phrase *k'ul ahaw* or 'holy lord' (see overleaf). In all living beings the sacred essence was believed to be located in the blood.

Particular features of the landscape were thought to possess formidable sacred powers. Springs, lakes, cenotes and above all caves were magical places, seen as thresholds to the nether regions, where offerings were made to the ancestors and the gods of the Underworld. Some especially awe-inspiring locations became centres of pilgrimage, such as the 'Sacred Cenote' at Chichén Itzá or the enormous painted cavern of Naj Tunich in the southeastern Petén, which was visited by kings and nobility from Calakmul, Caracol and other important cities and where accomplished scribes among the royal retinue left records of their devotional descents into its recesses in broad black brushstrokes on the cave walls.[2] Just as potent as points of contact with the sacred were mountains, connecting the earth to the gods of the sky, and perceived as the source of rain and thus by extension of life itself, and directly linked in Maya myth to concepts of human origins. Certain of the living creatures of the Maya environment – the jaguar, cayman, snakes and birds of prey, for example – were viewed as especially powerful because they had attributes people did not possess: the ferocious jaguar could see and hunt by night; snakes shed their skin and seemed miraculously to give birth to themselves. Many animals could also move freely, in the way humans could not, between the different domains of earth, sky and water. Thus it was that Maya rulers, people who were considered to have particularly strong blood or *k'ulel*, used animal images and associations, notably that of the jaguar, as symbols of their own superhuman capacities and dominant position in society.

A Maya lord dancing – part man, part jaguar – from a Late Classic painted vase.

Such a view of the world, sensing the divine in natural things and conceiving of human society as an integral part of the processes of nature, must be traceable back to the very first hunters and gatherers who entered the Maya region and sought to impose some sort of order upon their surroundings and explain their place in the scheme of things. Essentially, this vision never changed. Nor did the need to communicate with unseen forces in order to maintain equilibrium between man and the divine and thus ensure the continued well-being of Maya people. The individual who originally took on this responsibility would have been the shaman, a person of special knowledge who had the ability to influence the world of the spirits. Over time, however, with the growth of ever larger permanent settlements and the evolution of more complex, centralized forms of society, political and religious leadership came to be inextricably linked and the kind of esoteric knowledge once possessed by the local village shaman appears to have been codified and reinterpreted for more 'public' consumption. The earliest expression of a more centralized religious ideology of this kind is visible in the precocious art of the Olmec. By this time the rulers of a community appear to have led the most important rituals and conveyed the sacred messages to their people. If the Olmec laid down something of a pattern for future centuries, it was the Maya during the Classic period who elaborated the most brilliantly complex forms of religious expression in all of ancient Mesoamerica. Different cities produced their individual interpretations of commonly held beliefs, and in each one the king was presented as the central player, the intermediary between his community and the gods.

Getting to grips with the gods of the Maya is no easy task. In 1904 Paul Schellhas first identified some of the major Postclassic deities through study of the codices.[3] Although their characteristics differ in significant ways, many of the same gods are visible in art of the Classic period, and his alphabetical list of Maya Gods A–P is still used as a convenient, universally understood reference since the Maya names of some are still a matter of debate. In recent years, however, many scholars have argued that this kind of classification, which tends to suggest a divine family or pantheon of discrete deities in the Graeco-Roman mould, is a somewhat misleading simplification of more elusive Maya concepts of 'divinity'. Gods could be created in a number of different ways, for example as tutelary deities representing political or social groups, or as the deified spirits of important ancestors. But as we have seen, many features of the Maya environment were held to possess a divine force or vitality. Sacredness was a widely dispersed phenomenon and many gods appear to have arisen as personifications of those forces identified in nature. This may help to account for the sheer quantity of Maya deities, some representing very localized objects of veneration. It is very difficult to know how best to approach them – as separate from one another, or, as some suggest, as all representing different facets of a divine 'oneness' at the heart of Maya religion. This idea of the one and the many probably best enables us to cope with the perplexing ambivalence of Maya religious thought, which has frustrated Western attempts to fit it neatly into pigeon-holes ever since the arrival of the first Spanish missionaries.[4]

There is little doubt that the principal, universally recognized supernatural beings among the Maya originated as embodiments of the most powerful of all natural forces, such as the planets, rain, lightning or the divine personification of maize. But these gods are in themselves extremely complex, or at least they became so over time. For the major deities can appear in a daunting profusion of forms, as elusive as the multiple manifestations of Hindu deities. They can have human or animal characteristics, sometimes both, and possess numerous and often diametrically opposed aspects. In different guises they can be benign or malevolent, male or female, young and old, have distinct forms by day and by night, and be associated with different colours and cardinal directions. In this way one Maya god can be seen to encapsulate or in a sense to reconcile, within its own manifold nature, a series of fundamental dualities or oppositions. This seems to have represented a key principle at the heart of Maya thought, that the continuity of all things was dependent on the yin- and yang-like co-existence of complementary opposites. Ultimately, in starkest human terms, the life of Maya people was dependent on death, the sacrifice of other human beings.

The visible world inhabited by humans was conceived as a flat plane divided into four quarters corresponding to the cardinal directions. That this was so in the Classic period is revealed in one of the tombs of Río Azul, where each wall is painted with a separate glyph for north, south, east and west. These same glyphs appear in the Postclassic codices, where the world directions are given distinct attributes and powers. The east, where the sun rose, was connected not unnaturally with birth, fertility and with the colour red. The west stood for the setting, dying sun as it slid into the Underworld. Black was its colour. The north, whence came the longed-for annual rains, was given the colour white and was conceptually associated, as we have seen, with 'up' and the direction of the heavens, whereas the south, its colour yellow, was down and the direction of the Underworld. Each cardinal direction also possessed its own individual protector god, its own associated bird and tree and one of the sky-bearer gods – 'Bacabs' or 'Pauahtuns' – held up his quarter of the world. The earth as a whole could be envisaged as many things – a four-sided maize-field, the back of a crocodile or a turtle shell – since it was thought to float in a vast expanse of primordial ocean.

There are in fact five dimensions to the Maya world. The fifth was the centre, the great axis or the point at which the sky was thought to have been raised from the ocean at the moment of creation. This was often conceived as the 'World Tree', a giant ceiba or silk-cotton tree, with its roots in the Underworld and branches spreading up into the heavens, that magnificent cruciform image seen on Pakal's sarcophagus and within the temples of the Cross Group at Palenque. This sacred centre had the colour *yax*, the range of blue-green that appeared in so many precious things such as water, the sky, jade and young, growing maize. The fundamental Maya concept of the earth in the form of a 'quincunx', with four corners and a centre, survives to the present day. In the highlands of Guatemala, for example, a shaman or *chuchk'ahaw*, before he embarks upon any ritual, will first build in front of him a small model of the world, recreating with candles, flowers and copal incense the four-fold structure with its centre as an essential, age-old pattern of right order and balance (see plate section, p.19).

The nine-layered Underworld, 'Xibalbá' or 'Place of Fright' in Quiché Maya, was entered after death. It was a chilling, dreadful place pervaded by the stench of rotting corpses, each level ruled by one of the 'Bolontik'u', the fearsome lords of the Underworld. All Maya came here, saints and sinners alike it would seem, and the grave goods buried with them by their family equipped them for the journey ahead and the trials they faced. Rulers would be provided with food, pottery, textiles, sacrificed retainers on occasion and great quantities of life-giving jade and cinnabar to speed their resurrection. More humble Maya were lain to rest with only a few simple pots, but even they might carry a jade or greenstone bead in the mouth as a form of currency for the afterlife; some were even accompanied by the family dog to guide them on their way, a custom still observed until recent times by the Lacandón. It is none too clear how Xibalbá was truly conceived, nor how many could hope to escape from it. Apparently most were doomed to spend eternity within its rank halls, unless they could outwit the Lords of Death or unless they died in war, through sacrifice or in childbirth. Only then would they be given an easy birth within the Underworld itself or be resurrected and take an immortal place amongst the thirteen levels of the Heavens. Powerful royal ancestors were envisaged climbing up the World Tree to their rebirth in the sky. Here it was that the great celestial deities were to be found: the Sun and the Moon, Venus, the Pleiades, and the Milky Way, the latter so eminently visible in the American tropics and viewed as a night-time manifestation of the World Tree, a great 'white road' across the sky and a kind of umbilical cord between Earth, the Heavens and the Underworld. The Milky Way is similarly regarded as a 'celestial river' by many other ancient cultures of the Americas. The arch of the heavens was also often depicted in Maya art as a double-headed serpent, whose markings included the signs for the various heavenly bodies. A similar 'serpent bar' was carried by Maya kings.

The functioning of the universe was directed by a great number of gods. The most significant can be identified with reasonable precision, and a number of them we have come upon before. K'inich Ahaw, the 'Sun-faced Lord' was the Sun God, whose name and attributes were often adopted by kings. The Sun God possessed many aspects, related to the stages of the planet's daily journey above and beneath the earth and connected conceptually with ideas of life, death and rebirth. The transformation of the Sun God most widely seen in Maya art is his night-time aspect as the 'Jaguar Sun' of the Underworld. Chak, the ancient god of Rain, with reptile features and a downward-turning snout, also appeared in different guises and these were often associated with the cardinal directions – hence the 'White Chak of the North' or the 'Yellow Chak of the South'. In his most benevolent form he was associated with agriculture and fertility, and still today in the northern Yucatán, before planting and the coming of the rains, offerings are made to Chak. This often involves the construction of a ceremonial altar, bounded by ropes and saplings, another recreation in miniature of the age-old, four-cornered structure of the Maya universe. What Chak provided he could also withhold, or provide in excessive, disastrous quantity. For, in his malevolent aspect, he was also the bringer of drought and hurricane.

The still mysterious Itzamná or 'Lizard House', a god of human aspect in the guise of an elderly man with a hooked nose, appears to have been of great significance (see above). Early Colonial accounts talk of him as the Maya high god and as creator of the universe. Recent decipherments and Itzamná's documented appearances in Classic Maya art, ceramic art in particular, suggest that he was conceived in earlier times as the god of writing and learning, as the archetypal shaman and as the most important of a number of creator gods. Ix Chel or 'She of the Rainbow' may have been regarded as his wife. She, too, was associated with curing, with medicine and childbirth, and at the time of the Conquest was greatly venerated on Cozumel island and the Isla Mujeres. Those statues of women discovered on the latter island by some of the first Spanish explorers were no doubt images of Ix Chel. 'God K' in the Schellhas classification, known as 'Bolon Tzacab' at the time of the conquest, or 'K'awil' as he was probably called in Classic times, seems to have been a special patron of Maya kings. Often represented as the 'Manikin Sceptre', a figure held in the hand of rulers and endearingly termed a 'puppet on a stick' by Alfred Maudslay, he has an upturned snout, an axe buried in his forehead and one leg in the form of a snake. It was with these attributes of K'awil that the young Kan Balam was presented by his ancestors on the front piers of Palenque's Temple of the Inscriptions.

The commonly venerated deities also included Venus, brother of the Sun, and the Maize God, to whom, along with the various Lords of the Underworld, we shall return. Dozens of other deities are recorded, and at the time of the Spanish Conquest these included a wide range of patron gods such as 'Ek Chuah' or 'Black Scorpion', the god of merchants, and other deities that oversaw different aspects of Maya life such as hunting, fishing, singing, dancing and the keeping of bees.

The multi-layered Maya universe with all its deities may seem to us a place of some confusion. To the Maya themselves, more specifically perhaps to that intellectual élite within society who amassed and passed on sacred, esoteric knowledge, this was not the case at all. They watched and recorded everything in the natural world around them in the belief that through such observation they might grasp the divinely ordained order and meaning of the cosmos. The giving of godly names to so many natural phenomena was in a sense a form of classification, identifying the component parts of the functioning universe. Nowhere was this potentially fathomable structure more manifest than in the skies, where the movements of the heavenly bodies followed repeated and dependable patterns. The risings and settings, the reappearances of the planets and stars were perceived as stages in the journeys of the gods, who ceaselessly played out their roles and went through their own cosmic cycles of life, death and rebirth. Their celestial journeyings marked the passage of time, which was captured in that astonishing achievement of ancient time-keeping, the Maya calendar.

All ancient peoples looked into the skies intently. The heavens were clear, shimmered brilliantly, and the presence and movements of celestial bodies were a constant challenge to understanding. From earliest times agriculture was scheduled by planetary movement. The fact that ancient civilizations across the globe shared an interest in particular constellations or stellar alignments is not evidence of transoceanic contact or shared origins way back in the mists of antiquity, as latter-day Atlantis enthusiasts might have us believe, but of the unity of all early societies in their fascination with the stars. The Maya seem to have been more fascinated by them than any other civilization in human history.[5]

They scanned the sky with the simplest technology. They had no telescopes, clocks nor measuring devices as far as we know, simply the naked eye. There are illustrations in certain Central Mexican codices that give us an idea of the techniques they probably used for observing heavenly bodies. In the Codex Nuttall appears a man within a temple, itself decorated with star symbols, looking out over a pair of crossed sticks towards the horizon (see below). In another codex, an eye is drawn between a very similar pair of sticks. Thus it would seem that Maya Flamsteeds and Halleys sat in what may indeed have been 'royal' observatories and patiently plotted the heavens, perhaps using both foresights and backsights to record the extreme position of a body on the horizon at a certain time. When the particular planet or star returned to that position, the length of the synodical cycle was established.

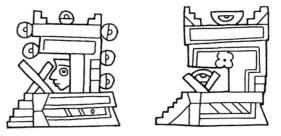

Astronomical observation in the Codex Nuttall and the Selden Codex.

Natural features on the horizon were undoubtedly used to aid the process of recording. At Yaxchilán, for example, it seems that from the tops of the hills at the centre of the site an impressive view could be gained of another series of hills to the east. Charting the appearance of the sun in relation to these would obviously have helped them to follow the progress of the solar year. From one particular building, Structure 41, the sun can be seen to rise on the longest day of the year directly from a cleft between the two highest hills in the range. Carolyn Tate, who has carried out a series of measurements here, believes that the overall planning of the city was carried out with solar orientations in mind, particularly to the summer and winter solstices.[6] She also suggests that what was possibly an original Maya name for Yaxchilán, 'Place of the Split Sky', may be a reference to those twin mountains from where the sun was seen to emerge.

At the site of Uxmal, a man-made fixed point on the horizon was used, this time for tracking the movements of Venus. Most of the buildings of Uxmal are aligned roughly north–south. But one impressive structure, the beautiful 'House of the Governor,' faces away from the centre of the city towards the south-east. Taking a line of sight through the central doorway of this building at the time it was constructed, around 900, Venus would have risen at its maximum southerly point as morning star at a horizon spot marked by a pyramid at the site of Cehtzuc, about five kilometres away. The importance of Venus to the ruler who built the House of the Governor, known as 'Lord Chak', is abundantly apparent in the decoration of the upper façade of the structure. There are two hundred stone mosaic masks of the Rain God and each of them is carved with the glyph for Venus on the god's eyelid. The significance of Venus about a century later to the people of Chichén Itzá has now been conclusively proved at the famous 'Caracol' building, whose purpose has been long thought to have been that of an astronomical observatory (see plate section, p.19). The whole structure is aligned to the planet's northerly extremes and a number of Venus sightlines have been documented from the interior through doors and windows.[7]

Venus, as we have seen in previous chapters, was the most sanguinary of planets. The connection between Maya war and Venus was first made by Floyd Lounsbury at Bonampak, where he discovered that the battle depicted in the murals took place on 2 August 792, which marked an 'inferior conjunction', the time at which the planet passed in front of the sun. A little later the captives were displayed, on the precise day when Venus reappeared as Morning Star. Why Venus in particular should have had such a relationship with war and sacrifice is still unknown. But after the Sun it was always, throughout Mesoamerica, the celestial body of greatest significance. Together they were envisaged as the 'Hero Twins' of Maya myth, as we shall see below, who accompanied each other through the sky, Venus either rising before the Sun at dawn or setting after it at dusk.

Man-made solar observatories dating from the Preclassic period are known at cities such as Uaxactún, Tikal and Calakmul (see overleaf). Today there is evidence from a number of other sites that systematic observation of the heavens began at an early stage in Maya history and

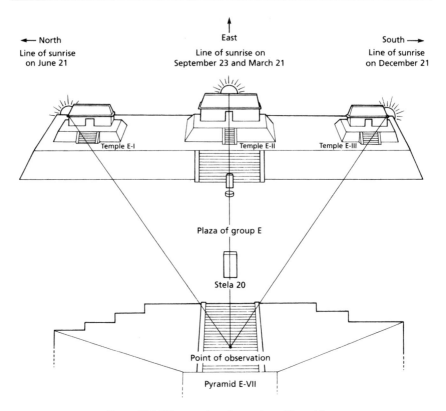

Pyramid E-VII as a solar observatory, Uaxactún.

was built upon down the centuries. Of course this is a crucial factor, since it is the sheer accumulation of knowledge over a very long period of time that would have enabled people with a simple technology to formulate accurate calendars. The Maya possessed the other essentials: a sophisticated enough knowledge of maths to enable them to make complex calculations and, in the codices, a means of keeping permanent records which could be handed on to their descendants. In recounting how he felt obliged to burn so many of them, Diego de Landa tells us that they contained their 'antiquities and their sciences'.

The Maya tracked not only the sun and Venus, also the cycles of the moon. Lunar data were always included, for example, amongst the extra-calendrical information provided with Long Count dates on Classic-period stelae, the reference normally being to whether the lunar month was considered to be either twenty-nine or thirty days in duration. It appears that over time they came to a finer and astonishingly accurate calculation for the average lunation, reckoning that 149 moons were equivalent to 4400 days. In other words, the average lunar month was made up of 29.53020 days, as against 29.53059, which is the calculation made today with the use of atomic clocks. Their Venus Calendar, though not perfect, was accurate to within one day in 500 years, and they also successfully followed the movements of Mars, Jupiter, Mercury and Saturn. Particularly remarkable to modern astronomers are their eclipse tables, based on calculations made over many generations and still usable today.

A solar eclipse, as represented in the Dresden Codex.

The bedrock of Maya time was provided by the unerringly faithful movements of the sun. The same word, *kin*, means both sun and day. But all the celestial cycles, of varying lengths, were important since each one seems to have been connected, like that of Venus, with distinct areas of Maya life. Thus each required particular sequences of appropriate ritual observance. Convinced that the universe represented a finely tuned whole with all its parts interlocking, the tracking of so many cycles was also a means of further plumbing its secrets and ensuring that the cosmic machine they observed continued to run smoothly. Thus they were particularly concerned to grasp how all the movements of the heavenly bodies fitted together. Here Maya maths and multiplication tables were fully exercised. Fortunately, the best, and to the Maya the most significant, example of this 'commensuration' is a fairly simple one. This is the connection between the cycles of Venus and the Sun. The cycle of Venus was particularly fascinating and mysterious, since it regularly disappeared from sight and then reappeared again. The Maya divided its movements into four phases, which are not in fact quite the same as we would recognize today. It appeared as Morning Star for 236 days, followed by 90 days when it was out of sight during 'superior' conjunction. It then featured as Evening Star for 250 days before hiding its face for 8 days during 'inferior' conjunction. This made a total of 584 days for the complete cycle. They realized that five such cycles were equivalent to eight 365-day solar years. As a result, they devised an eight-year almanac which ran both cycles together and which was one of the most important tools of the calendar specialist or diviner.

The Maya formulation of calendars, their perseverance and ambition, generation after generation obsessively observing and refining their knowledge of the skies, represents the application of a remarkably pure scientific method. It enabled them to advance knowledge of the observable world to a degree unmatched by their contemporaries in Europe. In our understanding of the word – and this should not imply any nit-picking denial of their achievements – Maya 'science' stopped when it came to using the data they amassed. Like other early civilizations prior to the Greeks, they had no concept of the natural world as an objective reality that might be tested and hypothesized about as an end in itself. Maya astronomy was pursued in the service of astrology, to predict what the future might bring. For the recurring movements of the planets and stars within the parameters of time delineated by the calendar revealed a cosmic order that was predictable. Everything functioned in cycles, came around again. And if the very structure of the universe revealed itself in this way, as an endless process of repetition, then the trajectory of human affairs had to follow the same course. To Maya minds, the logic of this was incontestable. Thus the purpose of almanacs and calendars was to have both past and future time immediately to hand, so that observed patterns in the past, both the doings of the gods revealed as celestial events in the skies and recorded occurrences on earth, would help to plot their likely repetition within the recurring cycles in the future. This might involve detailed analysis of every portion of time down to the smallest *kin* or day unit in order to work out the myriad influences of different gods and the precedents from the past that might have a bearing upon future events.

The *Tzolkin* or 260-day Sacred Almanac, thirteen numbers coupled with twenty day names, had no connection with any celestial cycle. But it was the most ancient and important calendar throughout Mesoamerica and the essential tool to the diviner. Still running in step with the cycles once observed in Classic Maya cities, it survives today in the highlands of Guatemala and is used by the shaman or 'day-keeper' to perform divinations on behalf of his clients. The contemporary shaman's activities would seem to represent the survival, in simplified yet essentially comparable form, of very ancient practices. The use of the 260-day calendar is combined with a number of other divinatory aids such as seeds and crystals which are cast onto a table and then counted up and matched with the numbers and day names to produce an augury. The day-keeper may be asked for his opinion as to whether a specific day is propitious for a business or family activity, for instance the appropriate time for a baptism. Among certain communities he can be involved in the timing of agricultural activities, providing a divination as to the most favourable day to complete a harvest, for example, which may mean that a family has to work extremely hard to meet the deadline. The day-keeper keeps his own charts of the days, his personal almanacs filled with notes on the complex influences brought to bear on each segment of time: the particular character of each day name and number, information about the phases of the moon, the relationship of the solar year with the *tzolkin*. And today Christian saints and the traditional 'earth lords', associated with the forces of nature and particular features in the landscape, both have a part to play in mapping out Maya destiny. Importantly, the role of the day-keeper is not simply to predict what may come to pass, but also to influence affairs through judging the right time to act and to perform certain efficacious rituals, which may involve the burning of candles and incense, the offering of liquor to the lords of the earth, on occasion the killing of a chicken, the nearest modern equivalent to ancient blood sacrifice. As in ancient times, not everything is predetermined. Through ritual, through effective communication with the sacred, people can hope to bend destiny to their will.

In the Classic period hundreds, probably thousands, of bark-paper books must have been produced, and one can guess that a large percentage would have been devoted to divination and prophecy. Almost all have been destroyed. Great numbers may well have been left to rot at the time of the Maya 'Collapse' in the ninth century. Those that avoided this fate, or were copied or compiled anew in the Postclassic era, would have ended up on Diego de Landa's bonfires or were eliminated by other extirpators of idolatry in the early Colonial period. But at least we have those four priceless, fragmentary survivals to remind us of what has been lost. Of these, the Dresden Codex is the masterpiece of the group, a monument of calendrical and ritual esoterica. Once thought to have been produced in the twelfth or thirteenth century, it now seems that it dates from only a short time before the Spanish Conquest, since recent research has revealed the mention of specifically Aztec names and deities. Michael Coe suggests that the calligraphic style and quality of the Dresden Codex is very much as it would have been in the Classic period and that it shows the scribal tradition to have been kept alive and flourishing in the centres of Maya culture of late Prehispanic times.[8] The Dresden is one strip of fig-bark paper about 3.5 metres long and almost 10 centimetres high, folded into 39 leaves and painted on both sides on top of the covering of white gesso. It contains tables recording and predicting eclipses, data on the synodical cycles of the planets, Venus in particular, including long lists of its rising and setting dates accompanied by illustrations of the gods relevant to those particular days (see plate section, p.3). In large part it is made up of a series of 260-day almanacs that provide day-by-day auguries.

The Maya may not have been true scientists, but neither were they unworldly gazers at the stars. Time was no mystery that was to be worshipped in some way. Skilfully handled, the calendar was an indispensable guide for action on this earth and those who possessed the specialized knowledge of the workings of the cosmos and the supernatural, who could chart what was foreshadowed in the past and predict the future, were an integral part of the governing apparatus of Maya society.

CREATION AND THE BLOOD OF SACRIFICE

Observation of the heavens and the natural world helped to answer questions about how the divine universe worked. More fundamental ones concerned the origins and nature of human society and how best to maintain good relations with the gods. They had created all life, and humans continued to depend on them for their survival and well-being. Equally, Maya people themselves had an active role to play in maintaining order and balance in the world.

The relationship between gods and men is best explored through the remarkable creation mythology of the Popol Vuh, the 'Book of Council', which was set down in the Roman alphabet in the mid-sixteenth century by descendants of the lordly lineages of the Postclassic Quiché kingdom. This was the document which was painstakingly copied and translated into Spanish in about 1702 by the Dominican friar Francisco Ximénez and published in Europe in the middle of the nineteenth century by Brasseur de Bourbourg. Scholars have to be circumspect in their use of the Popol Vuh, for a number of obvious reasons. Firstly, there is an enormous distance in both time and space between the sixteenth-century Quiché Maya and the centres of lowland civilization of Classic times. The Quiché were a highland Maya group who, over the centuries, received strong cultural influences from Central Mexico. The post-Conquest authors had already, in a formal sense at least, been partly Christianized; the original sixteenth-century text is lost and all we have to go on is the transcription of a Spanish friar. Nevertheless, in the 1970s Michael Coe began to trace certain clear correspondences between stories in the Popol Vuh and mythological scenes on fine pottery of Late Classic date. Today, although the vast majority of these pots have been looted, have no scientific context and find their way through dealers and auction rooms into private collections (prompting a number of more self-conscious purists to take a moral stand and have nothing to do with them), the number available for iconographical study has been greatly enlarged. Assisted by advances in decipherment, there is now incontrovertible evidence that major Popol Vuh themes were familiar and in common currency in the lowlands in Classic times. What is more, stone sculpture and architectural stucco ornament with Popol Vuh references have been identified from as early as the Late Preclassic, from highland sites such as Izapa and from the cities of Nakbé and from El Mirador in the lowlands.

In using the Popol Vuh, one also has to bear in mind that it can only act as a key to one particular cycle amongst what was originally a much larger body of ancient Maya mythology. There are, for example, many scenes on funerary ceramics that clearly relate to other myths that are now lost and which may never be understood. There are also narrative incidents depicted on the pots which, although they involve identifiable characters from the Popol Vuh, treat of episodes not recounted in the Quiché document. Bearing all this in mind, however, the vast majority of scholars now accept this uniquely powerful, poetic work of native American literature as a legitimate source of very ancient religious concepts, to which people throughout the Maya world subscribed. Indeed, the modern translator and greatest authority on the Popol Vuh, Dennis Tedlock, suggests compellingly that parts of it derive directly from an original Classic-period codex and that the document Ximénez saw may even have included both illustrations and some hieroglyphs.[10]

The second half of the text as it comes down to us describes the ancestral wanderings of the original heads of the Quiché lineages, the establishment and later history of the Quiché kingdom. What concern us here are the first sections of the book which deal specifically with creation and the attendant adventures of the 'Hero Twins', stories that Coe compares with *The Iliad* and *The Odyssey*, the Hindu Ramayana or the Norse sagas, where gods and heroes stride the same stage and where the deeds of heroes provide a 'charter' or certain behavioural models for the élite groups that ruled these societies.[11]

The impressive, sonorous opening of the Popol Vuh, following Tedlock's translation, presents the earth before its peopling as a featureless void:

> There is not yet one person, one animal, bird, fish, crab, tree, rock, hollow, canyon, meadow, forest. Only the sky above is there; the face of the earth is not clear, only the sea alone is pooled under all the sky; there is nothing whatever gathered together. It is at rest; not a single thing stirs. It is held back, kept at rest under the sky.[12]

In this serene quiet the gods who inhabit the sea and sky come together to conceive of creation, expressed as the 'sowing and dawning' (see below). First, the gods' very words generate the mountains, forests and

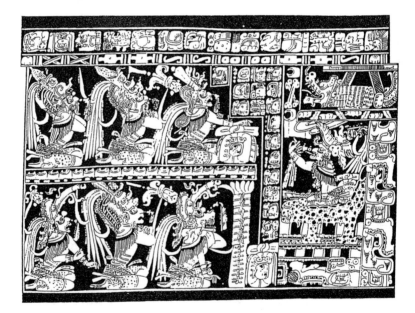

Vase of the Seven Gods: six supernaturals, before another enthroned god, are gathered together in the darkness before creation. The vertical text lists their names, each followed by the glyph *k'u*, meaning 'sacred' or 'god'. At the beginning of this text appears the date of Maya creation in the Calendar Round 4 Ahaw 8 Cumku.

earth from the all-encompassing waters. Then they decide to people the earth, but only with beings who conform to certain specifications. They must praise the gods, tend to shrines, make offerings and regulate their lives by the sacred calendar. To begin with, however, the gods' efforts are not very effective, an unsuccessful series of false starts, a pattern common to stories of creation throughout the ancient Americas. First they fashion creatures who do little but howl and squawk. Since they cannot speak and worship the gods properly, these are clearly inappropriate. But they will be allowed to live on as the animals of mountain and forest to provide for the improved models who come after them, those who can acknowledge, worship and are thereby of use to the gods. Next they attempt to make a being from clay, but its body is feeble and eventually crumbles. After this second failure the creator gods consult an old couple, called Xpiyacoc and Xmucane, who are the original mythic prototypes of soothsayers or diviners. These two cast lots and scan their books of days, and their divination prompts an attempt to create men from wood and women from rushes. The wooden people are an improvement. They look like humans, talk and procreate like them, but they do not respect or pray to the gods in the manner that is required. They are destroyed by a great flood, by fearsome monsters who tear them apart and even by their own dogs and household utensils who rise up to crush them. The descendants of what is left of these wooden people will become the monkeys of the forest.

There is now a pause in the narrative, for we are on the threshold of the final, successful attempt at creation. Now the Hero Twins enter the story. For it is their role to pave the way, in effect to rid the world of malevolent forces and provide the proper material out of which humans will be fashioned. The Hero Twins saga is complex and the action switches rapidly and somewhat confusingly between different generations and between the surface of the earth and the Underworld. The main protagonists are known in Quiché Maya as Hunahpu and Xbalanque. But there is another set of twins, their father and uncle, known as Hun Hunahpu and Vucub Hunahpu, who are the sons of the diviners Xpiyacoc and Xmucane. These first twins are great players of the ball-game. But they make such a noise in their ball-court on the surface of the earth that they anger the lords of the Underworld below. Owl messengers are sent to summon them to the terrible halls of Xibalbá. There they are challenged to a series of games, defeated, and eventually sacrificed. They are then buried beneath the great ball-court of the Underworld, the 'Place of Ball-Game Sacrifice', all save the head of Hun Hunahpu, which is hung from a calabash tree as a grisly trophy. Such swaggering on the part of the denizens of the Underworld is justly repaid, however, for there is to be a curious and fortunate outcome. 'Blood Moon', the daughter of one of the Xibalbán lords, goes to look at the strange fruit hanging in the calabash tree. The decapitated head spits into her hand and impregnates her. Fearing for her life when she becomes pregnant, she flees out of the Underworld to the surface of the earth and takes refuge with the first twins' mother, Xmucane. There it is that Blood Moon gives birth to Hunahpu and Xbalanque, who will gain revenge on behalf of their sacrificed relations.

The Hero Twins, Hunahpu with his characteristic spots, and Xbalanque distinguished by patches of jaguar skin on his face and body. From a painting in the cave of Naj Tunich.

The twins grow up in the house of Xmucane and there, one day, they retrieve the ball-game equipment that their father and uncle had hidden in the loft of the house before their departure for Xibalbá. They become just as proficient at the game, and equally noisy. Once more the Underworld lords are furious at the din and summon the pair to Xibalbá. But this set of twins are much better prepared and quicker-witted than their predecessors. Surmounting extremely unpleasant and deadly obstacles on their journey to Xibalbá, such as rivers of blood and torrents of pus, they too are made to play a series of ball-games against the Underworld gods. This they do by day, and manage to hold their own, and at night they are put through a sequence of trials in different, potentially fatal 'Houses', including a House of Fire and Cold, a Jaguar House, a House of Flint Knives and a House of Killer Bats. Surviving all these tribulations, they continue to outwit the lords of Death. Finally one of the Twins succeeds in decapitating the other and then bringing him back to life. Extremely impressed and excited by this, the Underworld lords queue up to have the trick performed on them. Only this time, of course, resurrection is not on offer. The remaining denizens of the Underworld are spared on condition that never again will they enjoy the powers they once possessed. No more will they have any influence over the earthly abode of men: 'Such was the loss of their greatness and brilliance. Their domain did not return to greatness. This was accomplished by little Hunahpu and Xbalanque.'

The whereabouts of the bodies of Hun Hunahpu and Vucub Hunahpu are then revealed, buried under the Xibalbá ball-court. They are revived and assured that in the future they will be revered as honoured ancestors by all humans, as yet unborn. Having purged the forces of the Underworld and secured the resurrection of their father and uncle, the Hero Twins rise up into the sky as the Sun and Moon, or as many scholars now believe, the Sun and Venus. Thereafter, for all time, they will continue to re-enact at dusk and dawn their epic descent and re-emergence from the Underworld, the metaphorical triumph of life over death. One can only imagine the power of this myth for Maya people, as they watched the sun sink every night beneath the forested horizon.

In the text of the Popol Vuh the focus switches back to the creator gods after the exit of the Twins from Xibalbá. For the stage is now set for the final, successful attempt at the creation of humankind. From the heart of a sacred mountain the gods retrieve maize – two complementary kinds of corn, white corn and yellow corn. Old Xmucane, diviner and midwife, grinds the two mixed with a little water to make dough. It is from this substance, the mixture of maize and water, that the first true people are formed.

As we noted above, however, mythological narrative scenes on Classic period painted pottery suggest that the colonial Popol Vuh text represents only one version of an epic story that in earlier times must have been interpreted in different ways at different Maya cities and with many variations upon the central theme. An extremely significant variation was first identified by the iconographer Karl Taube and it would seem to illuminate what in Classic times must have been one of the fundamental meanings of the story of the Hero Twins.[14] It concerns the role of Hun Hunahpu, the Hero Twins' father, whose head was cut off and hung in the calabash tree. Taube has clearly established that Hun

Hunahpu and the Maya Maize God were one and the same. On a famous Late Classic painted bowl, for example, one of a group of comparable images, Hun Hunahpu, identified by a name glyph, is adorned with the distinctive jewellery and corn foliage headdress of the Maize God. Flanked protectively by the Hero Twins, he is seen emerging from the split shell of a turtle, in other words through the surface of the earth (see below). A glyphic skull below confirms that he is indeed rising up from the Underworld. This provides a more direct connection between the Hero Twins and the creation of humans. For not only have they revived their father but they have also in effect brought maize, the material from which mankind is to be formed, into the human sphere, the plane of the earth. Indeed, the Maize God is represented here sprouting forth as a personified Maize plant, Xbalanque watering the sprout from a large ceramic jar. Thus Hun Hunahpu, the Maize God, also came to be regarded as 'First Father', direct ancestor of humans.

The stories of the Popol Vuh, and the painted elaboration of them we see on Classic period pottery, thus explain the creation of the world and the origins of society. In so doing, they also convey further truths, as the Maya would have seen them, of human existence. One of the most fundamental is the ever-present sense of doubt and impermanence in the world. For the present order is but the latest in a series of creations and

Hun Hunahpu, as depicted on a painted interior of a Late Classic pottery bowl.

destructions, reflecting that deep-rooted Maya perception that all things go through inevitable cyclical processes of birth, growth and decay. Who is to say when the present world will come to an end? One of the messages of the Popol Vuh is that the only way to ensure any permanence and order, and to avoid cataclysmic destruction in the future, is to maintain a harmonious relationship with the gods.

Among the Maya, the relationship forged between gods and men at the time of creation was an extremely close one, in that both had need of each other. For the gods, it will be remembered, were very precise about what they required of the future inhabitants of the earth. They sought to people it with beings who would recognize their achievements, worship and make offerings to them. They tried unsuccessfully a number of times, until finally they fashioned the flesh and blood of humankind from maize and water. Essential to this is the suggestion of an original covenant that bound humans and the divine order together. People were created from and are, literally, what they eat: maize and water. In return for the elements of their creation, and continued sustenance in the form of rain and the products of their corn-fields, humans must constantly praise the gods and nourish them, by returning that which they received in the first place, the sacred gift of blood. In an extraordinary process of reciprocity and the recycling of the substance of life, feeding the gods so that they in turn continue to provide for humans, the whole order of the universe would be maintained. It is a remarkably simple and economical concept, using maize agriculture, the source of Maya livelihood and the very origins of their civilization, as the central metaphor to encapsulate their relationship with the divine. Furthermore, people were indeed just like maize. They sprouted, lived and died, but carried in their blood the seeds of their own regeneration.

It is easy enough to understand that humans should depend upon the gods. What is very different, and indeed quite alien to most modern religions where omnipotent creators transcend their creation and have no need of any form of human assistance, is the idea that people themselves have an active part to play in sustaining the gods, indeed that without human participation the very existence of gods and the world order might be threatened. Of course this also explains why the letting of blood, the seat of *k'ul*, was the central religious rite of Maya life.

At the time of the Conquest Diego de Landa observed that from childhood all Maya regularly drew blood from various parts of the body and offered it to the gods. In the Classic period the practice was almost certainly just as widespread. Most famously, we know from Maya art and from archaeological retrieval of some of the paraphernalia involved, that members of a royal family pierced their tongues, their ears or the fore-skin and the blood, collected on strips of bark-paper, would be burnt, transformed into smoke and rise up to the heavens. So sacred were these rites of personal blood-letting that the piercing instruments used – obsidian, bone or sting-ray spine – were depicted as deified ritual objects. If personal blood-letting was an offering, it was also associated with the vision quest, supernatural communication with a god or deified ancestor, in the way that Lady Xoc is represented at Yaxchilán conjuring up a visionary manifestation of the royal founder Progenitor Jaguar. Excessive blood loss on its own can induce a trance-like state, but in certain rites this was almost certainly enhanced by other means – through strong tobaccos, still used in this manner until recently by the Lacandón, and other hallucinogenic substances. The important deci-pherment of the *uay* glyph demonstrates that the Maya had a concept of spiritual alter-egos or 'co-essences', which many have interpreted as supernatural identities that an individual could be seen to take on. In other words, through trance experience and shamanistic 'transforma-tion' he could enter and interact with the spirit world. It would thus appear that shamanism endured from early times as a central element of Maya religious practice, and that the Maya ruler was regarded as chief shaman in his society, able to communicate with and influence the supernatural for the benefit of his community. Where such contact with the spirit world was made was almost certainly in places remote from public gaze. Beneath the Palace at Palenque, for example, are a series of damp and murky underground passageways and rooms fitted out with stone benches. Descending here is like entering one of the levels of the Underworld. 'One can surmise that these passages might have been used for a little religious hocus-pocus', observed Eric Thompson many years ago. Today we can speculate with rather more confidence about what this 'hocus-pocus' may have involved.

Personal blood-letting, as an offering and as part of a process of com-munication with the divine, was not enough to repay in full the blood-debt to the gods. What they required was the more substantial sustenance afforded by human sacrifice. Ever since the conquistadores first encountered the practice, the idea of the institutionalized killing of other humans has repelled and mystified us. As the older, benign image of the Classic Maya has been superceded, the more sanguinary 'new view' patiently pieced together by scholars has inevitably became sensationalized. The Maya possessed an innate lust for blood; they were a people just as 'bloodthirsty' as the Aztecs. Clearly, such simplifications do not further any greater understanding of what we have seen was a complex component of their religious life, which had endured throughout Mesoamerica at least since the time of the Olmec.

It is difficult to know the true extent of human sacrifice practised by the Classic Maya. The stelae and paintings may deceive, since we cannot be certain that the individuals or small groups depicted were the only victims involved in a particular rite or whether they are representative of larger numbers that were put to death. The former appears much more likely, and that Maya sacrifice was an occasional affair that accompanied only the most important of religious rituals. It was certainly never on the same chilling, industrial scale as that perpetrated by the Aztecs. What is perplexing among the Maya, however, is the preparatory torture of individuals that is evident in their art. Victims were beaten, mutilated, their finger-nails torn out, and they were subjected to prolonged bouts of blood-letting before eventually being killed. The most prized prisoners, nobles or kings like K'an Hoy Chitam of Palenque, men who possessed particularly powerful and efficacious blood, could be held captive for years, their life-blood periodically tapped before an auspicious date was selected for their death. The final method of despatch was normally decapitation (see plate section, p.19), though it is evident that heart excision, the Aztec mode, was also practised. But as an alternative, or a preliminary, men could be disembowelled, scalped, burnt, strapped to wooden scaffolds and shot with arrows, besides being trussed up as balls and bounced down stairways. The idea of a religion whose most sacred rites involved the death of other human beings is unsettling enough, but that victims should be routinely tortured beforehand and their suffering recorded in painting and sculpture is even more disturbing. Yet some have found, in that very art, a certain mitigation. For victims intended for sacrifice can be accorded a remarkable nobility, portrayed with a human sensitivity that elsewhere in Maya painting and sculpture seems, to our eyes, extremely rare – in the terrible beauty of the naked figures in the Bonampak murals for example, pleading on the stairs, their hands outstretched and fingers spurting with blood or, from Tikal, the tiny image incised in bone of a standing captive studying the ropes that bind him with a proud indifference. What can one conclude from this poignancy? The captive's predicament was certainly pitiable on the one hand, but also deserving of considerable respect. For it would appear that sacrifice among the Maya was conceived as a celebration not of death alone but of what came out of it, of rebirth and the origins of life. Those who faced sacrifice could thus be seen as actors who, on a savage but glorious stage, replayed the epic struggles from the time of creation. And each could be assured of an honoured place in the afterlife. It is not the job of archaeologists to make moral judgements about the people they study, and from this distance we will never adequately resolve the conundrum of human sacrifice and its accompanying cruelties. In this sense the Maya remain as mysterious as they ever were. All we can do is acknowledge the sophistication of their thought and suggest that somehow they were able to confront and reconcile, since we cannot believe they did not distinguish them, certain concepts that are irreconcilable to most of us; to see good attendant upon evil and beauty in brutality.

RELIGION AND THE STATE

Human sacrifice was a public spectacle, a collective experience. The softening up and torturing may have gone on in more private, exclusive surroundings, but for the final despatch on the chosen ritual occasion crowds would have pressed into the plazas of Maya cities. The victim met his end either in the ball-court or at the top of a pyramid, the lifeless body quite possibly cast down the stairs on a symbolic tumble to the Underworld. Sacrifice represented the recycling of sacred energy, the blood that was shed bringing divine power into the immediate world to make the crops grow and bring prosperity to the community at large. Of course the whole procedure also bestowed enormous power on the small number who organized it all, who mediated between humans and the gods, in other words, Maya kings. The drama of human sacrifice was but one element in the display of their religious and political authority, which were indivisible.

Rulers referred to themselves on their monuments as *k'ul ahaw*, translated as 'holy lord' but more commonly rendered as 'divine king'. What this actually meant to Maya themselves, the kind of awe with which a loin-clothed farmer gazed up at the magnificent figure of his ruler emerging from a distant temple, is impossible to gauge. Was he looking at a man or a god? Perhaps both.[15] For our more clear-cut concepts of divinity are not particularly helpful, as we have seen. In a world where gods and men were thought to inhabit the same all-inclusive existence and regularly communicated with each other, and where all things shared in a sliding scale of the sacred, possessing differing degrees of *k'ulel*, the difference between humans and divine beings was perhaps more quantitative than qualitative. In fact gods themselves revealed very human frailties. They could grow old and die, and could be outwitted and vanquished by mortals, as the saga of the Hero Twins showed. As mythic protagonists, the latter occupy a characteristically ambivalent position as heroes of an amorphous in-between time before the present creation. Represented as proto-humans, they served to demonstrate how certain outstanding and particularly resourceful individuals could hold their own amongst the gods, overcome the forces of death and destruction and achieve resurrection as powerful celestial beings. This was the perfect pattern for Maya rulers – people who were more power-ful and 'sacred' than anyone else in their community while they were alive and at their death took their place in the divine firmament. At least that appears to be how Maya kings saw it. For of course the myth of the Hero Twins was their own creation, which they used to help justify their right to rule. All we are able to do is follow, in images and texts, their own projections of themselves.

It is no coincidence that the Hero Twins first appear in Maya art in the Late Preclassic period, at the time when Maya kingship was taking shape. By the Late Classic it is easier to identify them as the role models for kings, who on important ceremonial occasions would assume their guise. The ballcourt, the original place of sacrifice and confrontation with the gods, with its sloping side walls conceived as a great crack in the earth and point of contact with the Underworld, was the key arena for performance of this kind. At the time of creation the Maize God was brought back to life by his sons. Although resurrected, he seems to have been perceived as remaining in the earth, staying on beneath the ball-court of the Underworld; in effect, he was still there just under the ground in the ballcourt of every Maya city. And so, taking on the identity of the Hero Twins in a renewed struggle against the forces of darkness, Maya kings, through the ritualized execution of captives, were seen to despatch the Lords of Death and revive the Maize God, providing him with sustenance in the form of sacrificial blood and thus ensuring the future fertility of the earth.

Kings portrayed themselves with the aspects of a number of different deities and, dressed in masks and elaborate costume, they took on their powers and 'became' these gods for a while. One of the commonest of such associations was with the Maize God, the way that 18 Rabbit, for example, represented himself on Stela H at Copán. Painted ceramic vessels show Maya lords in the god's apparel. Sometimes they are dancing, the fantastic plumes that issue from their headdresses and 'back-racks' gently rippling and mimicking the movement of the plant in the breeze. In the guise of the Maize God kings were many things. They were maize itself and the sustenance of humanity, they were young, beautiful and immortal. Jade was the colour of all of these and in this medium survive some of the most magnificent portrayals of both the god alone and of the king transformed into the god. At death the associations were particularly strong, conveying the idea of the ruler bound for resurrection and thus forever youthful. The carved bones from Hasaw Chan K'awil's tomb at Tikal depict him adorned as the young god in his canoe-borne descent to the Underworld, and from the same tomb comes an imposing vessel covered with jade plaques and topped by an exquisite, apple-green head of the man-god in the prime of life (see plate section, p.20).

The most extraordinary image of a king assuming the identity of the Maize God is that upon the lid of Pakal's sarcophagus at Palenque (see overleaf). When Alberto Rúz first confronted it in 1952, he saw simply a semi-reclining human figure surrounded by an array of still poorly understood symbols. He could have had little idea of the meaning of the scene or indeed of any necessary relationship between this central figure and the body that had been buried beneath. Since that time, interpretations have on occasion been far-fetched and trivial. The influence of Erich Von Daniken lingers on and some are still prepared to entertain the notion that this is a spaceman at the controls of his rocket. The iconography is rich and complex, and even currently accepted interpretations by scholars such as Linda Schele or Mary Miller[17] will undoubtedly come to be modified in certain details over the years. But we can now approach this unique sculpture with a firm grasp of the central ideas it was meant to convey, seeing it through the eyes of its creators in a way that would have been thought impossible in Ruz's day.

The slab, and the body beneath, were placed north to south, the king's head and the top of the design representing the direction of the heavens. The whole setting is a truly cosmic one, the scene framed by a continuous 'sky-band' bearing symbols of the most powerful celestial bodies. Within this frame, filling the open spaces, is an array of small symbols including shells, jade beads and flowers, precious objects all

The lid of Pakal's sarcophogus in the Temple of the Inscriptions, Palenque.

emblematic of that *k'ulel* or pervasive divine force which, concentrated here, help to suggest the sacred context of the action. At the very top, perched upon the 'World Tree', appears a large supernatural bird, a perplexing image that some still take to represent the upper limit of the sky but may be associated, as a kind of familiar, with the god Itzamná, the original shaman or sorcerer, the bird's presence thus further underlining the magical quality of what is unfolding below. The World Tree bears within its cruciform branches the double-headed serpent bar symbolic of the heavens and so often carried by Maya royalty. Beneath it Pakal, in the netted jade skirt of the Maize God, tumbles into the jaws of the Underworld, upon a large bowl of the kind used to hold the implements of sacrificial blood-letting and which bears the night-time visage of the Sun God. Frozen here is the moment of Pakal's death, the point at which he enters the Underworld. As he does so, the World Tree, the central axis that connects all the levels of the cosmos, is brought into being and rises up behind him. He enters the earth as a 'kernel of regeneration', as Miller has put it, that in effect spawns the tree of life. There are other connected symbols here, typical of the metaphorical density and ambiguities of Maya art. Like that of the Maize God, Pakal's death is represented as a sacrifice from which life and renewal flow. In a sense, too, he can be seen to become the Tree, the great connector or conduit between the human and divine. And, assisted by his sons, in particular Kan Balam (whom we see with his diminutive father in the Underworld in the principal panels of the temples of the Cross Group), he will be resurrected and ascend the tree to his place as an ancestral deity in the sky. The curious position of Pakal on the sarcophagus lid presents a final ambiguity. He is clearly falling into the Underworld. But Schele noted that in certain scenes from ceramic art of the Classic period, this posture is associated with childbirth. There are perhaps two ways of interpreting this. He is either 'giving birth' to the World Tree, or he tumbles to his death in a manner that signals his own rebirth.

The arboreal metaphors continue around the sides of the sarcophagus. For here Pakal's ancestors are represented, each accompanied by a tree that emerges from a crack in the earth. But these trees are different. They are all varieties of fruit tree, such as avocado, guayaba or cacao, conveying the slightly different idea, human and domestic now rather than cosmic, that the spirits of the ancestors were always close by on earth, amongst the orchards and gardens that surrounded the homes of their descendants.

On the lid of his sarcophagus Pakal placed himself, at his death, at the very centre of the Maya universe. But every Maya king while he was living proclaimed that he was the great pivot, the focal point of his community, and surrounded himself with elaborate cosmic symbolism, conveyed most obviously and publicly in the very fabric of a Maya city. Reproducing the structure of the world in miniature is an enduring Maya practice. Thus the contemporary shaman erects his ritual altar to replicate the four-sided world with its centre, the design on a woman's *huipil* can represent the pattern of stars in the sky. These are aids to religious thought or reminders in the more everyday world of the wider scheme of things. Using architecture in this way is not, of course, unique to the

Maya. Within European culture, medieval church architecture represents to some degree an attempt to establish the structure of the heavens on earth. But few ancient peoples have turned their immediate built environment into models of the cosmos in the manner achieved by the Maya.

Firstly this is visible in the layout and orientation of architectural complexes, demonstrated in purest form by the 'Twin Pyramid' arrangements at Tikal, with their two celestial viewing platforms to east and west, nine-doored building to the south representing the Underworld, and the single open enclosure to the north containing the ruler's stela and whose text commemorated the passing of each *katun*[18] (see below). This more conceptual, two-dimensional plan comes alive if, for example, one superimposes upon it the design on Pakal's sarcophagus lid, north to south with the top of the World Tree upon the open enclosure and the jaws of the Underworld above the nine-doored structure. Then, spinning both of them 90 degrees on the east–west axis of the rising and setting sun, north becomes up, south down, and the Maya world picture emerges in three dimensions. At Tikal the same directional associations are repeated in the Great Plaza. Here, too, there was a single building with nine entrances to the south and facing it the North Acropolis, the royal burial ground and the place in the city conceived as nearest the heavens. Temples I and II, built at a later date to the east and west, effectively complete what became another Twin Pyramid complex writ very large.

Not every city repeated this kind of format in such an obvious way.

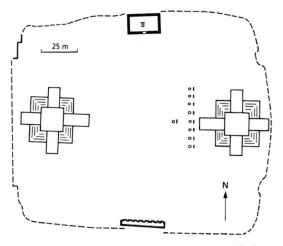

Plan of the Twin Pyramid complex 4E–4 at Tikal.

But even more striking, perhaps, and common to them all, was the formidable symbolic meaning, revealed by recent decipherments, attached to the individual architectural elements at the ceremonial heart of a city. Plazas represented the surface of the Underworld, and some may even have been purposely flooded in the rainy season to create an image of the great ocean that covered everything at the time of creation. The ball-court, as we have seen, was a crevice in the earth, the point of communication with the Underworld. Stelae were perceived as trees, the Maya phrase used to describe them being literally *te tun* or 'stone tree'. These in effect grew out of the Underworld and the trampled sacrificial victims often seen at their base were thus neatly positioned close to their destination at death. The standing figure upon the stela, the living ruler who had planted it, was the trunk, king as tree once more, the central pillar of his society. To complete this world view embodied in the stela, deified ancestors were often carved at the very top, above the king, floating in the celestial realms. If plazas were water on the surface of the Underworld and stelae were trees, pyramids, the most imposing features of the city centre, were mountains – where contact was made between the earth and the heavens, which were associated with creation in the Popol Vuh – and contained the tombs of kings. Thus the stacks of pyramids one on top of the other at Copán, for example, or Tikal, were perceived as ancestral mountain ranges, reflecting the very ancient idea, which survives among the Maya today, of hills as places inhabited by the spirits of the dead.[19]

Thus the *k'ul ahaw* or holy Maya lord strode, or more likely was borne on a litter dressed as a god, through an extraordinary artificial landscape, a mirror of the world order that he maintained. Against the back-drop of brightly painted temples and pyramids that served as awesome hoardings to advertise the power of kings, he re-enacted in elaborate ritual, in music and dance, the myths of creation and the histories of his ancestors. From this distance it is natural for us, too, to be overawed by the power and divinity that hedged a Maya king, where religion did not simply serve to explain the human condition and the secrets of the universe but presented the ruler as the most important secret of all, the exclusive channel of communication with the gods, upon whom the lives and livelihoods of all Maya people depended.

Naturally enough, one has to be very wary of this. A number of archaeologists continue to caution that the enormous research effort of recent years that has concentrated on the expression of the power of kings and the Maya élite and upon undeniably fascinating, and now understandable, religious ideology threatens something of a return to the bad old days of half a century ago, when disproportionate concern with kings and their major monuments produced that skewed model of a Maya society dominated by calendar priests and philosophers of time. Thus one has to maintain a critical perspective on the royal propaganda and attempt to get behind the façade, as we began to do at Copán in the last chapter.

The institution of 'divine' kingship, as it had become refined by the Late Classic, was the product of many centuries of development. It could not have evolved so successfully through coercion, but because it was based on broadly shared interests and common understandings held throughout Maya society. The management of the supernatural was a vital, practical aspect of Maya life, and had always been so. The services the king provided as broker with the divine would have been seen as essential by the community at large and, although a body of royal mythology had been superimposed upon them, the most fundamental of religious beliefs, in the gods as the powers of nature personified, had changed little since the days when communication with the spirit world was the responsibility of the village shaman. Above all, of course, the system endured for the simple reason that most sections of Maya society prospered. If that prosperity faltered and sections of the population ceased to benefit, it might be a different matter entirely.

Quite clearly, the community of a city-state was not held together solely by the successful religious and military performance of the king, however much their monuments might give that impression, but also by social and economic relationships between its constituent parts. There is still a great deal to be learnt about the Classic Maya social structure. Written records concern themselves solely with a restricted number of activities carried out by ruler and aristocracy, so we have to infer what we can about other groups in society from the archaeological evidence that emerges from houses and tombs, and from observations made by Landa and others at the time of the conquest. Traditionally, Maya society has been divided into two, élite and commoners. This was what the first Spaniards did, although they had little reason to look for any greater subtleties, being solely concerned with using what remained of the indigenous authority structure to control and convert the rest of the population. Very broadly, the twofold division can still be made. The upper stratum, no more than about 5 per cent of the population, would have included the ruler, his family, those connected by marriage with the royal dynasty and the nobility amongst the other lineages prominent in society, those with their hands on the levers of power. Among them were those *ahaws* and *sahals* that governed smaller centres on behalf of the king and presumably headed the military hierarchy. Such people lived in the more impressive houses, dressed in finer loincloths, capes, *huipils* and sandals, their tombs were well stocked and they were the conspicuous consumers of rare commodities such as jade, fine obsidian, feathers and cacao. They ate better than other people and did so off good quality pottery. This sector of the population, those with power and privilege and most of them literate, can thus be contrasted with those farmers, huntsmen, petty traders and perhaps a proportion of serfs or slaves, that made up the mass of commoners.

This is a considerable simplification. Here we might best approach Maya society through its major interest groups. Firstly one can talk about the king, members of the immediate royal line, his household and that service industry around his person concerned with the projection of royal power, which by the Late Classic period involved large numbers of people with different skills. Immediately around the ruler, of course, would have been those who prepared food, who worked as servants in the palace and perhaps entertainers such as musicians and dancers and even dwarves, who are often depicted in pottery scenes in the company of the ruler and his entourage and who would seem to have fulfilled that timeless role of keeping kings amused. Much more significant than these day-to-day retainers and support staff was the body of religious practitioners and advisers – scribes, diviners, astrologers, experts in oral performance, a category whose importance should not be underestimated, all of whom formed that group, many of their roles no doubt interchangeable, whose esoteric knowledge served to perpetuate the power and mystique of Maya kingship and keep the motor of dynastic rule running. Scribes form the most easily definable segment of the intellectual élite. *Ah ts'ib*, 'he of the writing' was the title used, although there were evidently women scribes as well, and Nikolai Grube has deciphered another phrase *ah k'u hun* or 'he of the holy books', which was evidently a very important role and would have approximated to something like the Keeper of the Royal Archives.[20] It seems very likely that there were special schools where the sons of rulers and the aristocracy were tutored in such skills as writing and calendrics. At the time of the Conquest, the Books of Chilam Balam record a series of tests and riddles in the 'Language of Zuyua', a kind of examination in esoteric knowledge and literacy, to identify those who were fit to serve as 'men of knowledge' and leaders in society.

It is possible to identify scribal abilities among Maya ruling families. We have already seen Hasaw Chan Kawil, great lord of Tikal, accompanied in death by his paint-pot. At Copán, for example, junior members of the dynasty have also been found buried with scribal materials, prompting the suggestion that this was a role often filled by younger sons. At Copán, too, the 'House of the Bacabs' was evidently the palace of a powerful aristocratic lineage of scribes, in the later eighth century headed by Mac Chanil, the mighty subject of king Yax Pac.[21] On its façade are sculptures of now headless individuals holding conch-shell ink-pots, and from within comes a magnificent stone figure, in the round, of a supernatural 'monkey-man' scribe, cross-legged and with brush and ink-pot in his hands. The word ts'ib means both writing and painting and undoubtedly scribes, like Ah Maxam from Naranjo, were often painters in the broadest sense, of pottery in particular.

Finely painted Maya pottery of the Late Classic period remains one of the great little-known glories of world ceramic art, as remarkable in technical quality and as rich in its historical and mythological subject matter as Greek pottery painting. So regularly plundered from tombs, the scientific value of most pots is extremely limited, as we have seen. But slowly the study of styles of pottery painting and of the chemical make-up of the pots is enabling researchers to define certain schools of painters and to trace the patterns of their distribution and exchange between cities.[22] Fine pots ultimately served as funerary vessels, but they were often presented as gifts by rulers, along with other precious objects such as jade, to aristocratic supporters or to allies in other cities to cement social and political relationships. A major importance of such ceramics is that the narrative scenes often help to display the richness and complexity of the upper echelons of Maya society, a cultured, aristocratic world of some style (see plate section, p.20). They depict rulers and their courtiers, their women and servants, nobility, scribes, painters and sculptors as well as warriors, tribute-givers and the ball-game. The study of the clothing and attributes of particular people in these scenes, which seem to present certain distinguishable kinds of uniform, along with the decipherment of the very difficult ceramic texts, may in the future yield considerably more information about the different roles of those who moved within the topmost social stratum and the diverse functionaries and emissaries that were received at a Maya court. The Maya élite, as more traditionally defined, was certainly not one monolithic group. There was considerable diversity, and inequality, within it.

Increasingly recognized today, and set out in an important recent book by Patricia McAnany,[23] is the likelihood of a constant, dynamic tension between the ruler, along with the family group, the royal lineage that surrounded him, and other powerful and long-established lineages within a city state. The centralizing success of royal dynasties almost certainly obscures the extent to which kings depended upon and negotiated with other political factions. For each dynasty of the Classic period had in earlier centuries been merely one among many such patrilineages or kin-groups. It is impossible to know with any precision how ruling lines established themselves at the end of the Preclassic period – as war-leaders, perhaps, or as mediators in local disputes. However they came by their authority, they could only have maintained it through consent and co-operation, despite the impression of absolute power that their monuments create. From the eighth century, at Copán in particular, there is now some evidence of the negotiation that must have gone on behind the scenes. There is little reason to believe that this kind of jostling was not seen in earlier centuries too. Local politics would differ from city to city, but one might presume that the Popol Na, the Council House, was a place of very real debate throughout the Classic period.

In the Popol Na the practical realities of Maya government would have been discussed. Since there are no extant written records that bear on this, and the evidence that archaeology provides can only be limited, very little is known about the mechanics of administration. The 'ahaws' and 'sahals' were clearly members of the royal house or the heads of other poweful lineages, but what their authority actually involved, aside from their having control over smaller, dependent centres is unclear. Another considerable area of uncertainty is the role of centralized royal authority in economic affairs. Trade in high-status commodities such as jade, quetzal feathers, rare shells of marine origin, even cacao may well have been controlled directly by the ruler and his closest supporters, since the redistribution of such items was an important element of patronage and the exercise of kingly authority. How the trade func-tioned in more utilitarian goods such as salt, grinding stones or chert axes is unclear, the likeliest answer being that groups of itinerant traders, perhaps forming their own independent guilds, controlled such affairs. Similarly, it is unknown to what extent central government had a direct

hand in the organization of agriculture. Kings surely directed the construction of canals and reservoirs around a city centre, but how far they
initiated the amplification of agricultural production in the countryside
is impossible to know. Rulers doubtless had their own extensive royal
lands, holdings based on what had always pertained to their particular
lineage. In this way, the appearance on his sarcophagus of Pakal's ancestors accompanied by a variety of fruit trees can be seen as a reference to
economics, to ancient rights to land and resources.

To support the elaborate centralized apparatus of dynastic rule kings
had to raise 'revenue', and here the co-operation of lineages and lineage
heads must have been essential. Firstly there would have been labour
obligation, the drafting in of hundreds, maybe thousands of people at
any one time to work on the building of temples and pyramids and the
maintenance of roads, reservoirs and canals. In fact this must already
have been underway on a vast scale in the Preclassic period, in the days
of Nakbé and El Mirador. In due course the Spaniards merely took over
the ancient system of labour obligation, Diego de Landa and his colleagues using it to build the early Colonial churches of Yucatán. If the
labour of thousands of ordinary Maya created the fabric of the great
cities, their tribute in kind kept their inhabitants fed. Ultimately, of
course, the ability of the whole Classic-period system to flourish
depended on the productivity of that vast majority of Maya people
whose existence is barely hinted at in monuments and inscriptions.

BEYOND THE PYRAMIDS

By the eighth century the simple communities of maize-farmers covered
the land between the major cities. Their way of life had changed very
little down the centuries. The basic social unit, as it still is today, would
have been the extended family. Typically, this might be made up of three
or four couples related through the male line, with children of differing
ages, a number of them able-bodied teenagers. There would be a few
remaining grandparents, including perhaps a venerated senior male recognized as the head of the family group. What the extended family
offered, and why it was desirable to have as large a one as possible, were
the co-operative skills and capacities of the different generations and,
above all, the sheer manpower required by the physical demands of
tropical farming. Men spent the bulk of their time in the fields, or

perhaps in hunting and such tasks as the building and maintenance of houses, while women were based more permanently around the home, minding children, tending gardens and livestock, preparing food and devoting some time to crafts such as weaving or making pottery. Such a family group would live in an arrangement of houses, maybe six to ten buildings in all, including kitchen and storage facilities, surrounding a patio or open area where most household tasks were performed and which would be the busy heart of the home. For apart from the rainy season, the Maya led essentially outdoor lives. The buildings themselves appear to have been much like they are today among many traditional farming communities, mostly single-roomed structures raised slightly off the ground on earth platforms, made of wooden posts plastered with mud, or sometimes of mud brick, and thatched with palm leaves. Such buildings could be put up by a family in a matter of days. They were cool inside and, as archaeological excavation would seem to demonstrate, kept scrupulously clean.

Maya households might be dispersed in various ways across the land-scape, but within a village an extended family compound would be one of a number of such households that made up a localized kin grouping or lineage, the basic unit of the Maya social structure as we have seen, and which might form a distinct ward or *barrio* within a settlement. Thus it was that over the centuries, as Maya society became more complex and hierarchical, one group of buildings belonging to an extended family amongst these lineage households might become larger and more impressive than the rest, often centrally placed and with one particular building elevated on a larger platform. This would be where a notable lineage head was buried and which had been turned into an ancestral shrine. At some sites archaeologists have been able to trace quite clearly the organic growth of a settlement. As villages became towns and towns grew into cities, particular lineages evidently prospered, began to domi-nate their society and ultimately became the ruling dynasties of the Classic period. But even then the household compounds of Maya rulers still possessed the same basic elements – one- or two-roomed buildings on platforms around patios or small plazas. By now, however, the plat-forms were more imposing, the structures were of stone and the burial places of lineage heads had become the great mortuary temple-pyramids of Maya kings.

Even humble households in ancient times followed the same funerary custom. Family members were not cremated, nor buried in cemeteries or particularly sacred locations in the landscape. They were interred beneath the floors of houses, or very close to the residence. Thus the ancestors still slept within the home and were ever-present amongst their descendants. Although land 'ownership' in our terms would have been an alien concept, ancestral bones in the familiar earth were in effect the title deed to their place in the world for generation after generation. Burial customs may have changed since the Spanish Conquest, but the loss of ancestral lands and in recent, violent years in Guatemala the enforced removal of whole communities to different locations, has proved a grievous assault upon the social and indeed the religious identity of Maya people.

For the ancient inhabitants of the lowlands a primary source of livelihood was the forest itself. The immense variety of trees provided many of the most essential raw materials – as fuel for fires, for cooking and to fire pottery. Hardwoods were employed in the construction of houses, for dug-out canoes and to make furniture, boxes, statues and other wooden objects, the vast majority of which have not survived. Palms, vines and different fibres were used to make rope, sandals, mats, woven baskets and bark cloth. The resin of the copal tree was formed into small cakes and burnt as incense. Kapok, the soft material surrounding the seeds of the ceiba or silk-cotton tree, served as padding for a number of purposes, for the stuffing of cushions, for example, often depicted next to the cross-legged figures of Maya lords on Classic painted pottery. The remains of kapok mattresses have been found in a number of tombs. Other trees would have been the source of dyes, medicines and foodstuffs. The forest was also home to an extraordinary range of wildlife, and game was hunted with blow-guns, traps and snares, both for food and in order to use the feathers, skin, bones and other by-products. For those who lived by coasts, rivers or lakes, fish, shellfish, turtles and other aquatic species would have been a major component of the diet. Dried fish may have been traded inland, though most of the archaeological evidence is of the movement of sea-shells for ritual rather than dietary purposes, notably the blood-red shell of the spondylus or spiny oyster, often discovered in burials or caches along with other exotic material of marine origin such as coral, shark's teeth and the sting-ray spines used for blood-letting.

Soon after man's arrival in the Americas the small horse, something like a Shetland pony, that was native to the continent appears to have been hunted to extinction. In the Andes of South America the Incas and their predecessors at least had the advantage of domesticated camelids such as the llama and alpaca. These were a prime source of food and fibre, and llama caravans were the principal medium for the transport of goods. In Central America there were no large mammals that could be domesticated in this way. Any form of cargo had to travel on men's backs or by canoe. The turkey and the dog, and perhaps the dove and Muscovy duck just prior to the Spanish Conquest, were the only domesticated animals, unless one includes the stingless bees which were kept in hives formed from hollowed-out logs. The dog seems to have played its universal role as pet, hunting companion and guardian of the home and, as in other parts of Mesoamerica, certain species, notably a hairless variety, were eaten. Deer bones are very common at many Maya sites and, if not fully domesticated, there is some archaeological evidence that deer may have been kept within fenced enclosures or encouraged to browse amongst the secondary growth of cleared fields.

Animal protein thus came from a range of both domesticated and wild sources, the latter including peccaries, monkeys, armadillos, tapirs, rabbit and rodents such as the agouti, a relative of the guinea-pig. Meats would have been roasted or prepared in soups and stews with vegetables, chillis perhaps and a variety of herbs. Turkey stew is much commented upon by early Spanish chroniclers and is still a favourite festive Maya dish today. But, lest we paint too attractive a picture of the richness and carnivorous variety of the ancient Maya menu, feasting on special occasions, which Landa describes as an enthusiasm common to all levels of society, was perhaps the only time that the bulk of the population consumed meat in any great quantity. The nature of the diet would have varied greatly from one region to another and over time, but certainly by the later Classic period wild resources may have been greatly diminished in many areas and domesticated animals carefully husbanded. The bulk of the Maya diet was made up of plant foods, in particular the well-balanced combination of maize, beans, squash and peppers.

Maize is still processed in the same special way. The cobs are normally left to dry, often on the lopped stalk in the fields, and then the kernels are removed and soaked in water and lime. The admixture of lime is critically important, since it releases essential amino acids and a form of vitamin B, which greatly enhances maize's nutritional value. The kernels are ground with a stone *mano* and *metate* (rocker and grinding stone) and the flour worked into a dough. This is then most often either parcelled up in leaves and steamed to form small cakes called *tamales* or flattened into the better-known tortillas which are baked over the hearth on a clay griddle.

Tamales are represented on some of the finest pieces of Classic painted pottery, where they appear served on shallow tripod plates at the feet of powerful-looking individuals within Maya palaces. Sometimes they are covered in a reddish sauce, perhaps chilli or *achiote* from the annatto tree, used as both a spice and a red dye. Besides occasionally depicting food in this way, such fine pottery will often be painted with a hieroglyphic text which directly states what the vessel was used for, thus providing confirmation of certain elements of the Maya diet, at least among the élite. The commonest example of this are the cylindrical drinking vessels whose texts say that they were for the drinking of different forms of cacao or chocolate. There are rounded bowls, too, that are labelled as being for another maize food, *atole*, a gruel of varying consistency often sweetened with honey, still a part of the Maya diet today. The tortilla is neither depicted nor referred to on Classic Maya pottery. Indeed, the griddles used to cook tortillas are not found in archaeological contexts at Classic sites and it is generally felt that the tortilla was a late import from Central Mexico, just before the Spanish Conquest. Today red or black beans are most commonly served alongside maize, either boiled whole or mashed into a paste and then fried. Along with the flesh and seeds of squashes, these provide most of the essential dietary proteins.

Agriculture maintained growing Maya populations over two millennia and there is no doubt that they were immensely skilful and adaptable farmers. But the critical question has always been how they did it, what agricultural techniques they used in the difficult tropical environment. Until about thirty years ago, as we have seen in earlier chapters, the most widespread and indeed the only form of ancient Maya agriculture was generally held to be slash and burn or 'swidden' farming, still practised by Maya farmers today: clearing an area of land, burning as much of the trees and undergrowth as possible, planting for a few years until soil fertility is depleted, and then moving on. The quality of the local soil will determine both how long the initial period of cultivation can be and the length of fallow time before an area has sufficiently recovered for it to be used again. This varies markedly from place to place. In the northern Yucatán, with its thin, poor soils and minimal rainfall, the required period of fallow could be up to twenty years. Much further south, in the southern Petén for example, fields might be cropped again within three or four years.

Swidden agriculture was employed by those very first agricultural colonists of the lowlands who penetrated inland along the major river systems. The picture often conjured up for this early period is of groups of families or small village communities operating within a vast area of virgin forest, which offered limitless opportunities for so-called 'pioneer' swidden, where an area is felled and planted and within a few years the farmer moves on to another patch of previously untouched, pristine forest. Of course reliance on shifting cultivation of this kind demands large areas of land and can only support relatively small and dispersed populations. Over the centuries, as populations grew and towns and cities emerged across the Maya landscape, the scenario of prodigal Maya frontiersmen slashing and burning swathes through the forest would have become increasingly impossible.

Swidden agriculture centred on maize cultivation remained the core element of Maya agriculture. But it was very soon adapted from the pioneer variety and, like contemporary practices, was carried out over more fixed plots of land that were always in variable states of fallow and were cleared and planted in rotation. Such lands were probably claimed by particular families or lineages. After the Conquest, Spanish administrative surveys, compiled to take stock of their new possessions, reveal how tenaciously individual Maya lineages in the Yucatán defended their claims to particular territories. But even a more 'disciplined' form of swidden would not have been compatible with the high levels of population that are suggested by the Late Classic period. More intensive forms of agriculture were essential. It must also be borne in mind that swidden agriculture would have been very demanding for the ancient Maya farmer, equipped only with stone tools as opposed to the steel machetes and axes of his modern-day equivalent. Thus, even without external factors such as population pressure, there would have been every incentive to look to other methods, firstly to make more concerted use of every available piece of land between the swidden field and the household compound.

A hint of how this might have been done and a suggestion of the sophistication of ancient Maya tropical forest farming has been provided by studies of the agricultural practices of the Lacandón.[24] Numbering only a few hundred today, they still live close to where Maudslay encountered them, in the rain forests of eastern Chiapas in

Mexico. The Lacandón speak Yucatec Mayan and are not the original inhabitants of this area. In the seventeenth or early eighteenth century they fled from the areas of Spanish domination further north in the Yucatán peninsula and eventually came to settle in the more remote forests here. Due to the massive scale of depopulation after the Conquest and the forced resettlement of many other native groups out of the Southern Lowlands in Colonial times, they represent almost the only original tropical forest Maya left in the region today. Change has come extremely rapidly to the Lacandón in recent years, but over the last century many studies have been made of their culture, including their agricultural traditions and techniques.

Lacandón methods of swidden farming do not differ essentially from those of other contemporary Maya communities in the Maya highlands or Yucatán. Between January and March they cut the trees and under-brush from the chosen *milpa* area. This will amost invariably be from *acahuales* or previously harvested plots that have been left fallow for between ten and twenty years, and which to the untrained eye will often seem indistinguishable from virgin forest. The cut vegetation will then be left to dry until April or early May, shortly before the arrival of the rains, when it is burnt and left in place to fertilize the field. Most nutri-ents in temperate forests are found in the soils themselves, but in the tropical environment 75 per cent of such nutrients are contained within the living biomass of the forest and only some 10 per cent in the soil. Thus the burning of the forest growth and its deposition as ash is a means of transfering nutrients to where they are most needed. In June, as the rains arrive, the farmer plants the field with maize, beans and squash. This is done without tilling the soil but, in time-honoured fashion, by simply poking holes through the ash with a digging stick and dropping seeds into each one. In the normal course of events, the harvest will be in September.

This kind of swidden agriculture is however only one element within an elaborate agricultural regime, and it is the wider picture of their exploitation of the forest environment which may offer certain parallels to ancient practices. The *milpa* is not devoted to maize, beans and squash alone. A great range of other crops are grown, planted alongside the maize at different times throughout the year. These will include chillis, tomatoes, garlic, other varieties of beans, root crops such as sweet pota-toes and manioc, tobacco – the list is an enormous one and in total fifty-six different cultivated plants have been recorded in Lacandón *milpas.* Spanish colonial accounts also indicate a large variety of crops grown alongside maize in the Southern Lowlands in the seventeenth century. The variety in the *milpa* keeps down weeds and minimizes risk through the failure of particular crops; the intercropping of different species can help to retain nutrients in the soil. A field that is sown purely with maize depletes the soil very rapidly.

Just as the greatest use is made of the *milpas* themselves, so too the *acahuales* or fallow fields are never totally abandoned. Parts of these will be used to cultivate fruit trees, herbs and medicinal plants. Other economic trees such as copal, chicozapote, palms and vines are left to grow where they can be regularly harvested, both in the *acahual* and the *milpa*. The *acahual* in its various stages of secondary growth also attracts animals such as deer, armadillo or the edible rodent tepesquintle and becomes an informal game reserve. Lacandón farming, then, does not involve the transformation of the 'wild' forest into a fully tamed, cultivated area in the way that people from temperate climes might envisage forest and field in a kind of opposition. Rather, it involves modification of the forest by introducing a harvestable range of plant species within it, mimicking, as some researchers see it, the bio-diversity of the forest itself. The Lacandón 'farm in the forest, they do not replace the forest', for, as many contemporary examples demonstrate, if you denude large areas of tropical soil of cover and leave it open to the sun it rapidly deteriorates.

Use of the land among the Lacandón continues right up to the backyard of the home. Around the house will be found a further range of useful trees and plants including perhaps bottle-gourd, cotton trees, other herbs, spices and fruit trees. Small plots of maize, beans and root crops are also planted. Being close to the house, the weeding and maintenance of such crops is relatively easy and they can be fertilized with household waste. By varying the species grown, they can be cultivated almost continuously.

Archaeological evidence of a very similar pattern of gardening and the cultivation of staples close to the home has come from a remarkable discovery on the fringes of the Maya world at Ceren, in western El Salvador.[25] Here in about AD 600 a volcanic eruption engulfed a small farming village and turned it into a tiny Pompeii. The inhabitants appear to have had warning of the impending disaster and managed to escape, but their houses, outbuildings, cultivated plants and gardens were buried beneath four metres of volcanic ash and wonderfully well preserved. A maize field was revealed, only about two metres from a kitchen; its ridges and furrows could be clearly identified and the casts of young plants remained in the ground just where they had been growing, probably in the month of July, judging by their size. Similar plots were discovered with cotton, agave, manioc, medicinal plants and evidence of young cacao trees. Wooden fences were also preserved, evidently erected to keep pests away.

Kitchen gardens and small orchards are a feature of Maya household compounds today, are described by Diego de Landa and other early Spanish colonial writers, and almost certainly account for the layout of Maya cities, where the spaces between groups of houses revealed by survey would have been too small for large cultivated fields but ideal for gardens with a selection of plants, shrubs and trees. Indeed, at sites such as Cobá, surviving concentrations of fruit trees suggest that these may well be the modern day descendants of ancient species cultivated close to residential areas.

Particular environments in the lowlands offered other possibilities for intensive agriculture, that is for the concentrated use of land with short or no periods of fallow. In favourable areas, such as the flood-plains of rivers in the south and east, like the Motagua and above all along the Usumacinta, well-drained, fertile alluvial soils replenished by periodic flooding may have allowed almost continuous cultivation. These areas could have become large-scale producers of food, perhaps exported to other regions.

But more marginal land was reclaimed and made productive. The most striking example of this is in perennially or seasonally wet regions such as swamplands (which form some 30 per cent of the total area of the Southern Lowlands), shallow lakes and the boggy margins of sluggishly flowing rivers. Here canals were dug through the saturated soils, sometimes simply to drain swampy areas for planting or, alternatively, by piling up the excavated earth in between to create elevated planting platforms or 'raised fields'. Areas of such fields seem to have become ingenious little micro-environments for food production. The canals themselves were home to fish and other edible aquatic creatures, and may even have been purposely stocked by the Maya in a form of fish-farming. The mud at the bottom of the canals would have been enriched with their excretions and other organic material and periodically lifted onto the fields as a fertilizer.

Experimental reconstruction of raised fields has proved how

productive they can be, allowing continuous cultivation of the same soils and yielding more than one crop a year. Pollen evidence has shown that they were used to cultivate maize, cotton and amaranth. Cacao was very probably grown on them as well. They are not unique to the Maya and are known in other parts of the Americas. The Aztecs used a very similar system of *chinampas*, sometimes called rather misleadingly 'floating gardens', in Lake Texcoco where Mexico City now stands, and in South America vast areas of raised fields around Lake Titicaca on the border between Peru and Bolivia and in lowland regions along the Bení river were the agricultural mainstay of civilizations long before the time of the Incas. In the Maya area they have now been documented from aerial photographs, followed up by verification on the ground, in northern Belize along the Hondo and New rivers, in swamp lands in southern Quintano Roo and along the Candelaria River in Campeche. Many of these systems date from the Preclassic period. Only small surviving traces of raised fields have been found in the Petén and southern Campeche, and their original extent has thus been a matter of some debate. But most scholars now think that the vast areas of *bajos* or seasonal swamplands around such cities as El Mirador, Calakmul or Tikal must have been exploited through this form of agriculture.

As well as intensive wetland agriculture, there is also evidence of the concerted modification of drier, hillier landscapes. In the Rio Bec region of eastern Campeche some 150,000 hectares of stone-walled agricultural terraces were constructed across gently contoured limestone country to check soil erosion and retain water in the soil. Terraces have also been found in small areas of the southern Petén, in the upper Belize river valley and in the foothills of the Maya Mountains in Belize, where 40,000 hectares of terraces were built close to the city of Caracol. On such terrace systems, regular maintenance would also ensure annual or short-fallow cropping.

Besides raising artificially the carrying capacity of unprepossessing areas of land, sophisticated methods were also devised for storing and managing water in and around urban areas. For the fundamental problem for those living away from rivers or lakes in the forested interior lay in the cycle of the seasons – superabundance of water in the wet season followed by months of drought. During the later Preclassic period at sites such as Edzna, Cerros and El Mirador, reservoirs and canals were built both to provide for domestic consumption and to irrigate nearby fields. Water was simply captured during the rains in enough quantity to last until the clouds gathered once more. In the Petén and at cities in Belize such as La Milpa, Vernon Scarborough and other researchers have shown how natural topography was used, by Late Classic times if not earlier, to facilitate the management of water.[26] Tikal, for example, was built around the tops of limestone ridges. La Milpa was likewise constructed on a natural hill. At both cities the main plazas helped to capture water during the rains and run it, by force of gravity, into large reservoirs immediately around the centre. By the beginning of the dry season these would have been filled. Over the next few months the release of water downhill from the reservoirs would provide for domestic needs and any left-over or waste water, as is evident at Tikal, would have been directed onwards into garden plots and fields on the edges of the city, thus ensuring the irrigated cultivation of these all the year round.

Before the 1970s most scholars envisaged a relatively low population of Maya farming families spread out in their hamlets across the forested landscape, whose traditional, unchanging methods of slash-and-burn agriculture serviced the 'ceremonial centres' of the Classic period. Today this image has been altered radically. The strategies employed by Maya farmers were in no sense static and they varied greatly according to local conditions. Through skilful adaptation to particular environments over the centuries, by maximizing all the means of producing food available to them and devising simple yet ingenious forms of agricultural and hydraulic technology, they managed to tame their forest surroundings and support burgeoning populations. Until, that is, both human ingenuity and the resilience of the land reached their limits. For although Renaissance artists often delighted in portraying the noble savages of the newly discovered Americas in a state of nature against the verdant backdrop of an earthly jungle paradise, the tropical forest was no Garden of Eden.

CHAPTER SEVEN

The Death and Rebirth
of Maya Civilization

To reach the ruins of Bonampak, a 300-kilometre round trip by a bad dirt road from Palenque, is a considerable challenge for most visitors to the Maya area. The Mexican authorities and the international community of scholars concerned about the future of the famous murals are doubtless happy for this state of affairs to continue. Such fragile masterpieces would be quite unable to tolerate any great volume of tourists. That they have survived at all is truly astonishing. They largely escaped any ancient iconoclasm; the building which houses them stood unscathed for more than a millennium while other structures nearby were reduced to rubble by the all-enveloping jungle and, paradoxically, a certain shoddiness in the building's construction led to the ultimate miracle of their preservation. Rainwater, seeping through the vault and absorbing lime from building stone and mortar on its way, gradually became deposited over the paintings as a hard, protective skin of calcite.[1]

Since their discovery in 1946 they have suffered greatly. Early visitors dowsed them in water and in kerosene to bring out the colours, which appears to have given sections of the murals a permanently purplish hue. Much worse, however, was the felling of the surrounding jungle and the erection of a tin roof above the structure, which served to alter radically the cool, damp micro-environment in which they had stood intact for so long. The calcifications began to dry out and flake off the walls, bringing the paint with them. In the 1980s the decision was made to scrape off this covering. Now it has gone there is apprehension and much debate about their long-term conservation. For the time being, the condition of the murals might best be described as stable, in the way of a hopeful hospital bulletin.

The site of Bonampak is unprepossessing as Maya ruins go, although recent investigations have revealed a series of previously unknown buildings and platforms in the surrounding forest which indicate that the city was not as small as was once thought. The centre is approached along a broad path through the jungle which follows the line of a *sacbe* that may well have originally connected the city with Yaxchilán, some thirty kilometres to the north and which was Bonampak's overlord for much of the Late Classic period. The path reaches a large plaza flanked by low platforms to east and west. In the centre of the plaza stand two stelae. One of these, Stela 1, is a broad and extremely tall limestone slab. At the bottom of this formidable monument the head and shoulders of the reborn Maize God can be seen, appearing from a great cleft in a personified mountain, with further profile images of the god to either side. Above, upon a horizontal band of glyphs, stands the ruler Chan Muwan, square on, his sandalled feet placed firmly apart, holding a spear and an elaborate masked shield and looking fiercely to his right. It is a posture duplicated in the murals. Here the bearing of the warrior-king is given added menace by the sneering curl to the mouth and the deeply drilled eye.

On the far, southern side of the plaza is a natural hill that was terraced to form an acropolis. A short way up, atop an initial flight of stairs, are two further stelae erected by Chan Muwan, one of them providing the date of his accession to the throne, AD 776. Only a few modest buildings are to be seen on the acropolis today. The largest is on the lowest terrace level to the west, a simple rectangular structure divided into three rooms. The exterior was originally decorated with stucco reliefs, but nearly all of these are gone. The ordinary nature of the building is very deceptive, however, for this is the home of the murals. Passing beneath finely sculpted lintels with scenes of captive-taking much like those at Yaxchilán, you enter the presence of the paintings, each series in its own separate chamber. Despite unfavourable opinions as to their current state from those fortunate enough to have seen them not long after their discovery, for the first-time visitor they are simply startling, their humble abode heightening the shock at the rare beauty and artistic ambition displayed here. Now that their protective coating has been removed, the surfaces look stripped and bare. In many places the surviving pigment is extremely thin and in Room 3, the most unstable part of the building, damage has been considerable and large sections are very hard to make out. Yet the colours, derived from plants and minerals that produced a range of ochres, reds and rusts and the magnificent pale turquoise or so-called 'Maya blue', remain remarkably vibrant.

A plastered masonry bench occupies much of the interior space of each room. Doubtless it was here that visitors were meant to sit and take in all that surrounded them. For paintings cover every stuccoed surface, from floor to ceiling. The narrative sequence begins in Room 1, to the left as one faces the building (see plate section, p. 5). The upper register, following the slope of the vault, depicts the presentation of the infant heir to the Bonampak throne to the assembled company of fourteen noblemen, standing in line in their white mantles. Above each of them is a slab of plain blue which was evidently designed as background for glyphic captions explaining who these individuals were. But most were never finished, so the lords remain anonymous, as do three figures seated upon a throne on the west wall. At one time it was thought that Chan Muwan and his wife, Lady Rabbit, were represented here. But now that advances have been made in the decipherment of many of the other very worn painted texts, we know that the celebrations went on under the aegis of Shield Jaguar II of Yaxchilán, Lady Rabbit's brother. It is thus very possible that he and his consort occupy the throne, in which case Chan Muwan himself does not appear in the paintings of Room 1.

The presentation of the royal child occurred on 14 December 790, so accompanying texts tell us. A second event took place 336 days later, on 15 November 791, at sunset, it would seem, on a day that Venus first appeared as Evening Star. It was the occasion for music, dance and pageantry both in honour of the heir and to mark the dedication of this very building, which would eventually be decorated with the murals. Part of the preparations for the performance can be seen in the upper register of Room 1, where three dancers are being readied by their attendants who, like busy couturiers, put the finishing touches to their costumes, lifting enormous headdresses onto their shoulders and smoothing down the feathers. In the lower register the same dancers are seen in action, performing what the texts say is a particular kind of 'feather dance'. They are flanked by a glorious parade of richly dressed onlookers and musicians who are banging drums, blowing long trumpets and shaking gourd rattles. In their midst appears a group of masked performers, each in wonderfully bizarre costume representing a different supernatural creature. One bears the head of a cayman, another is dressed as a pantomime crayfish, waving giant green claws in the air.

With its carnival-time exuberance and colour and the spell-binding costume of the participants, Room 1 is the most entrancing section of the murals. The material wealth visible here is prodigious. There are rare

ABOVE The Palace, the centrepiece of Palenque, with its arcades, interior courts and unique three-storeyed tower.

LEFT The Temple of Inscriptions at Palenque. At ground level deep within the pyramid lies the funerary crypt of Palenque's greatest ruler, Pakal.

One of the piers from the Temple of the Inscriptions, showing the child Kan Balam being held in the arms of one of his ancestors, his left leg transformed into a serpent.

ABOVE The Cross Group –
three temples built by Kan
Balam soon after the death of
his father Pakal – face onto their
own quiet plaza beneath the
forested hills of Palenque.

LEFT Limestone slabs with
images of captives stripped to
their loin-cloths from the East
Court of the Palace, Palenque.

The tomb of Pakal beneath the
Temple of the Inscriptions at
Palenque soon after it was first
opened in 1952. The massive
carved lid covers the stone
sarcophagus in which the king
was buried.

Don Manuel Pacheco is a Quiché chuchk'ahaw, literally 'mother-father', spiritual parent and guide to many of his community. Using candles, flowers and copal incense, he prepares his own altar or small model of the world, with four corners and sacred centre, before offering prayers to the 'Mundos' or forces that protect the land and Maya people.

ABOVE The 'Caracol' or Observatory at Chichén Itzá, positioned with curious but calculated asymmetry on two supporting platforms and from where Maya astronomers took sightings of the movements of Venus and other planets. The name Caracol, 'snail' in Spanish, derives from the form of a spiral staircase within the building.

RIGHT Decapitation was the commonest way of despatching a sacrificial victim. This detail from a remarkably well-preserved stucco panel at the site of Toniná in Chiapas shows the head of a Maya lord with typical aquiline nose and sloping forehead, the conventional ideal of male beauty. In this manner K'an Hoy Chitam of Palenque probably met his fate at the hands of Toniná.

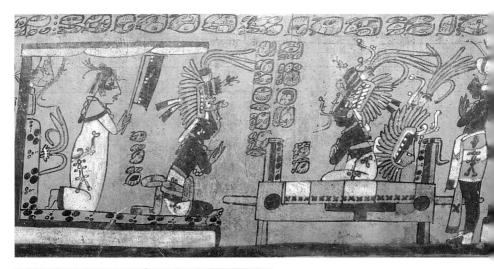

ABOVE Scene on a cylinder vase: a Maya lord on a litter visiting another ruler. A lady kneels holding a fan while someone looks on from behind a pillar beneath what appear to be curtains. Both the litter and furnishings of the palace are covered in jaguar pelts. The grey colour of quetzal feathers and jade jewellery would originally have been vivid green. The texts within the scene have not yet been fully deciphered but the horizontal text follows a conventional formula – blessing the pot itself and saying it was used for the consumption of a 'fresh' form of chocolate drink.

LEFT Vessel in jade mosaic, covering a ceramic interior, which was discovered in a tomb – possibly that of Yik'in Chan K'awil, 27th ruler of Tikal. A similar vessel accompanied the burial of his father, Hasaw Chan K'awil. Amongst the masterpieces of the Maya jade-workers' art, the youthful, god-like portrait represents the king as immortal, bound for resurrection.

The central doorway of the House of the Governor, Uxmal, decorated in typical stone mosaic. Above it are the headless remains of the figure of Lord Chak, sitting on a throne and wearing an enormous feather headdress.

A view across the Nunnery Quadrangle, the most beautiful complex of buildings at Uxmal, constructed during the reign of Lord Chak at the turn of the tenth century AD.

The Temple of the Warriors at Chichén Itzá. The rows of pillars on its southern and western sides are all that now remain of what were once colonnaded halls roofed with timber and plaster.

Chichén Itzá. The Castillo seen from the Temple of the Warriors, in the foreground the figure of a 'Chacmool'.

The walled city of Tulum, perched above the Caribbean, probably the first Maya city to be seen by the Spaniards. On the beach in the foreground Maya traders would have unloaded the merchandise from their canoes.

The Bonampak murals. The 'Judgement' Scene from Room Two showing tortured captives being presented to the triumphant ruler Chan Muwan.

The end of dynastic rule at Copán. The south side of Altar L, the only completed face of the monument, depicting the ruler Yax Pac to the left and U Cit Tok, the man who attempted to succeed him in AD 822, to the right.

Slash and burn agriculture. A section of forest in the foothills of Chiapas, cleared, burnt and planted with maize and other crops.

Sunday morning in Chichicastenango, Guatemala. A procession heads through the back-streets towards the plaza led by elders of one of the 'Cofradías', the religious brotherhoods who care for the images of the Saints.

A Tzutujil Maya farmer from Santiago de Atitlan with beans that he has collected, which he plants alongside his maize. Lake Atitlan is in the background.

quetzal and other exotic feathers. The fourteen nobles bear chunky jade pectorals and ear ornaments and blood-red spondylus shells from the Pacific Ocean dangle from their mantles. Each person's headdress is exquisitely finished and they sport fine, high-backed sandals. The cotton cloth that is exhibited, much of it dyed or embroidered, provides unique evidence of the range and quality of Maya costume. Women wear an array of mantles, underskirts and *huipiles*, men are equally impressive in their capes, patterned 'hip cloths' and the hint here and there of a fine loin-cloth beneath. Mary Miller describes the sheer quantity of fabric as 'awesome' and has calculated that in this one room five hundred square metres of cotton cloth is on display.[2]

Which room follows next in the sequence is still debated. In Room 3, at the western end of the building, many of the same characters reappear. There is another line-up of lords in white mantles in the upper register. But now the dancing which they witness takes place on the steps of a pyramid. This performance covers much of the wall space, involves even more extraordinary costumes and has become more frenzied. The main theme here is blood-letting. Miller suggests that the male dancers are letting their own blood and that long feather fans which jut out horizontally from the area of their groin may have been attached in some way to the penis. In contrast to this public exhibition of auto-sacrifice, there is a more restrained, private scene of three royal ladies sitting cross-legged on a throne in a palace interior and drawing blood from their tongues. Another woman beneath the throne is being handed a piercing instrument by an attendant. On her knees she holds a small child who spreads out his tiny fingers in front of him. Miller believes this to be a second representation of the heir to the throne, who may be about to undergo the rite of passage of his first blood-letting.

Room 3 may represent a continuation of the rituals connected with the designation of the heir seen in Room 1, or it may depict rites of blood-letting that served as a conclusion to the drama of Room 2. This central room is without doubt the most important of the three and here the most powerful message is conveyed. In essence it illustrates what Bonampak and its allies are capable of doing to their enemies and the formidable power that the young prince will inherit. Here is to be found the magnificent, tumultuous battle-scene which covers every wall and vault space except for the northern side of the room. Through a marvel of superpositioning, the chaos and horror of battle is conveyed. Bodies fly everywhere, spears thrust in violent diagonals across the scene and, in the midst of it all, Chan Muwan and other triumphant lords bring down their foes. These men, from a city that remains unknown, are depicted already half-naked, their lances shattered. Chan Muwan grasps one of them firmly by the hair, bringing those more static snapshots of capture from the stone monuments vividly to life.

The denouement, the famous scene of 'Judgement' on the north wall, took place we are told on 6 August 792 (see plate section, p.23). This was the centrepiece of the long-drawn-out celebrations in honour of the heir to the throne – the sanctification through sacrifice of his right to rule. In contrast to the mayhem of the battle, the action here is controlled, the atmosphere hushed. Upon a stepped pyramid, doubtless the acropolis here at Bonampak, Chan Muwan now stands centre-stage. A spear in one hand, he wears a jaguar-pelt jerkin and what appears to be a shrunken human head hangs upside down across his chest. Opposite him is a group of victorious lords. One of them, conceivably Shield Jaguar of Yaxchilán, holds out his hand to offer something to Chan Muwan. It is a single jade bead, that sacred material emblematic of life itself. Beneath the victors' feet, spread across the steps, is the group of captives, blood spurting from their finger ends, their protestations and looks of anguish futile and for whom little is in prospect but further torture and death. One figure is slumped sideways across the steps, unconscious or already dead. His right foot extends downwards and is almost touching a severed head, resting on a bed of leaves.

The painter, or painters, of the Bonampak murals were masters. But who they were is unknown. As yet no one has found their signatures in an unconsidered corner of the walls. Were they local people, or did they perhaps travel from city to city, painting to order from bark-paper pattern-books they carried with them? Another subject for speculation inevitably presents itself. Bonampak was never a major city. In wealth and power it was not in the same league as Yaxchilán, Piedras Negras or Palenque, let alone Tikal or Calakmul. As scholars bemoan the loss of Maya codices, so too we can only wonder how many other magnificent paintings crumbled and fell from the walls of ruined buildings many centuries ago.

The Bonampak murals encapsulate all the brilliance, the courtly splendour and the bloody drama that surrounded Maya kingship. But the events they chronicle took place as the last years of the Classic Maya golden age were closing in. Bonampak probably never won another battle. The paintings were left unfinished and, as Mary Miller has observed, the tiny heir whose future as a Maya ruler was celebrated here almost certainly never came to the throne. In reality, the murals are amongst the last great monuments of the *ancien régime*, of a political tradition and an era of Maya history that was doomed.

THE MAYA COLLAPSE

For the early explorers, the enigma of their downfall was perhaps the greatest of the Maya mysteries. The builders of the magnificent cities seemed to have vanished without trace. John Lloyd Stephens saw the 'shattered bark' of Maya civilization left adrift in the jungle, her crew perished and 'none left to tell what caused her destruction'. When had the forests engulfed the temples and pyramids and how had such glory come to pass away? A century later the first question was answered, although it only served to deepen the mystery surrounding the second. As men such as Sylvanus Morley assiduously tracked down dated inscriptions in the forests and excavations proceeded at some of the major sites, it became clear that dynastic rule at individual Maya cities had come to an abrupt halt during the course of the ninth century, now known as the 'Terminal Classic' period. No more monuments with dated inscriptions were set up and the construction of palaces and temples ceased. Yet this was more than the end of kings. For evidence was to accumulate that most of the major cities in the Southern Lowlands were abandoned, their populations never to return. Classic Maya civilization had folded utterly and the signs were that this 'Collapse', as it came to be called, had been a disaster of such a magnitude that it had little precedent in world history.

Today, now that the chronology from surviving inscriptions is more complete, we can plot the sequence as city after city announced its impending demise. The process seems to have begun to the south-west along the Usumacinta. At Bonampak, as we have seen, the last known date is 792. The last inscription at Piedras Negras is 795, that at Palenque was carved four years later. Yaxchilán fell silent in 808 and the tide of doom swept to the east and then north to the core area of Maya civilization in the Petén. At Quiriguá the end came in 810 and at Copán in 822. The last confirmed date from Calakmul is at present 810, though the city is mentioned at Seibal, some way to the south, in 849. The final known date from Caracol is 859 and then Tikal, one of the last to go, fell by the wayside in 889. The very last Classic Maya date of all, 909, comes from

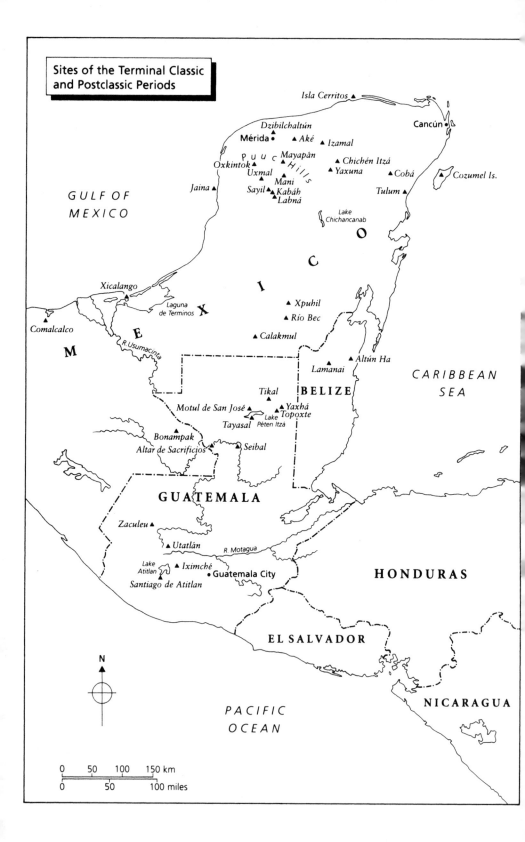

Sites of the Terminal Classic
and Postclassic Periods

Isla Cerritos ▲

Cancún •

Dzibilchaltún ▲
Mérida •   ▲ Aké   ▲ Izamal

P u u c   Mayapán
Oxkintok ▲   H i l l s   ▲ Chichén Itzá
         Uxmal ▲   ▲ Yaxuna   ▲ Cobá   ▲ Cozumel Is.
Jaina ▲   Mani ▲
         Sayil ▲▲ Kabáh   Tulum ▲
               ▲ Labná

GULF OF
MEXICO   Lake
                                         Chichancanab

                                              O

                                         C

                                    I

Xicalango   ▲ Xpuhil
         Laguna   X
         de Terminos   ▲ Río Bec

• Comalcalco   ▲ Calakmul

M   E   ▲ Altún Ha
         R. Usumacinta   Lamanai ▲   CARIBBEAN
                                                        SEA
                              Tikal ▲
         Motul de San José ▲   ▲ BELIZE
                              ▲ Yaxhá
                     Lake Topoxte
         Tayasal   Péten Itzá
   Bonampak ▲
Altar de Sacrificios ▲   ▲ Seibal

         GUATEMALA

   Zaculeu ▲

      ▲ Utatlán   R. Motagua   HONDURAS
Lake
Atitlan   ▲ Iximché
Santiago de Atitlan   • Guatemala City

                      EL SALVADOR

N

                                              NICARAGUA

PACIFIC
OCEAN

0   50   100   150 km
0   50   100 miles

the remote city of Toniná in Chiapas. The royal record before the fall of these cities offers little hint of impending catastrophe. No codices survive with prophecies of doom and there are few tell-tale signs of decline in Maya art, which remained vigorous until the end. All seems right with the world. Stelae commemorate victory in war, sacrifice and the turning of the *katuns* just as they had always done, until the last dynastic message is sent. Then communication is lost and silence descends.

Half a century ago a range of explanations had already been offered to account for what had happened, including plague, agricultural failure, earthquake, invasion from beyond the boundaries of the Maya world and peasant revolt. Today scholars shy away from presenting the fall of the Classic Maya as a tidy sequence of any single root cause and effect. For if factors can be identified which may ultimately have served to trigger the collapse of particular cities, these only operated because of deep-seated structural problems within the fabric of Maya society. In a pattern of cyclical inevitability that the Maya themselves would have understood, any civilization tends to accumulate imbalances and tensions within the very system that has created its success. The Maya were no exception, for centuries of growth produced intolerable strains which in the end proved socially and politically explosive. Yet if one had to select a fundamental 'cause', it must have lain in the glaring imbalance between the burgeoning Maya population and the productive capacity of their agriculture.

It is now well enough established that the population of the Southern Lowlands reached an all-time peak around 800. What this means in the way of overall figures is obviously highly debatable since the studies of settlement patterns upon which the conclusion is based have inevitably been limited so far to a very few cities and regions. These studies in themselves involve a number of assumptions, as we saw in Chapter 1, since they rely on counts of houses identified by survey or excavation, estimates of their contemporaneity and of the way that particular buildings were used in ancient times. Apart from the evidence of archaeology, supporting information is drawn from sources of the early Colonial period, in particular from censuses, which help to give one an idea of the size of the average family. These are further assisted by more modern ethnographic studies of traditional Maya communities. It is on this basis that at Tikal the core area of 120 square kilometres is thought to have supported some 65,000 people at its peak, with another 30,000 in the rural periphery within a radius of ten kilometres from the centre. The work done to date at Calakmul would suggest a similar, if not an even greater figure. These two were undoubtedly the largest of all lowland cities in the Late Classic, though Caracol at its height may not have been far behind. At Tikal the totals translate into some 800 people per square kilometre at the centre of the city, gradually reducing towards the out-skirts. Only a few other systematic population estimates of this nature have been made to date.[3] Quiriguá is thought to have housed rather less, 400–500 per square kilometre at the centre of the city. The reverse is true, to an extraordinary degree, at Copán. Here the immediate 23.4 square kilometre rural area of the Copán 'pocket' around the city centre may have contained 9500–11,500 at its Late Classic peak, a density of 400–500 per square kilometre. Intensive survey of the central urban area, however, has suggested that up to about 9000 people inhabited 1500 or so buildings covering only 0.6 square kilometres. Although this part of the valley is very constricted and must have contributed to the compression, the figure is quite staggering all the same. Thus the visitor to the site today, wandering through the spacious plazas and among the main ceremonial group of buildings, an area which would not itself have been densely populated, has to bear in mind that on every side by the end of the eighth century there would have been residential areas teeming with people.

The density of urban populations thus varied considerably from city to city. But just as important to gauge are the levels of population in smaller settlements, villages and hamlets between the cities. Here an important factor which has to be taken into account, and which often applies to urban areas as well, is that many of the earlier settlement surveys were done by counting 'house-mounds', the visible remains of the earth and limestone platforms upon which houses were constructed. More intensive surveys combined with excavation in recent years have shown that this may often have been very misleading. Many simple dwellings, which at some sites may have made up as much as a half of all domestic structures, were built directly on the ground surface, and thus are invisible without excavation. Hence the tendency now is not so much to err on the side of caution when making population projections, but to build in an 'invisibility' factor and inflate the figures that derive from pure survey. The most significant statistic to emerge to date from the rural areas between cities comes from a series of survey transects carried out across the central lakes area of the Petén. Here the estimate is of a population of some 200 per square kilometre during the later eighth century.[4] This is remarkably high. Few archaeologists are prepared to guess at the total population of the Southern Lowlands around 800, but postulated figures range from around 3 to as much as 10 million. Whatever the true figure, there seems little doubt that this region at the end of the Late Classic was one of the most densely inhabited parts of the ancient world. Many compare it to the demographic picture in pre-industrial China or Java.

This means that we have to shed many of our more romantic preconceptions. Because their ruins still lie amongst dense undergrowth and towering trees, the natural tendency is to think of the Classic Maya as a people who lived their lives within the embrace of the jungle. This had once been true. But the chances are that by the end of the Late Classic there was very little primary forest left, not just around the cities but in between them as well. If one had stood around 800 on top of one of the great temples at Tikal, as far as the eye could see would have been houses, secondary growth and people labouring endlessly in the fields. This kind of picture is not simply a presumption from the population estimates but is based on the study of pollen samples from cores taken from lake beds and swamps in the Petén and adjacent areas. They reveal the extremely high rate of deforestation by the end of the eighth century. The samples contain pollen from crops, weeds and secondary growth, but very little indeed from mature forest.[5]

If the evidence suggests that populations were increasing rapidly and that most available land was turned over to agriculture, the other element in the equation, the question of how much food the land could have produced, is of course impossible to answer. We now have an impressionistic picture of the range of Maya adaptations. We know that their agriculture was considerably more intensive than once thought, but any more precise understanding of the nature and effectiveness of cultivation across the Southern Lowlands will elude scholars for many years to come. Much as with population estimates, the evidence to date is limited and comes from scattered studies that have covered in detail only a tiny fraction of the region. And what they do reveal is great variability, that topography, differing soil fertility and localized weather patterns would have rendered conditions for agriculture very different from one area to another. There seems little doubt, however, that the land must have been under tremendous pressure. Over much of the region slash-and-burn agriculture would still have been the mainstay of the farming regime. Farmers who practise the same system today testify that even where a regular period of fallow is maintained, soils will naturally decline over the years in fertility and crop yields. The responsible farmer will see that from time to time fields are rested for longer periods. But with more and more mouths to feed and nowhere to move to, no other lands to till, this may have been impossible at the end of the Late Classic. Indeed many believe that the reverse was increasingly the case, that they would have been forced to shorten the period of fallow on already tired fields. This would have been an extremely risky strategy, courting disaster for short-term ends.

The increasing dearth of forest would have had a profound impact, firstly in encouraging soil erosion. But trees were also vital for so many aspects of life. Originally, of course, there would have been quite enough to go round and large areas of forest would have formed buffer zones between territories. Tracts of jungle must have been safeguarded and harvested as a renewable resource. But by the end of the eighth century one can well imagine strategic decisions being made to fell many of the remaining areas of virgin forest. The Maya were without doubt responsible farmers, with two thousand years' experience of conjuring harvests of maize from sparse tropical soils. They must have been aware of the impact they were having on their environment. But they could no longer afford to be enlightened guardians of forest and field. The picture that emerges is of the environment progressively degraded, of Maya agriculture reaching the very limits of its capacity and being unable to feed populations adequately. The key evidence comes from the bones of Maya people throughout the region. Studies from sites such as Tikal, Altar de Sacrificios and La Milpa tell the same story of an increasingly unhealthy and stressed population. Skeletons had shrunk, the life expectancy of children was beginning to decrease rapidly and disease was commonplace in a manner not observed in the more robust bones of earlier centuries. On the whole, kings and nobility continued to live well and remain healthy, but this would not be the case for long.

Another variable that has to be considered in the overall picture is that of climate change. Over the centuries the climate and patterns of rainfall in the Maya lowlands have been inherently unstable. Modern statistics reveal that rainfall varies considerably in quantity from year to year. Localized droughts are common and when the rains do come they can appear with extraordinary violence in the form of hurricanes that sweep in from the Caribbean. In 1961, for example, Hurricane Hattie wrecked Belize City and then headed inland to bring havoc to much of the Petén. At the time of writing, much of Nicaragua, Honduras and the Caribbean coast of Guatemala is still recovering from the devastating effects of Hurricane Mitch. Spanish accounts of the conquest period speak of an equally unpredictable climate and, in the northern Yucatán in particular, the common occurrence of drought. Diego de Landa was struck by this in talking to local people and records that in 1535 there was a terrible drought when 'such a famine fell upon them that they were reduced to eating the bark of trees... nothing green was left'.[6] Such uncertainties undoubtedly preoccupied the Prehispanic Maya and underlined the need, revealed in the codices, for effective divination and the right ritual action to be taken, in the way of suitable offerings for the gods, to avert such calamities.

Given the seemingly precarious situation at the end of the Late Classic, short-term changes in weather patterns or sudden natural disasters could have proved catastrophic in a way that they would not have done in previous centuries. There is now evidence that they may have been confronted by problems of a different order entirely. As we know to our cost today, the removal of large areas of tropical forest does not simply degrade the soil but also adversely affects the climate. Any more localized changes of this kind in the Southern Lowlands may be difficult to detect since, as Don Rice points out in his survey of the eighth century Maya environment, both human impact and climate change leave traces – in the pollen record, for example – which are very difficult to tell apart.[7] But in northern Yucatán, at some distance from the great Classic cities to the south, the analysis of sediments from the remote Lake Chichancanab has suggested that a period of consistent dryness set in throughout the Maya area between 750 and 800 and may have lasted for two centuries.[8] There is some evidence for longer term shifts or cycles of climate change in earlier periods. As we saw in Chapter 2, a notably dry episode may have contributed to the downfall of the Late Preclassic city of El Mirador. But that which began in the later eighth century appears to have been the most severe in the Maya region for thousands of years and could have brought prolonged droughts of a kind that the Maya would never have experienced before. Thus to people living on the edge, this may have acted as the final blow which led to social breakdown and disaster.

The exact circumstances and the pattern of events at each of the major cities as they fell apart undoubtedly differed from place to place.

The wealth of archaeological and epigraphic evidence from Copán and its region makes it the only example to date where it is possible to reconstruct plausibly and in some detail the end of a Classic Maya city. After its foundation by Yax K'uk Mo in 426, the city and royal dynasty at Copán flourished. To begin with it was a small centre amidst rich farmland overlooking the river. The abundance and increased prosperity amply justified the king's role as leader of his society. The 'semi-divine' authority, the lavish display and the trappings of Copán's kings increased. It was all a great success and the city attracted more and more people to it, even from as far away as central Honduras. But, as the population grew, the urban nucleus expanded over the most fertile bottomland into a continuous, densely packed residential mass. Gradually there became less and less good land available for cultivation and they began to farm the slopes of the surrounding hills, all the while making sizeable inroads into the local forest cover. Eventually the hills, too, were dotted with groups of houses and trackways, much as they are today, and as the eighth century wore on, Copán's farmers were forced to till the very poorest soils around the hill-tops. Finally, by the end of the century, deforestation, soil erosion and dramatically falling crop yields meant that the valley could no longer feed itself. For a time, perhaps the city was able to depend for food upon tribute in kind from the satellite communities that it dominated. But they, too, would have been feeling the strain, with little surplus to spare, and have been increasingly disinclined to support the demands of the centre.

Thus during the second half of the eighth century the pressures mounted, on the community at large and upon the royal dynasty. The latter's power and authority reached its peak under 18 Rabbit. But after his capture and sacrifice at the hands of Quiriguá in 738, doubts may already have begun to grow about how effective and useful kings actually were. The Hieroglyphic Stairway was completed and other building projects were to be undertaken as a public reassertion of royal authority. Stability was restored for a while. But Yax Pac, who succeeded in 763, appears to have inherited increasing political problems, surrounded by an aristocracy to whom he was obliged to concede more and more prerogatives and power in order to maintain his position. As the century came to its close, however, he may have been only too keen to distribute the blame as widely as possible. For with food in ever shorter supply, Copán was now an impoverished and sick society.[9] Extensive bone studies for this period have revealed severe malnourishment and disease here, throughout the valley, affecting not just commoners but royalty as well. Whatever attempts were made at power-sharing or other *ad hoc* political arrangements, the stark reality was that little could be done to halt the slide. In the end it was the royal dynasty which became the inevitable target for retribution. That order and prosperity, the equilibrium between men and gods, between humans and the forces of nature, that kings were supposed to maintain had gone from the world. Their old claims of a special relationship with the divine were proven to be spurious and their very existence could no longer be justified.

The end of dynastic rule at Copán is signalled by two most unusual monuments. The first is an unprepossessing, damaged stela of curiously rounded, columnar form known as Stela 11. It depicts the standing figure of the already dead Yax Pac descending into the jaws of the Underworld (see overleaf). On the back of the stone is a short inscription which has so far proved impossible to decipher in its entirety. But, following an abbreviated date which almost certainly corresponds to 820, the second glyph block features the verb *hom*, which David Stuart has interpreted as to 'dismantle' or 'destroy'.[10] The next glyph includes the word for 'founder', as it appears in the inscription on top of Altar Q, where it refers to the foundation of the Copán royal line some 400 years earlier by Yax K'uk Mo (see plate section, p.11). On Stela 11 this reference to the founder is coupled with the suffix *nah* meaning 'house'. Put together, what this would mean is 'the founder's house is destroyed', in other words the dynasty which began with Yax K'uk Mo had come to an end. If the interpretation is correct, this inscription is unique in actually announcing the termination of a royal line. It is an extraordinary and quite uncharacteristic admission of failure.

That the dynasty was indeed extinguished is confirmed by 'Altar L' set up two years later by an individual called U Cit Tok. Who this man was, whether related to the royal line or an upstart noble, is unknown. But there is little doubt that he was trying to take over power and to commemorate the event with a monument very like Altar Q. It is of comparable rectangular form and was clearly meant to display a similar line-up of seated Copán kings. To the right on the south side, cross-legged on his name glyph, sits the deceased Yax Pac, facing the similarly attired and seated U Cit Tok. Between them is the date 822 and the verb for 'seating' or accession to the throne. The monument is thus intended to mark the transition of power between the two men. But U Cit Tok's name or image appears on no other monument and this is the very last of all the

Stela 11, Copán.

known dates at Copán. Even more telling is that the altar is unfinished. The carving on the south side is completed well enough, but that on the north is merely roughed out and the two other sides and the top are completely blank, as if, as Schele and Freidel put it, the sculptor had picked up his tools and walked off the job.[11] Thus U Cit Tok failed in his attempt to establish himself. He could not muster enough support to keep the idea of royalty alive. This inconspicuous altar, which most visitors to the site tend to pass by, thus serves as an extraordinarily powerful metaphor for the downfall of the house of Yax K'uk Mo and the end of history at Copán.

There is no means of knowing what happened to the members of the royal family, although there is evidence that the residential compound of Yax Pac and his line may have been destroyed at about this time. Somewhat later, William Fash suggests, his tomb may have been looted and his funerary temple ransacked. There is no sign, however, of any major upheaval or of what might be termed a popular uprising. Fash believes that the political end-game at Copán amounted to a nobles' revolt.[12] Perhaps it was a takeover by the heads of those non-royal lineages who commanded popular support in the countryside and could distance themselves from the perceived failures of the ruling family. For the houses of these lineages continued to be occupied and indeed were added to over the following century. Thus at Copán rule by a single king seems to have devolved to that of the group. These leading families evidently attempted to stay on and revive the valley's fortunes. But after a century or so, perhaps because of renewed infighting and the continuing decline of agriculture, they appear to have drifted away to smaller, still fertile areas of land in the surrounding hills. At least here, on the less crowded fringes of the Maya world, they had somewhere to go. They reverted, it seems, to a simpler, decentralized way of life, of the kind that had existed before the onset of dynastic rule. Between about 1000 and 1200, the population of Copán fell away rapidly. From the evidence of their rubbish dumps and burials, small groups continued to inhabit parts of the city, but after this time the valley was largely abandoned.

The uniquely detailed picture that emerges from Copán offers a model of how some of the principal elements in the process of Maya 'Collapse' fitted together. Deterioration of the environment and the failure of agriculture imposed intolerable strains on the political system, which finally came apart and led to the toppling of royal scapegoats. In essence this pattern must have been repeated in many other cities, though elsewhere, where kingdoms jostled more densely together, the drift towards failure was more chaotic and more violent. Along the Usumacinta and Pasión rivers, and in the heartland region of the Petén and adjacent areas, the old system of alliances formed around Tikal and Calakmul had broken down by the middle of the eighth century. It is obvious enough today that the only thing which might have enabled the Classic Maya to surmount their problems was political unity and co-operation. This was clearly impossible. Under pressure the political system atomized, reverted to type, with each one of a host of now antagonistic city-states looking to its own interests in what became a struggle for survival. For in many areas, especially those away from the major rivers or lakes, the strain on the environment and the decline of agriculture was in all probability much greater than that visible at Copán. The only option that would keep kings in power and feed their populations was to take land and desperately scarce resources from others. Inscriptions suggest that the incidence of warfare and, most would conclude, its intensity, increased markedly during the latter part of the eighth century. The pattern may have been set with the destruction of Dos Pilas and the conflagration in the Petexbatún area that began in the 760s. This was all-out, brutal war that laid waste the whole region. Along the Usumacinta the last texts that survive from the major cities all speak of warfare, and at some of them there are signs of destruction. Buildings were burnt and monuments defaced at Piedras Negras, and at Yaxchilán archaeologists have recently discovered that a section of the city known as the 'Little Acropolis' was fortified with hastily erected walls, and projectile points covered the ground, suggesting that Yaxchilán, like Dos Pilas, may finally have fallen in war.

With the turn of the ninth century surviving inscriptions become fewer and fewer and it is extremely hard to follow the fortunes of the major cities as they each met their end. One can imagine, however, the contagion of war spreading from city to city in an atmosphere of mounting instability and fear. From a society likened to Ancient Greece in the jungle, the Maya world had become more like the twentieth-century Balkans. Victory in war, the plunder of another city-state perhaps brought temporary respite for rulers, a means of easing domestic pressures and rewarding their followers. But such success could only be short-term and there must have been less and less to fight over. There was ultimately no way out for beleaguered kings. Prisoners of their own propaganda, they had to maintain their prestige as semi-divine warrior lords, surrounded by what had become a bloated urban establishment, parasitic in its demands for labour, food and other material goods from a rural hinterland increasingly incapable of giving it. For centuries the social order of a Maya city-state had been maintained by the finely tuned string of reciprocity between rulers and ruled, mirrored in the relationship between men and gods. The population delivered their labour and products to the cities. Kings managed spiritual affairs and saw to the redistribution of goods and the disposal of manpower to keep the city-state running. Now, however, neither participant in this arrangement could fulfil their side of the bargain. Every individual family must have looked to their most fundamental, traditional loyalties – to kin group or lineage – in order to secure its own survival. In the end the whole system of royal government, such as it was, simply ceased to exist.

At Tikal the breakdown in central authority can be traced in outline. After the defeat of Calakmul, she had revived spectacularly and by the middle of the eighth century had re-established control over many other towns and cities in the region. This power-base may have approached in scale that of Tikal's Early Classic heyday. Construction in the city centre vastly increased and nearly all the great temple pyramids date from the second half of the century. By the mid-800s, however, the situation was very different. Tikal was evidently coming apart. Uaxactún had long before begun to erect stelae again, asserting its own independence, and now smaller cities within the Tikal orbit were doing the same – towns such as Ixlu, near Lake Petén Itzá, and Jimbal to the north. What is more, the jumped-up lords who commissioned these monuments used the Tikal emblem glyph and styled themselves 'Holy Lord of Tikal' (see overleaf). A shadowy figure, who took the great name, Hasaw Chan

Jimbal Stela 1

K'awil, appears to have ruled in the city itself at this time, remembered only by a worn stela erected in 869. By then, it seems, anybody with a strong enough private army could be king for a while.

By around 900 the ruling dynasty of what had once been the greatest city in the Maya world had been swept away, and so too, it seems, were all the petty pretenders. The centre of Tikal was abandoned. It is left to our imaginings as to how this happened. A bloody end is a probability, though re-education as simple maize farmers, Cambodia-style, may have been an uncomfortable alternative for what remained of the royal family. The speculative latitude that present ignorance allows might tempt one to suggest, somewhat romantically, that a few survived and fled to seek refuge elsewhere. Thus the last of the Tikal royal line, the remaining members of their household, the scribes and men of knowledge, holy relics and battered codices in bundles on their backs, made their final offerings to the ancestors on the North Acropolis and then simply wandered away. It would also be fine to imagine that they disappeared into the jungle whence their remote ancestors had come, nearly 2000 years before. But their escape more likely lay across a barren, shattered landscape where order had broken down, stunted crops grew only fitfully and where the king of the animal world, the jaguar, was also a refugee, driven to the point of extinction.

Yet if the last bearers of Classic Maya high culture at Tikal were gone, other Maya took their place. The poorer districts of the city were abandoned at the same time, but some of these families moved into the centre and occupied the palaces. Their simple pottery and the piles of garbage strewn untidily for archaeologists to find in compacted layers of 'midden' tell the story. This population of squatters lived on here for a century or more. They still seem to have revered the temples and plazas as sacred places and even moved some of the stelae around and set them up in more convenient places, although the writing must have meant very little since they re-erected a number of them upside down. Across the Southern Lowlands, remnant groups of ordinary Maya continued to live in and around the deserted cities and to worship in a similar manner amongst the decaying temples. The centre of Caracol, for example, was abandoned about the same time as Tikal, but some of the surrounding areas remained lightly occupied and until the eleventh century the centre was visited from time to time for religious ritual on a small, simple scale. The same appears to have been true at La Milpa further north in Belize, where at the time of first Spanish contact in the later sixteenth century a tiny population lingered on in the vicinity. Norman Hammond has observed an intriguing upsurge of stela veneration here at around this time, revealed by the quantities of Conquest-period pottery buried beneath them. As the Spaniards came nearer and nearer, perhaps dimly perceived ancestral forces resident in the stones were invoked to help resist the invaders.

It can sometimes be forgotten, however, that such a picture of wholesale disaster and abandonment, with a pitiful few peasants left camping amongst ruins, was not universal. To the south of Tikal for example, around Lake Petén Itzá and a series of smaller lakes to the east, where there were still enough sources of food to exploit and islands and peninsulas were readily defensible against the attacks of outsiders, the towns of Topoxté and Tayasal survived and remained inhabited until the Conquest. Tayasal, covered by modern Flores and so far little explored archaeologically, appears to have expanded considerably during the 'Postclassic' centuries until, by the time of Cortés' visit in 1525, it was the capital of a formidable, still functioning city-state. In remote parts, other favourably positioned settlements managed to cling on. The most notable and best documented of these is the city of Lamanai in northern Belize, excavated by David Pendergast and a team from the Royal Ontario Museum.[13] Here the 'Collapse' never happened. The city lay by a large lagoon on the upper reaches of the New River, an environment that could still support a sizeable population. A major trader in cacao and other commodities, Lamanai also seems to have been able to switch the emphasis of its commerce from land routes – a few of which still functioned – to canoe-borne trade northwards along the river to the sea, connecting with what would soon develop as flourishing networks all the way around the Yucatán peninsula. During the ninth century, when all was falling apart elsewhere, Lamanai was prospering. Temples were well maintained, new residential areas were built, religious ceremonial continued to be performed as before, and the tombs of rulers and nobility were well stocked with jades and other fine goods. How the city was able to cope with what one might presume were floods of refugees from elsewhere is unclear. Somehow, while their peers not far away were being toppled from their thrones, Lamanai's leaders proved extremely effective and resilient. By 1100 or so it was probably the only sizeable settlement left in the region, and Lamanai rulers continued to be laid to rest in their tombs until only a few years before the arrival of the Spaniards, although by then the city centre was not in its original location and the architecture was a shadow of its former grandeur. In the late sixteenth century a Christian mission was established amongst the last inhabitants of a settlement that had existed here continuously for some 3000 years.

Yet the above remain rare exceptions which prove the rule of the Maya Collapse: that in the overwhelming majority of cities across the Classic heartland, the phenomenon was total and irreversible. It must be a gauge of the scale of the catastrophe and the severity of damage to the environment that in the years to come no attempt was made to revive a single one of them. The forests may not have fully recovered until shortly before Cortés' crossing of the lowlands many centuries later.

ENDINGS AND BEGINNINGS

With the end of Classic civilization in the Southern Lowlands hundreds of thousands, maybe millions of people seem to have simply disappeared from the region. There are two answers to the question of what happened to them. The first must be that untold numbers died through war or disease and that the rate of infant mortality, already high enough at the best of times, increased dramatically in the prevailing, terrible circumstances, perhaps to as much as 60 per cent. This alone would have seen populations plummet within the century or so that it took for the process of collapse to run its course. The second explanation is that waves of people moved out of the disaster area to other places that offered the chance of a better life: to the highlands of Guatemala and Chiapas, to the coasts and, in particular it would seem, to northern Yucatán. For here, in the ninth century, just as the southern cities faded and died, populations swelled and centres such as Uxmal and Chichén Itzá enjoyed a phase of tremendous growth and prosperity. Although hard scientific evidence for northward migrations remains limited, many scholars now find it difficult to resist the conclusion that the two phenomena are connected. Certainly, all today would agree that what transpired after the Classic Collapse in the Southern Lowlands was not merely decline, decadence and, in northern Yucatán, invasion by militaristic peoples from central Mexico, as used to be thought, but a fundamental re-ordering of the Maya world, in which the north of the peninsula became the focus for the last great era of Maya civilization.

It is important to stress, however, as something of a precautionary preamble to the rest of this chapter, that, although nearer to us in time, considerably less is known about the Postclassic period, between around 900 and the Spanish Conquest, than the Classic centuries which preceded it.[14] To some extent this is due to the comparatively limited amount of archaeological investigation that has been carried out at sites that date from this time. But the major reason is that as the royal houses of the Classic period fell, so the tradition of recording dynastic history accompanied by Long Count dates on monuments of stone ceased. Monumental inscriptions survive from the ninth and tenth centuries in northern Yucatán, but they are rare and provide very little documentary information. This is not to suggest that literacy necessarily declined that markedly, or that there was no longer any interest in the chronicling of historical events. What seems to have happened is that painting on bark-paper now became the principal medium for such record-keeping. This can be interpreted as the result of political changes in the north during the Terminal and Postclassic periods which, at Chichén Itzá in particular, saw a shift from the sole rule of kings to more collective forms of authority, where the acts of individuals were no longer commemorated in public as they had been in earlier times.

The fact that the few surviving codices do not offer us anything in the way of 'history' is no reason to believe that those countless volumes consigned to the flames by Landa and his colleagues would not have done so. Indeed, we have his word that they recorded 'antiquities and their sciences'. Although its nature may have changed, historical consciousness did not die. This would have been impossible, for as we saw in the previous chapter, the recording of significant events and patterns in the past was essential in order to predict the future. History was inextricably bound up with prophecy, and it is in this form that the Books of Chilam Balam come down to us. Alongside the handful of traditional histories and legends recounted directly to Landa and a few other Spaniards, these are the only sources for piecing together the story of the concluding centuries of Maya civilization.

The books are so named after an original scribe or man of knowledge known as 'Chilam Balam', in translation 'Jaguar Spokesman' or 'Jaguar Prophet', who is supposed to have foretold the arrival of the Spaniards. They began to be set down in Maya but in the Latin alphabet soon after the Conquest by native scribes who were taught in the mission schools to use the written language of their conquerors. But these writings, much of them transcriptions or what was remembered from hieroglyphic originals that had been destroyed, were hidden away from Spanish eyes and jealously guarded. A dozen Chilam Balam books are now known to the outside world, each pertaining to a different northern Yucatán community. Others may survive in Maya hands and, in remote parts of Quintana Roo, they are still being added to. Those best known to scholars, such as the Books of Tizimin, Maní or, the most accessible and useful of all, the Book of Chumayel, appear to date for the most part from the eighteenth and early nineteenth centuries. Until that time they were constantly added to, amended and rewritten, snippets of pre-Hispanic history accumulated and used as the basis for prediction. For much of these books was organized around the 'Count of the Katuns', that cycle of some 260 years divided up into thirteen *katuns* or periods of nearly twenty of our years that were the principal means of prognostication and of time-keeping after the Long Count was abandoned. The language of the Books is highly metaphorical and difficult, containing all kinds of obscure allusions and even references to biblical teachings. And, because 'history' seems to have been rearranged selectively as the basis for prophecy, they have proved notoriously hard to interpret. The following, from the Book of Chumayel, is an example:

Katun 8 Ahau is the ninth Katun. The Katun is established at Izamal.

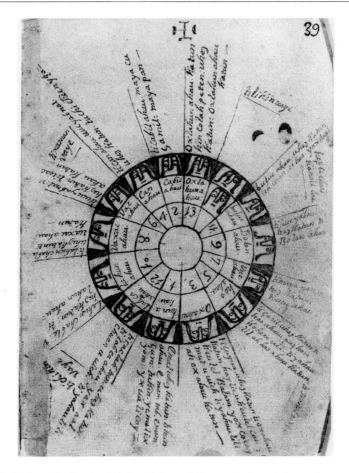

Folio 39 from the Book of Chilam Balam of Chumayel, late eighteenth century,
illustration of Katun wheel, displaying the cycle of 13 *katuns.*

There is Kinich Kakmo. The shield shall descend, the arrow shall descend
(upon Chakanputun) together with the rulers of the land. The heads of the
foreigners to the land were cemented (into the wall) at Chakanputun.
There is an end of greed; there is an end to causing vexation in the world.
It is the word of God the Father. Much fighting shall be done by the
Natives of the land.[15]

There are historical references here with which scholars continue to
tussle, notably the location of the place called 'Chakanputun'. But it is
hard to know which Katun 8 Ahaw in the past, which 260-year cycle is
being referred to. Neither can one be certain that over time events in the
past were not themselves shifted from one *katun* to another to accord

more neatly with a scribe's prophetic vision of the 'nature' of one *katun* as opposed to another. But, even if we cannot be sure when in the past particular events took place, the Books do consistently refer to certain important happenings in Maya history which can reasonably be taken at face value: the foundation of cities, wars between them, and the movements of peoples into and out of the northern Yucatán.

We shall refer to the Chilam Balam Books again below, but for our immediate purposes here they offer further backing to the idea of population movements from the south to the north at the time of the Collapse, of the intrusion of 'foreigners' and to the general instability of the times. The break-up of the Classic cities in the Southern Lowlands and the movement of their populations also has to be seen against a background of considerable and still little understood instability and change within Mesoamerica as a whole between about 700 and 1000. As we have seen in previous chapters, the Maya were never in any sense detached from developments beyond their boundaries. In the Early Classic, for example, Tikal and a number of other cities formed a very close relationship with Teotihuacan. The influence of central Mexico was absorbed and retained within Maya culture, periodically to re-emerge. In the new manifestations of Maya civilization that were to arise in the north, particularly at Chichén Itzá, strong outside influences are detectable, evidence of communication over long distances between Maya and Mexican societies. The question of how that communication operated leads us to a shadowy group of people on the western fringes of the Maya world who flourished at the time of the Collapse and who were to act as intermediaries or even perhaps as protagonists in the blossoming of northern Yucatán.

They are most commonly called the 'Putun', a title given them by Eric Thompson, or the 'Olmeca-Xicalanca', the Aztec name adopted in more recent times. Their homeland was along the coasts of Tabasco and southern Campeche, where they established a great commercial emporium or entrepot at Xicalango on the edge of the Laguna de Terminos. For first and foremost the Putun were traders, who between about 750 and the Spanish Conquest came to dominate the seaborne trade around the Yucatán peninsula.[16] They spoke Chontal Mayan, a variant of those Cholan Mayan languages found around the base of the peninsula, as opposed to the Yucatec Mayan of the regions further to the north. But though ethnically Maya they were heavily 'Mexicanized' culturally, due no doubt to their business as commercial linkmen between the two areas. Some also believe that, from the time of the fall of Teotihuacan in the later seventh century, the whole Gulf Coast and lower Usumacinta region became an extremely fluid kind of 'international zone' where migrant central Mexican groups settled and mingled with Maya such as the Putun. This kind of cultural mix, extremely difficult as yet for scholars to come to terms with, must account for the undoubted Maya influence seen in the striking murals of Cacaxtla, near Tlaxcala in the Mexican highlands. Here identifiably Maya individuals are represented in bird and jaguar costumes and even holding characteristic 'ceremonial bars'. One scene, comparable to the Bonampak murals both in content and to some degree in style, and which may indeed have been painted around the same time (about 800), depicts a battle in which Mexican warriors triumph over other individuals with distinctly Maya profiles, images which defy any easy explanation. Maya warriors or perhaps merchants are also depicted on the Temple of the Feathered Serpent at Xochicalco, south-west of Cacaxtla. Again, whether this reflects the activities of the Putun or another Maya group is impossible to say. But the Putun certainly appear to have been aggressive, militarized traders who, in the confused times of the late eighth and ninth centuries, made opportunistic inroads into many regions. They may well have taken over much of the trade that had once gone by river and across country through the great Classic Maya cities, diverting it around the coasts of the peninsula in their fast ocean-going canoes, of the kind that Columbus was to encounter in 1502.

Some have suggested a Putun incursion or 'invasion' into the heart of the southern Maya lowlands at the time of the Collapse. For at the city of Seibal in the Pasión valley there is evidence of a sudden spurt in population in the first half of the ninth century and marked changes in ceramic traditions, burial practices, architectural forms and in the iconography of stelae. In 849, for example, five stelae were erected here by a ruler who seems to possess facial characteristics strikingly different from more conventional royal Maya portraits. He has a rounded head with no sign of that upwardly elongated cranial deformation commonly visible among the Classic Maya, produced by clamping boards to a child's head during infancy, and he bears a moustache and certain other characteristics which appear decidedly 'foreign'. There was undoubtedly a major upheaval of some kind at Seibal, as there was at nearby Altar de Sacrificios, but whether this necessarily argues for a Putun invasion is hotly debated. David Stuart feels that the Seibal inscriptions of this period do not signify any major break with the past, and that even the portraiture can be compared with other local Maya traditions.

In this extremely uncertain period the conveniently mobile Putun have tended to be used as something of a catch-all to explain a variety of cultural anomalies. A major problem, however, is that their own homeland is very little known archaeologically. No Putun inscriptions of any kind survive, neither do they seem to have possessed any significant architectural tradition of their own. Despite their elusiveness, however, the 'Phoenicians' of the Maya world – as Thompson termed them – remain major players at this time, to whom we shall return as we look in more detail at developments in northern Yucatán.

Although the environment at the top of the peninsula is harsh and generally unfavourable for human settlement, with thin soils, low annual rainfall and little surface water, apart from that available in sink-holes or cenotes, a number of sizeable settlements had developed here by the end of the Early Classic period – sites such as Acanceh, Aké and Izamal, many of whose numerous pyramids and the famous but long-since disappeared stucco mask of the Sun God, engraved by Catherwood, would appear to date back to this time. The most important early cities seem to have grown up in areas devoted to specialized economic activities such as fishing, salt production, or the growing of cotton and sisal. These commodities would have been traded with peoples to the south, northern Yucatán receiving items such as obsidian, grinding stones, chert axes and cacao in return. Archaeological research has been limited here compared with the lavish attention paid to the cities of the south, and hieroglyphic texts are also few and far between. Two of the most impressive and better known Late Classic cities are Dzibilchaltún towards the coast to the north of Mérida, whose prosperity was evidently based on the salt trade, and Cobá on the eastern side of the peninsula. The latter is an enormous site, including impressive pyramids and an imposing ball-court, situated next to an unusual group of small lakes. It would have controlled a sizeable dependent territory, including its own port of Xelhá on the coast, in the manner of the cities to the south. From its centre radiates a network of broad *sacbes*, one of which, the longest Maya road known, runs 100 kilometres to Yaxuná in the west, which appears to have been constructed in the Postclassic period as a kind of border post between the realm of Cobá and that of Chichén Itzá. Twenty-three large but much eroded carved stelae have been found at Cobá, their style and the nature of their inscriptions comparing with those from the Petén and southern Campeche. Indeed, some think that the city may have been founded in the Early Classic period as a colony of a southern power. If this was indeed so, not just in the case of Cobá but other northern cities as well, then it may have been natural enough for southern peoples at the time of the Collapse to seek refuge with their connections in the north. The populations of established northern sites like Cobá certainly swelled at this time.

UXMAL AND THE PUUC CITIES

In the west, amongst the low, rolling Puuc hills south of Mérida, cities such as Uxmal, Kabáh, Labná and Sayil expanded greatly during the ninth century, and here were raised some of the most beautiful buildings ever conceived by the Maya. At Uxmal, Stephens and Catherwood spent longer than they did at any other Maya site, planning and sketching in detail precincts and palaces which in Stephens' eyes formed that 'new order' of architecture 'not unworthy to stand side by side' with the major traditions of the Old World. They have continued to impress visitors ever since. Indeed, in the 1920s, while the discovery of Tutankhamun's tomb inspired Egyptianizing forms of Art Deco, it was the architecture of the Puuc region which produced in the USA the brief florescence of what has become known as the 'Maya Revival Style', apparently given its initial impetus by the friendship between Pierre Lorillard, the tobacco magnate and Maya enthusiast who had sponsored Desiré Charnay's explorations, and Frank Lloyd Wright.

Maya architecture is various in its local traditions, from the stark grandeur of Tikal or Chichén Itzá to the gentler refinement of Palenque or Copán. But Uxmal, with its spacious courts and quadrangles, varied elevations and vistas and sense of proportion and balance between architectural form and ornament, displays a sophisticated aesthetic all of its own, where one directly senses the intelligence of architects at work. Who these architects were is quite unknown. Sculptors, painters and scribes are depicted on Maya pots, referred to on occasion in texts and sometimes signed their own names. Yet architects or master builders remain anonymous throughout Maya history. Neither are they singled out as a specialist class by chroniclers at the time of the Conquest. We also have little idea of architectural practice. The recent discovery at Tikal of a stone architectural model or maquette, a small block of limestone carved with miniature pyramids, stairways and a ball-court, has caused some excitement. Though this unique model appears to bear no relationship to known groups of buildings, it is widely thought to be more than a curious toy. Models such as this might well have been used in the discussion process before design decisions were made. The next stage, the process of construction, would have required extremely precise planning and calculation and must have presented a formidable challenge in man-management, the organization of enormous teams of labourers to work on the different stages of a building, since discrete sections would have been worked on at the same time. Excavations at Tikal have revealed lines drawn through the plastered floors of plazas as a guide for stone-masons to indicate where they should place the foundations for walls. Doubtless a corps of supervisors was continually occupied in checking the progress of different work gangs and reporting to the overseeing architect, who may indeed have had plans and specifications committed to bark-paper.

The architecture of Uxmal and the Puuc sites displays very distinctive technical characteristics, which in themselves reveal something of the division of labour and the 'industrial' manner in which construction must have been organized. Firstly, a solid structural fill was prepared which was self-supporting and held together by a kind of lime-based concrete. This was then faced with innumerable finely-cut stone 'mosaic' elements, which must have been mass-produced by teams of stone-carvers endlessly repeating the same standard pieces which made up the intricate patterns of lattice-work, step frets or, most famously, the masks of the Rain God Chak that decorate the façades and protrude from the corners of buildings. The House of the Governor at Uxmal, for example, was covered with some 20,000 separate stone elements. Yet, at Uxmal in particular, it is the restraint with which surface ornament is used, largely restricted to the upper part of façades, divided by sharp mouldings from plain lower sections, that is so appealing to modern sensibilities.

The southern tradition of tall temple-pyramids was not abandoned in the Puuc region, but they are rare. The great Pyramid of the Magician looms above Uxmal on the eastern edge of the city centre. It was constucted in five separate stages. On the west side, above an intimidatingly steep stairway, stands a temple with its entrance in the form of a monster mouth, in the style of the Chenés region to the south and also bearing comparison with the similarly elaborate monstrous doorway into Temple 22 at Copán. At first the pyramid seems somewhat out on a limb, but it does provide an effective visual counterpoint to the palaces and courts spread out beneath it. To the west of the Pyramid lies the first of Uxmal's two major glories, the 'Nunnery', made up of four rectangular range structures with multiple entrances, around a spacious interior court – hence the name bestowed on these buildings by the earliest Spanish visitors (see plate section, p.21). They were laid out corresponding more or less to the cardinal directions and appear to follow much the same cosmological pattern as architectural arrangements in the southern cities. Thus the northern range is placed on a different, higher level to the rest of the complex and has that heavenly number of thirteen exterior doorways. Sky serpents weave in and out of the upper façade amongst a series of models in mosaic relief of the thatched dwellings of ordinary Maya. The interconnected structures on the southern side of the quadrangle have nine entrances, corresponding to the tiers of the Underworld, including a central corbelled arch offering an impressive view towards the Uxmal ball-court. Jeff Kowalski, the greatest authority on the city's architecture, points out that a large stone column stood originally in the centre of the Nunnery quadrangle, representing the World Tree, further evidence of the cosmological programme that underlay the Nunnery's design.[17] Here also, on a platform near the Tree, was a Jaguar throne which would have been occupied by 'Lord Chak', identified as the ruler who oversaw the construction of the Nunnery at the turn of the tenth century.

Lord Chak was also responsible for the magnificent House of the Governor, constructed on top of three distinct artificial platforms and, as we saw in the previous chapter, facing east towards the most southerly rising point of Venus as Morning Star (see plate section, p.21).[18] The building is almost a hundred metres long, originally contained twenty separate rooms, and is divided with exquisite sense of proportion into three sections linked by grand corbelled arches. Amidst the elaborate mosaic decoration of the upper façade appears a number of seated human figures. That above the central doorway was the most impressive, although it is now headless. It depicts Lord Chak seated on a throne and wearing a huge feathered headdress. Radiating horizontally outward from the figure is a series of nine double-headed serpent bars, powerful symbols of royal authority and commonly carried by Classic-period rulers. Seven of these bear hieroglyphic inscriptions and the decipherable sections refer to constellations, elements of the Maya zodiac, visible in the sky at the time of the Venus alignment towards which the building is oriented.

Lord Chak commissioned the Nunnery quadrangle and the House of the Governor as residential or administrative buildings and both are associated with a few hieroglyphic inscriptions, whose dates range from about 890 to 910. This time-frame is also supported by a small number of radiocarbon dates from wooden lintels. References to Lord Chak appear elsewhere – upon a stone altar, for example, where he is referred to as a *K'ul Ahaw*, and on the best preserved of the few surviving stelae from Uxmal, Stela 14, where he is depicted in largely traditional pose standing upon two captives, although he is flanked by a warrior holding a circular shield comparable to contemporary images from Chichén Itzá.

The archaeological evidence indicates that Uxmal and the other major Puuc cities such as Sayil, Kabáh, Labná and Xcalumkin, along with many smaller sites, were first established during the eighth century. Before this time occupation of the region appears to have been limited. Although the Puuc soils are deeper and more productive than those in other parts of northern Yucatán, there are hardly any cenotes since the water table is at least 200 feet below the ground. The beginning of more concerted settlement here coincided with a technological innovation, the digging of extremely effective *chultunes* or small underground cisterns for water storage. These were lined with plaster, of swelling bottle shape with a constricted neck to counter evaporation and had a broad, sloping rim at ground level to catch the rainwater. At Sayil, archaeologically the best documented of the cities in the area, each individual household had at least one *chultun*, which would have seen them through the lengthy dry season. It is partly through the recording of chultunes that archaeologists have been able to estimate the population of Sayil by the ninth century. It had some 10,000 people within the urban heart of the site and another 7000 or so in the wider surrounding area. Through the centre of the city ran an impressive *sacbe* which linked the major architectural elements, including a ball-court, palaces and a platform where stelae were erected. The great Three-Storey Palace is the most beautiful structure that survives, comparable to the forms visible at Uxmal and making considerable use of rounded columns and clusters of rougher half-columns, represented bound together in imitation of the simple wooden-pole construction of vernacular Maya architecture.

The larger cities such as Uxmal, Kabáh and Sayil grew up to dominate smaller centres within their immediate region, and each would have been ruled by its own paramount lineage. A number of cities erected stelae, though the majority only survive in very eroded condition. Yet, like Lord Chak's Stela 14 from Uxmal, the Classic-period tradition of depicting single individuals surrounded by emblems of rulership appears to have been maintained, suggesting that after its demise in the Southern Lowlands the institution of dynastic rule lingered on in the Puuc region. But was it in fact brought here? For the difficult question remains: where did the peoples and rulers of the Puuc cities come from? The Books of Chilam Balam say that Uxmal was settled by a group of Maya called the Xiu, who migrated there from the south. If this is indeed true, it leaves open the matter of their more precise origins and when any such migrations occurred. If settlements were established here by the middle of the eighth century, the time when the distinctive Cehpech ceramics from this region began to be produced, could northward migrations really have begun this early? Or, as might seem more likely, were these cities swelled by refugees during the following century, at the time of the southern Collapse, when there is indeed evidence for a major increase in population and when Puuc art and architecture flowered so magnificently?

Uxmal became the largest and most powerful of the Puuc cities. By the later ninth century it may have directly taken over Kabáh and the smaller Nojpat, which are directly linked to Uxmal by a twenty-kilometre-long *sacbe*. Kowalski and other archaeologists believe that by the time of Lord Chak the city had become the centre of a powerful regional state and may have established some kind of alliance with Chichén Itzá. But by the middle of the 10th century rapid decline had set in and these cities would also be largely abandoned. Here, too, there is evidence that environmental factors may have played a part, and that population growth had once more outstripped the carrying capacity of the Maya landscape.

NEW ROME

Chichén Itzá has never been a 'lost' Maya city. When Diego de Landa came here, soon after the Spanish Conquest, much of it had obviously been abandoned, but pilgrims still visited to cast offerings into the Sacred Cenote. The 'Mouth of the Well of the Itzá', as Chichén Itzá is translated, was revered as a powerful, holy place across the Yucatán peninsula. Now thousands of tourists come here every day by bus from Mérida or the great Caribbean resort of Cancun and at the spring equinox Chichén Itzá becomes, like Stonehenge or Manchu Picchu, the teeming focus of a New Age pilgrimage – for at sunrise the pattern of light and shadow formed by the outline of the nine terrace levels of the pyramid of the Castillo conjures up the image of an undulating serpent slithering its way down the balustrade of the northern stairs. But although the most widely known of all Maya cities, Chichén Itzá is also one of the most perplexing. This was not always so in the minds of scholars. For until recent times ancient legend and the particular character and layout of Chichén Itzá's ruins combined, so it seemed, to tell the city's story.

The centre of Chichén Itzá can be divided into two discrete sections that possess markedly contrasting styles of architecture. To the south are buildings such as the Nunnery or 'Monjas' group and the 'Akab

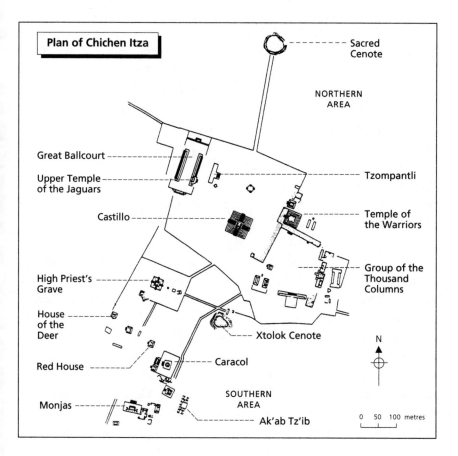

Plan of Chichen Itza

Sacred Cenote

NORTHERN AREA

Great Ballcourt

Upper Temple of the Jaguars

Tzompantli

Castillo

Temple of the Warriors

High Priest's Grave

Group of the Thousand Columns

House of the Deer

Xtolok Cenote

Red House

Caracol

N

Monjas

SOUTHERN AREA

Ak'ab Tz'ib

0   50   100 metres

Dzib' which, although they have none of the elegance of the palaces of Uxmal for example, are typically Puuc in appearance, with mosaic decorated façades and Chac masks at the corners. Other buildings here, such as the Red House and the House of the Deer, may not be so Puuc in style, but they are at least clearly Maya – temples on simple, relatively low platforms that have been compared with the Cross Group at Palenque in their design and relationship to each other. The Caracol is the only structure in this area which seems at all unexpected, though that might be put down to its purpose as an astronomical observatory.

To the north however, the style, scale and whole spirit of the architecture changes dramatically. At the centre of a vast plaza towers the Castillo, some 30 metres high, with stairways on all four sides and a bulky, flat-roofed temple at the top (see plate section, p.22). The entrance to the temple on the northern side is divided by two large columns in the form of feathered serpents, the open-jawed head of the snake at floor level, the body vertical and tail supporting the lintel of the doorway. To the east of the Castillo, about 100 metres away, stands the imposing Temple of the Warriors (see plate section, p.21). We have already seen the occasional use of columns incorporated into the architecture of cities such as Uxmal and Sayil. But here a whole forest of free-standing pillars leads from the south to the bottom of the temple stairway. A similar colonnade extends along the southern flank of the temple's supporting pyramid. From a distance they give this section of the site the look of a Hellenistic ruin. The columns are carved with repeated figures of warriors with curious 'pillbox' hats carrying spear-throwers, some with bunches of darts and the occasional club set with obsidian points. There are also images of what appear to be priests, a few of them women, bearing offerings and, close to the temple stairs, a group of prisoners. Their hands are bound together but they are standing and fully dressed, accorded some respect it would seem, in contrast to those stripped, humiliated captives found on the Classic period stelae in the south. Originally the pillars supported roofs of wooden beams covered with plaster, forming vast colonnaded halls. At the summit of the Temple of the Warriors a wide entrance is divided by two serpent columns, much like those of the Castillo, their feathered rattles once supporting an enormous wooden lintel. Here, at the entrance to the temple's outer chamber, lounges one of the famous Chacmools, a reclining human figure with a circular depression in the belly often conceived as a receptacle for sacrificial body parts. The head of this sinister sentinel is sharply turned to his left, staring grimly outwards across the enormous plaza.

In the direction of his gaze, at the far western end of the plaza, where the sun descends beneath the earth to face its nightly trials in the Underworld, lies the most unearthly of all Chichén Itzá's architectural complexes, the Great Ballcourt. One hundred and fifty metres in length and some thirty five metres wide, it is far and away the largest ballcourt known in the Maya area and an arena in which it seems almost inconceivable that the game could actually have been played, having more the feel of an enormous parade ground. The court has vertical sides, two rings carved with entwined snakes set high up into the walls and a series of stone reliefs at ground level which repeat almost identical scenes of ball-game sacrifice. Two groups of players confront each other, the leader of one team holding a flint knife in one hand and a decapitated head in the other (see below). The victim is on one knee opposite him. Streams of blood transforming into snakes' heads, one of them into a scrolling vine, gush out of his neck. Between the two figures appears a large ball, the outer skin encasing a ghoulishly smiling skull with a speech scroll emerging from between the teeth.

Overlooking the court at its south-eastern end, the Upper Temple of the Jaguars forms a grandiose viewing gallery, the entrance featuring further feathered serpent columns and more carvings of warriors. There were once fine murals here within the temple, including a series of battle-scenes commonly presumed to represent the successful wars waged by the people of Chichén Itzá. They are now all but gone,

Detail from the reliefs in the Great Ballcourt at Chichén Itzá

although a series of priceless copies were made by the English artist and traveller Adela Breton at the turn of the 20th century. Outside the ball-court, a short distance to the east, is a stone platform faced with repeating reliefs of stacked skulls pierced with poles, in imitation of a public skull-rack, known to the Aztecs as a *tzompantli*. Another platform close by bears friezes of jaguars and eagles devouring human hearts.

Although exaggerated by the lack of any forest cover – the mighty ruins of Tikal or El Mirador might create much the same impression bereft of the trees that surround them – the architecture of this part of central Chichén Itzá is overpowering and indeed quite intimidating compared with those structures conceived on a more human scale to the south. Combined with the brutal and seemingly alien sculptural imagery, the lack of hieroglyphic inscriptions or depictions of individual rulers, it all appears decidedly un-Maya.

This section of Chichén Itzá does however bear direct comparison with the architecture of Tula, over a thousand kilometres away just to the north of Mexico City. This was the home of the Toltecs, who created a sizeable empire in central Mexico between about 950 and 1150. Open, colonnaded structures, feathered serpent columns, Chac-mools, an apparent cult of warriors, of eagles and jaguars – all of these appear at Tula. The parallels between the two cities, first drawn by Desiré Charnay in the last century, are undeniable, thus it was that a very simple answer presented itself to explain the architectural peculiarities of Chichén Itzá. The 'Maya' buildings to the south, the part of the city which came to be termed 'Old Chichén', were earlier in date and repre-sented an initial native occupation. Then, around the turn of the eleventh century, the Toltecs invaded and brought with them their Mexican styles of architecture and fearsome ideology of war and sacrifice, displayed in so-called 'New Chichén' to the north.

Just as important, the legends of ancient Mexico transmitted via the Aztecs recommended the idea of an invasion. For they spoke of a Toltec king called Quetzalcoatl, or 'Feathered Serpent', who was said to have been forced out of Tula at around the end of the tenth century. He and his companions eventually sailed away to the east, where they were to establish a kingdom 'at the place of red earth'. From there Quetzalcoatl would one day return to exact his revenge, the story which Cortés famously manipulated to his advantage in conquering the Aztecs, who saw themselves as heirs to the Toltecs. What is more, the post-conquest native traditions of the Yucatán also spoke, somewhat vaguely, of the arrival at Chichén Itzá of a culture hero or great leader called 'Kukulcan', the Yucatec for 'Feathered Serpent'. When considered alongside the evidence of the architecture, it was only natural to presume that these stories must have had some basis in fact, reflecting real historical events.

However plausible and pleasing this solution may appear, it now seems that a Toltec invasion hypothesis of this kind cannot work. The most telling evidence to the contrary is provided by recently established chronologies for the architecture of the two cities. At Chichén Itzá the inscriptions in the Puuc-related buildings to the south are accompanied by dates that range from 832 to 881. But a key date has also been discovered upon a small monument from the great ballcourt, known as the Great Ballcourt Stone, which bears a much eroded scene very comparable in subject matter and style to the ballcourt panels discussed above. This date is 864, and it is now widely believed that the whole ballcourt complex must have been constructed at about this time. Furthermore, Carbon 14 dates and other archaeological evidence suggest that all the major buildings at the centre of the city, north and south, are roughly contemporaneous, spanning the period 800 to 950. In contrast, none of the major architecture at Tula was completed before the middle of the tenth century. Chichén Itzá was thus built first, and now of course the original hypothesis could be turned on its head, with Chichén in the role of donor rather than receiver. To many art historians this would be the more natural conclusion, since Tula's relatively unimpressive architecture seems little more than a 'provincial' copy of that of Chichén. Recent excavations at Chichén Itzá also indicate that the inhabitants of the city were Maya, who shared much the same indigenous forms of pottery and other aspects of material culture. Nothing has so far been encountered which would indicate any significant presence here of people from central Mexico.

With the general acceptance of the new time-frame for its construction and thus the elimination of the Toltecs from the equation, archaeologists have had to start all over again in addressing the major questions posed by Chichén Itzá. Who were the Maya who ruled here and, if it was not the Toltecs who brought it with them, how can the pronounced 'Mexican' influence in the city's architecture be accounted for? Archaeological investigations of the last few years demonstrate that the first settlement of Chichén Itzá of any consequence occurred around 650 to 700. Then, a century or so later, about 800, the population seems to have risen and a significant change is marked by the introduction of a pottery ware known as Sotuta, suggesting the arrival of new people. Over the next two centuries the city grew into a great metropolis, whose true extent is still imperfectly known. It covered at least 30 square kilometres and housed a population of many tens of thousands of people. Away from the centre were a series of secondary architectural complexes, each with its own cenote and arrangement of fine stone buildings, the houses of ordinary people scattered in between. These principal outlying groups, connected together by a remarkable network of *sacbes*, some seventy of which have so far been identified, may well represent the residential base of the powerful lineages who shared in the government of Chichén Itzá.

The inscriptions amongst the buildings to the south of the city centre help to explain how the political system at Chichén Itzá worked. They do not talk of dynastic rulers and their great deeds, as in previous centuries. Instead they mention a number of individuals, with names such as 'Kakupakal' or 'Kokom', in connection with the dedication of buildings and other ceremonies, often concerned with the maintenance of sacred fires and the drilling of 'new fire' on important occasions in the calendar. The glyph for sibling, *y-itah*, is used to describe the relationship between these people, suggesting rule by 'brothers'. Some may indeed have been related in this way and Diego de Landa also talks of the tradition of 'brothers' ruling at Chichén Itzá. But the phrase may best be interpreted to mean 'companions' or individuals each of roughly equivalent status. They are accorded the title *ahaw*, but significantly none is termed *k'ul ahaw* or supreme, 'divine lord'. What this would seem to represent is rule by council, by the heads of different lineages. At the time of the Spanish Conquest some small city states still used the term *multepal*, best rendered as 'group rule', to describe what was probably a very similar system. It may also be significant that the very centre of Chichén Itzá lacks any obvious stone-built 'palaces' or buildings that might have housed a ruling family. Likewise there are no stelae commemorating individual rulers and to date no identifiably 'royal' burials have been discovered. Thus the form of government here seems to have been quite different to that which had prevailed earlier in the south.

If Chichén Itzá was dominated by a council of lineage heads, where did these leading families come from? It is here that we must turn to the difficult matter of the Itzá, the people after whom the city is named.

They are clearly stated to have been the founders of Chichén Itzá by both Diego de Landa and the Books of Chilam Balam. They are described in the latter as 'foreigners' who only spoke the local Yucatec Mayan language 'brokenly' and, like the Xiu of Uxmal, they are said to have migrated from the south or south-west, in the Itzá case in two major waves, or so-called 'descents'. However, their more precise origins are not specified, nor is it possible, within the confusing framework of the 'Katun' histories, for scholars to be at all confident as to when these movements might have occurred. The Itzá were once equated with the Toltecs. Now they are most commonly interpreted as Putun Maya, those warrior-merchants from the Gulf Coast area, who are thought by many to have gradually established themselves in trading stations along the northern Yucatán coast and then to have headed inland to occupy Chichén Itzá.

More recently an alternative origin for the Itzá has been put forward, a very different reconstruction to previous theories. Linda Schele, Nikolai Grube and Erik Boot, in a reassessment of the Books of Chilam Balam and an attempt to tie them in with what is known of Late Classic history, propose that as early as 670 to 700 élite warriors and their followers, fleeing the increased intensity of wars between Tikal and Calakmul, were already moving north and may even have settled at Chichén Itzá by around 710.[19] They also speculate that these initial Itzá groups, the first wave or 'descent', may have been accompanied by refugee Mexican warrior castes from Teotihuacan, who were displaced after the fall of the great city in the second half of the seventh century. These early migrants settled down in northern Yucatán, amongst peoples with whom they may have had traditional connections of trade or even kinship, and were later joined by other refugees fleeing the Classic Collapse proper.

Furthermore, they suggest that it was Maya from the lakes region just to the south of Tikal, which had of course been the traditional Maya ally of Teotihuacan, who led the move north. They make a specific connection between the Itzá and and the site of Motul de San José, close to the northern shores of Lake Petén Itzá. Here Nikolai Grube has noted Classic period stelae that refer to the 'King of the Itzá' and the mention upon a looted ceramic vessel, believed to come from this region, of the child of an Itzá king.

The present name of the lake dates from the Colonial period, by which time the Itzá were undoubtedly living around its shores. These were the people whom Cortés came upon in 1525 when he visited their island capital of Tayasal, a Spanish corruption of 'Tah Itzá' or the 'place of the Itzá'. On subsequent occasions in the seventeenth century they told the Spaniards that their forebears had come from northern Yucatán not long before the Spanish conquest. This matches the accounts in the Books of Chilam Balam which say that the Itzá did indeed head south to the Petén, on a number of occasions it would seem, but most notably in the mid fifteenth century, a date supported by other sources and which was a time of political upheaval amongst the cities of the north. The new theories of Schele and her colleagues would of course put a whole new complexion on this fifteenth century migration. For in their view it was no flight to unfamiliar forests, but a homecoming. The Itzá had come full circle and finally returned to their roots by the lake.

Accounting for the anomalies of Chichén Itzá has proved a graveyard for a number of seductive hypotheses over the years and the proposition that the Itzá were refugees from the Petén, however compelling, still has to be more fully substantiated. Likewise, much work remains to be done at Chichén Itzá itself and on the still nebulous Putun before any more definitive answer emerges as to the Itzá's true identity. One might suggest however, that both groups of 'foreigners', southern lowland colonists and Putun Maya, each played a key role in the city's development. Chichén Itzá was above all a hybrid creation, a unique synthesis of different influences, both Maya and 'Mexican'. It has also become increasingly apparent that in its heyday in the tenth century Chichén was not only the most formidable power in the Maya world, but the largest and most renowned city in the whole of Mesoamerica. It is thus not unreasonable to imagine that its success may have been based on novel forms of co-operation between a number of different forces. Schele, Grube and other scholars such as David Freidel would contend that the Itzá newcomers from the south formed alliances with some of the existing major cities of the north-west such as Dzibilchaltún and Izamal. In due course, through force of arms, these alliances expanded and Chichén Itzá became the centre of a large confederacy which controlled most of northern Yucatán. Its only consistent opponents were the peoples to the east led by the city of Cobá. The form of alliance headed by Chichén Itzá was a very new political arrangement, a conscious attempt perhaps to break away from the old, failed system in the south of competing individual kingdoms headed by dynastic rulers. The ruling families of the confederacy, though they may have elected one nominal figurehead and perhaps a religious leader or high priest as well, met in session at Chichén Itzá in a more executive kind of 'Popol Na'. This might be seen as the successful achievement of that post-dynastic government by council that the nobility of Copán may have attempted to create on a smaller scale at very much the same time, though in the conditions of the southern Collapse it was doomed to failure.

The diversity of peoples involved in such a Chichén confederacy, both newcomers and natives of the area, would help to explain the varied forms of Maya architecture visible in the southern part of the city centre. In contrast, the major structures to the north might be seen to express the corporate, militaristic ethos of the confederate state as a whole. Thus the Temple of the Warriors has been interpreted as a symbolic seat of government, the carved pillars of the colonnaded halls at its base depicting ranks of warriors from the different cities of the alliance. Such military orders may indeed have massed in these halls and paraded through Chichén Itzá on ceremonial occasions to celebrate the successful wars that had created and sustained the conquest state. Rather than illustrating the victories of invading Toltecs over the local people of the region, as was once thought, it is these wars which are in all likelihood the subject matter of the murals in the Upper Temple of the Jaguars.[20]

In seeking to explain the 'foreign' influence in the architecture and iconography of Chichén Itzá we have to return to that broad picture of fragmentation and change throughout Mesoamerica between about 700 and 1000, the period immediately after the downfall of Teotihuacan and which then witnessed the collapse of the southern Maya cities. As we saw in Chapter 4, Teotihuacan had a unique place in the Mesoamerican psyche, as the first great imperial power in the region and above all as a place of origins, a cradle of human culture, recognised not just by the people of central Mexico but by the Maya as well. The eighth to tenth centuries proved to be much like the period after the fall of the Roman empire in the Old World, when political and religious systems throughout the region were in a state of flux and traditional boundaries came to mean very little. In these circumstances a number of cities emerged which, through the evidence of their art and architecture, seem to have been laying claims to the inheritance of Teotihuacan. These included Cacaxtla, Xochicalco, Cholula, eventually Tula in the Mexican highlands and Chichén Itzá itself. They all shared elements of what became for a short time a new kind of pan-Mesoamerican culture, where Maya influence is seen at Cacaxtla and Xochicalco and Mexican ideas and art styles at Chichén.

A central complex of images at these cities is that of the Feathered Serpent or Quetzalcoatl. The supernatural synthesis of serpent and bird dates back to the time of the Olmec. But the first, most famous manifestation appeared at Teotihuacan around 200 with the construction of the Temple of the Feathered Serpent, particularly associated it seems with warfare, human sacrifice and the birth of the calendar, by extension with creation itself. In a number of Mesoamerican religions, including that of the Maya, the Feathered Serpent was one of the leading creator gods, though the image of the deity is not prominent in Classic Maya art. In the ninth century however, some scholars see the worship of Quetzalcoatl emerging as a dynamic, revivified cult, a unifying divine force associated with the kind of political order emerging at Chichén Itzá and other cities – not that of the single dynastic ruler, but of the more anonymous power of the group, the very kind of warrior society first exemplified at Teotihuacan, where features such as military orders of jaguar and eagle knights, suggested at Chichén Itzá, originated. Much as Christianity and Islam were diffused along the trade routes of the Old World, so the cult of Quetzalcoatl may have been spread to different parts of Mesoamerica. It is here that the Putun Maya would enter the picture.

Directly north of Chichén Itzá, just off the coast, lies Isla Cerritos. On this small island the remains of an ancient sea wall have been discovered along with stone piers to which the canoes of merchants would have been tethered. Both 'Fine Orange' ceramics from the Gulf Coast, a trademark of the Putun, and the typical Sotuta pottery of Chichén Itzá have been found here. Isla Cerritos was the port that served Chichén Itzá and represented the city's major link with the wider world. Her trade relationships ranged far and wide across Mesoamerica. Amongst other commodities, Chichén received such precious things as green obsidian from central Mexico, jade from the Maya highlands and turquoise from what is now the southern USA. Copper and gold, found principally as offerings cast into the Sacred Cenote and much of it originating from Panama, Costa Rica and even Colombia, were arriving here from the ninth century onwards. If the Putun themselves were not the principal agents in the foundation of Chichén Itzá, at the very least they played a vital role as associates in the rise of the city and as both commercial middlemen and as cultural mediators, helping to transmit new ideas and images between northern Yucatán and central Mexico.

This traffic clearly worked both ways, though in a manner that is difficult to follow. In the case of Chichén Itzá and Tula there was a close trade connection. More than half the obsidian found at Chichén came from mines close to and controlled by the Toltec capital. As we have seen however, it would appear that, in cultural terms, Tula took from Chichén Itzá more than it gave. How then did Chichén itself come to generate such novel forms of architecture and iconography? One answer must be that it was in close contact with other Mexican cities before Tula's emergence. Many would also stress that much of the unusual architecture of Chichén Itzá has indigenous Maya precedents and that the traditions of Teotihuacan were for centuries a part of the Maya heritage. In earlier times the imagery of Tlaloc and the associated cult of war and sacrifice had been adopted by Tikal and other cities. The whole 'Tlaloc' complex, which included heavy sculptural use of skulls and other images of death, which would not look out of place at Chichén Itzá, reappeared, for example, at Copán in the time of Yax Pac in the late eighth century. This would indicate that, although dormant, the legacy of Teotihuacan lived on, to emerge at Chichén Itzá as a part of its own unique synthesis.[21]

The recent shift in perceptions of the Classic Maya also serves to make Chichén Itzá more understandable as a Maya creation. In a very different era it was thought by scholars such as Sylvanus Morley that people from the Southern Lowlands had indeed fled north at the time of the Collapse. There these peace-loving Maya refugees had been conquered by the warlike Toltecs. Now of course we know that war and sacrifice were as much second-nature to the Maya as they were to other peoples of Mesoamerica. So Chichén Itzá, however 'alien' it may still appear to most visitors, would seem to represent a unique though brief period in Maya history, when a single, cosmopolitan Maya city became the most potent political and religious force in the whole of Mesoamerica.

It was as a holy place, a centre of pilgrimage, that Chichén Itzá endured. Here the Castillo was to remain a key monument, as Diego de Landa observed. In age-old Maya fashion it is built upon nine terrace levels. It is also in essence a solar observatory which can be compared with those radial pyramids with four stairways constructed at Tikal and Uaxactún in much earlier centuries. The total number of steps, 91 on three sides and 92 to the north, equal the number of days in the solar year. The Castillo faces north and is joined by a broad sacbe to the main object of the Maya pilgrim's devotions, the Sacred Cenote.

Landa's descriptions of the sacrificial victims and treasures hurled into the Cenote prompted one of the last great self-taught pioneers of Maya archaeology, the American Edward Thompson, to probe its depths in the early years of the twentieth century. The US Consul for Yucatán and resident in the nearby Chichén hacienda, Thompson set up a derrick and dredge at the edge of the Cenote on its south side, 20 metres or so above the surface of the water. Remains of his machinery can still be seen around the site's 'visitor centre' today. He taught himself to dive, later hiring a professional Greek diver from the Bahamas sponge beds to help him, and between 1904 and 1908 painstakingly sifted through ton after ton of sludge from the bottom of the well. He found balls of 'pom' or copal incense, wooden 'idols' of the kind destroyed by Landa and the remains of 50 or so skeletons. The old tales of nubile virgins being the preferred subject for casting into the cenote were not borne out by analysis of the bones, which revealed that they were of all ages, both male and female, though there was a large proportion of juveniles. According to the traditional accounts, victims were dropped into the waters at dawn as potential vehicles for communication with the Underworld. If they survived until noon they were hauled out, bearing with them, perhaps, significant auguries from the supernatural. It may also have been believed that the surface of this impressive circular expanse of water, 50 metres or so across, acted as a giant mirror whose reflections were another aid to divination and prophecy. The array of precious objects that Thompson discovered included a large quantity of jade, notably some small masks and figurines, gold plaques, rings and discs, one with a scene of heart sacrifice, and such things as copper and bronze bells. The date that these offerings were made spans the whole period from the ninth to the sixteenth centuries.

But if the sacred power of the Cenote remained strong, the city-state of Chichén Itzá may have begun to decline soon after 1000. Still very little is known about how or why the city met its end. The Books of Chilam Balam talk of much political and inter-family intrigue among the Itzá and suggest that around 1220 it was attacked and defeated by the emerging city of Mayapan, one hundred kilometres to the west. There is now some archaeological evidence that this was indeed so, signs of destruction and the sudden appearance of ceramics of typical Mayapan form. The name of the lineage that ruled at Mayapan, Kokom, is mentioned in the inscriptions of Chichén Itzá. What seems to have occurred was a transfer of Itzá leadership from one city to the other, Mayapan now becoming the head of a similar kind of confederacy. Mayapan was a smaller city, completely surrounded by an impressive wall, seemingly a sign of the times, and the population of around 15,000 people was densely packed within. The architecture presents shoddily constructed, small-scale versions of that of Chichén Itzá, including colonnaded buildings and a small Castillo. Some sculpture was even taken from Chichén and incorporated within the fabric of the city.

For more than two centuries, in what appears to have been a period of increasing local conflict, Mayapan held its place as the dominant force in the western part of northern Yucatán. But the Chilam Balam Books say that an internal revolt within the confederacy, which led to the massacre of most of the leaders of the Kokom lineage, brought its violent destruction around 1440. It was then that large numbers of Itzá are said to have migrated south to the Petén. Thereafter most of the larger cities in the north declined and the region broke up into a series of sixteen or so independent states, those smaller-scale units that throughout their history seem to have been the most comfortable political system for the Maya.

On the western side of the peninsula the violence and competition appear to have continued. But to the north-east, along the mainland and on the island of Cozumel, the closing century or so before the Spanish conquest was a time of tremendous growth and prosperity when towns and small cities sprang up along the coasts, all linked into those trade networks, organized still by the Putun but dominated now by the new imperial power of the Aztecs. One of these was Tulum, perched on its rocky headland overlooking the Caribbean and with a pretty beach immediately to the north where the canoes of traders would have been paddled in through a break in the offshore reef to unload and display their cargoes. The Tulum 'Castillo', its back directly facing the sea, and the other tiny temples and colonnaded palaces here, enclosed within a neatly rectangular perimeter wall, have a unique charm. The architecture is eccentrically higgledy-piggledy and of no great aesthetic merit, although the interiors of some buildings still preserve sections of fine murals whose style compares with that of the Postclassic codices. Rather than 'decadent' or in decline however, most archaeologists today approach these ruins as those of a society which had simply acquired different priorities. The old concern with great public monuments, temples and ballcourts, with cults of war and sacrifice had evidently gone. The Maya here seem to have re-invented themselves once more, though this particular experiment in what seems to have been a more decentralized society, bent on making a commercial profit rather than war, had only a little time to last before Spanish sails appeared over the Caribbean horizon.

CHAPTER EIGHT

Conquest and Survival

Then with the true God, the true Dios, came the beginning of our misery. It was the beginning of tribute, the beginning of church dues, the beginning of strife with purse-snatching, the beginning of strife with blow-guns, the beginning of strife by trampling on people, the beginning of robbery with violence, the beginning of debts enforced by false testimony, the beginning of individual strife ... This was the origin of service to the Spaniards and priests, of service to local chiefs, of service to the teachers, of service to the public prosecutor, by the boys, the youths, of the town, while the poor people were oppressed.[1]

Thus the Book of Chilam Balam of Chumayel catalogues Maya suffering as it began in a Katun 11 Ahaw, the period between 1539 and 1559 in the Gregorian calendar, the years of the final subjection of northern Yucatán and the establishment of the new regime of the conquistadores.

Troubles for the Maya did not, of course, originate with the Spanish conquest. Over many centuries they had experienced bloody wars, natural disasters and migrations from their homelands. But, like the Hero Twins of myth who always managed to outwit the Lords of Death and survive the trials put in their way, Maya peoples adjusted in the face of upheaval and misfortune. At the end of the Preclassic period and again during the ninth century, at the time of the Classic Collapse, Maya civilization emerged changed but afresh from low points in the cycles of time.

In the sixteenth century however, an era of unparalleled and irreversible catastrophe came around. The sheer scale of mortality and human tragedy is still extremely hard to come to terms with. Diseases such as smallpox, measles and typhus swept through Maya communities. In the northern Yucatán alone at least half a million are thought to have died between 1520 and 1547. Statistics such as these have been translated into an overall population loss across the Maya region of some eighty percent by the turn of the following century. As occurred throughout the Americas, epidemics often spread with such speed that they far outstripped the advances of the Spaniards. The survivors of the unheralded holocaust were left demoralized and uncomprehending. And when the Spaniards appeared, they brought with them a new kind of warfare. The technology employed – crossbows, firearms, horses and vicious packs of hunting dogs – though terrifying enough, was of lesser significance than the ideology of all-out conquest war the Europeans introduced, where there were few rules, captive-taking was an encumbrance to be avoided rather than a religious obligation and terror tactics and destruction the norm. If the foreigners brought disease and war, they then proceeded, not simply to impose tribute as victors had done before, but to assault the very foundations of Maya society by seeking out and destroying the old gods and sacred knowledge that had been accumulated over the centuries.

The initial shock of conquest clearly brought a profound psychological crisis, a search for explanation. To Maya minds such terrible events should in some way have been signposted in the past. Calendar priests and writers of prophecy were thus bound to convince themselves either that they had foreseen the arrival of the Spaniards, as the original Chilam Balam or 'Jaguar Prophet' is supposed to have done, or, at the very least, that the signs had been there if only they had been able to read them. The manner in which the coming of the Spanish was incorporated within native histories seems to reveal something of the rationalisation that went on after the event. For example, in many instances in the Books of Chilam Balam there is a degree of ambiguity about the groups of historical 'foreigners' that are being referred to, as in this now famous passage: 'There was then no sickness; they had then no aching bones; they had then no harsh fever; they had then no smallpox; they had then no burning chest... At that time the course of humanity was orderly. The foreigners made it otherwise when they arrived here. They brought shameful things when they came.'[2]

These lines are naturally interpreted as an account of the pestilence unleashed upon the Yucatán Maya by the Spaniards. Yet they appear in a context where it is clearly the Itzá to whom reference is being made. But what may seem a confusion to us reflects the natural mode of thought to the Maya, who always sought out recurrence, repeating patterns in the past, both to explain the present and predict the future. In their search for precedent, the nearest equivalent they found to the

Spanish conquest – the appearance of outsiders and the disruption and suffering they caused – was the arrival of the Itzá in northern Yucatán many centuries before. Significantly, they associated this with an earlier Katun 11 Ahaw. Bracketing the European conquest with other historical events with which they were familiar, lodging it within their own structure of experience in this way, must have offered a kind of solace, helping them to face the terrible eventuality on something like their own terms and feel assured that the world had not spun completely out of control. And ultimately, once the conquest was positioned within the traditional, cyclical vision of history, there was always the hope that a future era would bring a reversal of fortunes and that the new arrivals might be defeated or return whence they had come.

The Spaniards did not go away of course, they were not to be defeated. But neither were the Maya, who, over the last five hundred years, have shown an astonishing capacity for survival. Today they may be long gone from their ancient cities, but they continue to live in the land of their ancestors and to worship amongst the old sacred places. Some Central American governments have in the past been reluctant to admit to the true numbers of indigenous people in their midst. Historians and sociologists have found census data hard to come by and often manifestly inaccurate when available. But a realistic present estimate would be of some seven to eight million speakers of Maya languages spread across the countries of the region, concentrated in northern Yucatán, the highlands of Chiapas and above all in Guatemala, where the Maya constitute more than half the country's population.[3] Infinitely resilient and adaptable, they have faced bloody repression, systematic assaults on their culture, the loss of ancestral lands and marginalization within modern nation-states dominated by elites of European origin. They have endured through a combination of outright resistance, flight to remote parts and subtle accommodation with their conquerors.

THE EARLY YEARS OF CONQUEST

In the Maya highlands concerted opposition to the Spaniards was to be brief, put down with great violence and loss of life by Pedro de Alvarado, whose reputation as the most pitiless and bloodthirsty of all New Spain's conquistadores, though inflated by the 'Black Legend' of

Spanish atrocities in the New World, seems well enough deserved and was even recognized by his compatriots. Cortés sent him to begin the subjection of the region in 1523. Backed up by a force of Mexican allies, Alvarado travelled through Soconusco above the Pacific coast and then up into the heart of the Guatemalan mountains. The most powerful kingdom here was that of the Quiché, their capital at Utatlan, just outside modern Santa Cruz del Quiché. Half a century previously their power had been challenged by the Cakchiquel to the south-east. Both were in diplomatic contact with the Aztecs, who in 1520 had warned the Quiché of the arrival of the Spaniards. For their part, the Cakchiquel evidently thought that by aligning themselves with the foreigners they might secure dominance over their rivals. They duly sent a delegation to Cortés to assure him of their friendship and support. This fatal division played into the hands of Alvarado, who in early 1524 met the Quiché armies on a great plain near present-day Quetzaltenango, an unusually favourable venue where Spanish horsemen could operate to advantage. In Maya tradition the tragic climax of this confrontation was a personal duel to the death between Alvarado and a Quiché warrior-leader called Tecun Uman, who appeared in battle magically transformed into a combination of eagle and quetzal. Although the Maya hero managed to down Alvarado's horse and flew up, it is said, to strike at the Spaniard, Alvarado pierced Tecun Uman through with a lance. With this fateful act Quiché resistance came to an end and today the drama has come to mark the symbolic defeat of all highland Guatemalan Maya, regularly reproduced in the 'Dance of the Conquest', a pageant performed in many highland towns.

The Spanish accounts talk of no such encounter, merely of the killing done by their men and the submission of the Quiché. After the battle Alvarado and his followers rode on to Utatlan where, informed of treachery and possible ambush, they retreated swiftly from the outskirts of the town. Then, with decisive brutality, Alvarado burnt to death two captured Quiché leaders and in due course massacred the remaining inhabitants of the city and razed it to the ground. Subjection of most of the highlands followed swiftly. The Tzutujil around Lake Atitlan were defeated with Cakchiquel help and by July 1524 Alvarado had established the first Spanish capital in the region, which he did simply by occupying and renaming the Cakchiquel city of Iximché as 'Santiago of the Knights of Guatemala'. This action, followed it seems by intolerable demands for gold, labour and other abuses, led to belated disillusionment among the Cakchiquel and to widespread revolts in the following few years. But from the 1530s onwards, barring isolated uprisings which occurred well into the nineteenth century, the highlands were to be permanently under Spanish control.

In northern Yucatán, at the beginning of the sixteenth century, Maya towns and cities were at odds with each other much as they were in the highlands. Epidemics began to spread through the peninsula as soon as the Spaniards set foot on Maya soil and when, after a pause to regroup and consider their tactics, the Montejos began a more systematic conquest in the 1540s, it was inevitable that the Spaniards would establish themselves as the new lords of the land. But, for a very long time, they were lords of only a part of the land.

By 1550 about a third of the Yucatán peninsula had been conquered – the very north and sections of the coastlines. The Spanish capital of Mérida lay in the north-west and three other towns, which fast acquired their church, town hall and residences built around the familiar Spanish plaza, were established as administrative centres. These were Campeche on the Gulf Coast, Valladolid in the middle of the peninsula east of Chichén Itzá and, in what is now southern Quintana Roo, the remote outpost of Salamanca de Bacalar. The number of Europeans in Yucatán at this time amounted to little more than 1500 people. Few were tempted to this unrewarding part of the Spanish empire and the figure increased only slowly. At first they were protected by Mexican auxiliaries who had borne much of the brunt of the conquest and were settled in their own quarters of the towns. For, despite the terrible decline in the native population, Maya still of course vastly outnumbered the Spaniards. They lived in their own traditional communities, many reduced to ghost towns by now, dotted amongst the dry, stunted bush between the isolated strongholds of foreign occupation.

The economic system imposed by the Spaniards, based on established pre-Hispanic practice, was that of tribute payment or the *encomienda*. The Spaniard, the *encomendero*, received a grant, not of land but of the labour of native people, who were obliged at appointed times to deliver commodities such as cotton, maize, honey, salt, turkeys and later, once they had become established, European crops and livestock. The second instrument of exploitation, again possessing convenient ancient precedent, though previously undertaken, one imagines, in a very different spirit, was the *repartimiento*. This amounted to forced labour to construct the roads, churches and town houses that the foreigners required. Much of the time, as in Mérida, and later in the construction of Landa's monastery at Izamal, it involved dismantling original Maya buildings and reusing the masonry in the fabric of the new Spanish establishment. The only obligation of the *encomendero* was to ensure the spreading of the gospel amongst the heathen allotted to him. At the time of Landa's purges and burnings of books in 1562, this became an oppressive burden and affront to Maya communities – the rooting out and suppression of every conceivable manifestation of idolatrous practice.

As in any form of foreign occupation, relations between Spaniards and Maya were complex. For Maya leaders on the north-western side of the peninsula around Mérida there was little option but to collaborate. Old ruling families such as the Xiu threw in their lot enthusiastically with the new regime and it was they who ensured the delivery of tribute. But in other parts many groups remained recalcitrant. And there was always the alternative of flight. To the south beyond the Puuc hills lay a vast area of jungle wilderness that was outside Spanish control. Here refugees from the oppression of the *encomiendas*, often led by charismatic native priests, established their own communities where they could worship the old gods in peace and dream of rebellion. Even if the chances of any effective resistance were slim, such hostile, fugitive settlements drained away tribute payers and labour and posed a constant threat. In 1546 there had been a last bout of resistance in the north-east and down towards Salamanca de Bacalar. Many Spaniards and their families had been slaughtered on their *encomienda* lands. The revolt was crushed, but it made the Spanish jumpy, in dread of insurrection and of being murdered in their beds. The Maya played on these fears. They possessed intelligence networks communicating between the runaway groups and their home communities. Prophecies of rebellion and rumours of Maya retribution would emanate from the rebel headquarters to the south and could quickly spread panic. In turn, the Spanish developed their own system of spies and informers. Occasionally there would be strikes into the forests to crush rebel settlements. Leaders would be executed, their followers dragged back to the *encomiendas* and hauls of idols destroyed. But often most of the fugitives merely retreated deeper into the bush.

THE LAST CITY

On its own, such irritation on the periphery of Hispanicized Yucatán might have been supportable. But much further to the south, amongst the now re-established tropical forests of the Petén, there lay a mysterious remnant of Maya civilization. This was Tayasal, island capital of the Itzá and centre of the last free Maya state, whose extraordinary history has now been documented in impressive detail by Grant Jones. [4] When Cortés and his entourage passed through here in 1525, they did not stay long. With a few companions, Cortés crossed Lake Petén Itzá to the city, though there is little surviving description of what they saw. Their accounts do reveal however that distributed around the lake, and smaller ones to the east and west, there was a sizeable number of towns and smaller settlements. It also became evident that Tayasal exercised control over a broad region to the east that included much of what is now southern Belize. The Itzá ruler Kan Ek spoke proudly of his cacao plantations at the foot of the Maya mountains. Continuing their journey in that direction, the Spaniards left behind bibles and other devotional material, since Kan Ek had supposedly vowed to give up his idols. Most famously, Cortés also left behind his sick horse. Six of the party remained at Tayasal, including three Spaniards who were unable, so it was said, to put up with further hardship. Nothing is known of the fate of these individuals, Jones notes, though they must have proved a useful source of information about the foreigners.[5] As to future intelligence of the progress of Spanish conquests, their trade connections with both the lower Usumacinta and the Gulf of Honduras, supplemented by reports from the north, would have kept the Itzá well informed of the way in which, beyond the forests that protected them, the old Maya world was crumbling.

For their part, aside from rumour and second-hand accounts through Maya informants, the Spanish probably knew very little about what was going on in Tayasal. Cortés never returned and it was to be almost a century before direct contact was made again. During these years the distant jungle kingdom thus took on mythical proportions as a land of fierce warriors, a bastion of idolatory and satanic practices such as human sacrifice, and as inspiration and place of ultimate retreat for any rebellious faction further north. The authorities in Mérida came to recognize that somehow Tayasal had to be dealt with.

By the end of the sixteenth century the Spaniards had established themselves in greater force around Salamanca de Bacalar in the east. From there, in a southerly direction, there ran a string of lonely mission stations. The most distant was Tipu, in what is now central Belize, close to the present border with Guatemala and less than one hundred kilometres due east of Lake Petén Itzá. Tipu became the launch pad for attempts to treat with Tayasal. The first direct overture was made in 1617 and seemed initially to have been enormously successful. A Franciscan called Juan de Orbita travelled with another friar to Tayasal. They met with Kan Ek (Tayasal's rulers were all called Kan Ek or 'Serpent Star') and apparently persuaded him that it was time to submit to Spanish rule. Indeed, they returned all the way to Mérida with 150 of Tayasal's inhabitants, some of whom, before they headed back home, were formally appointed as Indian officials by the Spanish authorities. Then, the following year, Orbita set off once more to Tayasal from Tipu, this time with another Franciscan called Bartolomé de Fuensalida. Significantly, 1618 was the beginning of a new *katun*, a Katun 3 Ahaw. The clear object seems to have been to further encourage Kan Ek and convince him that the prophecies for this *katun* were favourable for an accommodation with Spain.

However, negotiating through the prophecies was not to be so simple. Most Spanish accounts give the impression that Tayasal and the region that surrounded it was governed by a single ruler, from a line of Kan Eks. The political system was in fact much more complicated. Tayasal, the island in the lake, modern Flores, was the capital and religious centre of a confederacy. The overall territory that it dominated, some forty by twenty kilometres, was made up of four provinces that were distributed according to the cardinal directions, with Tayasal at its very centre. Each province had two rulers, one of whom resided most of the time at Tayasal. The city itself appears to have been divided into four quarters, with the holiest temples in the middle at the highest point of the island. Thus, in age-old fashion, political organization and the layout of the capital mirrored the quadripartite structure of the cosmos. If there were two rulers of each province, dual rule also operated at the centre, where presided the *ahaw* Kan Ek, whom the Spaniards related to as the 'king' of Tayasal, and a second more shadowy individual, the *ah k'in* Kan Ek, who appears to have been the high priest. It is clear now that although the *ahaw* Kan Ek was the political frontman or spokesman, he did not act alone. He represented a council of local rulers, very probably the same kind of government that had prevailed among the Itzá centuries before at Chichén Itzá and Mayapan.

There had evidently been deliberations at Tayasal since Orbita's previous visit. The response now was not a favourable one. Soon after their arrival, Fuensalida gave an expansive sermon on the gospel and the benefits of conversion to the true faith. But the friars were then told: 'that it was not time to be Christians [they had their own beliefs as to what that time should be] and that they should go back where they had come from; they could come back another time, but right then they did not want to be Christians.'[6] As a break in proceedings, the two Spaniards were taken on a tour of the island, which is roughly circular and of no great size, some four hundred metres across at its widest point. Today it is completely covered in more modern houses, restaurants, hotels and cobbled streets. Nothing ancient remains, though the sum of seventeenth century descriptions confirms that in those days too it was densely crowded with buildings. Plastered with lime, they shone brilliantly white and were visible for many miles around.[7] Fuensalida counted about two hundred more ordinary dwelling places clustered together close to the shore line. Passing through these, they climbed to the more prestigious buildings and the principal temples, about a dozen of them, 'where they keep the idols and are brought together for their dances and their inebrieties, which take place whenever they have to idolatrize or make some sacrifice.'[8] It was in this central part of the city, where Flores' main plaza, church and a large ballcourt, for basketball, are to be found, that they entered one temple and made a singularly bizarre discovery. They were confronted, not by images of the gods of maize or rain, but by the large statue of a horse. It was nothing less than a life-size replica of the lame animal that Cortés had left behind a century before. Many colourful legends surround the story of Cortés' horse, and different versions are still to be heard in communities around the shores of the lake today. In the village of San José, where live the very last surviving speakers of Itzá Mayan, they say that another statue toppled off a canoe and still lurks somewhere beneath the waters. There is no doubt that Cortés did leave his horse here. He says so himself. The most popular, if not the most authoritative Spanish story, which tends to inflate the simple credulity of the Itzá, relates that the people of Tayasal dutifully tried to care for it. They fed it turkey and bunches of flowers and, not surprisingly, it soon died. The statue was then fashioned in its honour and placed in the temple, where it came to be venerated as a manifestation of the rain god Chak, known as 'Tzimin

Chak' or 'Horse of Thunder and Lightning'.

Whatever the true circumstances behind its creation, the effigy stood in the temple, an important object of worship to the Itzá, until it met the inflexible gaze of Juan de Orbita. It is said that he flew into a rage, jumped up on to the statue and attempted to smash it to pieces with a rock. Such behaviour must have been a serious affront to local people and would not have rendered the Itzá any more receptive to the idea of Christian conversion. Indeed, before the two friars returned to Tipu, Kan Ek confirmed that, 'the time had not arrived in which their ancient priests had prophecied they would need to give up the worship of their gods, for the present age was one called *ox ahaw* [which means 'third age'] and the one that he had indicated to them was not arriving so soon.'[9] The following year Orbita and Fuensalida returned once more to Tayasal. Kan Ek himself remained conciliatory and even agreed to the erection of a cross outside his house. But his wife and other anti-Spanish factions were firmly against any more negotiations. The friars were escorted away from Tayasal by a party of warriors and told never to return.

Any hope that the Itzá might submit peacefully was gone and their intent was clearly demonstrated in 1624, when a party of Spanish soldiers accompanied by friendly Maya reinforcements from the north, who seem to have been on a freelance mission to 'pacify' the Tayasal region, were attacked by rebels while in church at a mission not far from Salamanca de Bacalar. A number of Spaniards were hanged and their leader was sacrificed. Other members of this party, led by a priest called Diego Delgado, had already gone ahead and in due course arrived at Tayasal. There his escort of twelve Spanish soldiers were killed, eighty Maya from Tipu were massacred and Delgado himself had his heart torn out and offered to the idols. Very soon rumours of insurrection and threats to Christianized Maya spread around Tipu and the other mission towns of Belize. Settlements were deserted as whole communities fled into the forests. Armed revolt and destruction consumed the region and for many years Spanish control of the area south of Salamanca de Bacalar was lost. By mid-century Tipu was directly controlled by the Itzá, whose policy now seems to have been to strengthen their isolation by creating a large buffer zone between themselves and the Spaniards.

For decades there was a stand-off, until in 1695 Martín de Ursua, the new Spanish Governor of Yucatán, decided upon more ambitious tactics, ordering the construction of a road, the prelude to invasion, straight through the forest between Mérida and Lake Petén Itzá. As it edged closer to the lake the pressure on Tayasal began to tell. In December of that year the nephew of the latest Kan Ek travelled to Mérida with an offer of submission and a request for priests to begin the process of conversion. At the very same time another Franciscan, called Andrés de Avendaño, headed for Tayasal, the first such visit since the ill-fated expedition of 1624. He and three other friars followed the newly-cleared road as far as it went, and were then guided the remaining hundred kilometres through the forest to the lakeside community of Chakan, close to modern San José. There they waited while their arrival was announced on the island.

There is an extraordinary romance today in the intrepid treks of the seventeenth-century friars, travelling back in time to the last living Maya city in the midst of the jungle. Avendaño seems to have had his own sense of this and of his dramatic role in great events, apparent in the vivid but markedly self-promoting description of the expedition that he wrote soon after his return. He was an unusual, gifted man, who spoke Yucatec Mayan fluently and, by his own account and that of his contemporaries, was extremely well-versed in the *katun* prophecies. Orbita and Fuensalida had been told to go away by the Itzá and come back some other day, 'for the time had not arrived'. But when would it arrive? Avendaño knew better than anyone that it was coming very soon. For in 1697 began a Katun 8 Ahaw, a truly portentous epoch which resonated throughout Itzá history as a time of trouble and upheaval. 'This was always the *katun*,' as the Chilam Balam Books put it, 'when the Itzá went beneath the trees, beneath the bushes, beneath the vines, to their misfortune.'[10] Way back in the past the original migration before arriving at Chichén Itzá was said to have occurred in a Katun 8 Ahaw. Their expulsion from Chichén Itzá was placed in the same calendrical era and so too their departure from Mayapan and movement south to Lake Petén Itzá. This latter migration had happened in the Katun 8 Ahaw of the previous cycle, some 256 years before the one that was fast approaching. Thus it was that Avendaño saw himself on a journey into the superstitious minds of the Itzá, and although offers of submission had proved worthless before, he convinced Governor Ursua that this time he could persuade the people of Tayasal to do what their prophecies told them.

Waiting on the shore at Chakan the friars eventually saw eighty canoes coming towards them, filled with painted and tattooed warriors. Kan Ek and some five hundred Indians disembarked. After preliminary speeches and protestations of friendship they set off for Tayasal. Avendaño says that he and the king became close friends. Kan Ek was constantly at Avendaño's side as they met with delegations from the different provinces of the kingdom. The Spaniard spoke to them, 'frequently and pleasantly, discoursing with them in their ancient idiom as if the time had already come (just as their prophets had foretold) for our eating together from one plate and drinking from one cup – we the Spaniards making ourselves one with them.'[11]

Avendaño displayed his intimate knowledge of Maya culture to his Itzá audience and, in professorial manner, he went through the prophecies with them, 'to find out what age the present one was (since for them one age consists only of twenty years) and what prophecy there was about the said year and age, for it is all recorded in certain books of a quarter of a yard high and about five fingers broad, made of the bark of trees, folded from one side to the other like screens … These are painted on both sides with a variety of figures and characters …' The Itzá, Avendaño says, were amazed at his familiarity with the ancient writing and his account suggests that he had already seen hieroglyphic books in the northern Yucatán, which must have escaped the purges of earlier years. In fact, Avendaño wrote a treatise on the calendar and Maya hieroglyphic writing, which was well known in his own time but which is now lost. Scholars today agree that, had it survived (there is the very remote possibility that it still might do in some neglected archive) Avendaño's work would have been of vastly greater value to decipherment than Landa's Relación.

The idea of Avendaño poring over codices with the Itzá at Tayasal introduces an intriguing discovery recently made by Michael Coe.[13] Looking closely at the Madrid Codex, he noticed that European paper had been incorporated into its first and last leaves, not as a repair but as part of the original manufacture of the book. Upon this paper there appear traces of Spanish writing, in a seventeenth-century hand. The Itzá had access enough to European texts, religious writings left behind for their use and other materials captured from Spaniards. Thus there seems a very good chance that the Madrid Codex was composed at Tayasal, the only place where the ancient tradition would have been maintained, at some point between the 1620s and 1697. It is as yet unknown how the book eventually found its way to Madrid. If produced at Tayasal, it could even have reached there through Avendaño's own hands.

Avendaño sermonized to the Itzá and baptized three hundred children, but he was to confront the same problems as Orbita and Fuensalida – divisions amongst the local leadership. Beneath all the talk of prophecies, as Jones demonstrates, different parties had distinct political agendas, including Avendaño. He had come to ensure that the Itzá gave up peacefully before any military confrontation, but he was also very concerned that the Franciscans, rather than the secular clergy, gain the prize of evangelizing them. Hence his hasty departure for Tayasal as soon as he heard of the Itzá mission to Mérida. Kan Ek, for his part, appears to have been keen to do a deal and ensure that he continued in place as ruler under Spanish domination. It appears that he had sent his nephew to Mérida without the knowledge of the rest of the Itzá council. Once the other leaders of the confederacy realised this the situation became extremely volatile. Avendaño recognized these divisions and says that Kan Ek had enemies, but he writes as if he did not fully understand, tending to attribute the local hostilities to the machinations of Satan, bent on thwarting his mission. Jones describes an extraordinary symbolic moment, revealing a degree of insensitivity and diplomatic bungling on Avendaño's part which today seems hard to credit.[14] For he had brought the king a suit of Spanish clothing, complete with colonial style hat and staff of office. Kan Ek appeared in this ridiculous outfit in front of the people of Tayasal. It was the kind of dress worn in northern Yucatán by Maya leaders subject to the Spanish crown. There could have been no clearer sign that Kan Ek had 'sold out' to the foreigners.

Avendaño had been at Tayasal for less than a week when hostility towards him threatened to turn violent. Kan Ek saw to his escape across the lake by night, the beginning of a terrible journey on foot through the jungle where he and his companions wandered lost and starving for days. At one point, struggling through a hilly stretch of country, he came upon buildings, some vaulted and in the form of cloisters and others that, 'though they were very high and my strength was little, I climbed up them...'[15] It seems quite possible that Avendaño was the first European to set eyes on Tikal. Finally they stumbled upon the road from Mérida. Avendaño took a long time to recover from his ordeal and never visited Tayasal again.

In some accounts of the end of Tayasal it is presumed that, with the approach of the fateful Katun 8 Ahaw, the very last Maya city-state gave up without a fight. This is the vision of the Maya as tragic victims, resigned to their fate, the prisoners of their prophecies. This was how Avendaño wanted to see it, how he felt these simple people should be behaving. But, not for the last time, an outsider had underestimated the subtleties of Maya thought and the degree of more practical reasoning that dictated their behaviour. Ironically, if Avendaño put so much faith in the Maya prophecies it was no doubt in part because he came from his very own, European prophetic tradition. The Franciscans saw themselves as the tools of Divine Providence, the religious order chosen to lead all the remote heathen to God before the Second Coming. If anyone was the prisoner of prophecy in this encounter it was not the Itzá but Avendaño.

As Grant Jones' study makes clear, the true story of the fall of Tayasal was a more complex, messy affair. The importance of prophecy cannot be discounted, but its role is in fact very hard to define. Although the Itzá had every reason to be fatalistic, they were in no sense supine. As had been the case at the time of Orbita and Fuensalida's visit, the prophecies were evidently viewed, even such portentous ones as those for the Katun 8 Ahaw, as matters of interpretation, to be discussed alongside other questions of policy. If anything, it seems that hard political bargaining positions were expressed in prophetic terms, rather than those positions being determined by prophecy. The great difference now, however, was that prophecy could no longer be used as a delaying tactic, to persuade the Spaniards to come back another time. Decisions had to be made, and in the end most of the Itzá decided to resist.

The conclusion was thus a military one. The road to the lake was finished, the Spaniards built a galley on the shore and then, after Ursua had made some last efforts at negotiation, the island capital was stormed and its inhabitants fled. Thus ended the last, still intact bastion of indigenous opposition to the Spaniards. And, if some recent interpretations are to be accepted, the Itzá represented an unbroken succession from the Classic period civilization of this region, the very heart of the ancient Maya world. The result of the conquest was painful for both Itzá and the Spaniards. For the Itzá the prophecies were of course fulfilled, for many of them fled once more, 'beneath the bushes, beneath the vines', into the forests. For the Spaniards there was conflict between Yucatán and Guatemala over jurisdiction in the area, and those who had to garrison Tayasal found it a terrible posting. There were intermittent Itzá raids and the region was not truly pacified for a decade or so. Disease struck, affecting the Itzá most terribly but the Spanish as well. By the mid-eighteenth century very few were living around the lake and it was not to be developed until cattle ranching slowly began here in the middle of the nineteenth century.

Kan Ek and one of his sons were amongst the few who survived the fighting and the epidemics. They were taken to Santiago de Guatemala (now Antigua) and there in 1700 were baptized in the city's cathedral as Joseph Pablo and Francisco. They became a familiar sight on the streets of the city, Jones relates, and were living in a boarding house with a few other Itzá in 1704. What happened to them after that is unknown, but it is curious to reflect that the very last readers of hieroglyphs and bearers of centuries-old Maya knowledge were rubbing shoulders with Europeans only a few decades before Palenque saw the arrival of the first 'archaeologists', who, eager for explanations but finding none to hand, came away with their notions of ancient colonization by Romans or 'Hindoos'.

THE CASTE WAR AND THE SPEAKING CROSS

The spirit of Maya resistance was not broken by the fall of Tayasal. But it was subdued for many generations. Bands of refugees, some of them the ancestors of the modern Lacandón, continued to roam the forests of the Southern Lowlands, the tenor of their stone age lives little different to that of their Preclassic ancestors more than two thousand years before.

In the north the *encomienda* system gradually evolved into what many historians now regard as a relatively comfortable relationship, compared to what came after it, between the descendants of the conquistadores and their subjects. The old Maya ruling families were left considerable autonomy as the agents of indirect rule and a sizeable educated Maya class emerged who collected tribute, were the judicial authorities within their communities and filled most of the posts in the local church hierarchy, acting as scribes and *maestros cantores*, literally 'choirmasters' but who supervised most church activities and, though formally barred from the priesthood, on occasion performed the sacraments. The role that these *maestros cantores* played was a subtle one and of great significance. Firstly, it enabled the Maya elite to maintain their traditional status in the eyes of their own people through a degree of spiritual leadership, which in Maya society had always been indivisible from political authority. This helped to maintain the social cohesion of local communities. But this spiritual function was crucial in another sense. After the early years of zealotry of Landa and his colleagues, Spanish priests learnt to be more tolerant in the way they sought to impart the Christian message. For the Maya did not reject Catholicism outright. It was not in the extremely fluid nature of their religion to do this. The Spanish conquest had proved the power of the Christian god and the saints that represented him. They thus sought to embrace Catholicism in their own way, much as they had adopted other foreign deities such as Tlaloc or Quetzalcoatl in Prehispanic times. The *maestro cantor* served as a crucial link in interpreting the new messages in terms both that the church hierarchy would approve of and that their own communities could understand and accept. What this came to mean was an acceptance all round that beneath new forms of worship and the symbols of crosses and saints, the essentials of many native beliefs lingered on. Today this kind of syncretism is most evident in the highlands of Guatemala, where the *cofradías* or religious brotherhoods, instituted by the Spanish in early colonial times, have charge of the images of particular saints, many of whom have acquired identities and powers that the Catholic church would not originally have intended. Carried in procession on feast days, it is easy to imagine them as the god images paraded on litters around ancient Maya cities. Significantly, a blend of belief systems also comes across in the Chilam Balam books, with their often eccentric mixture of traditional lore and references to the scriptures. It seems very likely that many of them were indeed written by *maestros cantores*, men of religious knowledge in between two worlds.[16]

As the *encomienda* endured, so life in the countryside changed, in essence, very little. New technologies had of course been introduced – machetes, iron and steel tools and European crops and animals – to the Maya's benefit, but families continued to be subsistence farmers cultivating land that pertained to local lineages, much as they had done before the conquest. And, something that the Spanish empire is often not given credit for, there were laws in place by the seventeenth century to keep such community lands inalienable and to protect Maya people from the worst kinds of abuses. It would be quite wrong to paint the colonial period in Yucatán as one of unalloyed contentment for the Maya. They were a subject people paying tribute to alien masters. But the essentials of traditional society, their land, sense of community, a degree of self-government, and to some extent their religious beliefs, remained intact.

The achievement of independence from Spain in 1821 changed all this. For the Maya, it was no independence at all. Far from it. With the mediatory presence of the Spanish crown removed, they were effectively abandoned to their fate at the hands of the only true beneficiaries, the local Hispanic elite. The main administrative alteration, already begun under the Bourbon kings, was the replacement of the old native authorities by *mestizos* or mixed bloods, whose allegiance was solely to the governing hierarchy and who were thereby accepted as 'Ladinos', the term used to refer to both whites and anyone else who was considered not to be culturally Maya. But, the most radical transformation that came after Independence was in agriculture and the system of land tenure, particularly in the poorer central and eastern parts of the peninsula where the *encomiendas* had lingered on. Laws were now passed which meant that much of the old lineage lands that had enjoyed the protection of the Crown were declared vacant. They were sold or simply expropriated and became *haciendas*, mostly devoted to sugar cane. Maya farmers could do very little. They were left with their own plots of land to till for their families, but for most of the time were obliged to labour on the new estates.

In the 1840s however, the increasingly oppressed and resentful Maya found, all of a sudden, that they were needed by the Ladinos. For the growing pains of the new Mexico brought increasing tensions over the degree of autonomy that Yucatán should enjoy. This led to war. Mexican troops that had garrisoned some of the major towns were driven out of the peninsula, Yucatán seceded from Mexico and then in 1842 was invaded by the Mexicans. Thousands of Maya were called up to fight. They gladly did so when guarantees were given that after the conflict was over their use of traditional lands would be ensured, burdens of taxes and church dues would be reduced, in short that the unchecked exploitation of their people would cease.

A complex period of confrontation and negotiation with Mexico lasted until 1846, by which time the latter was at war with the United States over Texas. In patriotic spirit, Yucatán's leadership in Mérida decided to reunite themselves with Mexico. But this prompted a revolt by opposition elements in the port of Campeche who feared their city might be blown apart by the heavy guns of the US navy. They now recruited Maya to their cause and began hostilities with Mérida.

Since they formed the great bulk of the population, Yucatán's leaders

had little alternative but to arm the Maya. The educated members of the
leading Maya families were given commissions and they and their men,
all of course from the same local communities, received military training
and were issued with firearms, which they became used to taking home
with them. The consequences are obvious enough now but were not
adequately foreseen at the time. Experience and success in combat gave
the native militias a sense of their own strength and potential as a Maya
force. But, just as their confidence grew, it became increasingly apparent
that, although they were fighting their wars for them, the promises that
the Ladinos made would not be kept.

A bloody foretaste of what was to follow came in January 1847 in
Valladolid, bastion of Hispanic traditionalism and the old Colonial city
which for three hundred years had controlled the centre of the peninsula. Two battalions of Maya troops went on the rampage for almost a
week, looting and killing before they returned to their villages. Over the
next few months, while Mérida and Campeche were still at odds with
each other, rumours of plots and uprisings were multiplying. A Colonel
Cetina appears to have begun negotiations with three Maya leaders –
Manuel Antonio Ay, Cecilio Chi and Jacinto Pat – seeking support for
what was in fact a Ladino revolt against the government in Mérida.
Once more, favourable terms were offered the Maya. But Ay was
arrested and executed in Valladolid by firing squad. Cetina suffered no
such fate, a clear example to the Maya of the nature of white justice. The
authorities attempted to track down Chi and when they could not find
him burnt and sacked his farm. Since Chi and Pat were both wanted
men and had little to lose they decided to come out in revolt on their
own. No more worthless deals with the Ladinos. They would attempt to
take power in the peninsula themselves.[17]

Meetings were held with other Maya leaders. One of these was raided
and five of the conspirators captured and summarily shot. Cecilio Chi
and his followers retaliated immediately by killing two dozen Ladino
families in the small town of Tepich. In turn government forces hurried
there and massacred all the Maya they could find. Events had spun out
of control and by August 1847 all-out war had begun. It was a war
rooted in specific Maya grievances. But the brutal and erratic responses
of the white government and the paranoia of the Ladino population as a
whole ensured that it became a race war of terrible, irrational ferocity
that brought an anarchy of killing and destruction all across northern
Yucatán.

Viewed in strategic terms, though grand strategy was not a particular feature of this conflict, the beginning of the fighting could not have been better timed as far as the Maya were concerned. In the first few months a coup in Mérida kept government forces in and around the city, while the Maya took over towns and plantations south of Valladolid. More importantly, Mexico was still at war with the United States, who maintained a blockade of the Yucatán coast. Very little in the way of weapons, supplies or reinforcements could reach the Ladinos, while the Maya shipped everything of value plundered from *haciendas* and churches to the border with British Honduras, where they were readily exchanged for firearms and gunpowder. By the end of the year the countryside around Valladolid had fallen and the city itself was under seige. Prospects for its defence were hopeless and during March 1848 the population was evacuated under military escort, harried all the way towards Mérida. The centre of the peninsula was in Maya hands.

Negotiations were now initiated by the desperate Ladinos. But these proved to be little more than a delaying tactic and an attempt to create divisions within the Maya leadership. Fighting was resumed and by the end of May most of northern Yucatán had been overrun. Chi and his forces took Izamal. Acanceh, less than fifty kilometres from Mérida, was soon to follow. Panic-stricken whites and *mestizos* crowded within the walls of Mérida and Campeche. Thousands had already left the country and others were desperate to find any boat that would spare them from the massacres that now seemed inevitable. Those who could not get away waited, expecting an attack any time. But nothing happened. They sent out a few nervous patrols, who returned to report the surrounding countryside strangely empty. Then two troops of scouts rode on towards Izamal. The city had been ransacked, houses were still burning, but apart from the occasional looter there was no one to be seen.

The peasant army of the Maya, loosely organized under their *batabs* or local leaders, was on the point of driving the descendants of their conquerors out of the peninsula, of reversing three hundred years of history. But their forces suddenly withdrew. No easy explanation emerges from the confusion of these times. It has been suggested that the Maya leadership, with the prospect of victory so close, might have fallen out amongst themselves over the future division of power. But there is little evidence of this. A more plausible factor might have been the refusal of Maya from the western provinces around Mérida to join the rebels. There was a long history of hostility between the two groups that stretched back into Prehispanic times. This could perhaps have contributed to a failure of nerve. But the traditional explanation, and the only extant Maya view, may account adequately enough for what happened. The story was told to Edward Thompson many years later by the son of Crescencio Poot, one of the Caste War leaders:

> When my father's people took Acanceh they passed a time in feasting, preparing for the taking of T-ho (Mérida). The day was warm and sultry. All at once the *sh'mataneheeles* [winged ants, harbingers of the first rain] appeared in great clouds to the north, to the south, to the east, and to the west, all over the world. When my father's people saw this they said to themselves and to their brothers, 'Ehen! The time has come for us to make our planting, for if we do not we shall have no Grace of God to fill the bellies of our children.'
>
> In this way they talked among themselves and argued, thinking deeply, and then when morning came, my father's people said, each to his *batab*, '*Shickanic*' – I am going – and in spite of the supplications and threats of the chiefs, each man rolled up his blanket and put it in his food pouch, tightened the thongs of his sandals, and started for his home and his cornfield…Thus it can be clearly seen that Fate, and not white soldiers, kept my father's people from taking T-ho and working their will upon it.[18]

The decision to go home is sometimes seen, somewhat romantically perhaps, as a reflection of the noble, but in this instance the tragically naive Maya mind-set – age-old adherence to custom and the farmer's sense of sacred duty to plant his maize, the 'Grace of God' that was the substance of life. However their concerns for their families were very real ones. The war had caused such terrible destruction of crops and stores of maize that there would have been a grave threat of starvation in their communities if they did not return. And, given their startling success of the previous months, it was doubtless easy to believe that once the planting had been attended to, they could become soldiers once more and claim the victory that was so close.

However, as their leaders knew full well, the strategic initiative was lost and there were larger forces at work that the Maya farmer would not have understood. The Mexican war with the United States ended in August and very soon Yucatán and Mexico were reunited again. The fortunes of those who had been trapped in Mérida and Campeche were transformed as arms, money and provisions began to pour into the peninsula. Chi, Pat and others tried to reorganize and when their men returned they held on in some areas for a while. But well-equipped government troops, reinforced by Maya from the western provinces and contingents of mercenaries, including almost a thousand American volunteers who had come on here from Texas in search of further excitement and freebooting opportunity, forced the rebels back. Valladolid and many of the towns around it were soon retaken. By the end of 1848, the year of revolution in Europe, the brief prospect of a Maya revolution in Yucatán was gone.

Such a swift reversal of fortunes now brought dissension among Maya leaders and in the following year both Chi and Pat were assassinated by their own people. Those who took their place decided that the only option left other than surrender was to flee south-east into the still remote, inhospitable forests of Quintana Roo. Though they had established themselves at Bacalar to the south, the Spaniards had largely left this poor region, little settled in Prehispanic times, alone. Now, in a great migration of the defeated, tens of thousands abandoned their villages in the centre of the peninsula and trecked here. With few horses or mules left between them, families carried what little they needed on their backs, the most precious commodity their seed-corn to plant in new clearings.

In the heart of the wilderness, where many of these desperate people gathered together, they found the solace they most needed. In the age-old sacred surroundings of a small cenote, a miracle occurred. By its opening there grew some mahogany trees, and on one of them was discovered the image of a cross, after which the place was given its name, 'Chan Santa Cruz' or 'Little Holy Cross'. It was to provide a religious focus and inspiration for the second, most successful phase of the Caste War, the establishment of a Maya state-in-exile. The Cross spoke, and through its first interpreter, a mysterious figure known as Juan de la Cruz, whose appearance later adherents were to equate with the Second Coming, it proclaimed that God would protect his chosen people and lead them to ultimate victory against the whites.

In the short term the reverse was true. The war continued haphazardly through the early 1850s, with both sides raiding each other. Twice punitive expeditions reached Chan Santa Cruz itself, though they were quickly forced to withdraw. But a peace born of weariness drew near. By now much of the country south of Valladolid was a wasteland of burnt and abandoned *haciendas*, villages and whole towns. Countless churches were in ruins, and still dot the landscape today. The overall toll of destruction in Yucatán had been terrible. Between 1846 and 1850 alone, war, disease and emigration is thought to have reduced the population from 500,000 to about half that number. The state government was bankrupt and its own troops on the brink of rebellion. So Chan Santa Cruz was simply left alone. The authorities claimed victory, but the war had not been won. Indeed, in 1858 the rebels enjoyed their last major success. They captured the city of Bacalar to the south, which secured their connections with British Honduras. Soon it meant the *de facto* recognition by the British of a Maya country which covered most of eastern Quintana Roo from Tulum in the north to the Rio Hondo in the south.

With the taking of Bacalar, the 'Cruzob', as they have become known, the 'People of the Cross' (the Spanish word coupled with the Maya plural suffix), turned to the consolidation of their new society and the transformation of Chan Santa Cruz from an armed refugee camp to a capital city. The total population of the Cruzob state was probably about fifty thousand by the 1860s. They were organized along military lines, on the model of Maya militias, fighting men and their families divided up into different companies. This helped to speed the social integration of people who came from many different villages all across the centre and east of the peninsula. At the top of the military hierarchy were four generals and beneath them conventional ranks down to corporal and ordinary soldier. All males provided regular military service at the centre.

Chan Santa Cruz came to consist of blocks of pole and thatch houses around a central plaza flanked by buildings of stone, including barracks, schools and residences for the city's leaders. It followed the model of a Ladino town and much of it was indeed built by Ladino prisoners, slave labourers toiling for their Maya masters. The outside world was in reverse here. On the east side of the plaza was an enormous barn-like structure, indistinguishable from other Yucatán churches, which housed the cult of the Cross, now moved a short way from its original location. Inside was installed a principal image of the Cross flanked by two others, the Speaking Cross as Holy Trinity it would seem. Each was dressed in the way that the saints were so honoured in other churches of Yucatán, though here the garments were distinctly Maya ones – the *huipil* and the typical petticoat worn by Maya women. The crosses were themselves called *santos*, but there were no other images here of the Catholic saints. The Cross alone was the focus of worship.

Contemporary accounts provide little detail, but it appears that ritual broadly followed Catholic practice and that the 'Interpreter' of the Cross fulfilled much the same role as the priest, officiating at a form of mass and at marriages and baptisms.

In no sense did the Cruzob return to the more obvious forms of pre-conquest 'pagan' religion. They adhered to the Cross, the most sacred of Christian symbols. But the Cross also represents in the post-conquest Maya world the most striking example of the merging of Christian and Maya images. For by its very nature the Cross became, quite effortlessly, the World Tree. On the surface, the two would appear to have some major differences in meaning – the World Tree representing the pivot holding up the cosmos and the Christian Cross the 'tree' upon which Christ was crucified. Yet both possess a dense array of symbols and the latter's associations with sacrifice and rebirth would have possessed a powerful resonance. Thus, unconsciously perhaps by this time, the Cruzob were in effect worshipping the Tree of Life of both religions. The name of the church of the Speaking Cross refers directly to indigenous traditions of thought. It was called 'Balam Na', or 'Jaguar House', the animal so associated with sacred power and authority in ancient times. At the time of the conquest, in the person of the original Chilam Balam or Jaguar Prophet, the connection is also made with divine revelation. Thus one can perhaps translate the name Balam Na another way – as the house of powerful, sacred speech.

Juan de la Cruz, the first Interpreter, had been killed very soon after the cult's establishment. But the Cross continued to communicate both verbally and in written form from the Balam Na. Images of gods talked and famous oracles undoubtedly existed in pre-conquest times. Some of the first Spaniards to arrive in Yucatán encountered on Cozumel island the large ceramic statue of a woman, seemingly the goddess Ix Chel. Behind it was a tiny room in which sat a priest or interpreter who 'spoke'. At Chan Santa Cruz, divine messages were transmitted in a similar way through a human medium. In the early years the cult was run by a triumvirate. This was made up of the so-called Patron of the Cross, who seems to have been the most powerful individual in the Chan Santa Cruz community, the Interpreter, who through visions and dreams was the vehicle for the receipt of divine communication, and another individual who acted as the ventriloquist and proclaimed the messages to the faithful. He seems to have operated from a small chamber disguised in a pit behind the three crosses. War, diplomacy, the internal affairs of the community were discussed by the triumvirate in consultation with the four generals. But all decisions and policy pronouncements emanated from the Cross itself. The word of God governed here.

Diplomatic approaches to Chan Santa Cruz had to be made directly to the Cross, either by letter or in person. The British gained some experience in this. After the capture of Bacalar, a group of officers went there to attempt to ransom some of the few Ladino survivors. They had to negotiate with a portable Speaking Cross which, much like older Maya god images or Christian saints, had evidently been taken into battle at the head of the Cruzob forces, after which it resided for a while in a house on the Bacalar plaza. In 1861 two Lieutenants, called Twigge and Plumridge, were sent to Chan Santa Cruz itself with a letter from the Superintendent in British Honduras complaining about Maya cattle-raiding. The experience was an unnerving one. It took them a week to reach the city from the Rio Hondo. Instructed to avoid any involvement with the mumbo-jumbo of the Cross, on their arrival it soon became obvious that there was no alternative. They were disarmed and locked in a guard-room from eight in the morning until midnight and then taken in darkness to the Balam Na, which was filled with praying Maya. They were made to kneel on the floor in front of the crosses. A voice addressed them, which they thought originated from somewhere up in the ceiling. They understood nothing, of course, and had to rely on a *mestizo* trader whom they had brought along with them as interpreter. He was so terrified by the angry tones of the Cross and the fierce reputation of the Cruzob that the original mission to register a complaint about cattle-raiding was forgotten and the party left Chan Santa Cruz having agreed on something completely different, to supply the Cruzob with one thousand barrels of gunpowder at the usual price.

If the Cross provided spiritual sustenance for the Maya in exile, it was undoubtedly British guns that sustained the war and enabled them to resist reconquest by the Ladinos. For their part, the British were happy to provide themselves with a buffer against the Mexicans, who did not recognize the existence of British Honduras, and, by acting as their quartermasters and remaining on cordial terms with Chan Santa Cruz, they were able to keep the Maya from interfering with their logging and other commercial interests. This special relationship with the tiny native state is an extraordinary footnote in imperial history. The Cruzob became intrigued by Queen Victoria and extremely well-disposed towards her. They sent letters addressed to the Queen and in later years even enquired whether Chan Santa Cruz might join the British Empire. But it appears that none of these communications reached the monarch herself. They never in fact got further than the authorities in Belize City.

The Cruzob were not the only Maya to escape into the jungles of Quintana Roo. Other smaller communities, who did not follow the Cross but were organized on similar military lines, sprang up in remote parts, some a long way to the south close to the border with Guatemala. In time these groups reached an accommodation with the authorities. They came to be known as the 'peaceful rebel Indians'. In contrast, the 'savage rebel Indians', the Cruzob themselves, held out until the end of the nineteenth century. In 1893 the British signed a treaty with Mexico which formally recognized the border with British Honduras. As a part of the agreement the arms trade with the Maya was halted. In 1901 the Mexican government resolved to deal with Chan Santa Cruz once and for all. Much as Governor Ursua had patiently cut his road from Mérida to the shores of Lake Petén Itzá two hundred years before, so General Nicolás Bravo now advanced deliberately and irresistibly through the bush. The Cruzob mounted hit-and-run attacks, but their antiquated weaponry had no chance against machine-guns and breech-loading cannon. The city was taken with ease, its inhabitants having fled once more deep into the forests.

But this was not the end. After little more than a decade of occupation, the army withdrew, the Mexican Revolution requiring its presence elsewhere. Briefly the Cruzob returned to their city. But for them it was now a very different place, having been taken over and defiled by the Mexicans. The Balam Na was no longer fit as a house of God. It had been used for stabling animals and as a prison, and the soldiers had burnt the image of the Cross. The Cruzob set out to destroy traces of the alien presence, blowing up a public reservoir, incapacitating a narrow-gauge railway that had been built from the Caribbean coast and finally cutting the newly established telegraph and telephone lines, thus ensuring their isolation from the outside world once more.

Shortly afterwards an epidemic of smallpox ravaged the region and reduced the remaining population from some ten thousand to less than half that number. It was interpreted as a punishment meted out by the Cross for their having permitted the city's occupation. In the following years the Cruzob were to be split into different groups in the surrounding countryside, each with its own individual shrine containing new versions of the Cross. Chan Santa Cruz is now called Carrillo Puerto and the Balam Na has been reconsecrated as the Church of the Holy Cross. But the People of the Cross and their cult still survive. The most flourishing centre is the village of Tixkakal Guardia, north of Carrillo Puerto.[19] Here a Cross is housed in an oval building known as *iglesia* or 'church', though it is a relatively humble structure, thatched like any other Maya house. The Cross communicates with its followers through an interpreter, who sleeps in the shrine and in dreams receives the divine messages. These are written down, left at the foot of the Cross and are then read out in the morning during what is still a version of the Catholic Mass. The Cross speaks as the Son of God, the Messiah, just as the very first Cross manifested itself as the saviour of oppressed and defeated Maya at the tiny cenote in 1850.

In a small sanctuary at the east end of the building are kept the shrine's most precious possessions. These are books, written in Yucatec Mayan but in the Latin alphabet, which record the prophecies of the Cross of Tixkakal Guardia along with other religious esoterica and fragments of historical tradition accumulated by the spiritual leaders of the community over the years. In the 1970s they included a copy of the original proclamation of Juan de la Cruz.[20] These are in effect Chilam Balam books, the very last in existence and still being compiled. In other parts of the peninsula the tradition ceased at the time of the time of the Caste War. But as the Maya refugees migrated to the forests of Quintana Roo, the scribal tradition and that of recording sacred knowledge in holy books travelled with them. The practice of hieroglyphic writing may have disappeared with the fall of Tayasal, but the present-day scribe and guardian of the books at Tixkakal Guardia, who in his own hand continues to add to the sum of ancient tradition, can be seen as the lineal descendant of the *ah k'u hun* or Keeper of the Holy Books of Classic times.

THE ANCIENT FUTURE

The descendants of the Caste War Maya still maintain themselves apart. Until recent times many continued to ask after the health of Queen Victoria to English-speaking visitors. They believed that the war was still going on and they were merely in a state of truce with the Mexicans, awaiting the call to arms to resume their struggle for the peninsula. But the battle they began was to be largely won for them by the Mexican Revolution, which reduced the power of the *hacienda* owners and has led in the twentieth century to a more integrated and open society in Yucatán. Today it is difficult to imagine the depth of hatred and fear between Maya and non-Maya that prevailed here one hundred and fifty years ago.

Such hatreds are far from forgotten, however, amongst the peoples of Guatemala, the country with the bloodiest history of violence against its indigenous population in all of Latin America. A Peace Accord recently signed between government and armed opposition groups has provided some hope that the the future may be set on a different course. But as recently as the 1970s and early 1980s, Guatemalan Maya found themselves engulfed by a war between guerrilla organizations, largely led by Marxist Ladinos from the cities, and the Guatemalan army, who, in the name of counter-insurgency, carried out terrible, systematic assaults against Maya communities. Tens of thousands were killed in these years and hundreds of thousands were forced from their homes, a great many fleeing as refugees to Mexico and neighbouring countries. There is a history of Maya revolt in Guatemala, notably in the later nineteenth century as a reaction to land appropriation and forced labour on the coffee plantations of the Pacific coast, but these have never been effective against the power of the landowning elite and the military, ever fearful and on the alert against the spectre of Indian uprising.

Yet, in the face of economic and political subjection, the Maya of Guatemala, along with their cousins in the neighbouring highlands of Chiapas, have maintained their cultural identity more tenaciously than any other group of Maya people. They have achieved this by turning away from the hostilities of the outside world to the solidarity of family, community, the Maya language and their religious beliefs. Long gone from other parts of the Maya region, in the Guatemalan highlands the 260-day sacred calendar is still observed, the count of the days scheduling every aspect of life in many communities. Shamans continue to act as intermediaries with the spirit world, performing rituals on behalf of both individuals and their communities at mountains, caves, springs and other sacred spots in the landscape. Candles and incense are burnt and their smoke rises to the heavens as a thanksgiving. The blood sacrifice of a chicken may be performed, with much the same symbolic meaning as in ancient times, to return to the gods of the earth the sustenance that humans receive from it. The prayers of the shaman can involve a mixture of invocations – to the ancestors, to the *mundos* or old gods of the Maya who since the conquest are believed to have gone underground, but also to Christ, the Virgin Mary and to Dios himself, or Dios Mundo as he is called among the Quiché. Embracing both Christian God and native Divinity, expressed as mother/father and one in many, Dios Mundo is probably best defined as *k'ul*, the divine force that animates all nature.

The remarkably vigorous survival of traditional Maya culture in Guatemala is immediately apparent to anyone who travels through the pine forests and volcanoes to the beautiful highland towns. The Quiché, Cakchiquel, Tzutujil amongst many other distinct groups still wear traditional forms of dress, cultivate their maize fields in time-honoured manner and trade agricultural products and craft goods along networks of trails that have been followed through the mountains for many centuries. Markets are one of the central features of Maya life and very attractive to foreign tourists. On Sundays or saints' days stalls will cover the main plaza and side streets of the larger highland towns. At Chichicastenango, most colourful and picturesque of all, the visitor sees crowds of local farmers and their families from the surrounding countryside who have brought their products to sell or exchange. Here, wandering among traditional Maya people – women in their brightly-coloured *huipiles* and wrap-around skirts, their long, sleek hair delicately braided; babies lying swaddled at their feet amongst sacks of different-coloured maize kernels; men lighting copal incense in small stone-built braziers on the steps of the two churches which face each other east to west across the plaza – it is hard to resist projecting such images of a seemingly living past back in time to people the silent ruins of ancient Maya cities, to conjure up perhaps a vision of market day at Tikal.

To imagine the Maya of today inhabiting a fossilized past is, of course, an illusion, though one that is gladly perpetuated by the tourist industry. Yet the perception has inevitably been encouraged over the years by archaeologists and anthropologists themselves. Concerned with explaining the mysteries of ancient Maya civilization, scholars have studied the contemporary Maya as living remnants who might bear keys to the meanings of the past. This is a perfectly legitimate, objective scientific endeavour. But the unwitting result, as many archaeologists and anthropologists now recognize, has been to fuel the popular notion that the modern Maya are a people locked in a time warp.

There are a number of lessons of contemporary relevance to be learnt from the study of the Maya past. The abrupt end of lowland Maya civilization in the ninth century is perhaps the most obvious. We can see now that population growth and environmental destruction spun out of control, bringing ecological disaster and social and political breakdown to the Maya world. It is a tragic irony that a society whose religion and whole culture was founded on an intimate relationship of reciprocity with what were conceived as the sacred forces of nature should in the end kill off so much of it. The warning is a stark one. But if this is in a sense a negative lesson, there is a positive side as well. The ultimate Maya failure was the inevitable result of their remarkable successes as tropical forest farmers. They devised many different forms of agriculture and used an array of crops which flourished in a productive equilibrium with their fragile environment for a very long time. Today, agronomists and environmentalists are slowly beginning to understand more about these achievements. And, as many highland Maya move down to colonize the forests, in the way the Kekchi from Guatemala are now opening up areas of the Petén that have not been cultivated for centuries, there is the opportunity for farmers and environmentalists to work together to utilize the lessons of the ancient Maya experience and to avoid further disasters in the future.

An awareness of the need to work with the contemporary Maya to preserve and study the remains of the past, to look upon the descendants of the ancient civilization not simply as informants but as collaborators, is now developing amongst archaeologists. For in the past research tended to be viewed as a detached intellectual exercise. Archaeologists, the vast majority foreigners, would fly in from their universities and museums, perform their fieldwork and, having collected sufficient data, fly out again to write up their theses. The new attitude, visible in many other parts of the world, comes from a sense of guilt that for too long Maya archaeology has been a cultural extension of colonialism, feeding off the past of another people. Now is the time to give something back, to encourage the Maya to be participators in what is after all the rediscovery of their own past.

Quite independently the Maya of today, in Guatemala particularly, are going through a cultural renaissance of their own, which in itself serves to demonstrate that they are not simply a folk culture living in the shadow of their ancestors. Led by Maya academics and professionals in universities and centres for indigenous studies, this is very much a product of the violence in Guatemala of the 1980s. For what has been termed the Maya 'diaspora' of those years helped to create a new pan-Maya solidarity that crosses international boundaries. The preservation and study of language is central to this reawakening. Here committed foreign scholars have become involved, helping to compile grammars and histories of the Maya languages. Increasingly, the 'Hieroglyphic Workshops' that Linda Schele pioneered, and which are now carried on by her colleagues, are being held in the countries of the region. Slowly Maya students are learning to decipher the ancient texts. Thus, as history continues to be written from the records of their ancestors that go back almost two thousand years, and as that history is fleshed out in the field by archaeologists, it is in the process of being reclaimed by the Maya themselves. The year 2012 sees the completion of the present Great Cycle of time in the Long Count calendar. In ancient prophecy this marks the end of the present world and the beginning of a new era. By then, perhaps, native Maya archaeologists and anthropologists will be at the forefront of their own field.

Appendices

The Maya Calendar

Before examining the workings of the principal calendars used in Classic times, a brief introduction to Maya numbers is necessary. They developed a mathematical system of genius, which was extremely simple and employed only three symbols – a dot for one, a bar for five and a shell motif for zero, the earliest appearance of a concept of zero, it would seem, anywhere in the world. Allied to the use of zero was the adoption of place notation, in which the position of a numerical symbol determined its value. Of course, we ourselves use place notation. In writing 654, for example, we mean four units of one, five units of ten and six units of one hundred, the values of the positions increasing by multiples of ten from right to left. In place of our decimal system, the Maya used a vigesimal system, base twenty, and their form of place notation was different. The values increased not horizontally, but vertically, from bottom to top. Thus, in the first of the examples below, a shell is placed in the initial, lowest position to indicate zero single units, above it a bar and three dots representing eight twenties and in the next position a single dot meaning one unit of four hundred, or twenty times twenty. In the second example one adds up seven single units, sixteen twenties, three four hundreds and five eight thousands, the next position up, to record a total of 41,527.

Diego de Landa observed this kind of vigesimal counting system being used by Maya merchants of his day and he describes how they did their sums on the ground or upon a smooth surface. Sticks, shells, maize kernels or cacao beans would doubtless have been used as counters. Beyond this reference of Landa's, however, there is no other surviving evidence of such everyday use of numbers and, aside from the very rare

8000s		——
400s	•	•••
20s	•••	≣
1s	〈Ⅲ〉	⎯ •

560	41, 527

appearance of numerals in name glyphs, such as three bars, three dots and an animal's head to represent the name of the Copán ruler 18 Rabbit, numbers only come down to us in calendrical expressions.

The Sacred Almanac and the Solar Year

The 260-day cycle, the 'Sacred Almanac', also called the *Tzolkin* – a word of modern invention meaning literally count of days – was used throughout Mesoamerica in ancient times. It was the key ritual calendar, forming the basis for prophecy and divination, and it is the *Tzolkin* which survives today in highland Guatemala, where the modern 'day-keeper' uses it for divinatory purposes. This calendar bears no relationship to any celestial cycle. Its origins are unknown, though it was in use as early as the sixth century BC among the Zapotec of Oaxaca, and the most widely accepted explanation for its adoption is that it approximates to the nine month period of human gestation. In ancient times people were named according to their birth date in this calendar, a practice which continues in many traditional communities today.

The days in the *Tzolkin* were divided up, not into months or weeks, but into a round of twenty day names combined with thirteen numbers. Each of the names and numbers had its own patron deity and supernatural associations. Both names and numbers turned continuously, so that the sequence would begin with 1 *Imix*, the number always prefixed to the name, and proceed 2 *Ik*, 3 *Akbal* and so on up to 13 *Ben*. Then the numbers would begin again while the names carried on – thus 1 *Ix*, 2 *Men* until the twentieth name was reached, which would be expressed as 7 *Ahaw*. This would be followed by a return to the first day-name prefixed with an 8, thus 8 *Imix*. The whole cycle would take 260 days to use up every possible combination, before starting up again with 1 *Imix*.

The 260-day almanac was used in conjunction with a 365-day

calendar corresponding roughly to the solar year. This was made up of 18 named 'months', each of 20 numbered days, plus 5 extra, nameless and unlucky days at the end of the year known as the *Uayeb* days. The Maya solar calendar had none of the leap days it would have needed to keep it in line with the true tropical year and over long periods of time the calendar simply drifted slowly across the seasons. The Maya New Year would begin with 1 *Pop* (the name of the month) and the days would carry on 2 *Pop*, 3 *Pop* and so on.

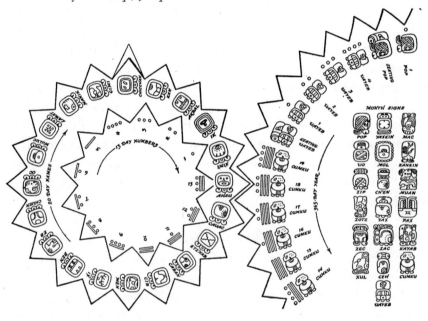

Both the 260-day calendar and the solar year carried on simultaneously, of course, so that any one day could be identified in both systems. The diagram above, in the form of an interlocking set of cog wheels, was first used by Eric Thompson. On the left appears a visualisation of the 260-day calendar, the 20 days on the outer wheel, accompanied by their hieroglyphic signs, and the 13 numbers expressed in bar and dot numeration on the inner wheel. As these keep on turning, so each new day of the 260-day calendar engages with one in the solar year, represented on the right. Here we see that the day 13 *Ahaw* (here spelt *Ahau*) meshes with 18 *Cumku* in the solar year. The hieroglyphs for the month names of the solar year appear on the right. We are approaching the end of the solar year in this diagram. After 18 *Cumku* comes 19 *Cumku* and then, not 20 *Cumku* but what is termed here the 'seating' of the *Uayeb*. This is because, in the Maya way of looking at time, where the divisions of the days were conceived as possessing their own individual natures, living entities in their own right, the influence of the *Uayeb* would already have begun to be felt on the last day of the preceding month. This 'seating' day is thus a day of transition between different categories of time. Similarly, the fifth *Uayeb* day was known as the 'seating' of *Pop*, before the new month proper begins with 1 *Pop*. This same seating convention applies at the end of every month.

Turning together in this way, the same permutation of dates in the two calendars will only come around again once in every 52 years. This 52-year cycle is known as the Calendar Round. Always written with the *Tzolkin* date coming first, in this case phrased as 13 *Ahaw* 18 *Cumku*, Calendar Round references are the commonest expressions of Maya time that have come down to us. For most Maya people, whose average life expectancy would have been less than a Calendar Round, this system, combining together ritual calendar and solar year, would have been perfectly adequate for ordering their lives. But their rulers, to record their dynastic histories unambiguously over much longer periods, adopted another method of time-keeping.

The Long Count

The origins of the Long Count are also obscure. The earliest Long Count date known is 36 BC and comes from a stela found in the foothills of Chiapas. Although the Maya almost certainly did not invent the Long Count, rulers of the Classic period took it on and made it uniquely their own. The key characteristic of the Long Count is that it is a cumulative count of time running from a fixed starting point, as we use the birth of Christ. But the Maya were not encumbered by solar years or lunar months in this calendar. It was a pure count of days that had elapsed since a base date thought to have been 13 August 3114 BC. Why this particular date was chosen is unclear, but it evidently marked the time of the present creation, when the gods set the world in order.

Expressions of time in the Long Count were invariably placed at the beginning of inscriptions, and they are easy to read. The amount of days that have passed since the base date, is recorded in a place notational system in periods of 400 years (known as *baktuns*), 20 years (*katuns*), 1 year (*tuns*), 20 days (*uinals*) and single days (*kins*). It should be noted, however, that the *uinals*, or periods of twenty days (one might call them months) are always multiplied by 18 rather than 20, thus breaking the conventional vigesimal system, in order to produce a year not of 400 days but of 360 and nearer to the true solar year. Thus, 20 *kins* make one *uinal,* 18 *uinals* one *tun,* 20 *tuns* a *katun* and 20 *katuns* a *baktun.*

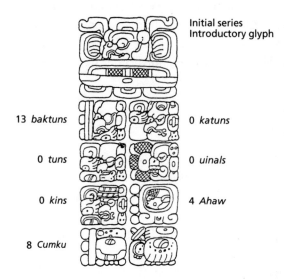

Initial series Introductory glyph

13 *baktuns*   0 *katuns*

0 *tuns*   0 *uinals*

0 *kins*   4 *Ahaw*

8 *Cumku*

Above is an example of a statement of time in the Long Count. At the top is placed the so-called Initial Series Introductory Glyph, which always serves to announce the appearance of a Long Count date. In this instance it takes up the space of two glyph blocks, but more commonly it will appear as no larger than each of the individual blocks below. The system of numerical place notation works downwards here, following the conventional Maya reading order. Thus we begin at top left with the expression for 13 *baktuns,* two bars and three dots to the left of a head, which stands for the *baktun* division. Further heads, each slightly different in detail, represent the other divisions. These are known as 'period glyphs', here in their so-called 'head variant' form, though other more abstract glyphic notations are often used. We then read left to right and downwards, recording 0 *katuns,* 0 *tuns,* 0 *uinals* and 0 *kins.* As is invariably the case, this is followed by an expression in the Calendar Round, 4 Ahaw 8 Cumku. Thus Maya time has been phrased in three different calendrical systems, the 260-day Sacred Almanac, the Solar Year and the Long Count. This particular example of the Long Count, from Stela C at the site of Quirigua, is a very special one, for it refers to the date of creation itself. Significantly, however, not all the divisions of time are set at nought. For it is registered that 13 *baktuns* have passed. The Long Count is to all intents and purposes a linear count of time, from this very base date in 3114 BC, but it was conceived as working in immense cycles of its own, cycles of 13 *baktuns*, in other words of more than 5000 years. Thus, creation here is in fact expressed as the completion of a previous cycle, a cycle perhaps of mythological time. The end of the present *baktun* cycle is imminent, since it is due to take place in 2012 AD. Then the *baktun* count will shift from 13 to 0 and another new era will begin.

APPENDIX 2

Rulers of the Classic Period

Listed here are the personal names and known dates of Maya rulers who appear in this book. For Tikal and Copán they are presented as dynastic sequences, though necessarily incomplete. The royal family tree of Palenque appears separately in Chapter 5 (p. 265). As decipherment proceeds, scholars are increasingly coming to agree on how the name glyphs of rulers should be read phonetically. However, in these pages we have retained the names by which Maya kings are most commonly known in the published literature, in guide-books and at archaeological sites. A number of these, like Pakal or Yax K'uk Mo, are phonetic readings that have been established for some years. Others, like Bird Jaguar or Curl Nose, often derive from the particular visual characteristics of the name glyphs as they appeared, in the early days of decipherment, to those who documented them. In the right hand column below are dates, other names by which a few rulers are still known (in brackets), and some more established phonetic readings. Numbers in brackets indicate where a position in the dynastic sequence is inferred but remains to be confirmed by Maya texts.

TIKAL

Name used in this book	*Dates and alternative names*
1 YAX MOCH XOK	Founder of the dynasty. Possibly reigning 1st *c.* AD.
2-13 RULERS UNKNOWN	Stela 29, dated AD 292, is attributed to a ruler called Scroll Ahaw Jaguar or Foliated Jaguar. This connection now challenged.
14 GREAT JAGUAR PAW	Ruled 317–378. Died at the time of the Teotihuacan 'takeover'. Phonetic name: *Chak Tok Ich'ak I.*
(15) CURL NOSE	Ruled 379–? (Curl Snout). Phonetic name: *Nun Yax Ayin I.*

16 STORMY SKY	Ruled 411–456. Phonetic name: *Siyah Chan K'awil.*
(17) KAN BOAR	Ruled *c.* 475. Phonetic name: *K'an Chitam.*
(18) JAGUAR PAW SKULL	Ruled *c.* 488. Phonetic name: *Chak Tok Ich'ak II.*
'LADY OF TIKAL'	Possibly ruled during this period.
19 CURL HEAD	Ruled *c.* 527. Phonetic name: *Kalomte Balam.*
20 UNKNOWN	
21 DOUBLE BIRD	Ruled 537–? Phonetic name: *Wak Chan K'awil.*
22 ANIMAL SKULL	Ruled *c.* 590. Phonetic name: *not established.*
23 UNKNOWN	
24 UNKNOWN	
(25) SHIELD SKULL	Ruled *c.* 657–679. Phonetic name: *Nun Uhol Chak.*
(26) HASAW CHAN K'AWIL I	Ruled 682–734? (Ruler A, Ah Cacao). Defeated Jaguar Paw of Calakmul and re-established the power of the Tikal dynasty.
27 YIK'IN CHAN K'AWIL	Ruled 734–? (Ruler B).
28 UNKNOWN	
29 CHITAM	Ruled 768–? (Ruler C). Phonetic name: *Nun Yax Ayin II.*
? DARK SUN	Ruled 810. Phonetic name: *not established.*
? HASAW CHAN K'AWIL II	Ruled 869. Last known king of Tikal, identified from Stela 11.

UAXACTÚN

| Smoking Frog | Principal figure in the 'takeover' of Tikal in 378. Almost certainly from Teotihuacan. Ruled at Uaxactún until *c.* 396. Phonetic name: *Ciak K'ak* |

COPÁN

1 YAX K'UK MO	Ruled AD 426–? 437. Founder of the Copan dynasty.
2 POPOL K'INICH	Ruled *c.* 436–? (Mat Head, Popol Hol).
3 UNKNOWN	Ruled ?–485.
4 CU IX	Ruled 485–*c.* 495.
5 UNKNOWN	
6 UNKNOWN	
7 WATERLILY JAGUAR	Ruled early sixth century. Dates uncertain.
8 UNKNOWN	
9 UNKNOWN	

10	MOON JAGUAR	Ruled 553–578.
11	BUTZ' CHAN	Ruled 578–628. (Smoke Serpent, Smoke Sky).
12	SMOKE JAGUAR	Ruled 628–695. (Smoke-Imix-God K). Phonetic name: *K'ak Nab K'awil.*
13	18 RABBIT	Ruled 695–738. (18 Jog). Phonetic name: *Waxaklahun Ubah.* Captured and sacrificed by Cauac Sky of Quirigua.
14	SMOKE MONKEY	Ruled 738–749.
15	SMOKE SHELL	Ruled 749–763. (Smoke Squirrel).
16	YAX PAC	Ruled 763–820. (Sun-at-Horizon, New Dawn, Madrugada, Yax Pas, Yax Pasah). Last of the royal line.
—	U CIT TOK	Pretender. Attempted to found a new dynasty in AD 822, but failed.

QUIRIGUA

CAUAC SKY	Ruled 724–785. (Two-legged Sky).

YAXCHILÁN

PROGENITOR JAGUAR	Acceded to the throne in AD 320. (Penis Jaguar). Founder of the Dynasty.
MOON SKULL	Believed to be the seventh king. Ruled 454.
SHIELD JAGUAR (II)	Ruled 681–742. (Itzam Balam, Shield Jaguar the Great).
BIRD JAGUAR (IV)	Ruled 752–768. (Yaxun Balam).

CARACOL

LORD WATER	Ruled 553–599. (Lord Muluc). Phonetic name: *Yahaw-te.* Led the defeat of Tikal in 562.

DOS PILAS

FLINT SKY	Ruled 645–698. (Flint-Sky-God K). Phonetic name: *Balah Kan K'awil.* Originally from Tikal, but as head of a rebellious faction left to found Dos Pilas. Ally of Jaguar Paw of Calakmul against Tikal.

CALAKMUL

JAGUAR PAW	Ruled 686–695. (Jaguar Paw Smoke). Phonetic name: *Yich'ak K'ak'.* Defeated by Tikal in 695 and, as most believe, sacrificed there.

BONAMPAK

CHAN MUWAN	Ruled 776–c.795. Protagonist of the murals and probably the last ruler of Bonampak.

Notes

INTRODUCTION: The Ancient Maya

1. Stephens, 1841, Vol 1: 104
2. Coe, 1992: 7
3. Put forward by epigraphers Stephen Houston, David Stuart and linguist John Robertson and noted in Coe and Kerr 1997: 6. 'Epigrapher' is the term conventionally applied to scholars engaged in the study of Maya hieroglyphic inscriptions.
4. Bernal, 1977: 20.

CHAPTER ONE: The Discovery of the Maya

1. Ferdinand Columbus, *Histoire* (Venice 1678), quoted in Sauer 1966: 128.
2. Cervantes de Salazar, *Crónica de la Nueva España*. Libro segundo. Cap. XXVII. In Tozzer 1941: 236. Although well documented for the Aztecs, evidence of cannibalism among the Maya appears extremely limited. See Jones, 1998: 334 and 498 n. 42.
3. For the early voyages of exploration and initial stages of Spanish conquest I have relied on Tozzer, 1941, Díaz del Castillo, 1963, Clendinnen, 1987 and Thomas, 1993.

4. Juan Díaz, quoted in Tozzer, 1941: 12, n. 62.
5. Tozzer, 1941: 15.
6. Montejo to the Crown, quoted in Chamberlain, 1948: 164.
7. Translation by Harold Jantz. In Chiappelli (ed.), 1976: 94.
8. Herrera 1726–30, V: 32.
9. Díaz del Castillo, 1963: 190–1.
10. Díaz del Castillo, 1963.
11. Tozzer, 1941: 170–1.
12. Ibid : 62.
13. Ibid : 179–81.
14. Ibid : 109.
15. Ibid : 171–2.
16. Ibid : 172–3.
17. Ibid : 169.
18. Quoted in Bernal, 1977.
19. Extracts from García de Palacio's letter are included as Appendix IV in Morley, 1920: 541–2.
20. Grant D. Jones pieces together Cortés' route, and the story of the journey based on the accounts of Bernal Díaz del Castillo and of Cortés himself, in Jones, 1998: 29–39. As Jones points out, Cortés could have chosen a much easier way of reaching the Gulf of Honduras, namely to travel round the peninsula by sea. But he decided upon the land route in order to discover 'unknown lands and provinces'. When he arrived in

Honduras the revolt had already been quelled and its leader Cristobal de Olid executed.

21. Florescano in Boone (ed.) 1993: 81–103.

22. For the story of early Maya exploration see in particular the very readable biographical accounts of Brunhouse, 1973 and 1975. For the first attempts at decipherment G. Stuart, 1992 and Coe, 1992. Willey and Sabloff, 1974 and Hammond, in Leventhal and Kolata, 1983: 3–32, provide overviews of the history of Maya studies.

23. For the accounts of Calderón and Bernasconi see Paillés Hernandez and Nieto Calleja, 1990. The explorers' original reports now reside in the Archive of the Indies, Seville.

24. Quoted in Paillés Hernandez and Nieto Calleja, 1990: 124.

25. Ibid : 126. Author's translation.

26. Del Río, 1822: 3.

27. Del Río, 1822: 19.

28. Dupaix's report appears in Kingsborough, 1830–48. Vol. 6. 421–86.

29. Quoted in Brunhouse, 1973: 15–16.

30. Dupaix and Castañeda, 1834: 73, quoted in Bernal 1977: 29.

31. Brunhouse, 1973 and Baudez, 1993.

32. Brunhouse, 1973: 82.

33. For the best account of what is known of Galindo's life and work see Graham, 1963.

34. Ruins of Palenque, 'The Literary Gazette and Journal of the Belles Lettres', No. 769, October 15, 1831. See Brunhouse, 1973 for an extensive list of sources, both for Galindo and other early explorers.

35. 'A Description of the Ruins of Copán'. Included in Morley, 1920: 593–604.

36. The only extensive biographies of Stephens and Catherwood, somewhat lacking in sources, are by Von Hagen, 1947 and 1973. For Catherwood's experience in Egypt see Jason Thompson, *Sir Gardner Wilkinson and His Circle*, Austin, University of Texas Press, 1992.

37. Quoted in Von Hagen, 1973: 109–10.

38. Stephens, 1841, Vol. 1: 14.

39. Quoted in Pendergast (ed.), 1967: 31.

40. Pendergast, 1967: 100.

41. Ibid: 175.

42. Stephens, 1841, Vol. 1: 99.

43. Ibid: 97.

44. Ibid: 102.

45. Ibid: 102.

46. Ibid: 104–5.

47. Ibid: 115.

48. Ibid: 119–20.

49. Ibid: 141.

50. Ibid: 159–60.

51. Stephens, 1841, Vol. II: 292.

52. Ibid: 343.

53. Ibid: 356.

54. Ibid: 413.

55. Ibid: 429–30.

56. Stephens, 1843, Vol 1: 278–92

57. Stephens, 1843, Vol II : 206–7

58. Stephens, 1841, Vol II : 443

59. Ibid: 439

60. Ibid: 442.

61. Ibid: 456–7

62. Quoted in G. Stuart, 1992, 10 and in Coe, 1992, 83.

63. For the best description of the four surviving codices, a summary of their history and of recent advances in our understanding of them see Coe and Kerr, 1997: 169–82.

64. From a letter by Brasseur to de Rosny quoted in Brunhouse 1973: 133.

65. G. Stuart, 1992: 22.

66. Stephens, 1841 Vol II: 195

67. Maudslay field notebook, 1881.

68. See Graham, Three Early Collectors in Mesoamerica in Boone, 1993: 49–80.
69. Maudslay field notebook, 1882.
70. Adamson, 1975: 193.
71. Charnay, 1887.
72. Maudslay field notebook, 1882.
73. Spinden, 1913: 15.
74. For examination of changing scholarly attitudes to the ancient Maya in more recent times see Coe, 1992, Sabloff, 1990 and Schele and Miller, 1992.
75. Thompson, 1950: 155.
76. Bronowski, 1973: 188–90.
77. Thompson, 1954: 89.
78. Thompson, 1950.
79. For an introduction to the Tikal Project's work see Coe and Larios, 1988.
80. See, for example, Willey et al., 1965.

CHAPTER TWO: The Origins of Maya Civilization

1. For an excellent introduction to the subject see Fagan, 1987.
2. See Byers (ed.), 1967. MacNeish was also involved in the work in Belize and the Santa Marta rock shelter mentioned above.
3. See Pohl et al., 1996.
4. Pohl et al., 1996.
5. For the transition from coastal gathering to farming in Chiapas see Lowe, 1975.
6. For the Olmec see Coe and Diehl, 1980, Sharer and Grove, 1989 and David Grove and Susan D. Gillespie, 'Ideology and Evolution at the Pre-state Level: Formative Period Mesoamerica', pp.15–36 in Demarest and Conrad, 1992.
7. Hammond (ed.), 1991. Also a good summary by Hammond 'Unearthing the Oldest Known

Maya', National Geographic Magazine 162 (1): 126–40, 1982.
8. Hansen, 1991 and 1992.
9. For the first major investigations at El Mirador, see Matheny, 1986, and also Dahlin, 1984.
10. Schele and Freidel, 1990: 96–129.
11. For a more detailed description of these early Mesoamerican scripts and discussion of the origins of Maya writing see Coe and Kerr, 1997: 63–70.
12. Personal communication, Richard Hansen.
13. See the contributions by Nicholas Dunning and Richard Adams in Grube (ed.), 1995.
14. Sharer, 1994: 132–3.
15. Grube in Grube (ed.), 1995: 1–5.

CHAPTER THREE: Cracking the Code

1. The most internationally renowned of the latter are the 'Hieroglyphic Workshops' hosted every year by the University of Texas. They were begun in 1978 by the late Linda Schele, the great motivator and popularizer behind much of modern decipherment. Other American universities and museums now hold similar events and Europe has begun to follow suit, the British Museum mounting its first such workshop in 1996.
2. Throughout this chapter I rely heavily upon Coe, 1992 and G. Stuart, 1992.
3. The Lintel 21 text, originally drawn by Eric von Euw and published in the 'Corpus of Maya Hieroglyphic Inscriptions' Vol. 3, Pt. 1, 1977, has been re-drawn after Schele and Mathews, 1993: 67 with up-dated captions.

422 THE LOST CHRONICLES OF THE MAYA KINGS

4. Thompson, 1972: 9–10.
5. Morley, 1946: 259.
6. Thompson, 1962.
7. Morley, 1946: 259.
8. Berlin, 1958.
9. Berlin, 1959.
10. Proskouriakoff, 1961: 14.
11. Roys, 1933: 75.
12. Proskouriakoff, 1960: 470.
13. Proskouriakoff, 1963, 1964.
14. Proskouriakoff, 1961: 16.
15. Quoted by G. Stuart, 1992: 35.
16. Coe, 1992: 138.
17. See Coe, 1992: 139–44 for a full account of Knorosov's use of Landa's 'alphabet'.
18. Mathews and Schele, 1974. The Mesas Redondas at Palenque, conceived by Merle Greene and her husband Lawrence Robertson, continue to be held and, like the Texas Hieroglyphic Workshops, have become an increasingly popular forum, attended by Maya scholars and enthusiasts of all nationalities.
19. Schele and Mathews, 1993: 34.
20. Houston and Stuart, 1989.
21. See Reents-Budet, 1994: 319, and also David Stuart, 'Hieroglyphs on Maya Vessels', in Kerr, *The Maya Vase Book*, 1989.
22. Coe and Kerr, 1997: 89–90 and 133.
23. Coe, 1992: 255–7.

CHAPTER FOUR: The Early Classic

1. For a guide to the ruins and the story of the archaeological investigation of Tikal see W. Coe and Larios, 1988 and Coe, 1963. More detailed treatment of excavations at the centre of the city appears in W. Coe, 1990. Also see Christopher Jones, *Cycles of growth at Tikal* in Culbert, 1991: 102–27. Tikal's monuments and inscriptions are covered in Jones and Satterthwaite, 1982.
2. Personal communication, Simon Martin.
3. Webster, 1993 for a discussion of Maya war and the different viewpoints of Maya scholars.
4. Berrin and Pasztory (eds), 1993 for recent thought on Teotihuacan.
5. Coggins, *The Age of Teotihuacan and its Mission abroad*, in Berrin and Pasztory, 1993: 140–55.
6. Schele and Freidel, 1990: 146–9.
7. Uaxactún Stela 5 and the text upon a stone monument or 'marker' from a Tikal ballcourt also commemorate the 'arrival' of Smoking Frog at Tikal on 16 January 378. The phraseology used in these texts is more direct and unequivocal than the still somewhat opaque expressions used on Stela 31 (personal communication, Simon Martin).
8. Martin and Grube believe that 'spearthrower-owl-shield' may well have been a ruler of Teotihuacan.
9. See Fash, 1991 for the archaeology of Copán.
10. For accounts of recent discoveries at Copán and interim conclusions see W. Fash, 1997, B. Fash, 1997, Agurcia, 1997 and George Stuart, 1997.
11. Agurcia and Fash, 1989. Agurcia, 1997.
12. The earliest indications from this analysis are that the bones of the male (in other words Yax Kuk Mo) are those of an individual who was not native to the Copán valley. In contrast, the female would appear to be from Copán itself.
13. See Folan, Marcus *et al.*, 1995 and Folan, Marcus and Miller, 1995.
14. The most significant recent progress

in understanding of the Calakmul inscriptions has been achieved by Simon Martin. See Martin, 1996 and Martin and Grube, 1995 and 1996.

15. Martin, 1997.
16. Martin and Grube, 1995 and 1996.
17. Chase and Chase, 1987 and 1992.
18. Martin and Grube, 1995 and 1996.

CHAPTER FIVE: The Late Classic

1. For the development of the city of Copán and its history during the Late Classic period see W. Fash, 1991 and Fash and Stuart, *Dynastic History and Cultural Evolution at Copán, Honduras* in Culbert, 1991.
2. Webster (ed.), 1989.
3. B. Fash, 1997.
4. Thomas, 1993: 311.
5. For the history of the ball-game in Mesoamerica see Scarborough and Wilcox, 1991.
6. Freidel, Schele and Parker, 1993.
7. See Marcus, 1976.
8. Webster (ed.), 1989 and Fash, 1991.
9. See Linda Schele and Peter Mathews, *Royal visits and other intersite relationships among the Classic Maya* in Culbert, 1991, 226–52.
10. Mathews, 1995.
11. Schele and Freidel, 1990: 262–305.
12. Coe and Kerr, 1997: 94.
13. Mathews, 1995 and Martin and Grube, 1996.
14. Mathews, 1995.
15. Schele and Freidel, 1990: 216–61.
16. The initial dynastic sequence presented in Mathews and Schele, 1974, has been considerably refined in Schele and Mathews, 1993.
17. Some of the Maya names for rulers here differ from those used originally in Schele and Freidel, 1990. We have adopted those currently employed by epigraphers.
18. See Schele, *Architectural Development and Political History at Palenque* in Benson, 1986: 110–38.
19. For magnificent documentation of the architecture and sculpture of the city see the four-volume *The Sculpture of Palenque*, Robertson, 1983–91.
20. Grube, 1996.
21. Grube, 1996: 5.
22. Schele, 1989 and Grube, 1996.
23. Jones, 1991.
24. For the history of Dos Pilas see Houston, 1993, Schele and Freidel, 1990 and Martin and Grube, 1996.
25. Haviland, 1992.
26. Demarest, 1993.
27. Martin and Grube, 1995 and 1996.
28. Carneiro in Demarest and Conrad, 1992: 185.

CHAPTER SIX: Gods and Men

1. For discussion of the concept of 'k'ulel' see Houston and Stuart, 1996: 292–3.
2. Coe and Kerr, 1997: 25.
3. Schellhas, 1904. Excellent introductions to Maya myths and divinities are Miller and Taube, 1993 and Taube, 1993.
4. Houston and Stuart, 1996.
5. For the Maya as astronomers see in particular Aveni, 1980 and 1997, Freidel, Schele and Parker, 1993 and Bricker and Bricker, 1998.
6. Tate, 1992: 160.
7. Aveni, 1997.
8. Coe and Kerr, 1997: 175–9.
9. See Coe, 1973 and 1978.
10. Tedlock, 1996: 27–30.
11. Coe, 1989: 161.
12. Tedlock, 1996: 64.
13. Tedlock, 1996: 139.

14. Taube, 1985.
15. Houston and Stuart, 1996: 295–6.
16. For the Maya ruler as Maize God see Miller, 1992.
17. Schele and Mathews, 1998: 95–132, Miller, 1992.
18. Ashmore, 1992.
19. D. Stuart, 1997. Also see Vogt, 1969 and 1976 for the significance of mountains among the contemporary Maya of Zinacantan, Chiapas.
20. Described in Coe and Kerr, 1997: 91–6.
21. See Fash, 1991 and Webster (ed.), 1989.
22. Reents-Budet *et al.*, 1994. This volume is an exhibition catalogue, with fine photographs of Maya pots by Justin Kerr, and also includes important essays on ceramic styles and technologies, hieroglyphic texts and the subject matter of Maya pottery painting.
23. McAnany, 1995.
24. Nations and Nigh, 1980, McGee, 1990.
25. Sheets, 1992.
26. Scarborough, 1994, Scarborough *et al.*, 1995.

CHAPTER SEVEN: The Death and Rebirth of Maya Civilization

1. See the introduction of Mary Miller's classic study of the murals, Miller, 1986, for the history of their discovery and issues concerning their conservation.
2. Miller, 1986: 160.
3. See Culbert and Rice (eds.), 1990.
4. Rice, 1993.
5. Ibid.
6. Tozzer, 1941: 185.
7. Rice, 1993.
8. Hodell *et al.*, 1995.
9. Rue, 1987.

10. D. Stuart, 1993: 344–6.
11. Schele and Friedel, 1990: 344–5.
12. Fash, 1991.
13. Pendergast, 1981.
14. For the Postclassic period see in particular Chase and Rice, 1985 and Sabloff and Andrews, 1986.
15. Roys, 1933.
16. Thompson, 1970: 3–47. Thompson was the first to draw attention to the 'Putun'. They are still largely his own construct since no-one since his day has been able to define them with any greater clarity.
17. Kowalski, 1998.
18. For the major study of the 'House of the Governor' see Kowalski, 1987.
19. Schele, Grube and Boot, 1995.
20. Schele and Freidel, 1990: 346–76 and Schele and Mathews, 1998: 197–255.
21. See Schele and Mathews, 1998: 197–255 for the case that the architecture and iconography of Chichén Itzá can be seen as a largely indigenous 'Maya' achievement.

CHAPTER EIGHT: Conquest and Survival

1. Roys, 1967: 77–9. The sonorous, rhetorical manner of this passage betrays the relationship between many of these writings and oral performance. 'Blow-guns' here is the Maya way of describing Spanish firearms.
2. Roys, 1967: 83.
3. See Lovell and Lutz, 1994.
4. Jones, Grant D., 1998. I have relied heavily on Jones' fascinating study in discussion of Tayasal.
5. Jones, 1998: 37.
6. Quoted in Jones, 1998: 44.
7. There are delightful echoes here of

that 'living' Maya city with 'turrets white and glittering in the sun' described to John Lloyd Stephens by the Spanish padre that he and Catherwood met in Cobán. It is quite possible that Tayasal was the original source of these legends.

8. Quoted in Jones, 1998: 72.
9. Ibid: 44.
10. Roys, 1967: 136.
11. Avendaño, 1987: 38.
12. Ibid: 39.
13. See Coe and Kerr, 1997: 181 and 220.
14. Jones, 1998: 207–10.
15. Avendaño, 1987: 61.
16. Coe and Kerr, 1997: 220–2.
17. For accounts of the Caste War see the classic study by Reed, 1964 and Bricker, 1981.
18. Quoted by Reed, 1964: 99.
19. See Nikolai Grübe's description of Tixkakal Guardia in Freidel, Schele and Parker, 1993: 165–8.
20. Bricker, 1981: 186.

Bibliography

Acosta, José de
1589 *Historia Natural y Moral de las Indias,* ed. Edmundo O'Gorman, Mexico City, 1962.

Adams, Richard E. W.
1977 (ed.) *The Origins of Maya Civilization,* Albuquerque, University of New Mexico Press.

Adamson, David
1975 *The Ruins of Time,* London, George Allen & Unwin.

Agurcia, Ricardo
1997 'Rosalila, An Early Classic Maya Cosmogram from Copán', *Symbols,* Spring Issue, 32–7. Cambridge, Mass., Peabody Museum and the Dept. of Anthropology.

Agurcia, Ricardo and William L. Fash
1989 'Copán: A Royal Maya Tomb Discovered', *National Geographic,* 176 (4), 480–7.

Andrews, Anthony P.
1983 *Ancient Maya Salt Production and Trade,* Tucson, Univerity of Arizona Press,
1993 'Late Postclassic Lowland Maya Archaeology', *Journal of World Prehistory,* Vol. 7 (1), 35–69.

Ashmore, Wendy
1981 (ed.) *Lowland Maya Settlement Patterns,* Albuquerque, University of New Mexico Press.
1992 'Deciphering Maya Architectural Plans'. *New Theories on the Ancient Maya,* eds E. C. Danien and R. J. Sharer, 173–83, Philadelphia.

Avendaño y Loyola, Fray Andrés
1987 *Relation of Two Trips to Petén,* tr. Charles P. Bowditch and Guillermo Rivera, ed. Frank E. Comparato, Culver City, California.

Aveni, Anthony F.
1980 *Skywatchers of Ancient Mexico,* Austin, University of Texas Press.
1992 *The Sky in Maya Literature,* New York, Oxford University Press.
1997 *Stairways to the Stars: Skywatching in Three Great Ancient Cultures,* New York, John Wiley & Sons.

Baudez, Claude
1993 *Jean Frédéric Waldeck, peintre: Le premier explorateur des ruins Mayas*, Paris, Hazon.

Baudez, Claude and Sydney Picasso
1992 *Lost Cities of the Maya*, London, Thames & Hudson.

Benson, Elizabeth P.
1968 (ed.) *Dumbarton Oaks Conference on the Olmec*, Washington D.C.
1986 *City-States of the Maya: Art and Architecture*, Denver, Colorado, Rocky Mountain Institute for Pre-Columbian Studies.

Benson, Elizabeth P. and Gillett G. Griffin
1988 (eds) *Maya Iconography*, Princeton, Princeton University Press.

Berlin, Heinrich
1958 'El glifo "emblema" en las inscripciones Mayas', *Journal de la Société des Americanistes*, Vol. 47: 111–19.
1959 'Glifos nominales en el sarcófago de Palenque'. *Humanidades* 2 (10): 1–8. Guatemala, University San Carlos.

Bernal, Ignacio
1977 'Maya Antiquaries', *Social Process in Maya Prehistory*, ed. N. Hammond, 1943.

Berrin, Kathleen and Esther Pasztory (eds)
1993 *Teotihuacan: Art from the City of the Gods*,

Boone, Elizabeth H.
1993 (ed.) *Collecting the Pre-Columbian Past*, Washington D.C., Dumbarton Oaks.

Brasseur de Bourbourg, Charles Etienne
1864 *Relation des choses de Yucatán de Diego de Landa*, Paris.

Bricker, Victoria R.
1981 *The Indian Christ, the Indian King: The Historical Substrate of Maya Myth and Ritual*, Austin, University of Texas Press.

Bricker, Victoria R. and Harvey M. Bricker
1998 'Calendrical Cycles and Astronomy', *Maya*, eds Peter Schmidt, Mercedes de la Garza, Enrique Nalda, Bompiani, Italy.

Bronowski, Jacob
1973 *The Ascent of Man*, London, BBC Books.

Brunhouse, Robert L.
1973 *In Search of the Maya: The First Archaeologists*, Albuquerque, University of New Mexico Press.
1975 *Pursuit of the Ancient Maya, Some Archaeologists of Yesteryear*, Albuquerque, University of New Mexico Press.

Byers, D.
1967 (ed.) *The Prehistory of the Tehuacan Valley*, Vol. 1: Environment and Subsistence, Austin, University of Texas Press.

Carmichael, Elizabeth
1973 *The British and the Maya*, London, British Museum.

Carneiro, Robert L.
1970 'A Theory of the Origin of the State', *Science*, 169: 733–8.

Catherwood, Frederick
1844 *Views of Ancient Monuments in Central America, Chiapas and Yucatán*, London.

Chamberlain, Robert S.
1948 *The Conquest and Colonisation of Yucatán, 1517–1550*, Publication 582, Washington, Carnegie Institution.

Charnay, Desiré
1887 *Ancient Cities in the New World*, London.

Chase, Arlen F. and Diane Z.
1987 'Investigations at the Classic Maya City of Caracol, Belize 1985–87'. Monograph No. 3., Pre-Columbian Art Research Institute, San Francisco.
1992 (eds) *Mesoamerican Elites: An Archaeological Assessment*, Norman, University of Oklahoma Press.

Chase, Arlen F. and Prudence M. Rice
1985 (eds) *The Lowland Maya Postclassic*, Austin, University of Texas Press.

Chiapelli, Fredi
1976 (ed.) *First Images of America*, Berkeley and Los Angeles, University of California Press.

Clancy, Flora S. and Peter D. Harrison
1990 (eds) *Vision and Revision in Maya Studies*, Albuquerque, University of New Mexico Press.

Clendinnen, Inga
1987 *Ambivalent Conquests: Maya and Spaniard in Yucatán 1517–1570*, Cambridge, Cambridge University Press.

Coe, Michael D.
1966 *The Maya*, fifth edn 1993, London, Thames & Hudson.
1973 *The Maya Scribe and His World*, New York, The Grolier Club.
1978 *Lords of the Underworld: Masterpieces of Classic Maya Ceramics*, Princeton, Princeton University Press.
1989 'The Hero Twins: Myth and Image'. *The Maya Vase Book*, Vol. 1 (ed. J. Kerr), 161–84, New York, Justin Kerr Associates.
1992 *Breaking the Maya Code*, London and New York, Thames & Hudson.

Coe, Michael D. and Richard A. Diehl
1980 *In the Land of the Olmec*, 2 vols., Austin, University of Texas Press.

Coe, Michael D. and Justin Kerr
1997 *The Art of the Maya Scribe*, London, Thames & Hudson.

Coe, William R. and R. Larios
1988 *Tikal, a Handbook of the Ancient Maya Ruins*, second edn, Philadelphia University Museum, University of Pennsylvania.

Coggins, Clemency C.
1975 *Painting and Drawing Styles at Tikal: an Historical and Iconographic Reconstruction*, PhD thesis, Harvard University.

Coggins, Clemency C. and Orrin C. Shane
1984 (ed.) *Cenote of Sacrifice: Maya Treasures from the Sacred Well at Chichén Itzá*, Austin, University of Texas Press.

Culbert, T. Patrick
1973 (ed.) *The Classic Maya Collapse*, Albuquerque, University of New Mexico Press.
1991 (ed.) *Classic Maya Political History*, Albuquerque, University of New Mexico Press.

Culbert, T. Patrick and Don. S. Rice
1990 (eds) *Precolumbian Population History in the Maya Lowlands*, Albuquerque, University of New Mexico Press.

Dahlin, Bruce
1984 'A Colossus in Guatemala: The Preclassic City of El Mirador'. *Archaeology* 37 (5): 18–25.

Danien, Elin C. and Robert J. Sharer
1992 (eds.) *New Theories on the Ancient Maya*, Philadelphia, Philadelphia University Museum.

Del Río, Antonio
1822 *Description of the Ruins of an Ancient City, Discovered Near Palenque, in the Kingdom of Guatemala in Spanish America*, London, Henry Berthoud.

Demarest, Arthur A.
1993 'The Violent Saga of a Maya Kingdom', *National Geographic*, 183 (2): 95–111.

Demarest, Arthur A. and Geoffrey W. Conrad
1992 (eds) *Ideology and Pre-Columbian Civilizations,* Sante Fe, New Mexico, School of American Research.

Diaz Del Castillo, Bernal
1963 *The Conquest of New Spain*, trans. and intro. by J. M. Cohen, Harmondsworth, Penguin.

Dunning, Nicholas P. and Jeff Kowalski
1994 'Lords of the Hills: Classic Maya settlement patterns and political iconography in the Puuc region, Mexico'. *Ancient Mesoamerica* 5: 63–95.

Dupaix, Capt. Guillermo and Jose Castaneda
1834 *Antiquités Mexicaines*, 2 vols, Paris,

Edmonson, Munro. S.
1982 *The Ancient Future of the Itzá: The Book of Chilam Balam of Tizimin*, Austin, University of Texas Press.
1986 *Heaven Born Mérida and its Destiny: The Book of Chilam Balam of Chumayel*, Austin, University of Texas Press.

Elliott, J. H.
1970 *The Old World and the New, 1492–1650,* Cambridge, Cambridge University Press.
1989 *Spain and Its World 1500–1700*, New Haven and London, Yale University Press.

Fagan, Brian M.
1987 *The Great Journey*, London, Thames & Hudson.

Farriss, Nancy
1984 *Maya Society Under Colonial Rule: The Collective Enterprise of Survival,* Princeton, Princeton University Press.

Fash, Barbara W.
1997 'Sculpting the Maya Universe: A New View on Copán', *Symbols,* Spring Issue, 18–21. Cambridge, Mass., Peabody Museum and the Dept. of Anthropology.

Fash, Barbara W., W. L. Fash, S. Lane, R. Larios, L. Schele, J. Stomper and David Stuart
1992 'Investigations of a Classic Maya Council house at Copán, Honduras', *Journal of Field Archaeology,* 19 (4): 419–42.

Fash, William L.
1991 *Scribes, Warriors and Kings: The City of Copán and the Ancient Maya,* London, Thames & Hudson.
1997 'Unearthing an Ethos: Maya Archaeology and Maya Myth', *Symbols,* Spring Issue, 22–7, 40. Cambridge, Mass., Peabody Museum and the Dept. of Anthropology.

Flannery, Kent. V.
1982 (ed.) *Maya Subsistence,* New York, Academic Press.

Florescano, Enrique
1993 'The Creation of the Museo Nacional de Anthropologia of Mexico and its Scientific; Educational and Political Purposes', *Collecting the Pre-Columbian Past,* ed. E. H. Boone, Washington D.C., Dumbarton Oaks.

Folan, William J., Joyce Marcus *et al.*
1995 'Calakmul: New Data from an Ancient Maya Capital in Campeche Mexico', *Latin American Antiquity,* 6 (4), 310–34.

Folan, William J., E. R. Kintz and L. A. Fletcher
1983 *Cobá, a Classic Maya Metropolis,* New York, Academic Press.

Folan, William, J., J. Marcus and W.F. Miller
1995 'Verification of a Maya Settlement Model through Remote Sensing', *Cambridge Archaeological Journal,* 5, 227–83.

Freidel, David
1986 'Maya warfare: an example of peer polity interaction'. In *Peer Polity Interaction and Socio-Political Change,* (eds) C. Renfrew and J. Cherry, 93–108, Cambridge, Cambridge University Press.

Freidel, David, Linda Schele and Joy Parker
1993 *Maya Cosmos: Three Thousand Years on the Shaman's Path,* New York, William Morrow.

Goodman, Joseph T.
1905 'Maya Dates', *American Anthropologist,* 7: 642–7.

Graham, Ian
1963 'Juan Galindo, Enthusiast', *Estudios de Cultura Maya* 3: 11–35, Mexico, Unam.
1967 *Archaeological explorations in El Petén, Guatemala,* Publication No. 3, New Orleans, Tulane University, Middle American Research Institute.

1971   *The Art of Maya Hieroglyphic Writing,* Cambridge, Mass., Peabody Museum of Archaeology and Ethnology.
1977   'Alfred Maudslay and the Discovery of the Maya', *Collectors and Collections,* London, The British Museum Yearbook 2.

Graham, Ian *et al.*
1975–99   *Corpus of Maya Hieroglyphic Inscriptions,* 16 vols to date, Cambridge, Mass., Peabody Museum of Archaeology and Ethnology.

Graham, John A.
1997   'Discoveries at Abaj Takalik, Guatemala'. *Archaeology,* 30, 196–7.

Grove, David and Robert Sharer
1989   (eds) *Regional Perspectives on the Olmec,* Cambridge, Cambridge University Press.

Grube, Nikolai
1995   (ed.) 'Transformations of Maya Society at the end of the Preclassic: processes of change between the predynastic and dynastic periods', *The Emergency of Lowland Maya Civilization,* 1–5, Mockmuhl, Verlag Anton Saurwein.
1996   'Palenque in the Maya World', (1993), Merle Greene Robertson, Martha Macri and Jan McHargue (eds) *The Palenque Round Table Series* Vol. 10, San Francisco, The Pre-Columbian Art Research Institute.
1998   'Observations on the Late Classic Interregnum at Yaxchilan', *The Archaeology of Mesoamerica,* 116–27, Warwick Bray (ed.), London, British Museum Publications.

Hammond, Norman
1977   (ed.) *Social Process in Maya Prehistory. Essays in Honour of Sir Eric Thompson,* London and New York, Academic Press.
1982   *Ancient Maya Civilization,* Cambridge, Cambridge University Press.
1991   (ed.) Cuello, *An Early Maya Community in Belize,* Cambridge, Cambridge University Press.

Hansen, Richard D.
1990   'Excavations in the Tigre Complex, El Mirador, Petén, Guatemala', *Papers of the New World Archaeological Foundation,* 62.
1991   'The Maya rediscovered: the road to Nakbé', *Natural History* 5: 9–14.
1992   'El proceso cultural de Nakbé y el area del Petén nord-central: las epocas tempranas', *V Simposio de Investigaciones en Guatemala,* 81–96, Guatemala City.

Harrison, Peter D. and B.L. Turner II
1978   (eds) *Prehispanic Maya Agriculture,* Albuquerque, University of New Mexico Press.

Haviland, William A.
1992   'From Double Bird to Ah Cacao: Dynastic Troubles and the Cycle of the Katuns at Tikal', (eds) Danien and Sharer, 1992: 71–80.

Henderson, John
1981   *The World of the Maya,* Ithaca, Cornell.

Herrera, A.
1726–30   *'Historia general de los hechos de los Castellanos en las islas i tierra firme del mar oceano,* 5 vols, Madrid.

Hodell, D. A., J. H. Curtis and M. Brenner
1995   *Nature,* 375, 391–4.

Houston, Stephen D.
1989 *Maya Glyphs,* London, British Museum Publications.
1993 *Hieroglyphs and History at Dos Pilas: Dynastic Politics of the Classic Maya,* Austin
      University of Texas Press.

Houston, Stephen D. and David Stuart
1989 'The Way Glyph: Evidence for "Co-essences" among the Classic Maya',
      Research Reports in Ancient Maya Writing No. 30, Washington D.C., Centre for
      Maya Research.
1996 'Of gods, glyphs and kings: divinity and rulership among the Classic Maya',
      Antiquity, vol. 20 (268), 289–312.

Houston, Stephen D. and Karl A. Taube
1987 'Name Tagging in Classic Mayan Script'. *Mexicon,* 9, 2. Berlin.

Humboldt, Alexander von
1810 *Vues des Cordilléres, et monuments des peuples indigenes de l'Amerique,* Paris.

Jones, Christopher
1991 'Cycles of Growth at Tikal', 102–27 *Classic Maya Political History,* (ed.) T.
      Patrick Culbert, Albuquerque, University of New Mexico Press.

Jones, Christopher and L. Satterthwaite
1982 *The Monuments and Inscriptions of Tikal: the Carved Monuments,* Tikal Report 33A,
      Philadelphia, University Museum, University of Pennsylvania.

Jones, Grant D.
1989 *Maya Resistance to Spanish Rule: Time and History on a Colonial Frontier,*
      Albuquerque, University of New Mexico Press.
1998 *The Conquest of the Last Maya Kingdom,* Stanford, Stanford University Press.

Justeson, John S. and Lyle Campbell
1984 (eds) *Phoneticism in Mayan Hieroglyphic Writing,* Publication No. 9, Albany NY,
      Institute for Mesoamerican Studies.

Kelley, David H.
1976 *Deciphering the Maya Script,* Austin, University of Texas Press.

Kerr, Justin
1989–97 *The Maya Vase Book,* Vols. 1–5, New York, Justin Kerr Associates.

Kingsborough, Edward King, Viscount
1830–48 *Antiquities of Mexico,* 9 Vols, London, James Moynes and Colnaghi,
         Son and Co.

Knorosov, Yuri. V.
1958 'The Problem of the study of the Maya hieroglyphic writing', *American
      Antiquity,* 23, 284–91.
1967 Selected chapters from 'The Writing of the Maya Indians', (trans. Sophie D.
      Coe, ed. Tatiana Proskouriakoff), *Russian Translation Series,* Cambridge, Mass.,
      Peabody Museum of Archaeology and Ethnology.,

Kowalski, Jeff K.
1987 *The House of the Governor: A Maya Palace at Uxmal, Yucatán, Mexico,* Norman,
      University of Oklahoma Press.
1998 'Uxmal and the Puuc Zone' *Maya,* (eds Peter Schmidt, Mercedes de la Garza
      and Enrique Nalda pp. 401–25, Venice, Bompiani.

Landa, Diego de
(See Tozzer, Alfred M.)

Leon-Portilla, Miguel
1973 *Time and Reality in the Thought of the Maya*, Boston,

Leventhal, Richard M. and Alan L. Kolata
1983 (eds) *Civilization in the Ancient Americas, Essays in Honour of Gordon R. Willey*, University of New Mexico Press and Peabody Museum of Archaeology and Ethnology.

Lounsbury, Floyd G.
1982 'Astronomical knowledge and its uses at Bonampak, Mexico', *Archaeoastronomy in the New World*, (ed. Anthony F. Aveni), 143–68, Cambridge.

Lovell, W. George and Christopher H. Lutz
1994 'Conquest and Population: Maya demography in historical perspective', *Latin American Research Review*, London, Institute of Latin American Studies.

Lowe, Gareth
1975 *The Early Preclassic Barra Phase of Altamira, Chiapas*, Publ. 39. Utah, New World Archaeological Foundation.

MacNeish, Richard S., S. Jeffrey K. Wilkerson and Antoinette Nelken-Turner
1980 *First Annual Report of the Belize Archaic Archaeological Reconnaissance*, Andover, Mass., Peabody Foundation.

Maler, Teobert
1901–10 Reports on his researches in *Memoirs of the Peabody Museum of Archaeology and Ethnology*. Vols. 2 and 4, Cambridge, Mass., Harvard University.

Mangelsdorf, P. C., R. S MacNeish and W. C. Galinat
1967 'Prehistoric wild and cultivated maize', *The Prehistory of the Tehuacan valley*. vol. 1, 178–200, (ed. D. S. Byers), Austin, University of Texas Press.

Marcus, Joyce
1976 *Emblem and State in the Classic Maya Lowlands*, Washington D.C., Dumbarton Oaks.
1992 *Mesoamerican Writing Systems*, Princeton, Princeton University Press.

Martin, Simon
1996 'Calakmul y el enigma del glifo Cabeza de Serpiente', *Arqueologia Mexicana*, 3, 18, Mexico City, INAH 42–5.
1997 'The Painted King List: A Commentary on Codex-style Dynastic Vases', *The Maya Vase Book*, Vol. 5, 846–67, (ed. Justin Kerr), New York, Justin Kerr Associates.

Martin, Simon and Nikolai Grube
1995 'Maya Superstates', *Archaeology*, 48, (6), 41–6.
1996 *Evidence for Macro-Political Organisation of Classic Maya States*, Manuscript on file, Washington D.C., Dumbarton Oaks and University of Bonn.

Matheny, Ray
1986 'Investigations at El Mirador, Petén, Guatemala', *National Geographic Research* 2, 332–53.
1986 'Early States in the Maya Lowlands during the Late Preclassic Period: Edzna and El Mirador'. *City States of the Maya*, (ed. E. P. Benson), 1–44, Denver, Rocky Mountain Institute for Pre-Columbian Studies.

Mathews, Peter

1980 'Notes on the Dynastic sequence of Bonampak. Part 1', *Third Palenque Round Table*, 1978, Part 2, 60–73, (ed. Merle Greene Robertson), Austin, University of Texas Press.

1991 'Classic Maya Emblem Glyphs'. *Classic Maya Political History*, 19–29, (ed. T. Patrick Culbert), Albuquerque, University of New Mexico Press.

1995 *War in the Western Maya Lowlands*, paper presented at the 1995 Mesa Redonda de Palenque.

Mathews, Peter and Linda Schele

1974 'Lords of Palenque: The Glyphic Evidence', *First Palenque Round Table*, Part 1, 63–76, (ed. M. G. Robertson), Pebble Beach, California.

Maudslay, Alfred

1889–1902 *Biologia Centrali-Americana: Archaeology*, 5 vols, London, R. H. Porter and Dulau and Co.

1881–2 Unpublished field note-books, British Museum, Dept. of Ethnography, transcribed by A. K. Miller 1986, London, Royal Anthropological Institute Library.

Maudslay, Anne Cary and Alfred Maudslay

1899 *A Glimpse at Guatemala and Some Notes on the Ancient Monuments of Central America*, London, John Murray.

McAnany, Patricia

1995 *Living with the Ancestors*, Austin, University of Texas Press.

McGee, R. Jon

1990 *Life, Ritual and Religion among the Lacandon Maya*, Belmont,

Miller, Mary Ellen

1986 *The Murals of Bonampak*, Princeton, Princeton University Press.

1986 *The Art of Mesoamerica from Olmec to Aztec*, London and New York, Thames & Hudson (revised edn 1994).

1992 'The Ancient Americas: Art from Sacred Lanscapes', *The Image of People and Nature in Classic Maya Art and Architecture*, (ed. Townsend), 159–69.

Miller, Mary Ellen and Karl Taube

1993 *The Gods and Symbols of Ancient Mexico and the Maya*, London and New York, Thames & Hudson.

Millon, René

1981 'Teotihuacan: City, State and Civilization', *Supplement to the Handbook of Middle American Indians*, Vol. 1: Archaeology, 198–243, (ed. J. A. Sabloff), Austin, University of Texas Press.

Morley, Sylvanus G.

1920 *The Inscriptions at Copán*, publication 219, Washington, Carnegie Institution of Washington.

1937–38 *The Inscriptions of Petén*, 5 vols, pub. 437, Washington, Carnegie Institution of Washington.

1946 *The Ancient Maya*, Stanford, Stanford University Press.

Morris, Walter F. Jr.

1987 *Living Maya*, New York, Abrams.

Nations, James D., and Ronald B. Nigh
1980 'The Evolutionary Potential of Lacandon Maya Sustained-Yield Tropical Forest Agriculture', *Journal of Anthropological Research*, 36: 1–30.

Pailles Hernandez, Maria de la Cruz and Rosalba Nieto Calleja
1990 'Primeras expediciones a las ruinas de Palenque', *Archaeologia* 4 1990, 97–128, Mexico City, INAH.

Pendergast, David M.
1967 (ed.) *Palenque: the Walker-Caddy Expedition to the Ancient Maya City 1839–40*, Norman, University of Oklahoma Press.
1981 'Lamanai, Belize: summary of excavation results', 1974–80, *Journal of Field Archaeology*, Vol. 8, 1. 29–53.

Pohl, Mary
1985 (ed.) 'Prehistoric Lowland Maya Environment and Subsistence Economy', *Papers of the Peabody Museum of Archaeology and Ethnology*, Vol. 77, Cambridge, Mass., Harvard University.
1990 *Ancient Maya Wetland Agriculture: Excavations on Albion Island, Northern Belize*, Boulder, Colorado, Westview.

Pohl, Mary *et al.*
1996 'Early Agriculture in the Maya Lowlands', *Latin American Antiquity*, 7, 4, 355–72.

Pope, K. A. and B. Dahlin
1989 'Ancient Maya Wetland Agriculture: new insights from ecological and remote sensing research', *Journal of Field Archaeology* 16. 87–106.

Proskouriakoff, Tatiana
1946 *An Album of Maya Architecture*, Pub. 558, Washington, Carnegie Institution of Washington.
1950 *A Study of Classic Maya Sculpture*, Pub. 593, Washington, Carnegie Institution of Washington.
1960 'Historical implications of a pattern of dates at Piedras Negras, Guatemala', *American Antiquity*. 25 (4). 454–75.
1961 'The Lords of the Maya Realm', *Expedition* 3 (4), 14–21.
1963 'Historical data in the Inscriptions of Yaxchilan. Part 1', *Estudios de Cultura Maya* 3, 149–167, Mexico UNAM.
1964 'Historical data in the Inscriptions of Yaxchilan. Part II', *Estudios de Cultura Maya 4,* 177–201, Mexico UNAM.

Puleston, Dennis
1977 'The art and archaeology of hydraulic agriculture in the Maya lowlands', *Social Process in Maya Prehistory*, (ed. Norman Hammond), 449–69, London, Academic Press.

Rafinesque, Constantine Samuel
1832 'Second letter to Mr Champollion on the graphic systems of America, and the glyphs of Otulum, or Palenque, in Central America – elements of the glyphs', *Atlantic Journal and Friend of Knowledge*, 1 (2), 40–44, Philadelphia.

Redfield, Robert and Alfonso Villa Rojas
1962 *Chan Kom, a Maya Village,* Washington D.C., Carnegie Institution of Washington.

Reed, Nelson
1964 *The Caste War of Yucatán*, Stanford, Stanford University Press.

Reents-Budet, Dorie *et al.*
1994 *Painting the Maya Universe: Royal Ceramics of the Classic Period*, Durham, New York and London, Duke University Press.

Rice, Don S.
1993 'Eighth Century Physical Geography, Environment and Natural Resources in the Maya lowlands', *Lowland Maya Civilization in the Eighth Century AD*, 11–63, (eds J. A. Sabloff and J. S. Henderson, Washington D.C., Dumbarton Oaks.

Rice, Don and Prudence M. Rice
1984 'Lessons from the Maya', *Latin American Research Review*, 19, 7–34, London.

Robertson, Merle Greene
1974–1996 (ed.) *Palenque Round Table (Mesa Redonda) Series*, 1–8.
1983–1991 *The Sculpture of Palenque*, 4 Vols, Princeton, Princeton University Press.

De Rosny, Leon
1876 *Essai sur le déchiffrement de l'écriture hieratique de l'Amerique Centrale*, Paris.

Roys, Ralph L.
1967 *The Book of Chilam Balam of Chumayel*, Norman, University of Oklahoma Press.

Rue, D. J.
1987 'Early Agriculture and Early Postclassic Maya occupation in Western Honduras', *Nature*, 326: 285–6.

Ruppert, Karl and John H. Denison
1943 *Archaeological Reconnaissance in Campeche, Quintana Roo and Petén*, Pub. 543, Washington D.C., Carnegie Institution of Washington.

Ruppert, Karl, J. Eric. S. Thompson and Tatiana Proskouriakoff
1955 *Bonampak, Chiapas, Mexico,* Pub. 602, Washington D.C., Carnegie Institution of Washington.

Rúz Lhuillier, Alberto
1973 *El Templo de las Inscripciones, Palenque*, Mexico City.

Sabloff, Jeremy A.
1985 'Ancient Maya Civilization: an overview', *Maya: Treasures of an Ancient Civilization*, (ed. C. Gallenkamp and R.E. Johnson), New York, Abrams.
1990 *The New Archaeology and the Ancient Maya*, New York, W. H. Freeman.
1997 *The Cities of Ancient Mexico*, revised edn, London, Thames & Hudson.

Sabloff, Jeremy A. and E. Wyllys Andrews
1986 (eds) *Late Lowland Maya Civilization: Classic to Postclassic,* Albuquerque, University of New Mexico Press.

Sabloff, Jeremy A. and John S. Henderson
1993 (eds) *Lowland Maya Civilization in the Eighth Century AD*, Washington D.C., Dumbarton Oaks.

Sahagún, Fr. Bernardino de
*c.*1565–1585 *Florentine Codex: General History of the Things of New Spain*, trans. Arthur J. O. Anderson and Charles E. Dibble, 12 books in 13 vols, 1951–82, Santa Fe, School of American Research and the University of Utah Press.

Sauer, Carl O.
1966 *The Early Spanish Main,* London and New York, Cambridge University Press.

Scarborough, Vernon L.
1994 'Maya Water Management', *National Geographic Research and Exploration,* 10 (2): 184–99.

Scarborough, Vernon L. *et al.*
1995 'Water and Land at the Ancient Maya Community of La Milpa', *Latin American Antiquity* 6 (2): 98–119.

Scarborough, Vernon L. and David R. Wilcox
1991 *The Mesoamerican Ballgame,* Tucson, University of Arizona.

Schele, Linda
1982 *Maya Glyphs: The Verbs,* Austin, University of Texas Press.
1989 *Some Thoughts on the Inscriptions of House C,* paper prepared for the Seventh Palenque Mesa Redonda.

Schele, Linda and David Freidel
1990 *A Forest of Kings: The Untold Story of the Ancient Maya,* New York, William Morrow.

Schele, Linda, Nikolai Grube and Erik Boot
1995 'Some suggestions on the K'atun Prophecies in the Books of Chilam Balam in the light of Classic Period History', *Texas Notes on Precolumbian Art, Writing and Culture 72,* Austin.

Schele, Linda and Peter Mathews
1993 *Notebook for the XVIIth Maya Hieroglyphic Workshop of Texas,* Austin, University of Texas.
1998 *The Code of Kings,* New York, Scribner.

Schele, Linda and Mary Miller
1992 *The Blood of Kings,* Fort Worth, Kimbell Art Museum 1986, London, Thames & Hudson.

Schellhas, Paul
1904 *Representations of Deities in the Maya Manuscripts,* Harvard, Peabody Museum Papers 4:1.

Schmidt, Peter, Mercedes de la Garza and Enrique Nalda
1990 (eds) *Maya,* Venice, Bompiani.

Sharer, Robert J.
1990 *Quiriguá. A Classic Maya Center and its Sculptures,* Durham, N. C., Carolina Academic Press.
1994 *The Ancient Maya,* fifth edn, Stanford, Stanford University Press.

Sharer, Robert and David Grove
1989 (eds) *Regional Perspectives on the Olmec,* Cambridge, Cambridge University Press.

Sharer, Robert J. and David W. Sedat
1987 *Archaeological Investigations in the Northern Maya Highlands, Guatemala,* Philadelphia University Museum, University of Pennsylvania.

Sheets, Payson
1992 *The Ceren Site: A Prehistoric Village Buried by Volcanic Ash in Central America*, Fort Worth, Harcourt Brace Jovanovich.

Siemens, Alfred H. and Dennis Puleston
1972 'Ridged fields and associated features in Southern Campeche: new perspectives on the lowland Maya', *American Antiquity*, 37. 228–39.

Smith, A. Ledyard
1950 *Uaxactun, Guatemala: Excavations of 1931–37*, Pub. 588, Washington D.C., Carnegie Institution of Washington.

Spinden, Herbert
1913 *A Study of Maya Art*, Memoirs 6, Cambridge, Mass., Peabody Museum of Archaeology and Ethnology.

Stephens, John Lloyd
1841 *Incidents of Travel in Central America, Chiapas and Yucatán*, 2 vols, New York, Harper and Brothers, London, John Murray, (reprint New York, Dover Publications 1963).
1843 *Incidents of Travel in Yucatán*. 2 vols. New York, Harper and Brothers, London, John Murray (reprint New York, Dover Publications 1969).

Storey, Rebecca
1992 'The Children of Copán: issues in palaeopathology and palaeodemography', *Ancient Mesoamerica,* 3 (1), 161–68.

Stuart, David
1987 'Ten Phonetic Syllables', *Research Reports on Ancient Maya Writing*, No. 14, Washington.
1988 'The Rio Azul Cacao pot: epigraphic observations on the function of a Maya ceramic vessel', *Antiquity,* 62, 153–57.
1992 'Hieroglyphs and Archaeology at Copán', *Ancient Mesoamerica* 3 (1). 169–84.
1993 'Historical Inscriptions and the Maya Collapse', *Lowland Maya Civilization in the Eighth Century AD,* ed. J. A. Sabloff and J. S. Henderson, Washington D.C., Dumbarton Oaks.
1997 'The Hills Are Alive: Sacred Mountains in the Maya Cosmos', *Symbols,* Spring Issue, 13–17. Cambridge, Mass., Peabody Museum and the Dept. of Anthropology.

Stuart, David and Stephen Houston
1994 'Classic Maya Place Names', *Studies in Pre-Columbian Art and Archaeology*, No. 33, Washington D.C., Dumbarton Oaks.

Stuart, George E.
1981 'Maya art treasures discovered in caves', *National Geographic,* 160 (2), 220–35.
1992 'Quest for decipherment: a historical and biographical survey of Maya hieroglyphic investigation', *New Theories on the Ancient Maya,* ed. E. C. Danien and R. J. Sharer. 1–63, Philadelphia, Philadelphia University Museum.
1997 'The Royal Crypts of Copán', *National Geographic,* 192 (6) 68–93.

Sullivan, Paul
1989 *Unfinished Conversations: Mayas and Foreigners Between Two Wars,* New York, Knopf.

Tate, Carolyn E.

1992 *Yaxchilán: The Design of a Maya Ceremonial Center*, Austin, University of Texas Press.

Taube, Karl A.

1985 'The Classic Maya Maize God: a reappraisal'. *Fifth Palenque Round Table*, (ed. M. G. Robertson and V. Fields), Vol. 7. 171–81, San Francisco, Pre-Columbian Art Research Institute.

1993 *Aztec and Maya Myths*, London, British Museum Publications.

Tedlock, Barbara

1982 *Time and the Highland Maya*, Albuquerque, University of New Mexico Press.

Tedlock, Dennis

1996 *Popol Vuh*, second edn, New York, Simon & Schuster.

Teeple, John E.

1930 *Maya Astronomy*, Pub. 403, Washington D.C., Carnegie Institution of Washington.

Thomas, Hugh

1993 *The Conquest of Mexico*, London, Hutchinson.

Thompson, J. Eric S.

1950 *Maya Hieroglyphic Writing: An Introduction*, Washington D.C., Carnegie Institution of Washington.

1962 *A Catalog of Maya Hieroglyphs*, Norman, University of Oklahoma Press.

1963 *Maya Archaeologist*, Norman, University of Oklahoma Press.

1963 The *Rise and Fall of Maya Civilization*, Norman, University of Oklahoma Press.

1970 *Maya History and Religion*, Norman, University of Oklahoma Press.

1972 *Maya Hieroglyphs Without Tears*, London, British Museum Publications.

Tozzer, Alfred M.

1907 *A Comparative Study of the Mayas and the Lacandones*, New York.

1941 (trans. and ed.) 'Landa's Relación de las Cosas de Yucatán', *Papers of the Peabody Museum of Archaeology and Ethnology*. Vol. 18, Cambridge, Mass., Harvard University Press.

Townsend, Richard F.

1992 (ed.) *The Ancient Americas: Art from Sacred Landscapes*, Chicago, The Art Institute.

Turner, B.L. II

1974 'Prehistoric Intensive Agriculture in the Maya Lowlands', *Science*, 185, 118–24.

Turner, B.L. II and Peter D. Harrison

1983 *Pulltrouser Swamp: Ancient Maya Habitat, Agriculture and Settlement in Northern Belize*. Austin, University of Texas Press.

Villacorta, J. Antonio and Carlos A.

1997 *Codices Mayas*, Guatemala City 1930 (new edn 1997).

Vogt, Evon Z.

1969 *Zinacantan: A Maya Community in the Highlands of Chiapas*, Cambridge, Mass., Harvard University Press.

1976 *Tortillas for the Gods: A Symbolic Analysis of Zinacanteco Rituals*, Cambridge, Mass., Harvard University Press.

Von Hagen, Victor Wolfgang
1947 *Maya Explorer: John Lloyd Stephens and the Lost Cities of Central America and Yucatán.* Norman, University of Oklahoma Press.
1973 *Search for the Maya, The Story of Stephens and Catherwood,* London, Saxon House.

Waldeck, Jean Frédéric
1838 *Voyage Pittoresque et Archaeologique dans la Province d'Yucatán pendant les années 1834 et 1836,* Paris.

Watanabe, John M.
1992 *Maya Saints and Souls in a Changing World,* Austin, University of Texas Press.

Webster, David L.
1976 *Defensive Earthworks at Becan, Campeche, Mexico,* Pub. No. 41, New Orleans, Middle American Research Institute, Tulane University.
1977 'Warfare and the Evolution of Maya Civilization', *The Origins of Maya Civilization,* ed. R. E. W. Adams, Albuquerque, University of New Mexico Press.
1989 (ed.) *The House of the Bacabs, Copán, Honduras,* Washington D.C., Dumbarton Oaks.
1993 'The Study of Maya Warfare: what it tells us about the Maya and what it tells us about Maya archaeology', *Lowland Maya Civilization in the Eighth Century AD,* ed. J. S. Sabloff and J. Henderson, 415–44, Washington D.C., Dumbarton Oaks.

Webster, David L. and A. Freter
1990 'Settlement History and the Classic Collapse at Copán: a redefined chronological perspective', *Latin American Antiquity,* 1, 66–85.

Willey, Gordon R.
1973 'The Altar de Sacrificios Excavations: general summary and conclusions', *Papers of the Peabody Museum of Archaeology and Ethnology.* Vol. 18, Cambridge , Mass., Harvard University Press.
1980 'Towards an holistic view of ancient Maya civilization', *Man* (NS), 15. 249–66.

Willey, Gordon R. *et al.*
1965 'Prehistoric Settlements in the Belize Valley'. *Papers of the Peabody Museum of Archaeology and Ethnology,* Vol. 54, Cambridge, Mass., Harvard University Press.

Willey, Gordon R. and Jeremy Sabloff
1974 *A History of American Archaeology,* San Francisco, W. H. Freeman.

Wren, Linnea H. and Peter Schmidt
1991 'Elite interaction During the Terminal Classic Period: New Evidence from Chichén Itzá', *Classic Maya Political History,* (ed. T. Patrick), Culbert Albuquerque, University of New Mexico Press.

Wright, Ronald
1989 *Time Among the Maya,* London, Bodley Head.

Index